AF674615

Saundaryalaharī

Other Books by Nataraja Guru

The Word of the Guru (The Life and Teachings of Narayana Guru, with translations of some of his poems)

The Bhagavad Gita (Translation and commentary highlighting the universal nature of the wisdom-science of Yoga as revalued by Vyasa)

One Hundred Verses of Self-Instruction: Translation and commentary of Narayana Guru's *Atmopadeśaśatakam*

The Philosophy of a Guru: An introduction to the *Atmopadeśaśatakam* as well as to the philosophy of Guruhood itself.

Vedanta Revalued and Restated

The Search for a Norm in Western Thought

An Integrated Science of the Absolute
Based on the *Darśanamālā* (A Garland of Visions of the Absolute) of Narayana Guru

Wisdom — The Absolute as the Adorable
(Collection of essays)

Experiencing One-World
(Includes: Towards a One-World Economics, World-Education Manifesto, Memorandum on World-Government and other essays based on a one-world vision)

An Anthology of the Poems of Narayana Guru
(Translations of nineteen poems)

Unitive Understanding (Essays)

Saundaryalaharī

(The Upsurging Billow of Beauty)

of

Śaṅkarācārya

English Translation and Commentary by

Nataraja Guru

(revised with original verses in Sanskrit,
transliteration and word-for-word translation)

Cataloging in Publication Data — DK
[Courtesy: D.K. Agencies (P) Ltd. <docinfo@dkagencies.com>]

Śaṅkarācārya, author.

Saundaryalaharī = The upsurging billow of beauty of Śaṅkarācārya / English translation and commentary by Nataraja Guru, revised with original verses in Sanskrit, transliteration and word-for-word translation. – Third impression.
pages cm

Text in Sanskrit (roman); translation and commentary in English.
Includes index.

1. Śaṅkarācārya. Saundaryalaharī. 2. Tripurasundarī (Hindu deity) – Prayers and devotions. 3. Hindu hymns, Sanskrit. 4. Hindu hymns, Sanskrit – Translations into English. I. Nataraja Guru, 1895-1973, translator, editor. II. Śaṅkarācārya. Saundaryalaharī. III. Śaṅkarācārya. Saundaryalaharī. English. IV. Narayana Gurukula Foundation. V. Title. VI. Title: Saundaryalaharī of Śaṅkarācārya. VII. Title: Upsurging billow of beauty of Śaṅkarācārya.

BL1225.T73S26 2017 DDC 294.543 23

ISBN 978-81-246-0267-6 (Hb) ISBN 978-81-246-0367-3 (Pb)

First Published in 1988, *by the East-West University, Varkala, India*
Revised edition published in 2005
Second impression of the revised edition published in 2008
Third impression of the revised edition published in 2017

Cover design: Faculty of Aesthetics, East-West University

Printed and published by :
D.K. Printworld (P) Ltd.
Regd. office : *Vedaśrī*, F-395, Sudarshan Park
ESI Metro Station, New Delhi - 110 015
Phones : (011) 2545 3975, 2546 6019
e-mail : indology@dkprintworld.com
Web : www.dkprintworld.com

Foreword

The *Saundaryalaharī* is the most important as well as the most intriguing of the hymns composed by Śaṅkarācārya, and perhaps also his last work. The present commentary by Nataraja Guru is equally intriguing and it is also his last (major) literary work.

Considering that Śaṅkara was a pure Advaitin, it is difficult to think that he would regard writing a lengthy hymn grounded in Tantra as a part of his life mission. Though we do not know much about the situation in which he felt compelled to write the *Saundaryalaharī*, we may assume that this condition arose out of a merging of thought, vision and circumstance.

The situation in which Nataraja Guru felt bound to write the present commentary is similar. In 'Preliminaries', he describes how he took up this task almost immediately after concluding that he has completed his life's work and has decided to set-off on a world tour!

Until the present commentary, the *Saundaryalaharī* was conventionally treated as a Tāntric hymn, and interpreted, both in the East and West, on those lines. However, Nataraja Guru thought otherwise; in his vision, the hymn represents Advaita Vedanta in a pictorial language, with the picture being painted on a canvas of Tantra concepts. When the peculiarities of the canvas are mentally negated, then emerges the picture of non-dual Reality, not in a conceptual form but in a perceptual one.

What is the ultimate goal of Advaita Vedanta? It is the unconditioned contentment or *ānanda* that the seeker experiences on realizing her oneness with the total Reality or *brahman* — an experience that is conceptual in status. In the Upaniṣads, this *brahman* is defined as *sat-cit-ānanda* (existence-consciousness-value experience).

What is *saundarya*? Though it is an experience of blissfulness, it is more perceptual in nature. *Brahman* — seen as an abstract reality — when realized in one's own being leads to an experience of blissfulness all through, equally abstract and conceptual, called *ānanda*. The same *brahman* can be perceived as having assumed the form of the perceptual world and the seeker's identity with it leads to an experience equally perceptual. This latter experience could be named *saundarya*. In other words, the conceptual *ānanda* transformed as a perceptual experience becomes *saundarya*, which may be translated as Beauty.

The ever-changing perceptual world must have a never-changing Substance for its basis. This all-underlying Substance is called *sat* in Vedanta. Being the source of everything, it is often poetically conceived as the 'Mother' and this poetic imagery is the origin of the practice of Mother-worship, known as *Devī puja* or *Śakti puja*. The whole of Tantra lives and moves around this Devī or Śakti. The Devī being the source of the perceptual world, the perceptual beauty of the perceptual world also becomes reduced to the perceptual beauty of the Devī. And this Beauty is the central theme meditated upon in the present hymn.

The perceptual world has a structural perfection of its own. It is but natural to think that this structure and its latent form are implicit in the base Substance of *brahman* as well. That this *brahman* as unconditioned Consciousness (*cit*) in essence is one of the basic tenets of Vedanta; then this *cit* must also have the latent structural peculiarities of the perceptual world. This *cit*, while finding expression as specific forms of knowledge and ideas, must have also reflected in them the same structural peculiarities.

The Devī-form, here meditated upon — the universal concrete cause underlying the perceptual concrete universe —

is also no exception in this respect. Attempts to give some verbal definiteness to this Reality should also have the same structural scheme implicit in it. Nataraja Guru's original contribution to philosophy is mainly in the context of making explicit the structural aspects hidden in the verbal expressions of world scriptures. The commentator, in order to make explicit how the *Saundaryalaharī* is a visual representation of Advaitic vision, resorts to eliciting structural details, both in the form as well as the content of the Devī principle. Familiarity with the structural language will be more helpful in appreciating the line of thought and beauty of this commentary.

Narayana Gurukula first published the Guru's commentary in 1988. Now it is being republished in a new format, re-edited by Swami Vinaya Chaitanya, a direct disciple of Nataraja Guru.

The word for word meaning, a new addition in this edition, has been prepared by Swami Vinaya. Structural diagrams and analysis for the first twenty-four verses, done by the Guru himself and first published in *Values* (1970-71); as well as the selections from the *Yogarāja Upaniṣad* and the *Saubhāgyalakṣmī Upaniṣad*, have been added to this edition as appendices. The translation of the appendices has been done by Dr. Hypatia Chaitanya. In adding these we have only fulfilled the wishes of the Guru.

Several other people have contributed to the preparation of this edition. Scott Teitsworth has contributed an article elucidating key structural features of the commentary. Swami Vyasa Prasad has prepared a comprehensive index and a bibliography. Sebastian Chiri has very ably updated the drawings. The Faculty of Aesthetics designed the cover. C.V. Ramesh and Kala Ramesh have been most helpful, as always.

D.K. Printworld of New Delhi have taken up the responsibility of bringing out this new edition, as they have done in the case of several other Narayana Gurukula publications. We are thankful to them, especially for their patience and cooperation with our editors.

It is our hope that this commentary will help banish long-standing misunderstandings about the great Advaitin Śaṅkara and this most valuable Advaitic work. May the unitive understanding that permeates the book help humanity regain the peace and joy that is its birthright.

Varkala 3.6.2004 *Swami Muni Narayana Prasad*

Contents

The Structural Secrets of the Saundaryalaharī

By the time Nataraja Guru undertook the *Saundaryalaharī* commentary, he had already spent a lifetime refining and elaborating his profound reassessment of philosophy. The work is directed especially to his disciples, who were already well versed in what he called the Science of the Absolute. Because of this, the explanation of some of the key ideas found here would have been redundant to his intense intellect, which was always eagerly straining at the leash to explore new fields of wisdom and abstraction. Therefore, without the explication of at least the most crucial and essential structural lines of thought implied in this commentary, the reader who has not been exposed to Nataraja Guru's highly original style would be very quickly at a loss. Thus it is important to mention a few of the secrets used as building blocks in the Guru's analysis. For a complete initiation, the reader is directed to all the previous works of Nataraja Guru, especially *An Integrated Science of the Absolute, Dialectical Methodology* and *The Search for a Norm in Western Thought.*

The Guru himself was fully aware of the importance of a structural analysis of the *Saundaryalaharī*, as he points out in his preliminary comments:

> Each verse leaps into meaning only when the underlying structural features are revealed and brought into view, otherwise the hundred verses remain, as they have remained through the thousand years or more of their history, a mere challenge to vain pedantry or punditry. In other words, structuralism is the key that can make

> this work an open book, a scientifically valid work, with a fresh appeal to all advanced thinking modern men of the East or the West. It will be our task within the scope of the work itself to introduce the reader, as occasion permits, to further implications and intricacies of this structural approach, which perhaps is the one feature on which the value and success of this work would have to rest. — p. 29

First and foremost, Nataraja Guru thought dialectically. While dialectics has many definitions, the kind he employed is similar to a type that occurs in the West from Plato to Hegel, where polar opposites — a thesis and antithesis — are combined to effect a synthesis. The actual source for the Guru was the yoga of the Upaniṣads and the Bhagavadgīta, but he found it explicitly or implicitly present in Western philosophy also. Yoga is another name for the process by which opposite poles are viewed synthetically, to be united in a common scheme of understanding.

To Nataraja Guru, dialectics springs out of the notions of complementarity, reciprocity, compensation and cancellation. In logical terms, *a* immediately implies *not a*. When they are taken together, there is a balance, which in a sense produces a virtual zero that embraces the entire picture. The formula is simply: $a + (-a) = 0$. This zero factor is another name for the Absolute. By the use of dialectics to balance life elements, the Absolute is brought in as a unifying factor in each and every situation. Therefore, the task of the yogi is to constantly seek out the element *not a* or *not this* to add to whatever situation presents itself, and in so doing restore a state of harmonious balance. 'The verity that is thus neutral and central between two terms of reciprocal propositions may be said to represent the Absolute norm of that context. . . ' is how the Guru puts it in *Dialectical Methodology* (p. 7).

Because dialectical thought is dynamic, it tends to move upwards towards more sublime and uplifting insights, or downwards into more static and constraining states. Nataraja Guru's use of the terms ascending and descending dialectics refers to these movements.

Where linear thinking follows a one dimensional line of thought, dialectical thinking expands into two and three dimensions through the triad of thesis-antithesis-synthesis. These imply a triangular shape, which rotated becomes a cone.

At the core of Nataraja Guru's philosophy are the Cartesian coordinate axes, consisting of a horizontal and a vertical parameter represented by straight lines that intersect at right angles to form a cross. The point of intersection is arbitrarily called zero, with increasingly large numbers representing expanding negativity and positivity leading away from the zero point. The left side of the horizontal line is called negative, and the right side positive. On the vertical parameter, above the zero point is positive and below it is negative.

Of these two lines, the vertical one is understood as being made up of unitive values, representing the urge for inclusive transcendence, while the horizontal axis stands for the multiplicity of ever-proliferating transactional variety. The horizontal and the vertical actually intersect each other at any

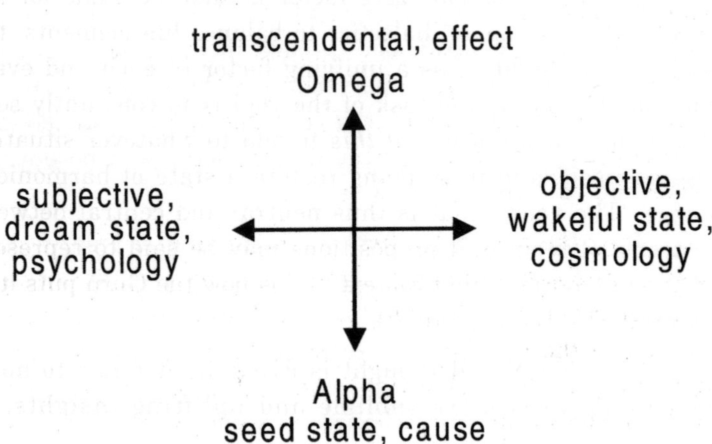

and all points, giving rise to a stable ground of participation between the outside and the inside, existence and essence.

Though they have been used in various forms throughout much of the history of thought, the adaptation of Cartesian coordinates to the philosophy of the structure of the universe was a stroke of genius of the Guru. Nataraja Guru's coordinate axes combine the three perceivable spatial dimensions into the horizontal, while conceptual ideas and time make up the vertical axis. The implications of this are profound.

Descartes himself set the initial parameters that Nataraja Guru developed in his Science of the Absolute, although due to certain unshakable prejudices Descartes was unable to develop the system to as advanced a point as the Guru. To him *res cogitans,* or thinking substance, was the vertical factor, and *res extensa,* or the extended, proliferated substance comprised the horizontal. In Nataraja Guru's interpretation of this, the horizontal is the physical universe (in its broadest sense) and the vertical is the metaphysical. Where the horizontal is vast, the vertical is an almost infinitely fine line or backbone, which knits the universe together in the same way that a fine thread holds together a string of pearls.

The Cartesian coordinates are not a fixed scheme but a tool for integrating seemingly divergent fields, so an endless series of dichotomies may be examined through them. If the horizontal represents the phenomenal, the vertical is the noumenal or the essential. Another integration is of *para* and *apara*, transcendent and immanent. The one and the many. Being and becoming. Essence and existence. And so on.

Breaking the axes down further, the horizontal positive may be treated as objective and the negative as subjective. The vertical parameter can run from the alpha at the extreme negative to the omega at the most positive, or from the dimensionless causal source to the dimensionless transcendental mystery. The journey from the alpha to the omega begins as a seed or point, grows in space until it is maximally horizontalized in the prime of life, and thereafter refocuses to the omega point at the termination of existence.

The horizontal positive is associated with the waking state, the horizontal negative with the dream state, the vertical negative with the deep sleep or seed state, and the vertical positive with *turīya* or the transcendental state. Using this scheme it is possible to graph all states of consciousness on the coordinate axes, as well as to monitor the progressive development of any aspect of creation.

Viewing this process in four dimensions produces an image of two cones placed base to base, with their bases conjoined at the horizontal axis. Viewed in cross-section they appear as equilateral triangles base to base. Since they are complementary,

The Śri Cakra

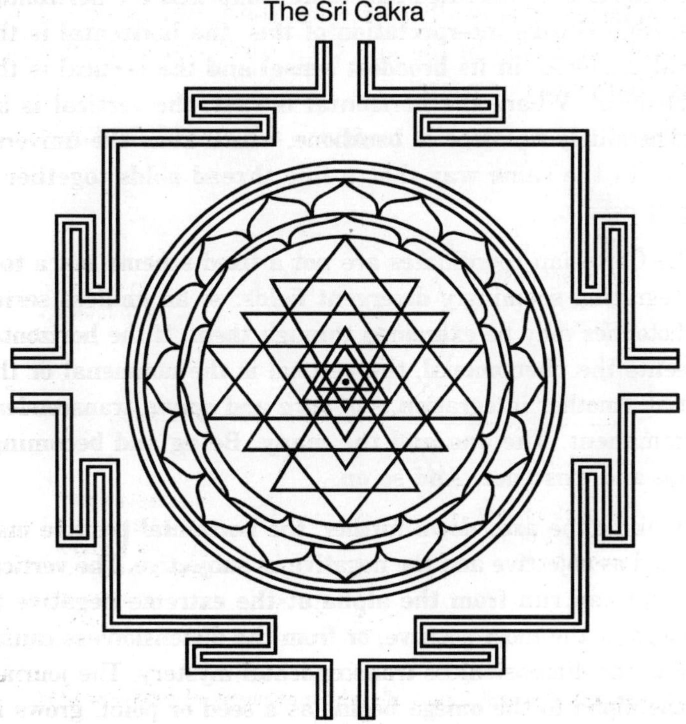

the triangles implicitly share elements of each other, which draws them to overlap to a degree. This is seen in the *śrī cakra*, which forms a central motif in the present work. The series of overlapping triangles that make up this pictorial (protolinguistic) device produce a virtual horizontal parameter at the intersection points between the overlapping bases, and a virtual vertical parameter running through the series of apexes. A glance at any *śrī cakra* will quickly reveal these virtual lines, as well as a number of virtual shapes.

Indian wisdom traditions reduce all possible philosophical questions to two basic ones: 'who am I ?' and 'whence this world ?' Of these, the 'I' refers to the vertical aspect while 'this' refers to the horizontal. The point where they intersect remains neutral as the core where the experience of both together takes place in an eternal time-space continuum. This is the state of the yogi/contemplative. The conflict between these two aspects is what makes for suffering in life and their unitive treatment is what brings happiness or peace.

The Guru occasionally mentions a figure-of-eight movement

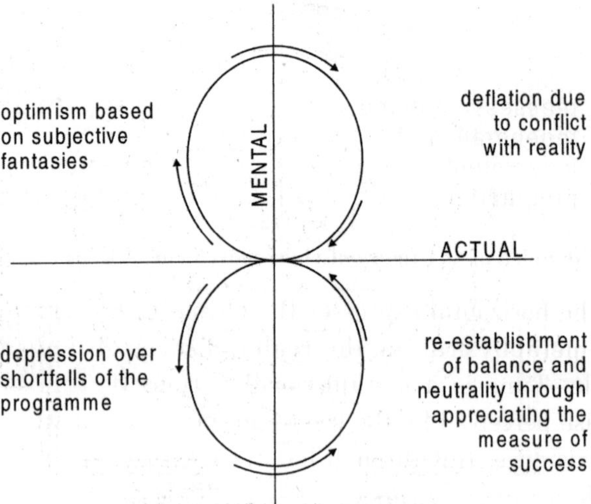

Examples of the figure-of-eight movement of consciousness.

of consciousness. When mental states are graphed on the Cartesian coordinates, the result is this type of figure. Picture the upper right quadrant as positive actually (horizontal) and positive mentally (vertical). The lower right quadrant is positive actually but mentally negative. The upper left quadrant is positive mentally but negative in actuality, while the lower left is negative both mentally and actually. As the psyche passes through these various stages, crossing from one to the next by passing through the zero point, a figure-of-eight pattern emerges.

It is possible to examine this oscillation either vertically or horizontally. Various exaggerations or minimizations can alter the size and shape of the figures:

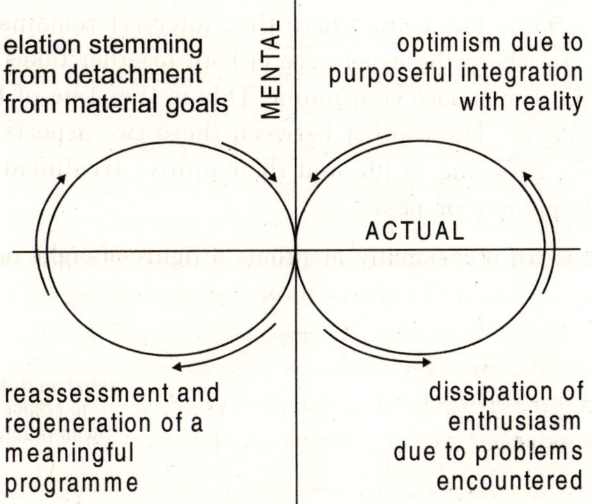

Examples of the figure-of-eight movement of consciousness.

If the horizontal expresses the physical, the vertical pertains to the metaphysical, or the realm of ideas. Take time for an example. Time is a metaphysical notion. It can't be seen or otherwise perceived by the senses in any way, yet we are certain of its existence. But through habitual acceptance, we have come to think of time in terms of clocks. A clock is a physical item, an actual representation or image of the metaphysical truth of time.

In using the clock we have unconsciously substituted an idolatrous, graven image for the original. And we have not just done this with time, but with nearly everything. Even in matters of spirituality — call it essential thought if you prefer — we have made this fatal error. Where the Absolute essence simultaneously transcends and includes both the vertical and horizontal, once conceptualized it becomes a vertical notion. When spirituality is further exteriorized into perceptual forms, it becomes the subject of religion, where it can be physically represented on the horizontal plane. In other words, religions use graven images in various guises to symbolize the transcendental, which has already been limited by being represented in thought patterns. Paradoxically, some religions that prohibit idolatry even worship graven images!

Of course, just as we use clocks and the movement of the sun to represent time for our personal convenience, there is a certain limited benefit to the use of images of the divine as reminders of the invisible Absolute from which we all spring. The problem comes when we forget to dialectically restore the essence to the form. Then we fight, or at least become unhappy. If we realized that horizontalized images are certain to differ but the vertical spiritual essence they represent is the same, then we would not have conflict. Instead, we try to foist our own favourite images on people who have different ones, and they defend their own favourite images in return. This process inevitably builds up tension that is very often discharged through warfare or other extreme forms of violence.

Since the interactions of multiple axes are vastly complex, let's examine a single axis in isolation. For it to remain in balance there has to be a state of equilibrium between the positive and negative elements, taken as a whole. As mentioned, Nataraja Guru often speaks of complementarity, reciprocity, compensation and cancellation, to include the various ways that the system remains in balance. If you have a plus two on the right and a minus three on the left of the horizontal, for instance, there would be an imbalance towards the subjective side, violating the four above-mentioned principles. Only a plus three will cancel a minus three. If an imbalance occurs, the system rapidly compensates to restore the balance; in fact, it can never really get out of balance, as an 'equal and opposite reaction' is instantaneous and eternal. The plus and minus elements are reciprocal, in that there is an implied relationship between them and together they add up to unity. Moreover, they are complementary because you cannot have one side without the other; in a sense the existence of one leg automatically produces or at least implies the other.

One helpful idea to keep in mind while reading the *Saundaryalaharī* is that the Guru spoke and wrote the way he thought, scrupulously observing reciprocity and complementarity in his sentence structure. Moreover, he was extremely careful not to favour one aspect of the universe over another. This will assist in decoding some of the complexities of his writing style.

In Western psychology an object is perceived by a subject, after which an image is produced within the mind of the subject. In Indian psychology, energy vibrates rapidly between the subject and object, like the fluttering of the wings of a bee, to produce a virtual image between them. The sum total of all virtual images, along with the very process of their production, is known as maya. The latter theory represents the postulated unity of the horizontal axis more accurately than the former.

It appears that the only realm of the universe where imbalance occurs is in the horizontal component of the human mind. When objects and their conceptualization go together harmoniously, complementarity remains in balance, but when there is a mismatch between percepts and concepts the system goes out of balance, and various psychological disturbances result. The quest of the yogi is to intelligently reattain the state of perfect mental equipoise through acceptance of valid relations and rejection of false ones.

The fact of reciprocity further implies an inner connection between apparently disparate elements, which has puzzled philosophers down through the ages. It is immediately clear to everyone that up has no meaning without down, bad has no meaning without good, and so on. These factors are therefore *relative* to each other. The idea resembles a teeter-totter, which requires the ends being connected on a single pole, and also to have an independently fixed fulcrum for the system to operate on.

Logically, then, some connection must be present between opposite poles, but where is it to be found? Nataraja Guru, squarely in the non-dual Indian tradition, understands this inner coherence to be provided by the Absolute as a universal ground or fulcrum. This approach is rejected by rationalist philosophers because of a tendency to insist on the visible proof of horizontal factors, while an absolute ground must necessarily be outside the limits of sensory experience. Historically, the great Indian gurus have had no such false modesty. They realized that if there is no inherent connection between polar factors, any assertion of their relative merit is arbitrary and thus false. But by postulating the Absolute as that which unites opposites in the equation, values immediately become possible.

In the present work Śaṅkara focuses on the blissful experience of Beauty as the emergent value-form of the Absolute, most intriguing to human beings. In his preliminary comments to the *Saundaryalaharī*, Nataraja Guru makes reference to this matter:

> Cancellation of counterparts is therefore one of the main features of this work. It is neither a god nor a goddess that is given a unilateral importance here. It is an absolute neutral or normative Value emerging from the cancellation or neutralization of two factors, named Śiva and Śakti respectively, that is noticeable consistently throughout this composition. If Śiva is the vertical *reference*, Śakti is the horizontal *referent*. Understood in the light of each other, the non-dual in the form of

> Beauty becomes experienced. Next to the principle of the quaternion — there are two parameters of reference, the vertical and the horizontal, which have to be clearly distinguished within the structure of the Absolute, which latter would be otherwise merely conceptual or empty of content. The phenomenal and the noumenal have to verify each other for the Absolute value to emerge into view. It is the absolutist character of the value of Beauty as understood here that justifies Śaṅkara's use of the term *laharī*. — p. 34

When ambivalent factors are brought into harmonious balance, the experience is of an upsurge of bliss. Śaṅkara treats the experience here as one of Beauty, and assigns it the colour *aruṇa* (magenta), Homer's 'rosy fingers of dawn.' This is the essential experience of non-dual union with the Absolute, in which 'night' and 'day' are in perfect equipoise, at dawn or dusk. Since Beauty is necessarily an actual experience, it must embody all attributes, even to the degree of having its own colour. The colour of the Creation-Goddess is, not surprisingly, the one resulting from mixing equal parts of infrared and ultraviolet light, the two poles of the visible spectrum. The expansive beauty of the full spectrum is thus epitomized in a single breathtaking colour-experience.

Relative factors taken dialectically reveal the Absolute ground between them. If sunrise is a thesis, sunset would be the antithesis. Combining them intelligently and rising to a scientifically higher vantage point, one can look down on the earth from space and see the sun shining constantly, while the rotation of the planet produces the seeming pluses and minuses of relative amounts of daylight. The constant of sunlight is the absolute ground on which the varying relative factors are played out on a rotating world.

Underlying all of Nataraja Guru's philosophy is the Absolute. Defining the Absolute is an impossibility, but it is revealed to the seeker as the emergent factor resulting from the cancellation of polarized elements. Unlike many philosophers who spend endless hours fine-tuning word meanings, with Nataraja Guru's terminology precise definitions are not only unhelpful but certain to leave much of importance outside their boundaries. His notions, like the Absolute to the yogi, arise as grand virtual images that are the sum total of a number of different, dialectically balanced perspectives. It is little wonder that Śaṅkara's great mystical poem, in which Absolute Beauty arises from yogic equanimity, would find the ideal appreciator in the Guru.

The modern day scientific thinker may stumble over the names of deities in the *Saundaryalaharī*. It is a simple matter to update these fanciful terms to the straightforward style of the present, and Śaṅkara would likely permit it. But we must take care not to undermine the poetic beauty of the work by so doing. Certainly, Beethoven's philosophic ideas for one of his symphonies could be summarized in a short essay, but we would have lost everything. It is the very beauty of the presentation that moves us; the power of that beauty converts dull and academic word images into a form that conveys the immense and transformative impact of their meanings. Such is Śaṅkara's leap with the *Saundaryalaharī*. After a lifetime of verbal arguments and cerebral interpretations, this was his Ninth Symphony, his ecstatic poem of divine experience. The philosophic structure is only the skeleton on which the glory of the Goddess is supported.

Everything begins with the Absolute, simultaneously all and nothing. Mathematically, it is the meaning of zero, in all its possible ramifications. The ancient rishis, having much more poetic imaginations than modern rishis, used the name Śiva instead of the Absolute. Śiva has multiple roles in the drama. Alone he is the Absolute, standing for the mysterious ground of existence. Then, in order for the universe to spring into existence with its big bang, Śiva splits into two: energy and matter, or creator and created, called by the ancients Śiva and Śakti.

Creation is known by many other names. She is the Devī, Śiva's wife Pārvatī, Aruṇā, Umā, or simply the Goddess or the Mother. And there are a number of others. The relationship of Śiva and Śakti is exactly the same as matter and energy, which are merely transformations of each other into different states.

A mathematical point has no dimension, and is therefore a pure abstraction. Creation becomes an accomplished fact when a point moves along a single dimension, creating a line. Such movement implies a time factor, which while being called the fourth dimension, has to be present from the instant the movement begins. A second line intersecting the first produces a second dimension and generates a plane. As lines multiply, they form a three-dimensional solid structure, which along with the time factor give us the substratum of our familiar four-dimensional universe.

The primary focus in this work — as in any work of science — is on the created world, here known as the Goddess. Anything created undergoes three stages of existence: generation, a period of manifestation, and final dissolution. These stages are traditionally named Brahmā, Viṣṇu and Śiva. One can see the secret development of the numbers 0, 1, 2, 3, in this process. Four emerges from the quaternion structure of creation itself, symbolized by the equal-armed cross or the Cartesian coordinates. Further specification of the Absolute into the five basic elements produces the next number. And so on. Nataraja Guru himself is much more a mathematician than a religious thinker, and his commentary is aimed primarily at a modern mentality. Further elaborations are well explained and comprehensible as soon as one catches on to his old-fashioned style of writing.

A pair of terms that occur frequently in Nataraja Guru's work and are almost certain to be unfamiliar to the lay reader are hypostatic and hierophantic. The former refers to the heaven worlds, peopled with gods and goddesses and the essences of things, and the latter refers to the world of priests, ritual worship, and prayer. Ritualists reach up, as it were, towards the heavens, while their corresponding divinities bestow boons from on high down to their supplicants below. Such high/low interaction necessarily takes place along the vertical axis, with hypostatic elements imagined at the vertical positive and hierophantic elements at the vertical negative pole.

From the point of view of Tantra, as in most religions, the duality between a god or gods and their supplicants is justified as laying the groundwork for a pathway to salvation in the heavens. Advaita (non-dual) Vedanta, however, does not countenance duality. Herein lies the crux of one of Nataraja Guru's arguments for Śaṅkara's authorship of the *Saundaryalaharī*. In the very first verse there is the claim that no amount of merit or number of divine boons is sufficient to enable the worshipper to bridge the gap with the Absolute in the form of the Goddess. She is beyond all such considerations. It is clearly an Advaita Vedanta position that non-duality can never be attained by dualistic means. In contrast, the dualistic or religious commentaries on the *Saundaryalaharī* universally misinterpret this verse to claim that only one with exceptional amounts of heaped-up merit would be able to properly worship the Goddess. This is not an idea that either Śaṅkara or Nataraja Guru would entertain for a moment. Anyone claiming such a notion as true is by definition a dualist, and their comments can be treated as merely derailing this ineffable work of philosophy into the backwaters of religious thought. To the Guru this 'implies a gap that is in the minds of the critics rather than in the work itself.' (p. 282). Nataraja Guru touches on this distinction in his verse 9 commentary:

> In the Patañjali system, which is based on the dualistic Sāṁkhya philosophy, the dynamism of yoga is in terms of a gradual process of spiritual progress, in eight grades of discipline, ascending to what is marked by the word *kaivalya* (aloneness) at the culminating point. This kind of gradual process of spiritual progress between two points,

> representing ends and means, is repugnant to the more dynamic unitive view proper to Advaita Vedanta, where no vestige of duality could be tolerated, whether in ends or in means. Ends and means have to be treated together. This is the correct Advaitic approach of the Upaniṣads and the Bhagavadgītā. (p. 111)

Nataraja Guru often speaks of numerator and denominator elements in a non-traditional way. As part of his mathematical approach to the Science of the Absolute, he expressed certain relationships as fractions. As in ordinary mathematics, the denominator represents totality, and the numerator the fraction of the total that is under consideration. Where the denominator represents unity or the whole, the numerator stands for plurality or the part. Again, the denominator is the cause and the numerator the effect. Occasionally, the Guru uses numerator to simply mean above the horizontal median, and denominator to mean below it.

When the numerator and denominator are of equal value, they cancel each other out in unity, symbolic of the Absolute. Perfection in Advaita Vedanta therefore is one. On the other hand, the denominator of Buddhism, "there is no Self," is zero, and anything divided by zero is an indeterminate form of zero. While both one and zero can symbolize the Absolute, the difference between them may be said to be the essence of the distinction between Advaita Vedanta and Buddhism.

While there are a seemingly infinite number of excellent points to be made regarding the Science of the Absolute, we will now bow out and leave what remains to the greatest expositor of them all, the Guru himself. *Auṁ*.

2004, Portland Gurukula Scott Teitsworth

Key to Transliteration

अ *a* (but)	आ *ā* (palm)	इ *i* (it)
ई *ī* (beet)	उ *u* (put)	ऊ *ū* (pool)
ऋ *ṛ* (rhythm)	ए *e* (play)	ऐ *ai* (air)
ओ *o* (toe)	औ *au* (loud)	ळ* ḷ
क *ka* (skate)[1]	ख* *kha* (blockhead)[1]	ग *ga* (gate)[1]
घ *gha* (ghost)[1]	ङ *ṅa* (sing)[1]	
च *ca* (chunk)[2]	छ* *cha* (catch him)[2]	ज *ja* (john)[2]
झ *jha* (hedgehog)[2]	ञ *ña* (bunch)[2]	
ट *ṭa* (start)[3]	ठ* *ṭha* (anthill)[3]	ड *ḍa* (dart)[3]
ढ* *ḍha* (godhead)[3]	ण* *ṇa* (under)[3]	
त *ta* (path)[4]	थ *tha* (thunder)[4]	द *da* (that)[4]
ध* *dha* (breathe)[4]	न *na* (numb)[4]	
प *pa* (spin)[5]	फ* *pha* (philosophy)[5]	ब *ba* (bin)[5]
भ *bha* (abhor)[5]	म *ma* (much)[5]	
य *ya* (young)	र *ra* (drama)	ल *la* (luck)
व *va* (vile)	श *śa* (shove)	ष *ṣa* (bushel)
स *sa* (so)	ह *ha* (hum)	क्ष *kṣa* (*kṣatriya*)
त्र *tra* (*trishūl*)	ज्ञ *jña* (*jñāni*)	

अं (ं) *ṁ* (*saṁskṛti*) *ṁ anusvāra* (nasalisation of preceding vowel)

अः *ḥ* (*prātaḥ*) *ḥ visarga* (aspiration of preceding vowel)

* No exact English equivalents for these letters.

[1] guttural [2] palatal [3] lingual [4] dental [5] labial

Preliminaries

In the autumn of the year 1968 I was preparing for a long voyage round the world. As the first step towards this adventurous project, I had booked a passage to Singapore on the British steamer *S.S. Rajula*. This date remains a memorable landmark in my mind because I had by that time finished all the series of major items of a dedicated life-work, projected by me, having bearing on the teaching of my teacher Narayana Guru, to which I had devoted more than four decades already.

I thought I had no more ambition in that same direction when I found myself sitting in front of a bookshelf of the library that was just being started at the Gurukula Island Home, bordering the sea in the Cannanore District of Kerala on the west coast of India. Two volumes of the works of a Malayalam poet called Kumāran Āśān attracted my attention, almost as if by the promptings of some vague principle of chance. I glanced at the two volumes listlessly and without purpose for some time. Before long my attention seemed to linger over the pages at the end of one of the volumes which happened to be a translation of the *Saundaryalaharī* into Malayalam. It was attributed to Śaṅkarācārya, and from the introductory remarks of Kumāran Āśān I found that the date of his translation coincided with the time he had returned from his training in Calcutta to become the first disciple and successor to Narayana Guru himself. At that time they were living together as Guru and the most favoured *śiṣya* (disciple) in a riverside ashram at a place called Aruvippuram, about fifteen miles south of Trivandrum, the capital of Kerala.

The initial scrutiny of the contents of the translation, each verse of which was printed side by side with the original Sanskrit of Śaṅkara, intrigued me and stimulated my curiosity to such an extent that I became more and more engrossed and involved in its study. In spite of not being a Sanskrit scholar of any standing whatsoever, I could discover slight discrepancies here and there between the intentions of the original author and the understanding of the translator. It seemed to me that he was engaged in an almost impossible task, as a result of which all his efforts seemed to be getting repeatedly frustrated or compromised, often with meanings miscarried. This was sufficiently evidenced by the fact that even the barest of a sequential, consistent or common sense meaning did not result, in spite of the tremendous efforts that seemed to have been lavished on the subject matter. Neither the content, context, purpose nor the person kept in mind as the proper student for these verses could even be roughly guessed.

The more I read these verses and tried to make at least some bare meaning out of them, the more enigmatic each verse seemed to become to my eyes. Strangely, too, my understanding seemed to progress inversely to the increased effort that I tried wholeheartedly to apply to this strange text. When I also remembered in these circumstances that Kumāran Āśān might have undertaken this impossible task at the instance of Narayana Guru himself, a belief which was gaining ground with me every time I read the work, my interest in this enigmatic work became all the more heightened.

It seemed to stare at me challengingly, as if to question my critical understanding of a text from a philosopher like Śaṅkara, whose other writings were already somewhat familiar to me. Furthermore, the short introduction by the author of the Malayalam translation, given to justify his understanding, referred to a group of religious people in Kerala, the 'Kerala Kaulins' as he calls them, for whose benefit, according to him, the great philosopher Śaṅkara undertook this apparently onerous task. My self-respect, not to say pride, in considering myself as a person sufficiently capable of understanding in the ordinary course a philosophical text, was stung, as it were, to the quick. And this is how I became personally involved in the work which now remains, even after three and a half years, a major challenge to my common sense or to that degree of average intelligence with which a man of my generation could be expected normally to credit himself.

Even at the moment of writing this (8 January 1972), the enigmatic nature of this work of great absorbing interest still stares me in the face. And it is with certain apologies to many worthy scholars anterior to me and with some hesitations that I enter now on this task of presenting to the modern world the one hundred verses of the *Saundaryalaharī.*

The Original Text and its Commentators

The first forty-one verses have to be distinguished, evidently according to the author himself, as the *Ānandalaharī,* within the totality meant to be entitled more generally as the *Saundaryalaharī.* In Sanskrit, *laharī* means 'intoxication,' or 'overwhelming subjective or objective experience of an item of intelligence or of beauty upsurging in the mind of man'. The word *saundarya* refers to aesthetic value appreciation. Such an appreciation of beauty must necessarily belong to the context of the Absolute if the name of Śaṅkara, the great Advaitic commentator, is to be associated at all with this work, however indirectly it may be. On this point we shall presently have more to say. *Ānanda* (delight) and *saundarya* (beauty) are the two possible perspectives of absolute Value appreciation. When the absolute Value is subjectively appreciated it is *ānanda*, and when it is objectively appreciated it is *saundarya*.

This work has puzzled pundits and professors such as Lakṣmīdhara, Kaivalyāśrama and Kāmeśvara Soori of India, and Sir John Woodroffe and Norman Brown in the West, through the centuries, and continues to do so to the present-day. It cannot be said, however, that the interest in it has ever flagged since it saw the light of day. On the contrary, it has spread far and wide as evidenced by the various editions of different dates and regions — some of them containing elaborate Persian, Mughal and Rajput paintings — and the increasing number of modern editions, mainly nurtured by a great revival of interest in that strange form of Indian spirituality known as Tantra. There is every indication that such an interest is still on the increase. Any light, however feeble, that I might be able to throw on such a subject will not, therefore, be out of place.

My Involvement and Confrontations

Between the date of my first getting involved in this interesting text and the present, I have travelled as much by inner exploration as perhaps to the extent that my physical wanderings were widely distributed. The intensity of my involvement with this text became more and more absorbing.

My first plan was to go around the world by ship. The first lap of my journey was accomplished according to this and I found myself travelling in South-East Asia, giving lectures on the *Saundaryalaharī* in out of the way places, both in Singapore and in various parts of Malaysia. During this period, when I found myself moving from place to place, I did not relax even one day from the uniform and sustained pressure which I applied to the study of the text. Each morning exactly between half-past five and seven o'clock I kept up the habit of sitting with interested listeners, with cups of black coffee and biscuits, trying to delve deeper into the meanings of each verse. I have done so for three and a half years and in the meanwhile have had to change the course of my world tour. Instead of crossing the Indian Ocean and trying to go towards Honolulu, I came back to India and adopted a revised itinerary by which I could include Moscow, Ghent, Luxembourg, Iceland, New York, Chicago, San Francisco, Honolulu, Fiji and Sydney, and be back in India through Malaysia once again, thus, spending nearly a year in all my wanderings.

Wherever I had a fairly long stop-over, my coffee classes continued and what was even more strange, I could notice that my lessons were evidently of greater attraction to others than to myself. Crowds gathered round me even at the unearthly hour of 5 a.m. and listened to me with remarkable avidity of interest. I could not solve many of the problems that seemed to crop up one after another as the studies continued. I began to differ from almost every book that I came across. The whole subject bristled with endless controversial questions and there were moments of despair in which I felt that I was hopelessly involved in some vain task. Some of the questions that came to the surface could be initially and summarily stated as follows:

1. How could Śaṅkara, who is known to be an Advaita philosopher, be credited with the authorship of this text which evidently is of the form belonging to the context of Tantra śāstra?

2. Why should he have written these verses after his great commentaries, which are by themselves sufficiently monumental for supporting his fame as a Vedantic philosopher?

3. If Śaṅkara gave primacy to wisdom, as is well known, how is it that he seems to have come down to the vulgar or popular level of a worshipper of the beauty of a goddess?

4. The *śrī cakra*, which figures in the text very prominently, seems to be the hallmark by which Tantra texts are recognizable. What has this geometrical design to do with Advaita Vedanta, which believes only in the purest form of reason?

5. What is the place of eroticism in the context of the austere sannyasa (renunciation) which Śaṅkara stood for so uncompromisingly?

6. Was Śaṅkara interested in yoga śāstra (the science of yoga) also?

7. If not, why does he take the trouble of describing the various details of chakras (synergic centres) as seen in the verses of this text?
8. If non-duality is the teaching of Śaṅkara, how is it that he postulates Śiva and Śakti as two distinct factors, principles or entities?
9. Was Śaṅkara a religious man at all?
10. How far are the verses compatible with the doctrines developed in his other works?
11. Did his followers give any importance to this work so as to adopt its teaching in any way in their lives as inmates of various ashrams in which they practised their spiritual disciplines?
12. Why does he employ a purāṇic and mythological language here?

Conventional Traditional Approach

Because of the above-mentioned and various other miscellaneous difficulties, even highly painstaking and correctly critical scholars like Professor W. Norman Brown of Harvard University have doubted the authorship of these verses. He has gone into the reasons for doing so in very great detail in Volume 43 of the Harvard Oriental Series, and takes care to indicate in the title page of the work, in all academic cautiousness, that the *Saundaryalaharī* is only 'traditionally ascribed to Śaṅkarācārya'. If we turn to another great authority on Tantra literature, Sir John Woodroffe, the points are not clarified any better. Even a strict word-for-word translation of this work is not so far available, not to speak of a satisfactory versification. Every translation or commentary that I have examined so far, whether in Malayalam, English or in the original Sanskrit, has not failed to reveal here or there some appalling state of ignorance in respect of the main intent and purpose of these verses. Except for borrowing rather lightheartedly the *śrī cakra*, found in verse eleven of this work and described in minute geometrical detail, the whole work seems to be otherwise treated with scant and stepmotherly respect, both by Tāntric pundits and professors alike. When I allude to pundits and professors at one and the same time, I am not unconscious of the fact that there are present in Bengal and in South India, especially in Kerala, many who claim to be authorities on Tantra generally, not excluding the *Saundaryalaharī* in particular. I have had occasion to consult quite a few of these authorities, and I can assert with a certain pleasure that they have tried their best to clarify their respective positions in a conventional and traditional manner proper to punditry and pedantry in India. I must at least mention a few names, like those of Pandit S. Subrahmanya Shastri and T.R. Srinivasa Ayyangar of the Theosophical Society, Kandiyoor Mahadeva Shastri, E.P. Subrahmanya Shastri, besides Lakṣmīdhara, Kaivalyāśrama and Kameśvara Soori.

The greater part of Sir John Woodroffe's prolific volumes itself is based, directly or indirectly, on what some pundits gave him to understand. It would not be wrong to say that these parts are based on hearsay and, therefore, lack that direct appeal or apodictic certitude necessary to make us treat them with the seriousness which the subject deserves. The interest of the present writer is not the same as that of a pundit or professor. Even the question of Śaṅkara's authorship of the work would take at least as much trouble to prove as to disprove. I, therefore, do not wish to enter into any polemical dispute with anybody, and would content myself with taking a position by which I could say that all the great scholars who have devoted their energies in clarifying this text, though they are right only as far as they go, do deserve our gratitude.

My own personal interest in this subject is based on two considerations only. Firstly, it is a unique work in which, for the first time, Śaṅkara is seen to adopt a non-verbal, protolinguistic approach to philosophy, as when Marshall McLuhan would say, 'the medium is the message'. Secondly, I believe that most of the controversies referred to above could be seen to arise from the fact that the text is usually looked upon as if it were a statically given doctrinal statement, instead of being considered as the dialectical revaluation of some anterior position prevailing at the time the author wrote it. The history of religion, as Professor Mircea Eliade of Princeton University has succeeded in proving in his monumental work on the subject (*Patterns of Comparative Religion*), is a series of dialectical revaluations of anterior positions in terms of posterior doctrines. Viewed in the light of such a dialectical revaluation it is not difficult, at least for me, to see that here Śaṅkara adopts a non-verbal protolinguistic medium to restate the message of Advaita Vedanta for which he has always stood, here as well as in his great commentaries.

When these two features are fully understood by the modern reader, it will be seen that most of the controversial problems that have puzzled both pundits and professors melt away altogether. The authorship of Śaṅkara could then be easily proved by a certain type of logic acceptable to Buddhism and Vedanta alike, which is called 'the argument by the impossibility of being otherwise', known as *anupalabdhi*. This kind of logic belongs to the order of axiomatic thinking, and therefore, is still understood even by phenomenological philosophers like Edmund Husserl, only with a certain degree of mistrust. No wonder, therefore, that the world of modern thought is involved in a characteristic puzzlement belonging to the same general intellectual and cultural malaise, the growing evidence of which is beginning to be recognizable wherever we turn, more especially in the world where modern youth express dissatisfaction because of a general gap that they feel existing between themselves and their elders.

This brings us to the next most important consideration that has made me all the more interested in this strange and almost impossible text that I have been trying to understand in all earnestness. There is a new generation of young people, variously called 'beatles', 'beatniks', 'hippies', 'flower people' or 'drop-outs'. They are unconventional members of a new generation, generally with long hair and free ideas about sex, variously influenced by Eastern religions. They believe in miracles and supernatural powers. Inner space is more important to them than outer space. Mind-expanding drugs are everyday luring them deeper into themselves. Such drugs are said to have a 'psychedelic' effect. Yoga and discipleship to a guru are taken for granted by them. Besides yoga, they are also interested in the secrets of what is called Tantra. Most of them are genuine seekers for a new way of life, although some of them are seen to be freaks or misfits. Whatever the explanation of such a widespread social disadoption might be, it is clear that the movement requires sympathetic understanding and guidance. What they call 'institutional life' is their common enemy, and coming into clash with it produces various forms of bad blood, repression or discontent which is at present becoming a problem to all concerned, most especially to themselves. A revision and rearrangement of basic values in life seems to be what they are asking for. Discoveries in science have disrupted the conventional standards in ethics, aesthetics, economics and even in education. Human ecology itself has to be reconsidered and revised. The *Saundaryalaharī*, as I soon discovered, lent itself readily to be the basic ground on which human values could be rediscovered, rearranged, revalued and restated normally and normatively. It is this discovery that became more and more clear to me each day as I taught in my travels, that made this work all the more dear to me.

Side by side with this it also dawned on me with equal force that this mainly non-verbally conceived text was just the one that suited the most modern means of man's communication, which is none other than what is coming to be known as 'expanded cinema'. The magnetic videotape and the advances in computer science, with all the numerous contributions by young and intrepid spirits who are at present engaged in this process which we have called 'expanded cinema', have been so spectacular in their development that now it is possible to say that this mass medium would inaugurate what is beginning to be known as

'Palaeocybernetic Age', expected to revolutionize the whole individual and collective life of man within a few years.

Man can examine the workings of his own mind, not to say the Self, through the intermediary of this wonderful new medium where line, light, colourful vision and audition could help in the process of the marriage of sheer entertainment with the highest form of so-called spiritual education. The availability of such a medium could be said to be just round the corner now. The only snag in this matter is that we need a new kind of literature that could be most advantageously fed into the machine when it becomes available. The answer to this kind of demand for a new kind of literature is already found in the *Saundaryalaharī.* This is the second discovery that came to me by chance. The possible appeal of the *Saundaryalaharī*, more especially to the drop-out generation, became immediately evident to me. My ambition, therefore, was not primarily to write a new and more learned book on this work, but rather to avail myself of the wonderful possibilities of computerized chromatic magnetic tape for putting across to the new generation the valuable contents of this rare book, where the message and the medium already coexist without any contradiction.

The highest purpose of life, which it was the privilege hitherto of the religious bodies to be able to cater to the public by way of spiritual nourishment, thus comes into the hands of every true educator. What is more, 'education' and 'entertainment' become interchangeable terms. The success of the *Saundaryalaharī* could be expected to open the way to many other possibilities of the same kind. What is called 'self-realization' can be made possible, as it were, by a strange irony of fate, through startling advances in the world of mechanistic technology itself. Evil shall thus be cured in and through itself, by its own cause.

What is called 'salvation' results from the cancellation of the non-Self by the Self. Beauty is a visible value in which lines, light and colour can cooperate to reveal man's true nature to himself. When thus revealed, that final cancellation of counterparts can take place which is capable of removing the last impediment to what we might soberly call 'unitive understanding'. This is none other than emancipation, or final Freedom with a capital 'F'. This is the promise that the wisdom of the Upaniṣads has always held out as the highest hope of man. There is both inner beauty as well as beauty 'out there', as it were. The former is that of the yogi and the latter that of the speculative philosopher. Both are capable of effecting cancellation of counterparts between the Self and the non-Self, resulting in that samadhi or satori which marks the term and goal of intelligent manhood.

Having stated now the nature of my main interest, let me take one by one the questions that I have raised above and answer them as shortly as I can manage, without getting lost in too many unnecessary bypaths.

1. Śaṅkara's great commentaries are primarily metalinguistic while this work is protolinguistic. Tantra is only a structural, protolinguistic, non-verbal approach to Indian spirituality at its best, when taken as a whole. We have to think of mantra, yantra and Tantra at once as presupposing one another, if we are to enter into a sympathetic and intuitive understanding of the dynamism that Tantra essentially represents. This dynamism is none other than the mutual participation of yantra on the one side and mantra on the other. Thus, Tantra is the 'know-how' or *savoir faire* by which yantra and mantra could interact mutually and produce what we call 'the fully real experience of unitive understanding', by a double correction. Yantra is associated with a wheel or machine, while mantra stands for uttered syllables or sounds. Each mantra involves a *devatā* or presiding deity that is specially invoked for attaining the efficient result of what is sought. The term *devatā* should be distinguished from *deva* (literally, 'shining one'), which referes to a god or demiurge. All the *deva*s of the Hindu pantheon can be given their correct positions

as monomarks in the context of the yantra, which is essentially a geometrical figure called the *śrī cakra.* Letters of the Sanskrit alphabet could also be used in place of monomarks to indicate structural aspects of the Absolute within the context of erotic mysticism, where beauty is the most prominent prevailing value.

In the erotic context of Tantra there are four functional monomarks commonly used which are: the goad and the noose, referring to the spatial dynamism applicable to an elephant, together with the sugarcane bow and five flower-tipped arrows which indicate the limits of the horizontal world of erotic pleasure. Many of the Tantra texts quoted or alluded to in the writings of Sir John Woodroffe make use of these monomarks and protolinguistic devices profusely, and to such a point of intricacy that the modern reader could easily get lost in their ramifications and complicated implications. For a clear statement we have to go to the *Mahānirvāṇa Tantra,* which perhaps owes its inspiration to Buddhist as well as to proto-Aryan Tantric sources.

One sees very clearly from this particular Tantra how the colour of the dark monsoon cloud which hangs over the whole west coast of India, from Ujjain to Kanyakumari, has a place in the context of Tantra. There is a temple situated on this coast, halfway between Gujarat and the Cape, which could be considered to be among the most ancient of epicentres from which this kind of spirituality could be imagined to have spread its influence far and wide, through the Mahayana Buddhism of central and northern India, reaching Tibet and finally nourishing the roots of the Śakti cult of present-day Bengal.

Tantra is a discipline which combines the secrets of yoga side by side with other esoteric teachings. To the lower strata of society, the five *tattva*s proper to its practice — *matsya* (fish), *māṁsa* (meat), *madya* (liquor), *maithuna* (copulation) and *mudrā* (gesture) — are to be considered both natural and normal. When this lower form of Tantra was subjected to revaluation and restatement in the light of Veda and Vedanta, it gave rise to further subdivisions and graded stratifications, such as the *Pūrva Kaula, Uttara Kaula, Samaya* and fully Vedantic versions of Tantra. Thus, Tantra is a complex growth in the spiritual soil of India.

Śaṅkara, as a great dialectical revaluator of the Hindu spirituality of his time, could easily be imagined to have attempted a final restatement of the same body of spiritual wisdom, which he proposed to clothe in a special kind of non-verbose language. As a result, there were two texts from his pen, the complementary works named *Saundaryalaharī* and *Śivānandalaharī*. The former presupposes a negative, ascending dialectical perspective, while the latter presupposes the same absolute Value when viewed from a more positive position conceived in terms of a descending dialectic. The final contents of both remain the same, although the starting postulates might seem diametrically opposed to each other.

Beauty, especially when it is colourful and full of significant lights and lines, lends itself to be considered the most tangible content of the otherwise empty or merely mathematical notion called 'the Absolute'. Truth and value, thus, are made to fulfil the same function: to give fully tangible content to the Absolute. In short, metalinguistically stated Advaita coincides here with what is protolinguistically understood.

2. As Śaṅkara himself states in verse sixty-two of the *Vivekacūḍāmaṇi*, verbosity is a bane which could even cause mental derangement.

3. To the third question, the simple answer is that no visible goddess is directly envisaged in any of the verses in the series here. Certain picturesque situations are, of course,

presented here and there in such a way that when the numerator and the denominator aspects of the same are cancelled out, we are left with an overwhelming sense of sheer absolute Beauty, independent of any anthropomorphically conceived goddess. The first and the last verses of the series, when read together, absolve Śaṅkara completely of any possible charge of being a theist, deist or even a ritualist in the ordinary religious sense.

4. The *śrī cakra* is a structurally conceived linguistic device. Just as a graph can verify an algebraic formula, there is no contradiction between the Advaita as Śaṅkara has elaborated metalinguistically in his commentaries (*bhāṣya*s) and that which the same Advaita represents in the form of a *schema* here.

5. The proper theme of all poetry or even art could be said to be love. No love, no art. One cannot think of beauty without the form of woman coming into it. Thus, the relevancy of erotic mysticism stands self-explained. The best proof in this matter is the high place that Kālidāsa's poetry occupies to the present day.

6 & 7. Yoga properly pertains to a dualistic school called Sāṁkhya. When revised in the light of Advaita Vedanta, abstractions and generalizations of the various stable syndromes and synergisms proper to the dynamism of yoga discipline refuse to resemble other texts on yoga such as *Gheraṇḍa Saṁhitā, Haṭhayoga Pradīpikā* or even the *Aṣṭāṅga Yoga* of Patañjali. Thus it is, that Śaṅkara's treatment of yoga seems different from other yoga disciplines. He merely restates it in a more respectable form acceptable to an Advaita Vedantin. The *Vyāsa bhāṣya* and *Bhoja ṭīkā* applied to Patañjali yoga are supposed to effect the same corrections and revaluations. Careful scrutiny of the Śākta Upaniṣads and the Yoga Upaniṣads will clarify any further doubt that might linger in the minds of keen and critical students in respect of the purport of these verses.

8. In the Sāṁkhya philosophy there are the concepts of *prakṛti* and *puruṣa,* the former being not imbued with intelligence, while the latter is the fully intelligent principle. Thus we find a heterogeneity between the two categories, which it is the purpose of the revised epistemology and methodology of Advaita to abolish effectively. Śiva and Śakti, who are meant to be united in the present work, are to be understood as belonging together to the same neutral epistemological grade of the non-dual Absolute. They, thus, lose their distinctness and, when generalized and abstracted to the culminating point, could be treated as two perimeters or parameters to be cancelled out by their mere mutual intersection or participation. One has a vertical reference and the other a horizontal reference, while both exist at the core of the Absolute. When abstraction and generalization are thus pushed together to their utmost limit, the paradox is transcended or dissolved into the unity of one and the same absolute Value, which is here referred to as Beauty or Bliss. Thus duality, accepted only for methodological purposes, is to be abolished at each step by unitive understanding.

9. To the ninth question raised above, an unequivocal answer is to be found in the first and the last verses of the series. It is not difficult to see that Śaṅkara's Advaita transcends all ideas of holiness or ritualistic merit altogether. He seems clearly to wash his hands off any such derogatory blemish. The *Vivekacūḍāmaṇi* contains other similar unmistakable indications at the very beginning, which tend to show that the sacred and holy religious values are all repugnant and altogether outside the scope of the uncompromising spirit of Advaita that Śaṅkara has always represented.

10. Śaṅkara's other works, such as his great commentaries (*bhāṣya*s), are conceived on the basis of demolishing polemically a series of sceptics (*pūrvapakṣin*s) taken in a

graded and methodic order, in favour of a posteriorily finalized position called *siddhānta.* A careful scrutiny of each of the verses here will reveal that the same finalized doctrine is enshrined and clearly presented in almost every one of them, though clothed in a realistically non-verbal and visualizable form, based on the value of beauty that could be experienced by man, whether he is a learned philosopher or not. Just to give one example, we could say that the second verse corresponds to the second *sūtra* of the *Brahmasūtras*, where creation, preservation and resolution form the subject matter as phenomenal aspects born out of the same Absolute. Examples could be multiplied indefinitely.

11. It is well known that almost all the existing ashrams or *maṭh*s claiming allegiance to the teaching of Śaṅkarācārya, such as that of Śṛṅgerī or Kanchīpuram, still speak in terms of worshipping a Wisdom-Goddess, such as found in the Śāradā Pīṭha. The tradition started by Śaṅkara is tacitly or overtly adhered to by his followers, although the critical understanding in respect of such worship still remains questionable with most of them.

12. Letters of the Greek alphabet are now being advantageously used in scientific language. The large quantity of purāṇic literature found in Hinduism affords a veritable never-expended mine from which an intelligent philosopher like Śaṅkara could derive monomarks and divinities which could serve the same purpose as the Greek letters in the language of mathematics. Thus, he merely uses the available linguistic elements from mythology instead of deriving them from mathematics as modern scientists would do. From the Upaniṣads through Kālidāsa's poems, such as the *Śyāmaḷā Daṇḍakam* and his various longer poems like the *Kumārasambhava*, there is to be discerned a definite *lingua mystica* using its own cliches and ideograms, through the centuries down to our own time.

After Kālidāsa, Śaṅkara used it most effectively, and it was given to Narayana Guru to be the continuator of the same tradition in modern times.

Generalities

It is a hard task to give a real or tangible content to the notion of the Absolute. All disciplines, whether cosmological, theological or psychological, imply a notion of the Absolute, without which, at least as a reference, all philosophy or science tends to become incoherent, purposeless and inconsequential. Ethical, aesthetic or even economic values also require a normative regulating principle, which can be no other than the absolute unit, presupposed tacitly or overtly for ordering and regulating these disciplines. Over-specialization of science leads to compartmentalization of branches of knowledge, each tending thus to be a domain proper only to an expert or specialist. The integration of all knowledge is beginning to be recognized as important for the progress of human thought at the present moment.

There is a hoary tradition in India which refers to a Science of the Absolute, which is called *brahmavidyā*. It belongs to the context of Vedanta, which has been recently attracting the attention of modern scientists of the West, such as Erwin Schrödinger and others. There is, at present, a large body of modern thinkers who believe that a rapprochement between physical sciences and what is called metaphysics — which is independent of the senses — is possible, and that a Unified Science can thus be ushered into existence. Attempts have been made along these lines, especially at Vienna, Paris, Chicago and Princeton. What is called the philosophy of science and the science of philosophy could be put together into the Science of all sciences, in which many leading thinkers are interested. It is the central normative notion of the Absolute wherein lies the basis of any such possible integration. To give a precise content to the Absolute is, therefore, an important problem engaging the attention of all thinking men. The new physics of the West is tending to become more and more mathematical or theoretical. What is equally interesting is that Eastern disciplines, such as Zen Buddhism, Yoga and Vedanta hold at present a new interest to the Western scientist.

The present work is meant to insert itself in between these two trends in modern thought. The large number of people now breaking away from conventional standards and patterns of behaviour, both in the East as well as in the West, not to speak of the polarity between northern and southern temperaments, are now trying to discover themselves anew. Humanity has to catch up with its own proper bearings and gather together loose ends from time to time as 'civilization' takes forward steps. We are now caught in the throes of just such an agonizing process. New horizons and more extensive frontiers have to be included within the ken of the vision of the world of tomorrow. Myths have to be revised and new idioms discovered, so that fact and fable can tally to verify each other and life can be more intelligent, consequential and consistent. An integrated or unified science must fulfil the functions hitherto related as proper only to religion or to metaphysical speculation. Educated man is called upon to take his position, more intelligently than hitherto, vis-á-vis the great quantity of discoveries that are being made in both 'inner' and 'outer' space. While relating outer space with inner space we also necessarily and tacitly bring together East and West, besides unifying science and metaphysics.

The notion of this inner space brings us to just that new factor which has recently entered into the creative imagination of the present generation. Thermodynamics, electromagnetics, cybernetics, semantics and logistics, aided by newer and newer mathematics, are bringing into view vistas unfamiliar hitherto, in which it so happens that in many academic circles the intelligent student feels more at home than the professional teacher, whose main interest is often merely to keep his job or shape his career. The best of the students and the most original of the young professors feel that there is a widening gap between their own ambitions or legitimate urges and the prevailing standards, and have reason to complain that they are often obstructed in the name of outdated precedents or rules. Co-education has abolished much of the distance between the sexes. Girls need no chaperones, and the university undergraduate does not have to live up to any Victorian form of respectability or even to the chivalry of the days gone by. Adam prefers to keep the forbidden fruit in his hand, and naturally begins to treat the earth as a planet on which he must pass freely. Linguistic or racial frontiers, together with dinner jackets and wine glasses, are being left behind in favour of more individualistic patterns of dress or group conduct. Parisian fashions do not impress youth any more, and mind-expanding drugs are beginning to replace those other poisons like champagne that induce merely a feeling of lazy comfort. Public standards are floundering because of this accentuation of inner space, which is holding out new interests to allure the imagination of adolescents.

Inner Space and Structuralism

LSD and allied drugs, which have what they call a mind-expanding effect, have opened up a world that could be called 'pagan', as opposed to 'prophetic'. Sensuousness is no sin to Bacchus, while to a Jeremiah, prostitutes and idolatry, and all the existential values belonging to animism and hylozoism are highly repugnant. The golden calf had to be replaced by the tablet of commandments that Moses and Aaron held up before their chosen followers. The water of the Ganges is sacred to the Śiva worshippers of India, and this is the reason that they are spat upon as idolators and infidels, fit to be trampled upon by the elephants of the emperor Aurangzeb. As between the *logos* of the Platonic world of the intelligibles and the *nous* of the pre-Socratic Eleatics, two rival philosophies emerge into view in modern times, trying to determine the superiority of existence or essence. Psychedelics reveal a new vision of the negative aspect of consciousness where what is called the subconscious, and all its contents, become magnified and revealed to inner experience.

There are thus at present two rival minds to deal with: one that is interested primarily in percepts, and the other interested primarily in concepts. Both of these have to be accommodated together in an integrated picture of absolute Consciousness. A lopsided vision can spell nuisable situations. It is this discovery of inner space that is upsetting and disrupting the total scheme of values of the individualistic 'drop-outs' of the present day. Values do not all hang together with reference to the same point any more, and the double or multiple standards thus emerging must necessarily confuse people in the domains of ethics, aesthetics and economics, not to mention those of education and religion or spirituality.

Values, both positive and negative, have to be fitted into a fourfold structure, the limbs of which could be summarily indicated in advance as representing the conceptual, the perceptual, the actual and the virtual. This fourfold structure has been known to poets in the West since the time of Milton, and in India since the time of Kālidāsa. The *lingua mystica,* of whatever part of the world it may be, seems to have had this mathematical secret hiding within its semantic or semiotic structuralism — sometimes referred to under the term 'semantic polyvalence'. The Upaniṣads contain many passages that reveal unequivocally this fourfold structure, mentioned so directly in the *Māṇḍūkya Upaniṣad* when it states 'this Self is four-limbed' (*ayam ātmā catuṣpād*). The *schematismos* of Kant and structuralism as understood by post-Einsteinian scientists like Eddington, have brought this notion once again to the forefront, and it is offered as a kind of challenge for the modern man to accept or reject. Bergson, while remaining essentially an instrumentalist, is also most certainly a structuralist, as would become evident to any one making a careful scrutiny of the following paragraphs:

But it is a far cry from such examples of equilibrium, arrived at mechanically and always transitory, like that of the scales held by the justice of yore, to a justice such as ours, the justice of the 'rights of man', which no longer evokes ideas of relativity and proportion, but, on the contrary, of the incommensurable and the absolute.[1]

Across the time and space which we had always known to be separate and, for that very reason, structureless, we shall see, as through a transparency, an articulated space-time structure. The mathematical notation of these articulations, carried out upon the virtual and brought to its highest level of generality, will give us an unexpected grip on the real. We shall have a powerful means of investigation at hand, a principle of research, which, we can predict, will not henceforth be renounced by the mind of man, even if experiment should impose a new form upon the theory of relativity.[2]

Śaṅkara's *Saundaryalaharī*

Śaṅkara's *Saundaryalaharī,* when examined verse-by-verse, reveals many enigmas which come to light only when a structural analysis is applied to each of them. Otherwise it remains a closed book to punditry that has beaten its wings in vain trying to make the great poet-philosopher's words have even a mere semblance of coherent meaning. The *Saundaryalaharī* (Upsurging Billow of Beauty), together with Śaṅkara's other century of verse called the *Sivānandalaharī* treats, we could say, of the same absolute value from perspectives tilted 180 degrees from each other. The mythological elements that enter into the fabric of this composition, and the large array of Hindu gods and goddesses are pressed into service, as it were, by Śaṅkara

1. Henri Bergson, *The Two Sources of Morality and Religion*, Doubleday, 1954, p.74.
2. Henri Bergson, *Duration and Simultaneity,* Bobbs-Merrill Co., 1965, p.150.

to give a precise philosophical context to the supreme value called Absolute Beauty, which is the subject matter of these verses. This same subject can be looked at in the more positive or modern light of a structural and mathematical language where geometric or algebraic signs and symbols can verify a formula. This is the basis of the protolinguistic approach that we have adopted in conceiving this work. Line, light or colour, also biological, crystalline or radiated structures, can all be made to speak a non-verbal language with at least as much precision as in the case of essentially verbose commentaries, such as those of Śaṅkara himself. How successfully this series of verses can itself be treated as a sequence of visions is a matter that the success of the present work alone must prove hereafter. Meanwhile, it is not wrong to state that modern technical discoveries, such as the stroboscope, laser holograms and computer graphics, animation and devices such as collage, montage, mixing, merging and filtering of colours etc., could together open up a new age for both visual education as well as entertainment through the most popular medium of modern times: the film.

Large and verbose treatments of such subjects are likely to go into cold storage in the future, because the output of printed matter is too much for the busy person of the present to cope with. This work is meant, as we have just indicated, to be educative as well as entertaining. Its appeal is not, therefore, primarily to box-office patrons who might wish to pass an easy or comfortable evening of relaxation after a hard day's work; but to a more elite audience, which wishes to learn while looking for visual enjoyment. There are thus many features that are not conventional in the film world which have to be taken into account even now by the reader, anticipating its fuller film version.[3]

---

3. Nataraja Guru was deeply involved in preparations for a video-film, at the Gurukula Film and TV Research Institute, Bangalore, at the time of writing these words. Though Guru's

The first forty-one verses of the *Saundaryalaharī*, are distinguishable as such by the scrutinization of the nature of its content, as pertaining to the world of inner yoga. The mandalas, the chakras, the yantras, mantras and tantras, as representing stable psychic states or experiences of the yogi, figure here to the exclusion of beauty as seen objectively outside. Global perspectives of objective beauty are presented in the latter section of the *Saundaryalaharī*, this name being more directly applicable to verses forty-two to one hundred, inclusive. As against this second part of the work, we have the first part, of forty-one verses, which is distinguished by the name *Ānandalaharī, ānanda* (bliss) being a factor experienced from within, rather than from any outer vision. The title of the whole work of one hundred verses is justified in spite of this inner division, because that absolute value called Beauty, which has here the character of being upsurging or overwhelming in its wholesale appeal to the spirit of man, who wants to give tangible content to the notion of the Absolute, which would otherwise be empty, is still that unique value-content, whether subjective or objective, which remains the common subject matter or the object matter of this entire work as conceived by Śaṅkara.

Śaṅkara is well known in the context of Advaita Vedanta by his great commentaries on the three canonical texts of Vedanta: the Upaniṣads, the *Brahmasūtras* and the Bhagavadgītā. Although some scholars still doubt the authorship of the present sequence of verses and tend to attribute it to some others than Śaṅkara, anyone familiar with the doctrinal delicacies and particularities of the Advaita that Śaṅkara has always stood for, cannot for one moment doubt the hallmark that always distinguishes his philosophy unequivocally. The internal evidence available from almost every verse in this text, as well as the sister-work called

→ leaving the mortal coil interrupted the work, it is still hoped that the film project will be taken up and completed by disciples in the near future, through the grace of the Guru. (ed.)

Śivānandalaharī, attributed to the same Śaṅkara, can, in our opinion at least, leave no doubt about Śaṅkara's own authorship of these two exceedingly interesting and intelligent works. Moreover, Śaṅkara is unmistakably the correct continuator of the Vedic or Upaniṣadic tradition that has come down to us through the works of Kālidāsa to the present-day. There is an unmistakable family resemblance here which, when viewed in its proper vertical hierarchical perspective, exists between the idioms, ideograms, imagery and other peculiarities of a mystical language. One can recognize this masterpiece as representing the best of the heritage of the ancient wisdom of India preserved through the ages, and of which Śaṅkara is, truly speaking, one of the more modern continuators.

Śaṅkara as a Dialectical Revaluator

Śaṅkara is a great dialectical revaluator of all aspects of ancient Indian wisdom. Nothing of Sanskritic cultural importance has been lost sight of by him, including those of semantic, logistic or merely ritualistic importance. The authorship of Śaṅkara of these hundred verses at least need not be doubted if only for the additional and final reason that we cannot think of any other poet-philosopher or critic attaining, unmistakably, the high quality of this work and its sister-work *Śivānandalaharī*. The history of religion is nothing but the history of the dialectical revaluation of prior positions in terms of posterior doctrines. These two positions could be treated as complementary to each other.

In the Biblical context this same transition from the old to the new, as from the Mosaic law to the law of Jesus, is invariably marked with the words, 'You have heard it said — but verily, verily, I say unto you'. It is not unreasonable to think that Śaṅkara here takes up what was, till his time, known as esoterics — under the titles of Tantra, yantra and mantra, especially as understood in the Kaula and the Samaya traditions, both of Bengal and South India — and subjects them to his own critical and dialectical revaluation. He thus presents to us the restatement of those 'esoteric' doctrines in a fully 'exoteric' form in keeping, above all, with his own avowed position as an Advaita Vedantin. This view must suffice for us here to show that all those who hitherto treated *Saundaryalaharī* as some kind of text belonging to the Śākteya Mother worship cult would thus be culpable of a great inconsistency which they do not themselves explain, thinking that an avowed Advaita Vedantin could ever write a text which does not support his own philosophy. It is strange that even Sir John Woodroffe, who treats of this *Saundaryalaharī*, tends to belong to this category. Professor Norman Brown of Harvard has the same misgivings as revealed in the very subtitle of his work where the authorship is dubiously stated as 'ascribed to Śaṅkara'.

Modern man is interested both in post-Einsteinian physics as well as in the world that properly belongs to the discipline of yoga. Zen Buddhism opens up a world in which meditations and contemplative experiences from within the self have an important place. The Upaniṣads, and Vedanta too, are based on inner as well as outer experiences proper to the contemplative. When we think of inner experiences we are in reality referring to the mystical experiences of a yogi within himself.

The Nature of the Text

The *Saundaryalaharī* consists of one hundred verses and forms a sequence in Sanskrit poetry written in a heavy and dignified metrical form. The syntax and inflections of Sanskrit are especially suited to the use of highly figurative language, and there are often many layers of more and more profound suggestions as one layer of meaning gives place to another implied below or above it, in ascending or descending semiotic series. We are here in the domain where meanings have their own meanings hidden behind each of them and the mind sinks backward or progresses forward, upward or downward, within the world of poetic imagination and expression. A sort of meditation and a free fancy are presupposed in compositions of this kind, heavy-laden with suggestibility or auto-suggestibility. There is always a subjectivity, a selectivity and a structuralism that is implied.

Further Implications of Structural Language

With reference to this work, it is necessary to clarify the implications of what we call structural analysis. Poetry has the primary function of being pleasing or beautiful. Literary critics in the West tend to condemn metaphysical or moralistic poetry as inferior to pure poetry where enjoyability is its only desirable quality. In the world of Sanskrit literature, however, mysticism and the wisdom that goes with it have never been divorced from the function of poetic art. Aesthetics, ethics, and even economics can legitimately be made to blend together into a pleasing confection that can console or satisfy the love of bliss or joy that good poetry can give — without the compartmentalization of such branches into separate disciplines of literature. Moralist maxims such as found in *Aesop's Fables* or in Alexander Pope's writings have been condemned by critics in the West as being didactic in character and thus detracting from the pure function of poetry as such. We do not look for morals or precepts in poetry any more; much less do we expect, according to Western norms of literary criticism, to learn metaphysical truths from poems that must necessarily suffer from didactic tendencies which can never be reconciled with the proper function of poetry which is mainly lyrical or just pleasing. Metaphysical poetry in the West tends to be artificial or forced. The Upaniṣadic tradition has, however, quite a different history. It has always had the serious purpose of revealing Truth through its analogies and figures of speech. The one absolute Value that wise people have always been interested in explaining has been, for the Upaniṣadic rishis, the one single purpose of their innocent, transparent and detached way of high thinking exhibited through their simple lives. The degree of certitude that they possessed about this Value-content of the absolute touched a high watermark in their pure contemplative literature. They had no private axes to grind. Thus, Wisdom that referred to all significant life interests taken as a whole entered into the varied texture of these mystical and mathematically precise writings. Poetry and science were treated unitively here, as perhaps nowhere else in the world's literature, with a few exceptions perhaps, as in Dante's *Divine Comedy*, Milton's *Paradise Lost*, or Goethe's *Faust*.

The Upaniṣadic tradition has been compared to the Himalayas, the high source of the three great rivers of India, the Indus, the Ganges and the Brahmaputra. Like the Nile for the Egyptians, the snowy peak of Gaurīśaṅkara and the waters of the Ganges have lent their precious idioms, ideograms, and even analogies and figures of speech that have perennially nourished Sanskrit literature. Without the Himalayas and the figurative language in which the Śiva family is represented as living on Mount Kailās, Kālidāsa's poetry would be deprived of much of its grandeur and richness. Śiva is the positive principle of which the Himalayas is the negative counterpart. Pārvatī is sitting on his lap and the twin children represent between them the striking ambivalence of personal types. The white bull Nandī, the good and faithful servant and vehicle to the principle that Śiva represents, reclines nearby. This family can be seen by any imaginative or intuitive person to be a replica of the grand scene of the Himalayas as revised and raised to the dignity of divinity. When an absolutist touch is added to this implied quaternion structure of the Śiva family, with the bull representing the foothills of the central mass and the peak dominating the total content of the Absolute as structurally recognizable, we get a close and correct perspective by which we may examine this century of verses.

Each verse leaps into meaning only when the underlying structural features are revealed and brought into view. Otherwise, the hundred verses remain, as they have remained through the thousand years or more of their history, a mere challenge to vain pedantry or punditry. In other words, structuralism is the key that can make this work an open book, a scientifically valid work, with a fresh appeal to all advanced modern thinking persons of the East and the West. It will be our task within the scope of the work itself to introduce the reader, as occasion permits, to further implications and intricacies of this structural approach, which perhaps, is the one feature on which the value and success of this work would have to rest.

Theology permits man to say that he is created in the image of God. This is only a polite way of stating the same truth that 'The Kingdom of God is within you', or 'the Word was with God and the Word was God'. The bolder Vedantic tradition asserts the same verity when it says: 'Thou art That', or 'I am *brahman*'. A subtle equation is implied here between the relativistic perspective of the content of *brahman* and its more conceptual or absolutist aspect of the pure notion itself, so that the word 'Absolute' could have a tangible content. Such a content cannot be other than some high value because without value it cannot be significant or purposeful in terms of human life. When Keats says 'a thing of beauty is a joy for ever', we recognize a similar Platonic thought repeated on the English soil after the European Renaissance. To treat absolute Beauty as the content of the Absolute is fully normal to Vedantic or Advaitic thought. Both what is existent (*sat*) and subsistent (*cit*) must be covered, each in its turn, by *ānanda* (bliss or value factor) which could easily be equated to the high value of absolute Beauty. Thus, we see unmistakably the sequence of the reasoning justifying the title *Saundaryalaharī*. It becomes not only justified but lifted above all forms of lower ritualistic or Tāntric contexts to the pure and exalted philosophical domain of a fully Advaitic text, in keeping with the dignity of a scientific philosopher of the status of Śaṅkara. The pure and the practical, the noumenal and the phenomenal, the absolute and the relative, the transcendental and the immanent, *res cogitans* and *res extensa,* and all other such conjugates, whether in philosophy or science, could only refer to what is distinguished in Vedanta as *para* and *apara brahman*. Different schools of thought might have differing terms which have the same two intersecting parameters for their common reference.

Each of the hundred verses with which we are concerned here, when scrutinized in the light of this structuralism that we have just alluded to as also in the light of the equation implied in the *para* and *apara* (i.e., the vertical and the horizontal) aspects of the same Absolute, will bring to view as far as possible in non-verbose language, the content of the Absolute seen from the negative perspective of absolute Beauty as viewed *sub specie aeternitatis.* Thus, a book that has remained closed to punditry all these years will come to have a significant and practical bearing on our modern life.

Yantra, Mantra and Tantra

The word *Tantra* has to be understood with its associated terms — which belong together to a certain type of esoterics found in secret India — independent of formulated philosophical systems or doctrines. Just as the bed of a river contains precious deposits mixed with sand, cultures that have flowed down the ages over valleys or plains such as that of the Ganges or the Nile have often deposited rich nuggets of esoteric wisdom-value. The Hermetics, the Kabbalah and the Tarot represent such deposits near the Mediterranean cities of antiquity. As in the case of the *I Ching* of China, fortune-telling and astrology have their own vague contributions to this body of esoteric wisdom found in different parts of the globe. To change esoterics and present it in a more critically revised form as exoterics is impossible without a normative reference. Tantra, yantra and mantra are three of the fundamental notions connected with a certain type of esoterics found particularly in Tibet and also along the Malabar Coast and Bengal in India. The central idea of Mother worship and erotic mysticism has nourished this school of thought known as the Śakti cult, and has kept it alive through the ages without being subjected to the corrections of either Vedism or proto-Aryan Śaivite philosophy. Being full of secret mystery, thaumaturgists made use of the vague twilight in which its teachings flourished — mainly in the basements and cellars hidden under old temples or shrines — to participate in certain kinds of orgies where wine and women and flesh-eating figured to support a pattern of behaviour known as *vāmācāra* (a left-handed way of life), which the more learned brahmins would not recognize. They, under the general name of *Śākteya*s, came to include two sections — the more ancient and cruder section being called *kaulin*s, and the other section, which received at least some recognition from Vedic priesthood, being called *samayin*s. These schools indulge in exorcizing evil spirits and in correcting psychological maladjustments by preparing amulets or talismans, the word for which in Sanskrit is yantra. It often consists of a scroll of thin metal enclosed in a case of more precious metal, which is tied around the neck. Because of the lucrative nature of such a profession, priestcraft, as anywhere in the world, gave this school its patronage, and thus it has persisted on the Indian soil for ages, independent of any prevailing religious authority at any given time in history.

The yantras invariably contain geometric figures with magic letters marking angles, points, lines or circles. The letters would correspond to the notion of mantra, which depends on a symbolic chant or incantation. The figures themselves are attempted proto-linguistic representations of the same mystery, the technique of which is to be distinguished as Tantra. It is thus that the terms yantra, mantra and Tantra belong together to a certain form of esoteric mystery still attracting the attention of many people, both intelligent and common place, where mysteries naturally thrive in the twilight background of human thought.

Since Śaṅkara was a guru who wanted to revise dialectically and restate in a proper critically revalued form the whole range of the spirituality of his time, he did not overlook the claim of this particular form of esoterics. He wanted to salvage whatever was precious in it and bring it into line with the Upaniṣadic tradition. He had for himself the model of the great Kālidāsa, whose writings, as his very name suggests, belonged to the same context of Mother worship. Although Kālidāsa's works have become almost a closed book to even the best pundits of India in the present day, it is still possible to see — through a structural analysis of his works — the common lineage that links Śaṅkara with his forerunner Kālidāsa and thus take our minds backwards to the great source of all the wisdom contained in the Upaniṣads. Speculation had scaled very high in India at the time of the Upaniṣads, which centred around one main notion — the Absolute (*brahman*). The structural implications of the Absolute found in the mystical language of the Upaniṣads have served as a reference and have nourished subsequent thought down to our own times. In the light of the structuralism that has come into modern thought, as it were, through the backdoor of science, and through the precise disciplines of mathematics going hand in hand with the progress of experimental scientific findings, it becomes possible now to see these ancient writings as consistent with a fully scientific modern outlook. It is this discovery, if we may call it so, that encourages us at present about the possibility of presenting the contents of the *Saundaryalaharī* through the visual language of the film or magnetic tape.

The Meaning of *Laharī*

The title of this century of verses itself underlines its unique characteristic. Each verse when properly understood will be seen to contain two distinct sets of value counterparts. If one of them is to be called 'physical', the other can be called 'metaphysical'. When they cancel out against each other through a complementarity, compensation or a reciprocity which could be recognized as implied between these two counterparts, the resultant is always an upsurge of an experience which could come either from the inner or the outer pole of the total absolute Self. This resultant could even be called a constant, and thus an absolute belonging to a particular discipline and department of life. To give a familiar example, when heat and cold cancel out, climatic conditions can yield the possible absolute constant of that particular context. When heavenly values and earthly values cancel out by complementarity, alternation, or split-second cancellation, we can also experience another kind of beauty, bliss or high value factor. When viewed in its proper absolutist perspective, such a constant amounts to attaining the Absolute. Such an attainment of the Absolute would be tantamount to the merging of the Self with the Absolute in Upaniṣadic parlance, and can, even in principle, amount to merging in or becoming the Absolute itself.

Śaṅkara has named his work a *laharī* which suggests an upsurging or overwhelming billow of Beauty, experienced at the neutral meeting point of the inner sense of beauty with its outer counterpart. We have to conceive the whole subject always in its fourfold polyvalence to be able to experience this overwhelming joy or bliss, to produce which each word, phrase or image of each of these verses consistently strives, in its attempt to give a high value content to the Absolute. There is no mistaking that the present work is perfectly in keeping with the same Advaitic doctrine that Śaṅkara has laboriously stood for in all his other writings.

Cancellation of counterparts is therefore one of the main features of this work. It is neither a god nor a goddess that is given a unilateral importance here. It is an absolute neutral or normative Value emerging from the cancellation or neutralization of two factors, named Śiva and Śakti respectively, that is noticeable consistently throughout this composition. If Śiva is the vertical *reference,* Śakti is the horizontal *referent.* Understood in the light of each other, the non-dual in the form of Beauty becomes experienced. Next to the principle of the quaternion (referred to above), there are two parameters of reference, the vertical and the horizontal, which have to be clearly distinguished within the structure of the Absolute which would otherwise be merely conceptual or empty of content. The phenomenal and the noumenal have to verify each other for the absolute Value to emerge into view. It is the absolutist character of the value of

Beauty as understood here that justifies Śaṅkara's use of the term *laharī*.

The Alphabet of the World of Beauty

All philosophy is generalization and abstraction to give meaning to the Absolute. This meaning must have human value significance. 'Beauty' or 'Bliss' is the final term of speculation bringing us to the very doorstep which opens into the Absolute. Thus, there is the world of beauty in aesthetics, just as there is the world of discourse to which logic belongs, or the world of calculables to which mathematics belongs. Mathematics has its elements which can be algebraic or geometric in status. Similarly, linguistics can use either signs or symbols. A red light is a signal or a sign while the word 'stop' is a symbol, but both of these have the same meaning. In the same sense, percepts meet concepts and cancel out into one value factor.

Beauty can be analysed structurally to reveal its relational aspects, i.e., through geometric figures it could be given monomarks which might belong to any alphabet. The world of beauty has its alphabets or its lines or angles. It is in this sense that for the Pythagoreans the numerological triangle called *tetraktys* became a divine symbol, still worshipped in their temples. The alphabet understood as belonging to metalanguage and geometrical elements such as angles, points, lines or concentric circles can be used protolinguistically to reveal the content of the Absolute in universally concrete terms. This is the truth that Kant mentions in one of the footnotes in his work on pure reason by which he intends to state that *schematismos* can verify philosophical categories and vice-versa. Thus corrected both ways, in a back-to-back structural relationship contained within the paradox of the two parameters (vertical and horizontal), we could verify between them various algebraic formulae. Thus we have in our hands a rare instrument of research, about which Bergson speaks in the quotation already cited, on page twenty-three.

What we are concerned with is not only the alphabet of the world of beauty, which belongs to the metalinguistic or conceptual side, but also with its schematic counterpart which is of a more perceptual order. If the alphabet of the world of beauty, as monomarks or letters which are essentially symbolic in status, is metalinguistic, the schematic counterpart of the same world of beauty will be protolinguistic, consisting of geometric elements such as the triangle, the circle, the line or the point, together with the vertical-horizontal correlates having the figure-of-eight at its very core, to give dynamism to the total static structure. The various limits within which it lives could be named algebraically by the alphabets, as monomarks for each element. Elements of the world of beauty could belong together to the context of absolute Beauty conceived neutrally or normatively. We arrive in this manner not only at alphabets, but also at elements about which we shall speak in the next section. About the alphabets themselves we could say here in advance that they have a taxonomic value, helping us to name and recognize unitive factors in the context of absolute Beauty. Further implications of such an alphabet of the world of Beauty will become evident when we treat the actual verses in the present work at their proper places, such as verse thirty-two, linking letters with elements so as to verify each other and thus lead to the certitude about the content of Beauty which the interaction of these verses reveals, and which justifies the use of this kind of double-sided language of signs and symbols. All alphabets, however analytically understood, have still to be held together at the core of consciousness by the unifying letter *hrīṁ* which is the first letter of the word standing for 'heart' in Sanskrit. However varied the alphabets might be, they have to have the heart at the core of consciousness to hold them organically together, like the hub holding the spokes of a wheel. Thus structuralism and its own nomenclature belong together.

One has to be familiar both with the alphabets of Beauty as well as with the elements of Beauty, each from its own side of the total situation. Alphabets could be as many as contained in any language and could include vowels as well as consonants. Each letter could be made to represent a certain characteristic, forming a component unit or part of the total content of the Absolute. Each of the rays radiating from a point of light could thus have a letter attributed to it for purposes of recognition and nomenclature. Thus, these letters belong to the mantra aspect, while the yantra aspect is the structure itself. The *savoir faire* or the know-how aspect of imparting the knowledge about the Beauty could be called the Tantra aspect of the same. Thus, Tantra, yantra and mantra belong together and verify one another to make this sense or experience of Beauty surge up within one's consciousness with an overwhelming force. A sense of Beauty overpowers the person who is able to enter into the meaning of each verse both analytically and synthetically at one and the same time.

Elements of the Perceptual Components of the World of Beauty

Crystal-clear gems, when they reflect or refract or diffract light, represent beauty in the most evident sense. They have angles, points, lines and colours, and they make various beautiful combinations. Next to gem-beauty comes flower-beauty. The lotus has been the flower dear to the heart of the contemplative Indian mind through the ages. Thus, God is praised as having lotus feet, lotus eyes, lotus mouth, lotus in the heart and at the various psychophysical centres called chakras or *ādhāras*.

When structural features belonging to the biological world are abstracted and generalized, we enter the three-dimensional world of conics. Conic sections can be related at various levels to a vertical parameter running through the base of a double-cone, placed base to base. The triangle is only a particular two-dimensional instance comprised within the solid geometry of conics and the apex of each triangle could be turned inversely and a series of interpenetrating triangles could be placed within the cones for purposes of structurally analysing the total relation-relata complex in the light of which we are to examine the beauty contained in the Absolute.

A vertical symmetry and a horizontal symmetry, the former with a complementarity, the latter with a parity, could be included within the total possible structural perceptual patterns that emerge to view. Parity could imply a right-handed and a left-handed spin, twist or mirror-asymmetry, and complementarity could imply ambivalence, reciprocity or compensation of various intensities. The vertical axis is purely mathematical or logical in status in which degrees of contradiction could be admitted, for cancellation. Time can absorb space and space, time; this dynamism which is the basis of modern physics and the very essence of Cartesianism is to be kept in mind here by us. To use our own terminology, there is always to be attributed a polarity, an ambivalence, a reciprocity, a compensatory principle, a complementarity and finally a cancellability between the limbs of the quaternion structure here postulated. At its core, there is a vertical back-to-back relation and horizontally, there is what might be called a belly-to-belly relation. The latter admits of contradiction and is the basis of all conflict in life. Vertically, however, all shocks and stresses are absorbed and abolished, by mutual cancellation at whatever level of this two-sided parameter. There is a dialectical descent and ascent between the positive and the negative poles of the total situation.

Structure has thus to be conceived statically first, and then its own proper dynamism introduced or attributed to it so that we get a global view of all the perceptual component factors that make up the total picture in which the high value called Beauty is to be examined by us in each of the hundred verses. There are subtler factors that enter into the dynamism which we cannot enumerate exhaustively here. They will enter into our interest normally as we focus our attention on the representations implied in each verse.

A flashlight that we hold in our hand when walking through misty darkness can light only a circle within our visible area at a given time, although mist and darkness are not limited to what we can see. Contemplative minds, especially as understood in the logic tradition of India, thus justifiably think in terms of circular or global units of consciousness placed in a vertical series beginning from the bottom pole of this vertical axis and ending at the top pole. Although its physiological position may not correspond to psychological units in terms of consciousness, the vertebral column with a central strand of nervous energy called *suṣumnā nāḍī*, together with two other psychophysical strands, at the left and right, respectively called *iḍā* and *piṅgalā* is generally taken for granted in yogic literature. If we now imagine six zones of consciousness ranging from bottom to top we get the *ādhāra*s or chakras, sometimes described and elaborated in detail by geometrical and biological analogies such as angles and coloured petals in yoga books.

There are various schools of yoga, the most important one being that of Patañjali, which uses eight such centres. In the present work however, we find six centres prominently mentioned, each representing a point where the horizontal factors and the vertical factors cancel out to reveal a stable, neutral or normal aspect of the Absolute proper to that particular level. The ambivalent factors always cancel out to yield the same constant Absolute, however varied the pictorial context in which Beauty is appreciated might happen to be.

The Tarot cards consist of pictorial representations supposed to represent the alphabet of their kind of mysterious schematism of thought. Yoga books also indulge in a similar pictorial language, but on the Indian soil such pictures are mostly nourished by the mythology or analogies proper to the long Sanskrit tradition. This is to be treated only as incidental by the modern man, who can understand the same without mythology by a more positively revised protolanguage such as what we adopt and recommend here. The various gods of the Hindu pantheon happen to be themselves structural or functional components to be fitted together, giving us a content for the totality called absolute Value which is always the object of any speculation, independent of time or place. Śaṅkara can be seen to have taken full advantage of the implications of this mythological language not because he is religious himself, but because it lends itself admirably to the problem of giving beauty-content and full significance to the otherwise empty notion of the Absolute.

A word about the *Bindusthāna*, the locus of participation

The first forty-one verses of the *Saundaryalaharī* presupposes a contemplative yogi who is seated with shut eyes, representing an introspective withdrawal into the world of inner consciousness. The objective or the positive side of consciousness in relation to the Self will be the 'object matter' proper to the rest of the composition. When a person meditates properly, his mind attains one-pointedness. This very term presupposes a point, not necessarily on a blackboard but at a locus within one's self, which is referred to in Tāntric literature as *bindusthāna.* This focal point is where the global drop or essence of existence resides. When we think of a drop like *bindu*, we could think of it as being made of an absolute Substance, described also by Spinoza as a 'thinking substance'. We could visualize the same absolute Substance with its own vertical reference when we add to it the dimension of *res cogitans* as used by Descartes. This vertical element is often referred to in yogic or Tāntric literature as *nāda,* the essence of sound. *Nāda* and *bindu* together participate vertico-horizontally in terms of a thinking substance known as *nādabindu*, which is supposed to be the ontological starting point — the source or place of origination and dissolution — of all that comes to become or to be in the mental or the material world.

It is usual in contemplative Sanskrit literature to refer to *nādabindu* in terms of the tender lotus feet of a god or goddess. Only the tenderest part of our mind can participate with an equally tender part of that which we meditate upon, because any participation between subject and object, even in meditation, has to presuppose the principle of homogeneity, which is called *samāna adhikaraṇatva*. The soldering together of two different metals implies this principle; the base metal and noble metal can be made to participate intimately only when there is an equality of status between them. The tenderest devotion thus meets on equal terms the tender petals of the lotus feet of the god. It is, therefore, usual to put the two feet of the god you are meditating upon at the focal point, where mind and matter cancel out into the neutrality of the thinking substance. The two feet within a lotus could be placed at any point on the vertical parameter, which is cut at right angles by an implied horizontal forest of lotuses, which is independent of the *bindusthāna* of meditation. Thus a vertical series and a horizontal series of lotuses are presupposed for structural purposes in each of these verses. The horizontal dimension is incidental only, whereas the vertical reference is the essential parameter that links essence with existence — existence marking the lowest (hierophantic) alpha point, and essence marking the highest (hypostatic) omega point. The point of intersection represents the normative *bindusthāna* proper, but at whatever point in the vertical series (positive or negative) the feet of the adorable One might be placed by the contemplative, there is a constant value regulated by the central normative lotus which is always the constant reference.

These are some of the characteristics of this structural language adhered to by classical convention through a tacitly understood *lingua mystica,* coming down to us from pre-Vedic times through the Upaniṣads, through Kālidāsa and through Śaṅkara. It is impossible for us not to recognize the two sets of lotuses radiating from the central lotus at the *bindusthāna,* as suggested in verse twenty-one. A justification of all that we have said above is found in this verse.

Structural Dynamism

It is one thing to visualize the alphabets or the elements of structuralism *in situ*, and quite another thing to visualize this structuralism in living or dynamic terms. Yogic meditation is not a static fixation of the attention on objects such as a *bindu* which is mere mesmerism or crystal-gazing. The *bindu* must be thought of as a target to be reached by the mind that is comparable to a bow fitted with an arrow directed vertically upwards towards the omega point. It is reciprocally implied that the bowstring is pulled towards the alpha point. The bowstring when thus pulled, would tend to make its own hyperbolic triangular shape, with an apex pointing towards the base of the lower cone, implied in the static structural figure that we have suggested of a double cone placed base to base. The flying arrow reaches the target at the apex of the top cone, while its reciprocal negative dynamism is implied in the tension of the bowstring trying to attain the limit at the alpha point. The alpha point thus has a negative psychodynamic content in the form of an introspective or introverted, mystical or emotional state of mind full of tender feelings, such as the feeling between mother and child, shepherd and sheep, etc. This is the domain of the weeping philosopher and the agony of the mystic.

The stages marked on the plus side of the vertical axis represent brighter and more intelligent states of the psycho-physical or psychosomatic self. The coloration tends to be brighter and whiter as the emotional content transforms itself in its ascent by stages into fully emancipated states free from the weight of emotional impact. A rich magenta glory might thus be said to be present even to the normative or centralized psychosomatic vision, though only subjectively experienced by the yogi.

The arrow that flies upward at right angles with a momentum proportionate to the tension of the horizontal bowstring pulled toward the negative pole of the vertical axis, attains its maximum limit the more it approximates to the alpha point, when released with maximum tension. The speed and power of penetration of the arrowhead breaks through all barriers, cancelling out the arithmetic difference that might persist between the arrow and the target. Thus, there is a cancellation of counterparts along a vertical parameter, to be understood with its negative as well as positive content, but always with a central normative magenta glory for reference. Such are some of the dynamic features of the structuralism, which we have to insert correctly into the same context, when we have visualized the static structural features.

Psychostatics and psychodynamics have thus to belong together when we try to get to the bottom of the value that each verse reveals. Each of the six or eight positions usually distinguished as *ādhāra*s or chakras is to be looked upon as a stable cross-sectional point of equilibrium between counterparts which are always cancellable into normality or neutrality — just as a numerator number of whatever value could be cancelled out against a denominator value of the same set or category — yielding a constant that remains uniform at whatever position it might be along the vertical parameter. It is always the neutrality of the magenta glory that is revealed when vertical and horizontal factors cancel out within the core of the Absolute.

Other Miscellaneous Ideograms

There are many other ideograms besides the bow and arrow which bring into the picture the dynamic aspect of structuralism. We have seen how the lotus flower and the feet figuratively represent ideograms. Now we find a number of secondary ideograms which are consistently used as alphabets or elements or both together within the scope of the *lingua mystica,* which is the language employed in this work.

The bee drinking honey from the lotus always implies a factor on the side of the enjoyer (*bhoktā*), as against the honey as the factor on the side of the enjoyable (*bhogya*). There is a subtle dialectical interaction between these two sets of values: one referring to the subjective world and therefore vertical, the other to the objective world and therefore horizontal. At the point of separation between the vertical and the horizontal, we could imagine a row of bees sucking honey, with a flower for each bee. The horizontal parameter would be the line separating each bee from its flower or the drop of honey it seeks. Instead of a row of bees, sometimes we find rows of cranes or rows of elephants, which refer to the four quarters of the compass in a sort of vectorial space, to be placed within consciousness. Thus, we find the word *diṅnāga*s, which means 'four or eight elephants, each representing the four or eight points of the compass', to be imagined as playing havoc on or pushing their trunks into a central pole or axis. The crystal imagery, resembling that of a colour solid, properly belongs to the base of a vertical axis, while at the neutral zero point this same crystalline form would resemble a maze, or lattice or matrice of vertico-horizontal lines looking like a cage.

When we think in terms of radiating light that goes from a point to some universal here or elsewhere, the colour solid gives place to its counterpart, to be visualized in terms of two cones placed apex to apex. Thus crystal shapes, conic sections, radial arrangements in flowers, logarithmic spirals with complementary spins, inversions, transformations both vertical and horizontal, all enter into the complex fabric of the dynamics of the structural language employed here. Petals, like apexes of triangles, can represent, together with rays of light radiating outwards, elements of various abstractions or generalizations within the scope or content of the absolute value of Beauty here. The letters of the alphabet could be applied preferably to conceptual rays, while lines standing for relations of a here and now ontological character are proper to the crystal which serves to explain more ontological relation-relata complexes. The matrice at the centre of the axes serves to clarify the fourfold quadrant aspect. The most central dynamism could be the representation by a figure-of-eight, exemplified by the familiar pulsations in electromagnetic interference figures, and also by the systole-diastole function of the heart. Every pulsation could be biologically reduced in its double aspect to conformity with this figure-of-eight which depends on the sine function of waves or frequencies. Wavelengths are horizontal while frequencies are vertical, or vice-versa, as the case may be. When inserted together into the same space, they make this figure-of-eight structurally valid in terms of cross-polarized light.

All these figures trace their courses within the grand flux of universal becoming, which is the most basic phenomenal manifestation of the neutral Absolute. The universe becomes experienced in most general terms as a process or flux of becoming. This is what Heraclitus meant when he said that 'one cannot enter into the same river twice'. Bergson's philosophy supports the same flux in terms of the *elan vital.* Vedantins also think of the universe in terms of a process or flux of becoming when they refer to *maya* as *anādi bhāva rūpa* (of a form of a beginningless becoming), itself having an absolute status. Maya, as the negative aspect of the Absolute, however, could yield a normative Absolute which could cancel out the flux, but viewed from the side of relativity to which a living man naturally must belong, the universal flux of becoming is a reality that could finally be abolished only when the total paradox implied between physics and metaphysics is also finally abolished. In this grand flux of becoming, structuralism naturally enters as it does in modern physics, where space and time belong together as conjugates and can be treated as Cartesian correlates. The articulation of time gives us the vertical parameter.

Functional Monomarks of Graded and Duplicated Divinities or Presences

Dynamism presupposes functions. Eros is the god of Love who has the function of sending arrows to smite the hearts of lovers. Eros, thus, is a demigod or demiurge who is often represented by the bow and arrow held by him. The bow and arrow represent in visual language the monomarks belonging to his function. The three divinities, Brahmā, Viṣṇu and Śiva, have their functions of creation, preservation and destruction respectively, which take place within the total scope of the cosmological phenomena comprised within the pure notion of the Absolute. Thus Viṣṇu's function lies structurally in the middle zone, while Brahmā brings up the rear and Śiva functions as the destroyer of everything at the omega point of nominalistic over-conceptualization. Upward and downward logarithmic lines between the lower and the higher limits would indicate the ambivalence between the function of Brahmā and that of Śiva.

Eros, or Kāmadeva, must have his counterpart Rati as his virtual companion. Śiva can destroy Eros only when Eros' presence falls outside the vertical negative parameter. But when occasionalism favours him, as he takes refuge within the vertical negativity of the Absolute, he reigns invulnerably supreme by his own right (verse six). The divinities can be either hypostatic or hierophantic in their significance. Where they have a numerator value, they are represented as gods or demigods, but when they have a denominator value they are spoken of as 'presences' with an ontological or an existential status (verse eight).

The devotee, as Śaṅkara himself indicates in the first verse, is placed outside the scope of the holy or the sacred, at the bottom of the vertical axis, and beyond Śiva who marks normally the omega point. Parameśvara, who has a thinner and more mathematical status, is to be presupposed as the counterpart of the devotee, as his saviour. As prayer or worship always implies a benefit between the worshipper and the worshipped, we could imagine an endless series of devotees praying for benefits compatible with them, each placed in duplicate at points marking hypostatic or hierophantic values within the total amplitude of the two-sided vertical parameter. Each of the divinities involved could confer its benefit to the believer or worshipper who constantly meditates on it. All prayers correctly made from the denominator side must necessarily find their compatible response from the numerator side. Such is the time-honoured presupposition in all prayer.

Thus, a mathematical Paramaśiva beyond the omega point on the thin parameter has his counterpart in a footstool or cushion on the negative vertical side, either for the Devī or himself indifferently. From her toes to the top of her tresses there are subtler values to be arranged back-to-back. Nothing can be omitted, because the universal concrete that the Absolute represents enters even into the essence or existence of the toe-nails and the tuft of hair. Flowers could be hierophantic or hypostatic in origin, or both, according to the circumstances. The waters of the Ganges, representing the high Value, can pour down to purify or bless a total situation from the head of Śiva down to his feet. When originating at the zero point, in a lake represented by the navel of the goddess, this water flows horizontally like an actual or geographical river conferring benefits on cultivators. The seventh verse, when scrutinized, will reveal how these levels and dimensions are woven into the structural dynamism as adopted by Śaṅkara.

A Drama Unfolding within the 'Self' as in the 'Non-Self'

The present series of verses could be viewed statically as representing chakras or mandalas. The yantra could provide a dynamism because it suggests a wheel always going around. A picture as well as a drama may be said to be unravelling itself before our vision as the poem unfolds to our view various aspects of absolute Beauty. The dynamism thus superimposed on the structure makes the whole series resemble the scenes of a dramatic universe, to be thought of both subjectively and objectively at once. All drama involves personages who are also called characters. Besides the hero and heroine, who between them represent the vertical and horizontal references, there is a villain who is responsible for bringing in the complication which has to be resolved during the presentation of the action of the drama. When the classical rule of the unity of time, place and action is fully respected, as it used to be before the time of the romanticism of Victor Hugo, we get a more global perspective of a comedy or a tragedy, with many stratifications of paradises gained or lost, infernos or purgatories incorporated into the picture, with Dante and Beatrice, God or Satan, Faust or Mephistopheles as the main personages involved.

A clown or a chorus that can be used to interpret the scenes could add a touch of levity to the total scene. All the nine emotional attitudes known to Sanskrit aesthetics, ranging from masculine passion to the tenderest emotions of motherhood, could enter into the total picture that the drama thus unfolds to our view. In Aeschilus' play, the bound Prometheus supplies the central locus around which action develops radiating polyvalently in all directions. A clown could be an interloper functioning both as a villain as well as a tale-bearer. A strong man could add a Herculean touch in whom hierophany prevails over hypostacy. In the present composition all the corresponding personages of the Indian myth can be easily distinguished. Eros is recognized as a complicating character. The presentation and the resolution aspects of the drama have the same Eros involved in them in milder or modified forms as occasion demands. The antinomy between Zeus and Demeter is resolved in the present work by the attempt made in every verse to resolve the paradox involved between them, rather than to enhance the element of contradiction as in classical Greek literature. Śiva and Śakti participate in a gentle dialectical way so that a normative cancellation without conflict takes us beyond the contradiction of the paradox. Such is the interplay of the functions of the various characters which are seen to be enumerated in verse thirty-two by the author himself.

Part I
Ānandalaharī

1

शिवः शक्त्या युक्तो यदि भवति शक्तः प्रभवितुं
न चेदेवं देवो न खलु कुशलः स्पन्दितुमपि ।
अतस्त्वामाराध्यां हरिहरविरिञ्चादिभिरपि
प्रणन्तुं स्तोतुं वा कथमकृतपुण्यः प्रभवति ॥

śivaḥ śaktyā yukto yadi bhavati śaktaḥ prabhavituṁ
na cedevaṁ devo na khalu kuśalaḥ spanditum api ।
atas tvām ārādhyāṁ hari hara viriñcādibhir api
praṇantuṁ stotuṁ vā katham akr̥tapuṇyaḥ prabhavati ॥

śivaḥ — Śiva; *śaktyā yuktaḥ yadi* — if united with Śakti; *prabhavituṁ śaktaḥ bhavati* — becomes able to manifest; *evaṁ na ced* — if not thus, otherwise; *devaḥ* — this god; *spandituṁ api* — even to pulsate; *kuśalaḥ na khalu* — does not know indeed; *ataḥ* — therefore, thus; *hari hara viriñcādibhiḥ api* — even by Viṣṇu, Śiva and Brahmā; *ārādhyāṁ tvām* — adorable You; *akr̥ta puṇyaḥ* — one of ungained merit; *praṇantum stotuṁ vā* — to bow down or even to praise; *katham prabhavati* — how could be able

Śiva, united with Śakti, becomes able to manifest,
If otherwise, this god knows not even how to pulsate,
How then could one of ungained merit be able to bow to,
or even praise,
One such as You, adored even by Viṣṇu, Śiva and Brahmā.

This opening verse squarely poses the paradox of life. Sanskritic literary convention requires that the beginning of any work indicate: (1) the subject or content of the work, (2) the context of the work, i.e., where it belongs in relation to other disciplines or kinds of literature, (3) the overall purpose of the work, and (4) the type of person to whom the work will correctly apply. These requirements are correctly kept in mind by Śaṅkara in this opening verse of the *Saundaryalaharī*.

A paradox always implies two rival positions, both of which could be true alternately or when taken together dualistically. The wise man, the poet, the philosopher, or the spiritual guide has to face this paradox which lurks at the very core of life as its most central problem. It is of a highly subtle, speculative, or philosophical order. Other problems belong to human life in its numerous everyday aspects. In every case, an enigma lurks between two factors such as appearance and reality, mind and matter, theoretical and practical, noumenal and phenomenal, etc., as an endless series of antinomies. Man and woman, father and mother, husband and wife, cause and effect; these are conjugates of the same kind, their relation in every case being of a subtle and enigmatic order. Even a word and its meaning belong to each other inseparably, for they cannot be thought of disjunctly from each other.

The Bhagavadgītā refers to this duality in its own terms as the field (*kṣetra*) and the knower of the field (*kṣetrajña*). By abolishing the duality between them one attains the Absolute. Thus we come to the notion called the Absolute, which is the same as the *brahman* in Vedantic philosophy, with which Śaṅkara is most directly concerned. It is well known that he stood for Advaita Vedanta, a strictly non-dual philosophical position which admits of no reality outside itself. The doctrine of the *Saundaryalaharī* is the same philosophy that he has elaborated in all his great commentaries (*bhāṣya*s), although here it is presented in a non-verbose, visible, and colourfully real, protolinguistic form. Failure to appreciate this fact has made most scholars and authorities treat this work as pertaining only to the discipline of Tantra rather than of Vedanta, thus resulting in a wrong estimation altogether. We have explained this fact in the 'Generalities' earlier.

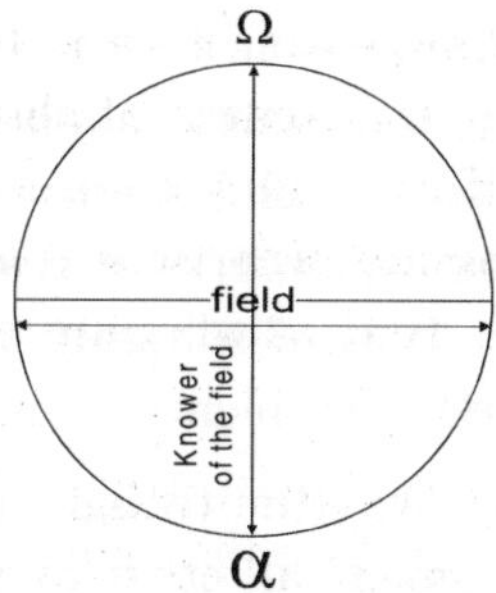

Śaṅkara makes Śiva and Pārvatī represent between them the highest of human values, as easily recognizable even in everyday conjugal life known to all men and women anywhere in the world. Śiva is not a demiurge here but has his place as the counterpart of his own negative aspect, represented by Pārvatī. The relation is a very subtle and enigmatic one. A word and its meaning belong together. The word is merely nominalistic or conceptual, but its meaning must refer to human experience without being a mere abstraction. We call the abstraction a concept, while the experienced aspect of the same would be a percept. Thus nominalism and perceptualism, which Vedantins refer to more simply as 'name and form' (*nāmarūpa*), meet and fuse together, cancelling out into what we appreciate as the meaning, which is neither a concept nor a percept, but is the result of the two-sided participation between these opposing aspects.

To give an example, truth and beauty can be thought of as human values resulting from the participation and cancellation of what is visible with what is intelligible. The status of the resultant meaning, represented by the words 'Truth' and 'Beauty' written with capital letters, falls within the aegis of the Absolute. All human values can be treated this way, as Spinoza says, *sub specie aeternitatis*. In the *Saundaryalaharī* Śaṅkara combines the beauty of Śiva and Pārvatī so as to give them together the human value of Beauty with a capital letter, by which it attains an overwhelming absolutist status, as suggested by the title of the work itself. Śaṅkara's aim here is to give to the abstract notion of the Absolute, the content of absolute Beauty. In doing so he reveals himself as a man of superior poetic genius, by virtue of which the Absolute, otherwise a mere abstraction, comes to have a concrete, real, and visible as well as a truly experienceable content.

Colour is a reality. And the twilight colour, magenta, has a special central status among all other colours, for it results from the meeting of the infrared and the ultraviolet. We find as the central theme of each of the hundred verses the personification of the value of absolute Beauty in the form of the Goddess who is directly equated with the colour magenta (*aruṇa*). (See verses twenty-three, fifty, eighty-four, ninety-two, ninety-three and ninety-eight.) Thus the author intends here to bring together two aspects: something fully real and visible on one side, the colour magenta, and that which is on the other side as its counterpart — a highly thin and mathematical abstraction which also represents the Absolute, not in visible but in purely intelligible terms. The universal concrete and the universal abstract are thus inserted into the same neutral or unified ground. By intersection we could say that magenta, as a universal reality, has a horizontal reference where it inseparably participates at the core of the field of consciousness with its own vertical parameter of a highly fourth-dimensional order. Such theoretical matters will become clearer as we proceed. Lesser degrees of abstraction and generalization could give us an endless series of intermediate positions. Each position could then represent, in a hierarchy of values, one item of value, always coming under the aegis of the Absolute when correctly placed and cancelled out within the fourfold structural situation. What we must understand is that Śiva and Pārvatī, who are mythological figures or divinities of the Hindu pantheon with specific functions attributed to them in the traditional literature of Hinduism, are here being exalted by Śaṅkara to the position of two ambivalent abstract principles — their intimate participation having a complementarity, a reciprocity, a compensation, and a cancellability between them.

All overt action or activity is horizontal in status, and therefore, must be relegated to the domain of the negative existential principle, which is the function of Pārvatī. Her reference is at the negative vertical limit of the fourfold structural whole previously described. The participation between Śiva and Pārvatī takes place at the very core of the total situation, ground or field. Śiva, as the positive principle within the same field, is to be visualized as a thin vertical parameter, having his reference at the hypostatic or positive vertical limit of this quaternion situation. No kind of action, except in the most purely mathematical sense, applies to him. He is a kind of 'unmoved mover' of Aristotle, who, like the catalyst in chemistry, while acting, is not really acting at all.

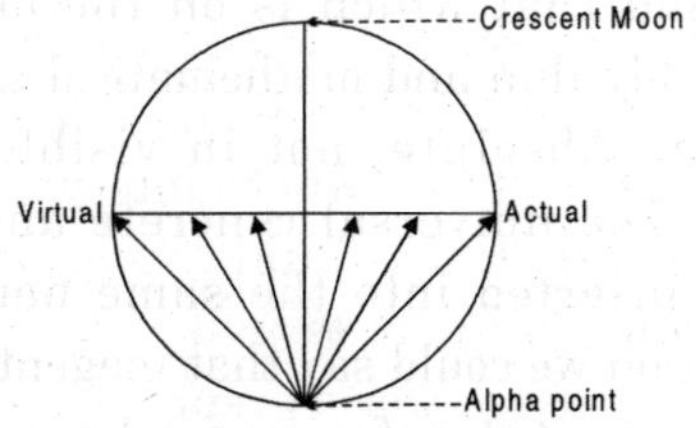

The distinction here can be compared to time-like and space-like functions. Horizontal action is space-like; while vertical action is time-like, spending itself in duration, which is purely conceptual in its status. If we abstract this paradox of concept and percept even further, it abolishes itself by double assertion or by double negation, both of which attain the Absolute which is beyond paradox. Such are some of the subtleties which must be kept in mind by the intelligent reader who examines the content of this century of verses, starting from this very first one. Without doing so, the reader is likely to make the error of treating this work as a theological or cosmological scripture or even a textbook of Tantra meant only for religious or philosophical study by persons lesser in their cultural interest than the uncompromising Advaita Vedantin, like Śaṅkara himself, who is to be kept in mind as the *adhikārī* (the type of person for whom these verses are meant). It is in this sense that Śaṅkara takes care to indicate that he is outside the scope of that kind of Vedic religious orthodoxy, which thinks in terms of holiness or meritorious works, when he says that he is incapable of praising or even saluting the absolute principle of Beauty here intended. The way of works and merits is unequivocally rejected by him in this verse as being outside his scope or intentions. We have to read the first verse together with the last verse of this work, where he again washes his hands of any intention to present a specific religious doctrine, which ordinary religious people might infer that he is tacitly supporting. The Absolute is proved by itself, and should be left alone to declare its glory to the world.

In this very first verse, the reader can see that Śaṅkara wishes to emphasize the necessity of thinking of Śiva and Śakti as belonging together to the one and only unitive context which is that of the value called absolute Beauty. It is a great mistake to separate the functions of the twin counterparts that are meant to enter into a unified non-dual function here. Mother worshippers in India are likely to make the mistake of saying that the beauty of the three worlds represented by the Goddess, sometimes referred to as Śakti or Tripura Sundarī, is to be given primacy over the Śiva principle. They tend to forget that the basic cancellability of status between these two counterparts (male and female, positive and negative, vertical and horizontal, conceptual and perceptual, etc.), is all-important to keep in mind throughout the unfolding of this sequence of verses. To forget this idea is to fall into the error of duality, the most repugnant attitude for Advaita Vedanta. The Kaulins, and perhaps the Samayins, were just such Sakti worshippers, whose unilateral positions Śaṅkara must have wanted to correct and revalue by undertaking the present work.

Another point to notice in this verse is that when Śiva is not united with Śakti, he has no function at all. Some commentators say he becomes *śava*, a dead body, when he is not united with the feminine principle. This is to forget that a correlating parameter running through the whole universe and able to order or ordain it, making cosmos out of chaos, is as important a function as any other function or aspect of the same Absolute. Here a form of pure verticalized action is implied as running through the world like the guiding thread of Ariadne, without which Theseus would never have been able to ascend out of the labyrinth of the Minotaur. Even the *Māṇḍūkya Upaniṣad,* which eliminates all functions and even predications when it refers to the highest Absolute in its final verdict — describing the ultimate Absolute as removed multi-dimensionally beyond all taint of relativity or predicability — still retains a certain auspicious value or attribute, referred to as *śāntam śivam advaitam* (peaceful, auspicious, non-dual). A further qualification is mentioned immediately anterior to these final epithets by the words *prapañcopaśamam,* referring to that principle which abolishes the phenomenal world, that is, all that has a horizontal reference. Thus, to distinguish clearly the implied paradox, so as to finally abolish it correctly without violating the requirements of an absolutist epistemology, methodology or axiology, is of great importance from the very start. Science and mathematics, physics and metaphysics, the visible and the intelligible, are all counterparts that have to be treated as belonging together to an absolutist whole.

There is, in this verse, a reference to the three gods, Brahmā, Viṣṇu and Śiva, who have three distinct functions to perform within the totality of the field in which Śiva and Pārvatī live together. The value of the union itself is the ground of the Absolute, and the three functionaries are to be inclusively contained therein as having only a secondary importance. With any number of other gods permissible under the aegis of the Absolute, this eternal union of male and female represents the resultant of the absolute value of Beauty. In mathematical terms this union is just a cancellation taking place between the vertical and the horizontal parameters, the latter of which can be thought of as a curved or asymptotic line (perimeter), while the former could be a straight line (parameter).

The three main functionaries represented here are fully justified and they could be recognized even by strict scientifically-minded persons when we treat them each as having the status of a factor with a function belonging to it, as when we say that $y = f(s)$ in algebra. Thus the mythological personifications can be disregarded as merely incidental to the exigencies of language. Other monomarks could be chosen to refer to these same functions, which are creation, preservation and destruction. These three functions are inevitable concepts in the context of the cosmological, psychological and axiological processes taking place in the universe, within the Self or the non-Self, when thought of in most general and abstract terms. Mythology is less positive than mathematics, as August Compte would put it. The positively-minded modern man need not take mythology seriously. These demiurges could be treated as monomarks for the three functions understood in the abstract, where the grand process of becoming in the universe can be thought of as coming under the inevitable functional phases or aspects of beginning, enduring and disappearing, to one or the other of which three phases, any process, inner or outer, must conform.

These three gods or demiurges belong to the Vedic context. Vedanta is outside mere Vedism but does not conflict with it, just as an expansive lake could hide within it a well. Vedism, with its distinctions of meritorious action and sin, based on the notions of the sacred and the profane, could be inclusively transcended or submerged within the scope of the more open and generous dynamism of the Advaitic outlook. We have to distinguish the two as limiting points within the scope of spiritual progress. (Just as the river Rhone expands into the lake of Geneva at one end, but passes out at the other end as a thin stream again — to use one of Henri Bergson's favourite examples — one could place oneself at the lower expanding limit of the river or at the upper contracting limit of the lake in a vertical perspective; without coming into conflict with less absolutist religious disciplines, which are vitiated by hedonistic or relativistic considerations.) This first verse marks the lower limit. By the time the discussion reaches the last verse, spiritual progress through 'works' has attained its maximum maturation, thus effectively abolishing its own importance, just as the same water can transcend the lake to become a simple river again. The three gods thus come into the picture only between the lower and higher limits of the total situation to be kept in our minds here. Śaṅkara himself prefers not to enter into the context where merits and demerits, or causes and effects, or obligations and taboos come into interplay within these two limits. The effects of good works accrue only at the upper limits. Śaṅkara, at the start here, correctly places himself before any action and reaction or cause and effect begin to operate. He wishes to remain a strict absolutist in keeping with his own neutral and normalized position, giving equal importance to both cause and effect. He takes his stand preferably even before the causes begin to operate. He is thus removed from all taint of the phenomenal process of becoming. Transcending this, he is again seen at the end to be outside the scope of the fourth-dimensional set-up in which alone good and bad could interact. This is the reason why he takes care to underline in this verse that he is one of unaccomplished merits, unlike the demiurges who are caught within the process and strive to attain the positive limit which is the culminating point for all meritorious actions.

Vedanta is a negative way (*nivṛtti mārga*). That is a further reason why this description, as evidently applicable to himself as well as to the correct reader, is treated as being outside the scope of both merit and demerit taken together. When speaking of himself in this manner, we are also justified in thinking that he is indirectly referring to the kind of person to whom this work applies (*adhikārī*), which refers to any member of the public having the same status as himself in the total situation to be visualized here. This could be done by what is called extrapolation in mathematics. The subject of this work is the value of Beauty under the aegis of the Absolute, as correctly seen in the context of Vedantic tradition, which transcends the Vedic context in which the three gods aspire for perfection by works of religious merit, being placed at the positive top limit of the structural vision. As a Vedantin, Śaṅkara himself takes his position initially on the negative side of the total situation, opposed to all aspiration, as is in keeping with the *nivṛtti mārga* of *brahma vidyā* (the Science of the Absolute) understood in the Upaniṣadic context.

There is a reference in the *Kena Upaniṣad* to the situation in which three gods — Agni (god of fire), Vāyu (god of wind), and Indra (the chief of the gods) — stand puzzled about the nature of a spirit (*yakṣa*) that presents itself in a vacant space before them. This, in fact, was *brahman*. This positive aspect of the Absolute is approached closest by Indra, the best of the demiurges. The same space then suddenly reveals the beautiful form of Umā, the daughter of the Himalayas, representing the negative aspect of the same Absolute without contradiction or mutual exclusion. The beauty of Umā (Pārvatī) here treated as interchangeable in value with what the Absolute represents, thus affords us a correct precedent acceptable to the teaching of the Upaniṣads, of which the *Saundaryalaharī* could be treated as a correct continuation.

Śiva worship is proto-Aryan and chiefly of South Indian origin, but the Upaniṣadic tradition blends both Aryan, proto-Aryan and Dravidian cultures, as is unequivocally implied in verse seventy-five. These comments on this first verse are to be taken as important preliminary clarifications for the understanding of the remaining verses also.

Structural Analysis

The analysis will reveal some more of the structural implications applicable to the aesthetic value of the Absolute when viewed from a negative rather than from a fully positive perspective. Note here that it is the totality that is indirectly adored or praised. The question of merit does not even arise when the total absolute Value

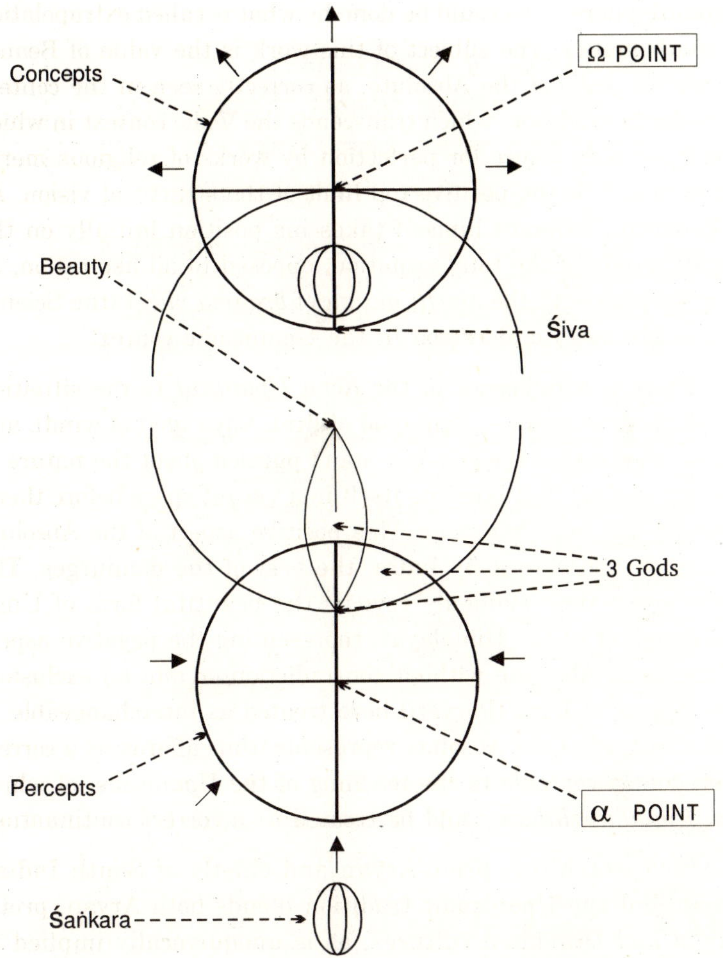

as intended here is understood. The manifesting function is that of the horizontal negative and the pure Absolute itself is beyond action as it is comprised within pure verticalized positivity. There is thus only an indirect praise of the Absolute initially at the start of the work, from a negative viewpoint.

2

तनीयांसं पांसुं तव चरणपङ्केरुहभवं
विरिञ्चिः संचिन्वन् विरचयति लोकानविकलम् ।
वहत्येनं शौरिः कथमपि सहस्रेण शिरसां
हरः संक्षुद्यैनं भजति भसितोद्धूलनविधिम् ॥

tanīyāṁsaṁ pāṁsuṁ tava caraṇa paṅkeruhabhavaṁ
viriñciḥ sañcinvan viracayati lokān avikalam ।
vahaty enaṁ śauriḥ katham api sahasreṇa śirasāṁ
haraḥ saṁkṣudyainaṁ bhajati bhasitoddhūlanavidhim ॥

viriñciḥ — Brahmā; *tava caraṇa paṅkeruha bhavaṁ* — arising out of Your lotus feet; *tanīyāṁsaṁ pāṁsuṁ* — the fine dust; *sañcinvan* — gathering up; *lokān* — the worlds; *avikalam* — entire, unimpaired; *viracayati* — creates; *śauriḥ* — Viṣṇu; *sahasreṇa śirasāṁ* — by thousand heads; *enaṁ* — this same; *katham api*- somehow or the other; *vahati* — (incessantly) he bears; *haraḥ enaṁ saṁkṣudya* — Śiva, having shaken it up; *bhasita uddhūlana vidhiṁ* — (his) ash-wearing rite; *bhajati* — accomplishes.

The fine dust arising from Your lotus feet,
Brahmā, gathering up, the worlds creates,
Viṣṇu incessantly bears them up somehow with thousand heads,
And Śiva, having shaken it up, accomplishes with it his ash-wearing rite.

In this verse the individual function of each of the three demiurges is fitted into a common scheme, as attributes of the same unifying vertical parameter running through their three functions. It is important to remember that it is not an ordinary universe which we have to presuppose or postulate in this verse, but rather the *monde affine* known to modern physics, which we have to visualize as the starting datum for the purposes of this work. There is direct reference to fine particles, whether in the form of botanical pollen, or matter seen in mineral crystals, or as finely divided matter independent of the states of solid, liquid or gas. Particle physics speaks an exponential language of many decimal points to describe the immensity or minuteness of the worlds of astronomy or quantum physics. The telescope and the microscope are magnifying instruments which bring nearer to our view the frontiers of the macrocosm and the microcosm, within which the observable world exists for us. Placed between these two worlds is our own mysterious universe, which is capable of expanding or contracting through processes of explosion or implosion, endosmosis or exosmosis, and entropy or negentropy.

Sources of cosmic rays have been found to be both bright spots and black holes, wherefrom streams of energy units like neutrinos may enter our cosmos and disappear through another hole. Modern physics presently speaks even in terms of particle and anti-particle and matter and anti-matter, yet the very structure of the space in which we live is still a profound mystery to the best of physical theorists to the present day. Particles of matter seem to have smaller planet-like bodies, with left-handed or right-handed spins (or both) floating round them, just as in the solar or galactic space. Here supernovae, red giants and white dwarfs, with their colour schemes based on a periodic law to which all matter is chemically subject, heighten the mystery even of the physical world which is the normal environment of us ordinary human beings. The wonderful colour patterns produced by cross-polarized light through the spectroscope reveal the structure of the minutest of crystals when polarized and analysed with the help of short wave rays. The red and violet shifts give us evidence, though indirectly only, of a universe expanding or contracting at a speed approximating the velocity of light. In modern times, it would not be incorrect thus to assert that there is little difference between scientific myth-making and the ordinary myth-making tendency so natural to man ever since literature began to influence human life. The creation of the universe is said to have taken place by a 'big bang', according to some advanced physicists, while other experts think of this creation in terms of a 'steady state'. Modern science is thus in the process of putting every favourite notion into the melting pot called scientific knowledge.

It is the task of the bold speculator to attempt to reconstruct a cosmos out of this kind of intellectual chaos. If he is not able to put some order into this diverse relativistic knowledge, there will occur disruption of human values, leading to a confused state of mind, the signs of which are already evident in modern society. Therefore, it is very important for the reader's understanding of verse two to try to look at the universe from a thoroughly revised perspective from that to which we have been accustomed by convention hitherto.

We have already said that absolute Reality could be viewed from either the conceptual or the perceptual perspective, the latter being placed at a lower point in the degree of generalization or abstraction implied. The increase of energy or voltage in the positive direction results in the higher version of the same Absolute without abolishing its basic content. The higher subsumes the lower and the lower assumes the higher. Within the lower Absolute, postulated for purposes of speculative scrutiny, we should first insert the three grand processes of creation, preservation and destruction as three horizontal stratifications which are traversed vertically by a single correlating parameter, without which they might fall apart and lose their global unity. The universe in the form of an eternal process or flux of becoming was understood by Heraclitus of ancient Greece, and finds approval even by modern critical philosophers such as Bertrand Russell, who calls Heraclitus the first scientific philosopher. Bergson supports the same hylozoist point of view and even goes to the extent of inverting 'topsy-turvy' the whole setup of the universe when he ends his work, *The Two Sources of Morality and Religion*, with the statement that 'the universe is a machine for the fabrication of gods'. The scientific perspective can be said to take a teleological starting point for its speculation. The former ascends from cause to effect and could be called ascending dialectics, while the latter takes its stand on end results or effects, teleologically, and employs descending dialectics to enter into the very heart of reality hereunder. Between the opposing forces of contraction and expansion, evolution and involution, entropy and negentropy, explosion and implosion and other such antinomial factors — all acceptable to present-day philosophers of science or scientific philosophers — the modern man stands, trying to decide which way to turn.

The three gods, Brahmā, Viṣṇu and Śiva, enter into the series of verses in several places, and it is necessary to fit their functions dynamically, as well as statically, into the overall context of the Absolute, before we can fill in this lower or negative perspective of the Absolute with a value significance or content, which is so necessary for intelligent living in an environment where a regulated hierarchy of human values enters as interests to choose from, within the scope of the total ecological setting within which we have successfully to live and move. Thus we have to view reality in its structural, functional, ontological, existential and even pragmatic aspects in order to do justice to all the opportunities that present themselves to us moment after moment in our lives. Everyday problems do not demand the same intelligence as the problem of final salvation, in which humanity has always been interested. Otherwise there would not be religions or churches, scriptures or rituals, towers or spires — all standing on modern utilitarian or idealistic institutional life. Brahmā here represents the aspirational, Viṣṇu the hedonistic, and Śiva the idealistic or tragic aspects of life. We have explained that if the mythological language of the Indian tradition should be repugnant to persons outside its normal climate, we could substitute more scientific and mathematical terms, idioms, ideologies and ideograms to describe the same meaning.

Brahmā is said to be a lotus-born god, belonging to a botanical or biological context. The lotus is the favourite flower, dear to the Indian mind, and its haunting beauty has enriched the similes and metaphors of poetry through the ages. A flower represents the dream of a plant, just as a crystal could represent the dream of a supersaturated liquid. A flower emerges from the otherwise dull background of the world of botany and looms into general consciousness, not unlike a colourful globe of light, displaying its variegated beauty to attract and please the eyes of man. It is the most basic object of beauty in this world, having its origin in mud and dirt, as is particularly true of the lotus-flower. Each flower is a global and structural unit, complete in itself, and if we put three circles around it and its beauty, as conceived in abstract and general terms, we could easily insert such a globe of light within our own total consciousness. It could occupy, at plus or minus levels, a position in the vertical axis or in any one of the ramified sets of possible positions. Brahmā, as the four-headed, lotus-born god, is to be placed within a qualitative space of the individual or collective consciousness of man and treated as a phenotype to mark the source of all creative activity. As the lotus blooms within time, the four-headed god, each of whose faces turns towards one of the four points of the compass, would give us a concrete image of creation as a visualizable process in the form of a personified agent with the specific function of creation, who is to be placed at the ontological negative vertical limit called the alpha point.

As the process of growth and division proceeds sufficiently forward in pure verticalized terms, we transcend the world of biology into another order where solidity of matter, characterized by mutual impenetrability of particles, initiates a horizontalizing exclusiveness between each unit. This results in what we understand as the terra firma which consists mostly of silicon dioxide crystals, each of which seems to be fighting to preserve its own space from being occupied by another crystal at the same time. Without this terra firma, the drama of life itself could not be acted out. All human aspirations must have a firm basis as a foothold, without which no value can ever be enjoyed even for a split second. This is the parameter, however thin in its functional amplitude, that we have to allow in favour of Viṣṇu, who is represented as sleeping on a thousand-headed serpent, Ananta, in a milk-ocean, symbolically representing the life-value of nourishment spread generously all around, at the basis of human life itself. Salvation would lose its meaning without such a basis. Viṣṇu as a universal concrete principle, is represented also by a small golden fish, *matsya*, who grew to immense proportions; by a tortoise, *kūrma*, who supported a mountain on his back for the churning of the milk ocean; and by a boar, *varāha*, who, by his hard tusks, killed the demon Hiraṇyākṣa and brought the earth back to the surface of the ocean. The fish, tortoise and boar, which are said to be successive incarnations of water-loving creatures, are evidently to be placed in a vertical series, beginning at the alpha point or negative limit. There are many Sanskrit texts which lend support to the view that Viṣṇu supports from below all the hypostatic worlds above. The horizontal expansiveness of space in terms of quantity stands for the firm earth; the schematic representation of the same would be the horizontal axis. Thus we arrive at a general notion of the function of Viṣṇu.

Now, when we pass over this horizontal parameter represented by Viṣṇu at the equatorial region of the total situation, and enter into the world of vertical values of a more teleological order, and pass through the immensity of empty space, i.e., the interstellar space of our own universe, the same vertical parameter followed far enough takes us to the domain of Śiva, as the universal principle of destruction. Creation would not have any meaning without its counterpart, dissolution. Heat and cold belong together; the same is true of birth and death. In the same manner, existence and essence have also to belong necessarily together, whether we wish to die early or not. If grandmothers and grandfathers refuse to die, what will be the lot of this world? Surely a somber and vegetative picture, full of sadness and frustration, would be the state of humanity if Śiva refused to function as the most 'generous' principle of destruction, at least in the paradoxical sense of Shakespeare's dictum 'sweet are the uses of adversity'. Every reality must have a container which has a lid at the one end, just as a jug cannot be open at both ends. This is known in Vedic literature as the principle of the inverted cup, or in the West, as the phenomenological principle of bracketing. Heat must be countered by cold, and creation by destruction, in any process conceived in its totality. Modern phenomenologists have tried to describe human life as an *epoche*, enclosed within brackets, one being evidently at the top and the other at the bottom. Śiva's function has thus to be put in its proper structural perspective. This task is not easy even for modern physicists, but in the sequence of verses that follows, the ancient speculative tradition of India takes up this challenge with at least as much confidence and dignity as modern theoretical physics.

Grey ashes and nourishing food such as rice and water, mark the limits or brackets between which human life is destined to fulfil itself. There is a complementarity, reciprocity, compensation and cancellation between these two limits as life unfolds, corrected and harmonized within these ambivalent tendencies. Ashes cancel out against nourishing rice and water into the central value represented by mother's milk, as so touchingly alluded to in verse seventy-five. Milk represents the generosity of the Absolute, viewed from the perspective of motherhood.

Śiva thus occupies the omega point or highest limit in the vertical axis of the total system of contemplative values. He is represented as dancing in the graveyard in the Śaivite literature of South India and in the world famous bronze of the dancing Naṭarāja, in the temple at Chidambaram dedicated to him. He is known as the City Burner, descending with flame in hand, while he himself is engulfed in the flames of his own austere way of life. Thus, he is not an auspicious god in the conventional sense, but one who can bring to bear on the total situation that positive touch, without which life would be meaninglessly lopsided. He represents the principle of tragic cancellation. Therefore, it is apt to describe him as smearing his body with ashes while revelling in the positive principle of tragedy. When cancelled against his own negative counterpart, the resultant absolute Beauty is both tragic and comic at once. The Absolute transcends both, and is beyond both good and bad, beyond all dualities. Such are some of the guidelines to be kept in mind when scrutinizing this second verse, by the light of which the three stratified functions within the total scope of the absolute Universe could be easily visualized by the reader without further explanation.

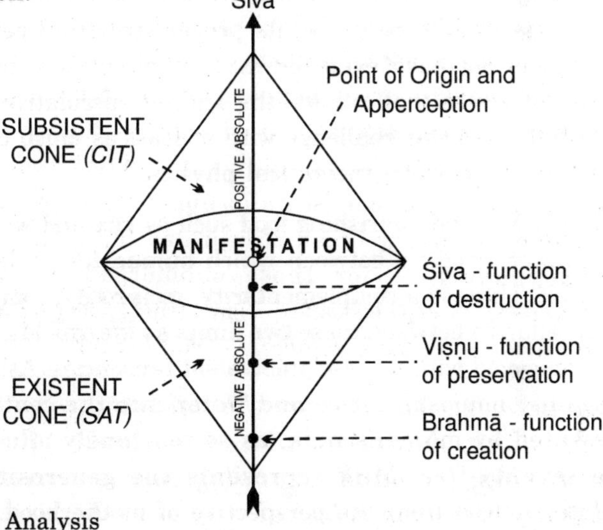

Structural Analysis

> In Śiva we attain the top conceptual omega or nominal limit of the total situation here schematically analysed. Existence here gives place to thin logical or rational subsistence merging into the value world of pure axiological status. Śiva the Destroyer is thus the omega point where actualities evaporate into thin mathematical nothingness of nominalistic though absolute Value. The thin dust of the feet is subjected to further refinement as suggested in the last line here so that it becomes the ritual ornament smeared lightly on the radiant body of Śiva. Thus existence, subsistence and value with a pluralistic, horizontal reference are all capable of structural recognition in this verse.

3

अविद्यानामन्तस्तिमिरमिहिरद्वीपनगरी
जडानां चैतन्यस्तबकमकरन्दस्रुतिझरी ।
दरिद्राणां चिन्तामणिगुणनिका जन्मजलधौ
निमग्नानां दंष्ट्रा मुररिपुवराहस्य भवती ॥

avidyānām antas timira mihira dvīpa nagarī
jaḍāṇāṁ caitanya stabaka makaranda srutijharī ।
daridrāṇāṁ cintāmaṇi guṇanikā janma jaladhau
nimagnānāṁ daṁṣṭrā mura ripu varāhasya bhavatī ॥

avidyānām — for the uninstructed; *antaḥ timira mihira* — inner darkness (banishing) sun; *dvīpa nagarī* — light city, mid-ocean placed; *jaḍāṇām* — to inert ones; *caitanya stabaka makaranda* — mind-expanding sweetness from within blossoms celestial; *sruti jharī* — the ooze, flow (of); *daridrāṇāṁ* — for indigent spirits; *cintāmaṇi guṇanikā* — a brood of philosophers' stones; *janma jaladhau* — in the ocean of repeated birth and death; *nimagnānāṁ* — for those submerged; *muraripu varāhasya* — of the boar of Viṣṇu (the enemy of Mura); *daṁṣṭrā* — the tusk; *bhavatī* — you become

To the uninstructed, You are the light-city, inner darkness banishing, mid-ocean placed;
To inert ones, the mind-expanding ooze of sweetness from within blossoms celestial;
While for indigent spirits, you become a brood of philosopher's stones,
And for those submerged in the birth-cycle ocean, the very tusk of Viṣṇu's boar.

A fourfold structure is evidently implied in this verse, although such a structure is not easy to imagine in rigid geometric lines on the surface of two-dimensional paper. There are presented within the scope of this verse, four types of spiritual aspirants. To place each of them correctly in their proper positions in the qualitative perspective of beauty, within which each has to find his own place, brings us face-to-face with a problem, which is important to solve correctly from the very beginning.

Vedantic literature knows of a similar fourfold distinction of types of aspirants, such as in the Bhagavadgītā, where we read of one who is steeped in affliction, another who has a desire to know the truth, a third is fond of gaining the goods of life, and the fourth represents a wise one. The same four types are presented here also, but their aspirations or interests are brought under more poetically elaborated value worlds representing the item of interest most attractive to each type of aspirant: they are the uninstructed, the inert, the indigent and the suffering. These four types are to be inserted into a fourfold frame of reference, with a one-to-one correspondence between what each one is in himself and what his aspiration represents. When a man's interest cancels out against what he is, his dignity attains a meaning which refers to his own proper absolute Value. Just as when Shakespeare says that the dress makes the man, or when the Gītā equates faith with the person who is faithful, there is an interchangeability and reversibility to be understood here between the Self and the non-Self. The passion of an Othello possesses him so completely that he becomes identical with it. In the same sense, Shakespeare elsewhere uses the expression, 'the play is the thing'. This way of treating Self and non-Self unitively and of placing them together within a subjective and contemplative world of value is quite a normal way in the literature of Advaita Vedanta. Each man is known by his master interest, just as each mathematical term is known by its function, or as a tree is known by its fruit.

The seeker of wisdom of the first line, described as the uninstructed, is the most respectable of the four types that are designated in a certain structural order of gradation. He could be thought of as one whose main interest is to know the truth; he believes in sayings like 'Thou shalt know the Truth and the Truth shall make thee free.' He aspires for that glorious day when emancipation will come to him. He is a dreamer, steeped in the darkness of ignorance, who envisions before him the beautiful circular structure described in this first line. The 'City of God' on high, called *De Civitate Dei*, is an idealized acropolis placed on the top of a hill in Augustinian imagination. Here, however, we notice that the 'city of light' is placed in the middle of an ocean. When we apply the structural frame of reference to this situation, we could imagine the perspective of this aspirant to be from a central position in any circular cross-section that we could take within the quarter of the apex of the lower cone, while the 'city of light' here can be seen as a cross-section at a corresponding position within the upper cone. The lower inverted cone is negative and can therefore represent darkness, from which this aspirant seeks the light from above the cross-sectional plane dividing the two cones, placed base to base. The meaning of this first kind of aspirant becomes clear to us when we visualize truth or wisdom as the non-Self on the positive numerator quarter, while the uninstructed ignoramus, as the counterpart of his own aspiration, can be seen to be on the negative or denominator side of the quaternion. We shall find this same mental island elaborated further in later verses.

To visualize the inert man of the second line, who is fond of the ordinary pleasures of life, and to correctly place him in his proper structural perspective, we have only to think of a day-dreaming fat boy type character, like Kumbhakarṇa of the *Rāmāyaṇa*, or Joe in Dickens' *Pickwick Papers*. Literature is familiar with many such fat boys. This kind of aspirant is interested only in the merriment of eating, drinking and sleeping, and he is never bothered by the harsh pinch of necessity. We could thus visualize this inert man on the left or virtual side of the horizontal parameter as the counterpart of the actual item of his fancy, which can be seen on the horizontal right side in the quaternion structure.

The third line refers to a man who is actually poor and 'cannot make ends meet' in his everyday life. The indigent spirit is haunted by the love of wealth which never actually reaches his hand. An example of this type of aspirant might be a kind of scholar gypsy, who, by too much book learning, is unable to make a livelihood. Having missed his occasion to succeed, he is troubled about somehow making good, without being serious about the philosophy which he espouses. He hopes one day to come to good luck and keeps dreaming about such a value in a Pharisaic or dilettantish manner. Such a type fits in the numerator side of the total fourfold situation.

The afflicted or suffering man of the fourth line, submerged in the birth-cycle-ocean, is stifled and suffocating due to lack of air to breathe. His repeated efforts only cause him to rise and sink alternately in this ocean of necessity. His main desire is to climb to a level where he could at least breathe fresh air, ridding himself of this suffocating world of necessity. To free himself from such a dire circumstance, he seeks only that which is factual, decisive or firm, with the ontological richness of the hard tusk of Viṣṇu's boar. As an example of this type of aspirant we could think of a person who has badly lost in business and suffered bankruptcy. In this state of mind his only desire is to stand up in the world as a solvent person once again. The afflicted spirit can thus be placed on the factual right side of the horizontal parameter.

The intention of the author in this verse is evidently to make the student sufficiently familiar with the implied quaternion structure. The further elaboration of its subjective implications should become more precise and convincing as we proceed in this work.

Structural Analysis

Each man represents in himself an aspiration vaguely felt as an intentional factor of interest. The ignoramus aspires for some light from the Absolute as its source. The indigent or poor man sees it negatively as a treasure of gems which would abolish his poverty and console him too as a high human value. The pleasure-loving man of lazy inert ways seeks something sweet to drink like the

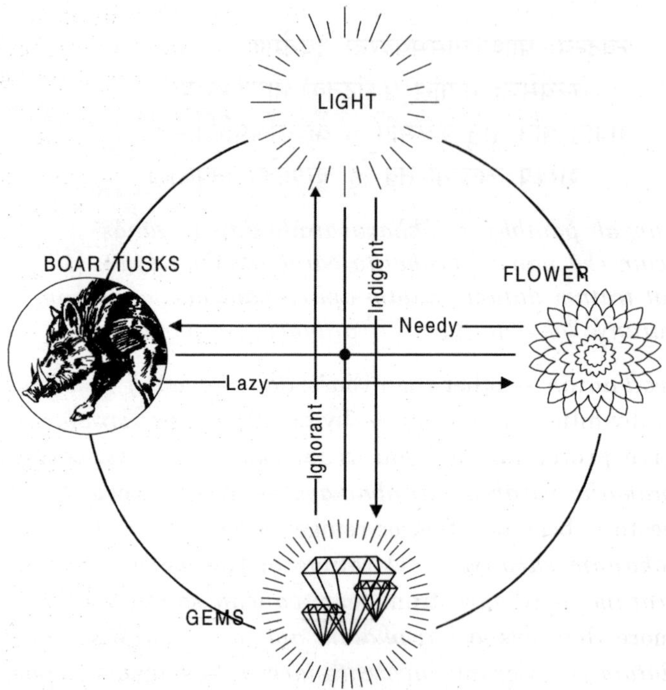

honey at the core of a flower. The man steeped in imperative or absolute needs in a very actual or real sense has to have something like the tusks of Viṣṇu's boar to hold him up and prevent him from sinking deeper into the sea of needs that might make him desperate. Conditioned by subjective states each sees only one aspect of the Absolute. In the figure please note the fourfold context of the structure of the Absolute as well as the double force acting on each interest, with equilibrium resulting in the consolation the Wisdom Mother represents.

4

त्वदन्यः पाणिभ्यामभयवरदो दैवतगण-
स्त्वमेका नैवासि प्रकटितवराभीत्यभिनया ।
भयात् त्रातुं दातुं फलमपि च वाञ्छासमधिकम्
शरण्ये लोकानां तव हि चरणावेव निपुणौ ॥

tvad anyaḥ pāṇibhyām abhayavarado daivataganas
tvam ekā naivāsi prakaṭita varābhītyabhinayā ।
bhayāt trātuṁ dātuṁ phalam api ca vāñchāsamadhikam
śaraṇye lokānāṁ tava hi caraṇāveva nipuṇau ॥

tvad anyaḥ — other than yours; *daivata gaṇaḥ* — classes of divinities; *pāṇibhyām* — by hands; *abhaya varadaḥ* — give protection or boon; *tvam ekā* — you alone are; *prakaṭita varāḥ abhīti abhinayā* — in acting overtly, by gesture, boon-granting or refuge; *na eva asi* — not thus; *lokānāṁ śaraṇye* — O refuge of the worlds; *bhayāt trātuṁ* — to save from fear; *vāñchā samadhikam* — more than asked for; *phalam api ca* — and also boon; *dātuṁ* — to grant; *tava caraṇāveva* — your feet alone; *nipuṇau hi* — are expert indeed

Hands of classes of divinities other than Yours can confer protection or boon;
You alone are unique in not acting overtly by gesture, the promises of refuge or boon.
What is more, Your feet, O sole refuge of the world of beings,
Are alone expert indeed in yielding more-than-asked-for boon.

This verse has its setting in the world of Hindu iconography. A visit to an Indian museum, such as the famous one in Madras, filled with bronze figures and statues of divinities, would verify for the reader the intention of the author here, while a visit to some of the temples of South India would be even more convincing for those seriously interested in such a study of images. Each image is meant to tell you something. The votary generally looks at the image from a short distance outside the temple doors, while camphor bits are waved before the icon. When a man goes to the temple for worship, he has in his mind a prayer most dear to him at that moment, referring to one of the four sets of values reviewed in the previous verse, where the prayer for wisdom denoted the most superior aspirant. At the many temples of South India there are multitudes of believers who kowtow before such images, asking for favours from the variety of divine representations or presences. All prayers are bound to be answered, for the simple reason that it could not be otherwise. Humanity would not have continued to build so many houses of prayer the world over if experience had proved that all prayer amounted to nothing at all. Man has had many centuries to test such an experience. If God had been dead and ineffective, man would have removed God from his life long ago. Even the Russian dictionary contains the word God, which shows that rightly or wrongly, faith in the efficacy of prayer still persists. Religion is a necessity for man, though not in the same sense as food. Other hungers also need satisfaction. Even if there were no God, we might have to create one and put Him there.

In this verse the author purposely brings into relief a pointed contrast involving a point that has an important and direct bearing on the philosophy of Advaita, especially that represented by Śaṅkara. This point is, however, not one of doctrinal importance but one that has to be understood in the methodology proper to Advaita philosophy. The question here is whether one has to give primacy to the cause, or rather to the effect, in the philosophical enquiry that would take one to the truth of the manifested world of appearance. Each manifestation has a cause lurking behind it which is not manifest. In our enquiry we can travel positively from effect to effect *ad infinitum*, which is the way of the Vaiśeṣikas (atomists) and others. There is another way which is distinguished as the *via negativa*. This way of enquiry, which is an approach to truth by eliminating the extraneous, is recommended in the Upaniṣads and is there called 'not this, not this' (*neti, neti*). By this method we arrive at the source of all manifestation at the negative limit or alpha point of the vertical axis. Otherwise, if we follow the positive way, of giving primacy to effects rather than to causes, we soon land ourselves in a world of plurality of effects in the visible world. We have, as Bergson puts it, to do violence to ourselves, in the effort of philosophizing, and not only enter into the heart of the reality that we are examining, but sink to its point of origin by a process of eliminating the plurality of horizontal manifestations.

Translated into the language of iconography, this methodological principle is underlined by Śaṅkara here in verse four. At the negative limit, marked by the feet of the Goddess in the context of this image language, resides the origin or source where individual manifestations remerge into unity. Mathematical structuralism, in the context of complex numbers, is familiar with this same idea when it puts the square root of minus one, ($\sqrt{-1}$) at the bottom of the vertical axis as understood with the help of Cartesian coordinates. Thus, the absolute Goddess is Negativity, while there could be innumerable classes and sub-classes of divinities which could answer prayers or grant benefits in an endless variety of gestures or favours. While at the numerator end the possiblilities are located in the infinity of possible effects, when the locus is fixed in the denominator aspect, at the feet of the Goddess, we could think of the one and unique end result or benefit of absolute Wisdom alone accruing to the votary, seeker or supplicant, to the exclusion of all other miscellaneous benefits that ordinary human beings may be interested in. Praying for particular favours is called *upāsanā* and because the value implied therein is paltry and transient, the absolutist Vedantin, who is more wholehearted, discountenances all such devotional conduct or behaviour and prefers only to know the Truth. Such are some of the methodological and doctrinal secrets which Śaṅkara wants to insist upon in this verse.

The reference to 'more-than-asked-for boon' in this verse may require some explanation. Ordinary prayer is answered according to the mechanistic law of action and reaction being equal and opposite, following an arithmetical way of justice of a 'tooth for a tooth' order. On the other hand, when one says that if a man asks for your shirt, give him your coat also, there is a generosity which is not arithmetical. The good Samaritan and the father of the prodigal son have a sense of justice and generosity which is of a higher order than a merely quantitative justice. Bergson distinguishes between natural Justice, with a capital letter, and the justice which is measured out quantitatively between the two scales of a balance. Absolute justice is natural and open-minded in its generosity. The absolutist attitude has been compared to that of a gambler in the Gītā and follows the law of 'partial stimulus, total response'. It is in this sense that the 'more-than-asked-for boon' given by the grace of a Goddess enjoying an absolutist standpoint contrasts with relativistic items of benefit derived from lesser divinities.

In the second line it is understood that hand gestures are part of the stone language by which the icons communicate to the votary. Generally it is by gesture with one or more hands that the response from the side of the deity is conveyed to the devotee. Such gestures are called *mudrā*s and the wisdom-gesture given by a guru to a disciple is the highest of them. There are four well-known gestures, each given by one of the four hands. The *varada*, that of boon-giving or benediction, is one. The gesture of protection is called *abhaya* in which the hand points at a foot to indicate that the devotee should surrender himself to the feet of the divinity for refuge. Another hand can carry a weapon, which is indicative of the anger or punishment involved. The fourth hand might carry a flame or some symbolic totem. Viṣṇu's four hands are distinguished by the conch, discus, mace and lotus. Subrahmaṇya is recognized by his lance, and Rāma by his bow. The rosary and book belong to Sarasvatī, while Kālī can have many arms and hands, as in Cāmuṇḍī. Four monomarks held by four hands, which are bow and arrow, noose and goad, belong to the structuralism of the absolute Goddess portrayed here, as presented to us in verse seven and others, where the hand gestures of this stone language are referred to. The foot or the twin feet have primacy over all such numerator value monomarks as the bow, arrow, noose and goad. Existence has primacy over essence, at least for methodological requirements.

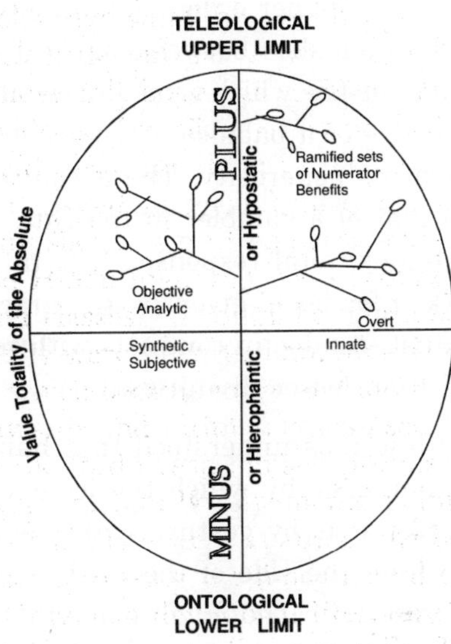

Structural Analysis

Theological divinities are many. They can protect votaries or confer boons in various pluralistic, relativistic or hedonistic contexts known to non-Vedantic or dualistic scripture. The Goddess represents the non-dual absolute Value which has rich ontological value but only negligible teleological or hypostatic significance in Vedanta. While the range of the ramified sets of gods or demigods which are numerous can grant hedonistic, relativistic or pluralistic benefits or securities, at the bottom of the vertical parameter of all values, rich ontology of real or universally concrete values comprise and comprehend all the miscellaneous and conceptual values of the hypostatic, axiological intentionalities and expectations. It is at the existent level that all essences merge into a unique value factor. As in the case of atomic structure, the neutrino or the neutron is richer in negative content than the electron particle. Indigence prevails on the plus side. Innate subjectivism is more important than analytic or positive objectivism.

5

हरिस्त्वामाराध्य प्रणतजनसौभाग्यजननीम्
पुरा नारी भूत्वा पुररिपुमपि क्षोभमनयत्।
स्मरोऽपि त्वां नत्वा रतिनयनलेह्येन वपुषा
मुनीनामप्यन्तः प्रभवति हि मोहाय महताम्॥

haris tvām ārādhya praṇata jana saubhāgya jananīm
purā nārī bhūtvā pura ripum api kṣobham anayat ।
smaro'pi tvāṁ natvā rati nayana lehyena vapuṣā
munīnām apy antaḥ prabhavati hi mohāya mahatām ॥

praṇata jana saubhāgya jananīm — the mother that bestows blessings on those that worship you; *tvām hariḥ purā ārādhya* — once Viṣṇu having adored you; *nārī bhūtvā* — taking womanly form; *puraripum api* — even to the City Burner; *kṣobham anayat* — caused agitation; *smaraḥ api* — Eros too; *tvāṁ natvā* — on worshipping You; *rati nayana lehyena vapuṣā* — with body licked into reality by the glances of Rati; *mahatām munīnām antaḥ api* — even to the minds of great recluses; *mohāya* — cause confusion of values; *prabhavati hi* — is able to bring indeed

Once Viṣṇu, having adored You, the Mother that bestows blessings on those who worship You,
Taking womanly form, even to the City Burner (Śiva), caused agitation;
Eros, too, on worshipping You, with body licked into reality by the glances of Rati,
Even to the minds of great recluses, confusion of values, indeed, is able to bring.

This verse brings us one step closer to the main content or subject matter of this series of verses. Since the central theme of this work is erotic mysticism, the god of love has to be understood first. Man finds woman beautiful and vice versa, because between their forms there is operative a subtle parity, reciprocity, complementarity or cancellability, in terms of pure action. The embrace of man and woman represents a form of pure and subjective action between values which could be called counterparts. The joy or the bliss that results therefrom is not a value to be excluded from the total scope of eternal or absolute values. There is an interaction between contemplative and worldly interests involved in this kind of conjugal joy. The Goddess cannot experience it by herself or by itself. The life principle that enjoys it has to participate with both the pure or sacred values on the one side and the more profane values on the other. The experience of love, which is so well known to young men and women, is such a serious matter that there is not one year in which some suicide pact between a young couple does not occur in one region or another. Like hunger, which has no limbs nor any exact position within the stomach only, love can pervade and possess the whole personality of a man or a woman at a given moment. This given moment is regulated by the principle of occasionalism, as known in Cartesian philosophy, by which the will of God and the disposition of man cancel out on occasions which are fully favourable. It is in this sense that Othello's passion fills him so completely that he becomes a tragic hero of the fullest stature. A Cosette and a Marius find themselves in each other's arms before they are even conscious of what they are about. Instances of this kind can be multiplied indefinitely from the world's best literature.

Love is a noble sentiment, laudable in one perspective, but not so much in another. Shakespeare's sonnets contrast the real difference between true and false love. The Upaniṣads do not treat legitimate love as a forbidden fruit, but include it within the scope of absolute joy that the soul of even a dignified man should be capable of enjoying. Kālidāsa's *Kumārasambhava* is perhaps one of the best classical examples on this subject. Śiva forever remains the leader of ascetics even though in the last verse of this work, he is represented as living eternally in the bedchamber of the Goddess, refusing even breakfast. Here the paradox of eroticism is faced squarely without making this subject either wholly profane or wholly sacred. It is the principle of the non-dualistic Absolute alone that can finally dissolve this paradox. Eroticism can have the dignity of mysticism only when the contradiction at the core of profane love has been fully abolished. This task is exactly what Śaṅkara undertakes in the present series of verses, and in this verse he clears the ground for viewing the subject of erotic mysticism in the structural perspective proper to it. Further, it is important that such a perspective falls correctly within the aegis of absolute Beauty, because it is the beauty of the female which is the very occasion for erotic mysticism to come to be talked about at all. The expression *sub specie aeternitatis* of Spinoza, explained elsewhere, describes this unitive perspective. The passion of Othello becomes a Passion, with a capital letter, when it falls within the ambit of the Absolute on a given occasion. This is the reason why men are said to 'fall in love', and justifies somewhat the popular saying that 'marriages are made in heaven'.

Eros, as known in the Greek context, is represented in some paintings as a winged angel that descends onto the body of a beautiful woman from above. The Sanskritic Eros is called *Anaṅga* and *Manasija* (The Limbless or Mind-born one.) His position in the structural set-up is in the peripheral region of the base of the lower, rather than the upper, of the two cones placed base to base. With his bow and arrow made of flowers, he lies in wait for the proper occasion to make young lovers fall for each other as they sit in a garden in the flowery season, called *vasanta* in India, when the cuckoos sing and mangoes put out their blossoms and tender magenta leaves. The *elan vital* in nature operates with highest pressure on this occasion, when mentally pictured with the gentle *malaya* breeze and other concomitant circumstances favourable to the function of this god. Details about the behaviour of Eros and his wife, Rati, are depicted in detail in Kālidāsa's *Kumārasambhava*. We shall have occasion to return to this same subject in the verse that follows.

Like hunger, love has no limbs. As an inner experience, it is an amorphous entity that can pervade all the limbs of one's body at a given moment. The mind-born god (*Manasija*) is thus considered limbless (*Anaṅga*). One might ask how he could send his flowery arrows without limbs. His bow and arrows are made of flowers, to show that his instruments as well as his limbs belong to a very tender and neutral order, in which matter and mind are interchangeable and can participate both ways. Life is the principle that links matter and mind, and it is exactly at this point of meeting that the mind-born god, Eros, has his being.

Without anticipating what we shall have many more occasions to elaborate, let us fix our attention in this verse on the divinity called Viṣṇu, who is said to have assumed a beautiful female form to distract the attention of Śiva on the occasion of the churning of the milk-ocean mentioned in the *Bhāgavata*. In this incident he was named Mohinī. By his intervention, Viṣṇu was able to avert a conflict that would have otherwise become a disastrous situation. Viṣṇu's structural position is more centrally located, perhaps a little below the middle of the vertical parameter. It is because of his special normalized absolute position, falling within the scope of the vertical parameter itself, which is of a fourth-dimensional order within the structural totality, that he is able to attract the attention of Śiva himself, in spite of the latter being the most austere of austere divinities. These mythological anecdotes or episodes are not to be directly depended upon by us in this commentary. We only allude to them in passing so that they could lend whatever verification they might to our approach, which is one that is primarily nearer to a mathematical structuralism proper to science, treated as integrating physics and metaphysics.

Though Eros is placed in the lower cone, with base upwards, the value principle implied in him can, at a particular moment, permeate the whole structural field, giving to it a red or magenta hue throughout. The recluses referred to in the fourth line are generally persons who have left their homes to live in Himalayan retreats for the purpose of practising various lukewarm degrees of austerities, usually to forget something in their past, like an unhappy married life. The intensity of their devotion to austere ways of life could be great, which would justify the epithet 'great recluses' in this verse, but it is to be understood that their detachment has not attained to the positive heights of that leader of all ascetics, Śiva. The influence of erotic values could still be dominant in the minds of such recluses, compromising their absolutist status, however great their lopsided dedication to an austere life might be. It is in this sense that the mountain-daughter, Pārvatī, is said in the *Kumārasambhava* to be respected even by recluses (*munis*). Even after leaving their homes the appeal of a beautiful woman can perturb their minds, causing some confusion of values within their hearts. Such a view finds support in the poetry of Kālidāsa, where a traveller from a distant land, separated from his once favourite wife, bursts into tears when reminded of his lost felicity even by the sight of a beautiful tree laden with flowers waving in the breeze. These recluses, as ordinary human beings, still belong to the horizontal plane and are to be situated somewhere peripherally between the bases of the two cones in the structure.

The reference to the body of Eros being licked into shape by his wife, Rati, may need some clarification before we leave this verse. Beauty in its four-dimensional fullness is the result of the meeting of two sets of light, as revealed in modern laser ray technique. Holographs have to be resolved, or made clear, by one cross-polarized ray meeting another at a certain angle. Eros, by himself, is an incomplete beauty without the admiration of his wife from another position, cutting at correct angles from one of the peripheral rims of one of the cones placed base to base. Cross-polarized light interferences create visibly living colour effects, as is familiar in modern crystallography. Spectral colours are revealed at the periphery, while magenta pervades the greater part of the remainder of the rim. Some structural explanations of this verse may be considered far-fetched, but our excuse for resorting to such descriptions is that we only intend to add some adequacy or validity to the otherwise 'negatively unscientific' or mythological language used here. Our attempt, as we have stated, has been to substitute a more scientifically acceptable version for the mythological language. Myths can verify mathematics and vice versa.

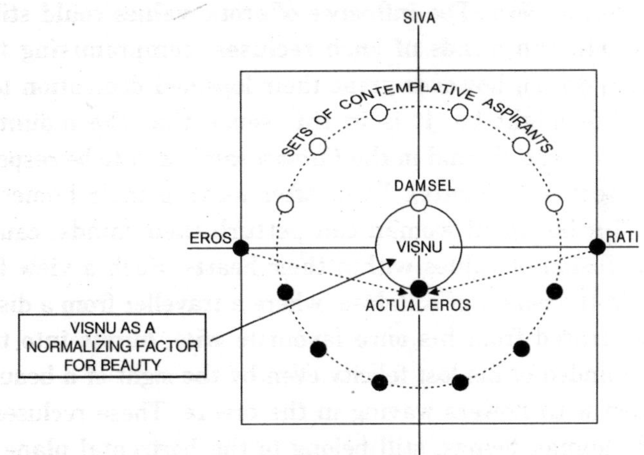

THE TOTAL STRUCTURE OF ABSOLUTE BEAUTY

Structural Analysis

There are two sets of double corrections to be thought of in terms of normalization and renormalization here. Beauty as an absolute Value is the central theme. This beauty could be viewed from two perspectives which are complementary or reciprocal counterparts, compensatory and cancellable into the final unity of the value represented by the Absolute as Beauty here.

Vertically, Śiva as the Burner of the City is the positive counterpart of Viṣṇu as the normalizing factor. Horizontally the virtuality of Eros has its counterpart in the actualizing light of his wife Rati. There are groups of contemplatives of different sets and sub-sets all round the central value who benefit spiritually or in actual terms from a contemplation of the Absolute. Śiva as an extremely uncompromising radical and positive principle must have the re-normalizing factor as its central counterpart which acts as a descending factor or function *vis-á-vis* this thin mathematical parameter at the omega point of the Absolute. A beautiful damsel in a worldly sense can participate in the Absolute and have a stunning effect on a recluse even of the status of a Śiva. Viṣṇu, as a neutrally placed normalizing influence, could be a simple damsel with stunning beauty or viewed theologically as the cosmic principle of preservation. The circling set of recluses are all aspirants who practise contemplation of various types that can be fitted into the scheme in endless gradation or variety of sets or sub-set ensembles.

6

धनुः पौष्पं मौर्वी मधुकरमयी पञ्च विशिखा
वसन्तः सामन्तो मलयमरुदायोधनरथः।
तथाप्येकः सर्वं हिमगिरिसुते कामपि कृपा-
मपाङ्गात् ते लब्ध्वा जगदिदमनङ्गो विजयते॥

dhanuḥ pauṣpaṁ maurvī madhukaramayī pañca viśikhā
vasantaḥ sāmanto malaya marud āyodhanarathaḥ ।
tathāpy ekaḥ sarvaṁ himagiri sute kām api kr̥pām
apāṅgāt te labdhvā jagad idam anaṅgo vijayate ॥

himagiri sute — O Daughter of the Himalayan peak; *dhanuḥ pauṣpaṁ* — (with) flowery bow; *maurvī madhukaramayī* — bowstring of bumblebees — *pañca viśikhāḥ* — five-flowered dart; *sāmantaḥ vasantaḥ* — minister, springtide; *malaya marut āyodhana rathaḥ* — south-west breeze for war chariot; *tathā api* — in spite of this; *anaṅgaḥ* — the limbless one, Eros; *te apāṅgāt* — from your side glance; *kām api kr̥pām* — whatsoever grace; *labdhvā* — having obtained; *idam jagat sarvaṁ* — this whole world; *ekaḥ* — one; *vijayate* — reigns supreme

O Daughter of the Snowy Peak, just deriving from Your glance askance
Whatsoever grace he could; with flowery bow and bumblebee bowstring, five-flowered dart and springtide for minister — all these as one withal;
Mounting the chariot of the mountain breeze,
He victoriously reigns, that god of love.

This verse continues and carries over the basic ideas just examined in verse five and adds a little more dynamism to the picture. The key to the understanding of this verse is in the principle of occasionalism, without which Eros would get a dignity out of all proportion to his importance in human life. All people do not fall in love at all times of the year. The component factors making up the totality implied in every absolute occasion in which they do, are enumerated and described realistically here, with some details. Let us examine them separately and together.

The primary requisite for Eros to reign supreme is stated in the first line as the glance, though only askance, of the Goddess. This kind of glance is very familiar in devotional Sanskrit literature where the votary, out of humility, does not dare to pray for a full frontal regard of kindness from the Goddess. Such a sympathetic side glance, well known as *karuṇā kaṭākṣa*, is all that a humble devotee can claim from an absolute Goddess. Though the glance is only partial in its nature, it is received with total gratitude on the side of the devotee. Thus what is lost on one side is compensated for on the other side. Śiva's love of Viṣṇu in female form, mentioned in the previous verse, is a richer and more direct relationship than in the case of Eros and the Goddess in this verse. Eros thus has a lesser status than even a demiurge or a divine presence. He tends to derive his dignity from the instinctive pole of the personality of the Goddess and, as such, is to be placed nearer to the elemental spirits, located at the pole of existence, ontologically rich, at the negative limit of the vertical axis. This is the reason why, as we shall see in later verses, the god of love is depicted as having his proper place within the legs of the Goddess. Above the horizontal line, Eros is exposed to too much light and heat or electricity coming from the topmost limit of the vertical axis. In this bright world of high energy his head is said to catch fire and he is obliged to jump into the navel of the Goddess, represented as a lotus lake in the mid-region of her body. Such details will come under more specific reference in later verses.

The reference to a bowstring of bumble-bees has its own structurally dynamic implications. Every flower of the *vasanta* season (spring-summer) carries a drop of honey at its core, and each drop of honey attracts a bee. Thus the basis of a dynamism such as what exists between a bow and its bowstring develops. A bee, very thirsty for the drop of honey from the flower, develops a kind of tension within its mind similar to the tension of a browstring when drawn away from its bow. In this picture the bow and the arrowhead are made up of choice flowers. The season spreads over the surface of the earth horizontally and evenly. The same scene, when viewed three-dimensionally, gives us a cross-section which contains the bowstring of thirsty bees sitting in a line along the horizontal parameter, thirsty for the drops of honey in the flowers which make up the bow. Enjoyment and the enjoyer, represented by the honey and the corresponding thirsty bees, are thus structurally placed as counterparts.

The arrow shoots vertically through this two-sided, totally horizontalized situation. When the trajectory of the arrow is perfectly verticalized, it can hit Śiva at the omega point, at the apex of the upper cone. It is Pārvatī who gives the perfect verticality to the arrow of the god of love, who has to lie in wait for his propitious moment, based on the principle of occasionalism in the total absolutist context. The five flowers of the dart represent the five sense interests. When they strike the victim altogether at the given occasion when everything else is favourable, even an austere god like Śiva is unable to escape their effect totally. The fate of us human beings who are lesser than Śiva could be thus left to the reader's imagination. The whispering breezes of springtide lend their support to endorse this power conferred on Eros by the occasion. The mountain breeze is also an important concomitant, finalizing the imperative character in the operation of such successful functioning of the god of love. It is in this sense that at a given moment alone, when the totality of favourable factors conspire together, that the god of love can triumph. The integrative principle belongs to both the principles represented by Śiva as well as by Śakti. Eros has neccessarily to hide and operate from the negative side. This dynamism gains support from the relational structuralism and vice versa; both must be treated as belonging to an Occasionalism with a capital letter.

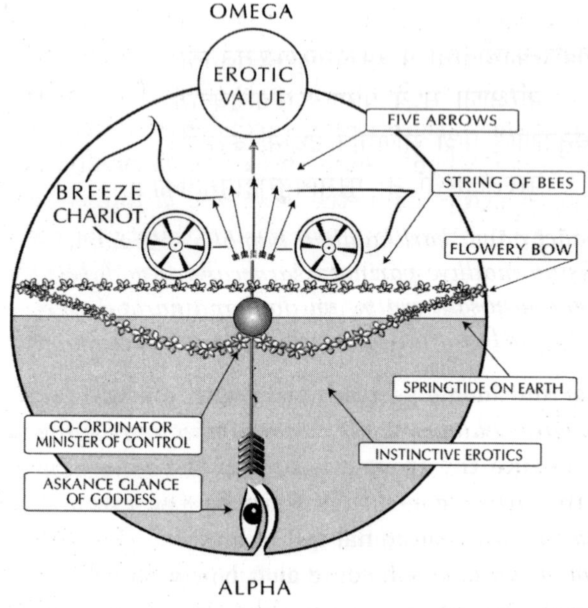

Structural Analysis

The total erotic situation can be schematically represented as the top and bottom half of a circle. The bow of iron when conceptualized becomes flower tender as a luxury springtime value. Flowers bring bees and the bumblebee is the conceptual aspect of summer love feelings in operation. The five senses with their afferent functional counterparts are represented by five darts that hurt the lovers' hearts subjectively or objectively. The total controlling factor giving purpose to erotic life is the season of spring and the more ineffable plus side of the situation is a wind-wafted chariot. The minister is a person here and now and thus has to take his position on the point where the vertical axis meets the horizontal at "O" point. Eros himself is an abstraction by the mind and thus he represents an erotic value under the aegis of the Absolute and could be said to radiate his essence over the whole of the conscious situation from the apex of the plus omega point, while the Devī herself, as his counterpart, occupies the rich ontological of the alpha point. Other structural implications ought to be clear.

7

क्वणत्काञ्चीदामा करिकलभकुम्भस्तननता
परिक्षीणा मध्ये परिणतशरच्चन्द्रवदना ।
धनुर्बाणान् पाशं सृणिमपि दधाना करतलैः
पुरस्तादास्तां नः पुरमथितुराहोपुरुषिका ॥

kvaṇat kāñcī dāmā kari kalabha kumbha stananatā
parikṣīṇā madhye pariṇata śaraccandra vadanā ।
dhanur bāṇān pāśaṁ sr̥ṇim api dadhānā karatalaiḥ
purastād āstāṁ naḥ puramathitur āho puruṣikā ॥

kvaṇat kāñcīdāmā — resounding with waistbelt of jingle bells; *kari kalabha kumbha stana natā* — recumbent by breasts like the frontal bulges of a young elephant; *madhye parikṣīṇā* — slim of waist; *pariṇata śarat candra vadanā* — with autumnal full-moon face; *dhanuḥ bāṇān pāśaṁ sr̥ṇim api* — holding aloft bow with arrow, noose and goad; *karatalaiḥ* — within the grasp of hands; *dadhānā* — bearing; *pura mathituḥ* — of the City Burner; *āho puruṣikā* — O wonder, the proud counterpart; *naḥ* — us; *purastāt* — in front of; *āstāṁ* — (let her) appear

Resounding with waistbelt of jingle bells, recumbent by
breasts like the frontal bulges of a calf elephant,
Slim of waist, with autumnal full-moon mature face,
By hands, holding aloft bow with arrow, noose and goad;
O let Her appear before us, that proud counterpart of the
City Burner.

Verse seven seems to imply a challenge by the author, and it is meant as a key to the structural dynamism applied to the content of beauty, having both name and form, at the core of the otherwise empty notion of the Absolute. Its position toward the end of the first ten verses is evidently meant to indicate the covering of the preliminaries in respect of this work. It is an appeal that apostrophizes directly the personification of absolute Beauty, who is the central figure for the whole of this work: 'Let her appear before our eyes in as concrete and real a form as we could possibly expect'.

Beauty has to be given some kind of visible form, either as a Lakṣmī, or a Sarasvatī, or even a Kālī, as conventionally known to the Indian mind, to confer on it a tangible meaning, if at all. Such divinities have all to be fused together into one abstracted and generalized dynamic personal expression, in which all the levels and fourfold aspects implied in each of them could be brought into active interplay together under a universal concrete perspective. The three previous verses could be seen to have prepared the ground step by step for this verse. All the six previous ones are synthetically put together and summarily reviewed here, to afford a firm basis for the further elaboration of the wisdom contained in the rest of the work. If we look at the eighth verse in advance, we can see there the emergence of a definite personality of the Goddess, seated on a couch and represented in a form suitable for the contemplative purposes of an actual yogi. Here, however, the author takes his stand on a more neutral ground between matter and mind.

Advaitic verity is neither real nor abstract, but is something that places itself at the core of consciousness; sometimes real, sometimes amorphous or abstract. The dancing Śiva in his sinuous movement represents the pure verticalized process of the cosmic flux of becoming. He is the City Burner who descends in all his burning glory into a situation, which is to be ontologically understood, at a lower level in the vertical axis. The last line of this verse makes direct reference to the Goddess, meant here to be a counterpart of the City Burner as a dynamic version at an ontological level. Her dance is not usually a masculine *tāṇḍava*, but is filled with a grace natural to the feminine principle, slow and heavy, known as *lāsya* — a dance which has a more gentle horizontalized grace. Here, however, as she still remains the wife of the City Burner, a certain degree of masculinity remains grafted on to her, to give a positive revaluation to her personality which is otherwise fully feminine.

No contradiction is implied here. There are many such features that we have to put together in order to enter into the full spirit of this verse, which, as we have said, is both a key and a challenge to us. Thousands of years of accepted Sanskrit as well as Tamil poetic conventions have been telescoped, as it were, into the four lines of this verse.

The paradox of the first verse is only heightened, before being abolished, at this stage of the work. The world of fine particles of the second verse is also to be presupposed here to get the neutral position to be revealed now in only a very thin outline. It is as if we see the television screen with streaks of silver light vaguely playing on it, instead of an actual bright, colourful scene. In between the over/under focusing, there is a neutral ground which is neither psychic nor physical. If it is visible at one moment, it is not visible at the next. The quaternion structure of the third verse is also to be retained here, as what is depicted is to be treated in its totality as representing the structural dynamism that the author has outlined up to this point. Besides the fourfold nature of the structural ground of the third verse, we have also to include the vertical dimension passing through the whole quaternion, by which cause is given primacy over effect. Finally, we have to insert the occasionalism implied in the fifth and sixth verses, by which divinities and demiurges could equally attain absolutist status when coming within the purview or aegis of this normalized Goddess, who is meant to be neither too hypostatic nor too hierophantic. She stands on the terra firma, while Śiva is the City Burner placed high above. To get a vision of absolute Beauty in female form in this thin and neutral light, as intended by the author in this verse, one has to place oneself in the same neutral subjective mood, so that the seer and the seen could experience the overwhelming upsurge of absolute Beauty, by the sudden cancellation of what the seer represents and what he sees in gleaming outline. When viewed in such a correct perspective, this verse gives up some of its enigmas, without which it may not make meaning at all, especially to a modern reader.

The first line refers to the sound of the jingling waistbelt bells as the starting point, conducive to making the vision appear to the reader in just that form intended by the author. The vision has only a schematic status, although it is dynamically presented here. Sound belongs to the conceptual side, while the schematic outline is a form. Thus the dance meant to be revealed before our eyes is, in principle, the same as the well-known Naṭarāja dance, conceived in a more normalized form, at a lower level. The sound of the waistbelt bells is heightened when the dancing girl plants her feet as she enters the stage for her performance. By the sound of these bells, the onlookers are introduced at once to a world in which concepts and percepts cancel out into a sheer beauty, expressed through the art of dancing. Touching terra firma first represents the ontological starting point of the dance, where sound meets form, and brings in the horizontality of the earth into the total schematic situation. This is known in Sanskrit as *jhaṅkāra* (sudden jingling of the ankle bells), the point where ontology has its impact and participation as between the earth and mind.

After marking thus the horizontal bottom limit in the very first line, the poet refers us to the heavy breast region, which is to be imagined as a horizontal line, schematically understood, on the numerator side of the situation. We also know at once that when it comes to the necessity of feeding a newborn baby, the breasts of a woman are better when they are big and ponderous, although the breasts of a young maid before her maturity need not have the same ponderousness as in later years of full maternity. These two versions are reciprocal. Time is telescoped here, and intervals tend to be abolished in terms of an eternal present or moment. That is why the author does not stop the dance movement at the transition point, in passing from the form of the Goddess where she is slightly bent forward, to one in which her breasts are compared to the frontal knobs of an elephant. This last reference is to lift the status of the breasts to a more hypostatic level of value content. There is a beautiful sinuous curve and a torsion as well as an inside-outside transposal to be imagined by us in this transition from the numerator breasts to their own denominator aspect. This figure-of-eight, which results from contraction, transposal, torsion between right and left, and front and back — independent of big or small, near or far — can be accentuated even further. The dancing girl's beauty on the stage is meant to fill the whole field of vision summoned to our view here. Dancing consists mainly of bending and stretching, where the hips and breasts of a woman fuse themselves into a structural yin-yang model, both bright and dark at the same time. The dynamism is meant to be of increasing voltage until an absolute limit is reached, passing necessarily through the second and third-dimensional perspectives, to the full stature of the fourth-dimensional version recognizable in the last line. In this last line the dancer and the Goddess attain to the maximum vertical height that it is possible to reach from the ontological side of the situation.

The *Daśakumāracarita* of Daṇḍin contains such a contemplative version of a dancing girl, in which she is first represented as beginning the dance by touching the ground with both her fingers. From this simple standpoint her performance becomes more and more elaborate, as the jingle bells help us to cancel the merely visual with the conceptual counterparts of the dance. Elaborations go on in endless variety and, as she is true to her name of Kandukavati, it is a magenta ball representing Eros that she plays with, dexterously manipulating it in great detail by bending and stretching with her beautiful torsion movements, so as to fill the whole stage or ground with her beauty. But the final feat of all is represented as one meant to make the ball go upward by hitting it with the back of her hands. The leap resembles that of Śiva's *tāṇḍava*, and it is referred to by Daṇḍin as the 'musical leap'.

The dancing girl represents an ideogram which has been relied upon by a long line of master poets on the Indian soil, to reveal the structure of the Absolute, long before Śaṅkara himself adopted this method here. It could be called the *Kandukavati* ideogram, which has influenced erotic mystical literature throughout the centuries, down from Umā of the Upaniṣadic times to what is represented here, and which has been taken up and continued by Narayana Guru in his *Kālī Nāṭakam.*

When the tempo or voltage of this dance attains to higher levels of expression, we pass from a three-dimensional level to a fourth-dimensional one. Weak reactions in nuclear physics when influenced by a cyclotron similarly pass to a perspective that is more fully verticalized, just as magnetism can do as it passes into electromagnetism. Thus the yin-yang structural pattern, with its vestige of duality between the two aspects, can progressively become abolished when electricity prevails more and more over the horizontal expression of weak magnetic fields. Both the frontal bulges of the calf elephant and the recumbent breasts could thus become absorbed into a central structural locus radiating light equally from all around the circumference. This is the full face of the Goddess, viewed in a verticalized perspective as a conic section. The limitation of paper and description would naturally make the tilting of the face of the Goddess from a vertical to a horizontal view negligible. This is why the mature autumnal moon-like visage of the Goddess is presented to the view of the onlooker without apology. The view thus obtained is a frontal one, resulting from the tilting of a conic section, which, if it needed explanation, would have unnecessarily landed us into the intricacies of three-dimensional conics and geometry, which is thus kept out by Śaṅkara for good reasons. If one should look at a face reflected from the top of a well, this circular conic section view would be justified.

After getting so far in our vision of the content of the beauty of the Absolute in three-dimensional terms, the remaining task is for Śaṅkara to make this vision fully fourth-dimensional, or even multi-dimensional, in its status. The fourth-dimensional status is revealed in the third line, where conventional monomarks of Indian iconography are attributed to the Goddess intended in this verse, conforming to the norms of a well-accepted iconographic language which has been developed through the ages and shaped finally by successive contemplatives who revised and revalued the basic ideogram. The hands holding aloft bow and arrow, noose and goad, are meant to mark the horizontal and vertical structural dimensions of the Goddess, now viewed together in a fully fourth-dimensional perspective. The bow and arrow have the target of making Śiva fall for her, but the goad and noose have between them a fully verticalized function of normalizing the movement of something of a dark and spatial or earthy order, like an elephant. They are, thus, the four regulative principles in the grand flux of becoming, to be imagined as taking place within the context of time and space in a fourth-dimensional universe.

Finally, in the last line, it is indicated that although she is a Goddess belonging to the so-called weaker sex, she is still capable of attaining high vertical heights in the same way as her husband, by means of her direct affiliation to him. They have equality of status in every respect, as we shall see maintained throughout this work.

The question now remains whether the vision here presented is to be treated subjectively or to be taken as objectively positive. We shall see that up to the limit of verse forty-one, inclusive, which is distinguished as *Ānandalaharī,* the descriptions of the Goddess apply to the inner space within the yogi as his own personal experience. Beyond the forty-first verse, the title becomes *Saundaryalaharī*, where the presentiment is on the side of the non-Self rather than the Self. We should, therefore, after the schematized dynamism has been presented in this verse, expect to see verses clothed in more realistic terms, so that they are to be placed inside or outside. This can be noticed in the very next verse. The last line refers to the 'proud counterpart of the City Burner', where we have to suppose that sex limitations are abolished and cancelled out. Śiva, as *ardhanārīśvara*, is androgynous — a half female, half male deity.

Conversely, Śakti is here the proud *puruṣikā*, where the word *puruṣa*, though normally applied to the male, is here applied to the female on the same reciprocal principle as above.

One more point remains which is the reference to the slimness of the waist. In other Sanskrit poems of Kālidāsa and Śaṅkara, we have this same feature more directly referred to as *mithyākalpita madhya* — the middle region having a false, conceptual status only. The absolute Goddess is not to have any waist at all. It has to be abolished in the name of her schematic status, because here, schematically speaking, is implied the meeting point of the apexes of two triangles, one representing the hypostatic or metaphysical, and the other representing the heirophantic or the physical. Like the sand particles in an hourglass, the delicate passage or osmotic interchange of existence and essence that is taking place between the two is both nothing and something at the same time. This is a secret aspect of structuralism to which Kālidāsa and Śaṅkara adhere throughout their works. Although abolished mathematically by its slim nothingness, we know that this waist region is the very part out of which everything is born. The paradox here is to be understood in its two rival structural reference points, one placed at the ontological end and the other at the opposite teleological limit. Ontologically, the double cones are placed base to base, while teleologically they are placed apex to apex. Both the positions are equally valid. It is the ineffable nothingness of the vertical axis, which passes from ontology to teleology without interruption, that represents the absolute value factor called 'Beauty' here. When such a parameter is produced positively or negatively, upwards or downwards, we attain to the fourth-dimensional or even multi-dimensional value worlds within ourselves or in the cosmos outside of us. Cross-sections taken at any point on this vertical parameter will reveal various mandalas or chakras, which could be of infinite variety. Here we are more concerned with chakras, while in Tibetan Buddhism the four-sided mandala language is favoured and adopted. The very next verse gives us a picture of the Goddess seated within a structure which is suggestive both of a mandala and a chakra.

Structural Analysis

At the centre of the schematic structure we have to place the radiant full moon as representing the face. The thin waist has a double correction and back to back inversion in which the positive ego of the City Burner cancels out the negative existential richness of the full breasts. A logarithmic curve joins the two halves into a unified whole for purposes of meditation of the absolute value-factor of sheer Beauty both hypostatic as well as hierophantic at once. The beauty of the Goddess represents complementary factors or functions in the context of the word and its meaning. The zero point induced by meditation on the sound of the waistband jingling bells represents the normal white light of absolute Beauty. We have put faces at both the alpha and omega points in order to respect the reciprocity and complementarity of the counterparts which could also be considered as cancellable or as compensatory in principle. The whole is to be treated unitively as a normalized value under the aegis of the Absolute under the caption of Beauty as a high human value.

8

सुधासिन्धोर्मध्ये सुरविटपिवाटीपरिवृते
मणिद्वीपे नीपोपवनवति चिन्तामणिगृहे ।
शिवाकारे मञ्चे परमशिवपर्यङ्कनिलयां
भजन्ति त्वां धन्याः कतिचन चिदानन्दलहरीम् ॥

sudhā sindhor madhye sura viṭapi vāṭī parivṛte
maṇi dvīpe nīpopavana vati cintāmaṇi gṛhe ।
śivākāre mañce parama śiva paryaṅka nilayāṁ
bhajanti tvāṁ dhanyāḥ katicana cid ānanda laharīm ॥

sudhā sindhoḥ madhye — in the midst of an ocean of nectar; *suraviṭapi vāṭī parivṛte* — surrounded by celestial trees; *maṇi dvīpe* — on a pearly-gem island; *nīpa upavana vati* — having a grove of *kadamba* trees; *cintāmaṇi gṛhe* — in a house made of contemplative gems; *śiva ākāre mañce* — on a couch of Śiva-form; *paramaśiva paryaṅka nilayāṁ* — with Supreme Śiva for cushion; *tvāṁ cidānanda laharīm* — You as the upsurging billow of mental joy; *dhanyāḥ katicana* — those rare fortunate ones; *bhajanti* — they meditate

Seated on a couch of Śiva-form and having the Supreme Śiva for cushion;
Placed within a mansion wafted round by the perfume of blossoms of kadamba *trees,*
Located within a celestial grove, on a pearly-gem island in the midst of a nectar ocean,
Some fortunate ones contemplate You as the upsurging billow of mental joy.

It is natural for wisdom seekers to aspire for a quiet place, far from the ignoble strife of common human life. This desire only means that they want to keep company with themselves, seeking a happiness that is more than the pleasure that could be derived from society. In aspiring thus for loneliness, some aspirants might think of a cave in the Himalayas, as Śiva is intent on finding in verse seventy-eight. Others might think of an island situated far away from disturbing contacts. We have already had a hint about this kind of natural aspiration in the third verse, where a city of light placed in mid-ocean corresponds to the dear dream of an ignorant man who strongly feels that he needs the consolation of wisdom or philosophy. This same idea is carried over for elaboration in this verse where the third line alludes to a 'pearly-gem island in the midst of a nectar ocean'. It describes in greater detail a mandala-like structure in which the Goddess is seated in dignity and grandeur on a couch. The island evidently has a well-furnished and well-ordered household in a mansion, surrounded by many varieties of trees laden with fragrant blossoms and ripe fruits. The grove itself is a holy place. The water of the ocean is not the usual salt water, but consists of rich life-giving nectar in great abundance. Poverty or indigence cannot touch such a place.

There are three familiar words in the context of yantra, mantra and tantra, which are mandala, chakra and *ādhāra*. In Tibetan mandalas we find the four walls or steps leading to four doors. A chakra would suggest a space enclosed by concentric circles, some more peripheral than others and generally three in number. The term *ādhāra* is used more specifically in yogic literature proper. There are six of them excluding the *kulakuṇḍa* and *sahasrāra*, which bring up the lower and upper limits. We can see, by glancing at the succeeding verses, that this verse prepares the ground for viewing these contemplative units within consciousness, as they could vary vertically or horizontally in a series, or in a hierarchy of sets or subsets. We shall have occasion to go into such details when we come to the verses treating of them.

For the present, we must note here that it is the state of mind within the consciousness of a yogi, who is meditating with shut eyes, which is the subject here. This island, thus represents rather a state of mind than a bit of geographical land. India itself is sometimes referred to as *jambudvīpa* (an island of rose apple trees, *Eugenia jambolana*) for contemplative reasons, outside of mere geographical considerations. The yogi thus meditating on the personification of Beauty within the scope of his own wisdom-awareness, finds the most precious personification of absolute Beauty in the first instance as seated comfortably on a couch. She is far removed from indigence or want. A yogi who feels that he is poor cannot meditate freely on the highest of values beyond all riches, which is represented by absolute Wisdom. It is for this reason that the seat of the Goddess here is at the very core of a situation in which all sense of necessity of everyday life is excluded from its realm. There is a level on the negative side of the lower cone where necessity can have its place, but the island here is to be imagined as occupying the position just between the bases of the two cones, placed slightly apart in close juxtaposition.

The walls of the mansion could be considered a square or four-sided orthogonal figure, but the island itself should preferably be imagined as a circle, because contemplation within consciousness is comparable to a torch in misty darkness, which clarifies only a globe of light around it. A burning lamp sheds its umbra and penumbra in circles. In spite of this circular or rather global shape in consciousness, when we think of the neutral level at which the mansion here is to be located, a square motif is not to be ruled out, because the world here is one that is viewed through lattices or matrices, as in a graph paper. Television technique and cybernetic matrices, as also gratings, microscopically studied, reveal the square shape based on the principle of orthogonality. The impossibility of 'squaring a circle' in mathematics also indicates that the square fits into an actual context of full horizontality, while the circle is more contemplative. Reference to actuality of this kind brings the status of the Goddess into a fully realistic perspective. Vedanta, as some people wrongly think, is not a form of idealism. The soul of man is supposed to fit, by both its existence and its essence, to the very tip of the hard nail, just as a razor fits tightly in its own leather case. The idea of the universal concrete is to be respected to its very limit, as when the *Chāndogya Upaniṣad* says that the nail scissors are made of steel without gradation in the homogeneity of its substance. Just as the steel fills completely the shape of the nail scissors, so *brahman* fills the whole universe. Nothing should be explained away as being not real or merely mental. Thus, a square mansion placed within a circular island is not repugnant to the ideal doctrine of Advaita Vedanta, as understood through Śaṅkara's commentaries. The numerous criticisms of Śaṅkara's Advaita, as tending to treat the world as unreal, are seen to be false when correctly understood in this way.

There is one special particularity in this verse which has to be examined more closely. The very first line seems to suggest that Śiva became a couch, and that a superior grade of the same Śiva became a cushion, for his wife to sit on. This offers a puzzle and an enigma which has to be explained before we proceed. In the common prayer of Christianity — 'Thy kingdom come. Thy will be done on earth, as it is in heaven', reference is made to two worlds placed at two limits of the same vertical parameter. Heaven is hypostatic, while the earth is its hierophantic counterpart. What is there as a value is also here as a value, but there lurks within these two sets of values, a subtle inversion which makes the one-to-one correspondence 'topsy-turvy'. Ancient hermetic symbolism, as in the Tarot cards, alludes to this structural secret of 'topsy-turvydom' by the picture of a man hanging head downwards. There is an inversion involved in the very structure of space, which is referred to as 'mirror reflection' horizontally, and 'handedness' vertically. These are two kinds of symmetries that have been noted by physicists within the basic structure of space. Ontological existence and teleological subsistence have to belong together within the total scope of absolute Space. Here a subtle ambivalence, a reciprocity, a compensation and a complementarity become evident. Existence and essence belong to two dichotomous poles of the total situation. Phenomenologists of modern times distinguish between *noetic, noematic* and *eidetic* presentiments. What they call the phenomenological *epoche* or *ghost* is to be contained within brackets, so as to enclose the value content within the inverted curves of the two brackets, which, facing opposite ways, are turned obversely and conversely. A blind man might take a water jug and, holding it upside down, say that it is useless because it has a hole at the bottom. He might then touch the bottom and say that nothing can be poured into it. Though the Absolute has to be contained as a value within consciousness, it has to avoid falling into the double errors of tautology and contradiction. These epistemological errors are referred to as impossibility (*asambhava*) and tautology (*ātmāśraya*). (See Narayana Guru's *Darśanamālā*, Chapter II. Verse 6.)

The difference between existence and essence, which has been the subject matter of much disputation between modern existentialists and the earlier scholastic philosophers who emphasized essence, is a problem that has been faced and solved by the Vedantic tradition long ago. When Vedanta refers to *sat cit ānanda*, the first term, *sat*, refers to existence or ontological reality, while the term *ānanda* corresponds to the essence of God as known in Western theology. It is between these two limits that logic, *cit*, rules supreme. In scrutinizing the meaning of *satyam jñānam anantam brahma*, Śaṅkara takes much trouble in his commentary to point out that *sat* is neutralized by *cit* in its meaning content, and *cit* is again modified by *ānanda* in its meaning content. Thus, between *sat cit ānanda* there is, what Bergson would call, a 'back-to-back correction' which we must apply to the situation. According to this correction, Bergson would even go so far as to say that accidents do not happen to us, but that 'we happen to accidents'. If this idea can be understood, the enigma here of Śiva becoming a cushion would be considered as quite in keeping with the views of such a modern pragmatist philosopher as Henri Bergson.

The hypostatic value of Śiva, when transformed to the denominator side would become a couch or a cushion. What is there is also here in a transformed or translated form, one as teleological essence and the other as ontological existence. As we have indicated already, Śiva comes down from the peak of Kailāsa looking for caverns for his austerities. He descends from the top of the structure to the middle of the parameter. The Goddess, on the other hand, has her reference at the bottom of the negative parameter. She ascends to the structural mid-region, and thus goes beyond all necessities, into the neutral ground between the base sections of the two cones, where the palace on a gem-set island in a nectar ocean is to be placed contemplatively by the votary. If this verse is read with this kind of double perspective in one's mind, most of the enigmas become self-explained. The fortunate contemplative of the last line gives us a standpoint with which we are to place the absolute goddess of Beauty at the *bindusthāna* or core of the contemplative situation to serve the purpose of fruitful yogic meditation. Śiva has only a conceptual status; it is his name that is more important than his form. Transposed to the negative side, he becomes a value that helps contemplative verticality to be promoted within consciousness. A couch and a cushion are objects which have their everyday value, which should not be excluded from the contemplative set of values.

The fragrant blossoms of special sacred trees and the sanctity of the grove itself, referred to in the second and third lines, could be fitted easily into the structural context at the mid-region, when we remember that they belong to the world of intentionality and not actuality. Cleanliness and godliness are sometimes used interchangeably. The sweet smell of flowers and a grove of trees are presences or influences which give to life an interest and a zest, lifting it or merging it within higher or lower stratifications of the total set-up of values. The peripheral trees forming a circle are more existential than essential, while the central trees, with the perfume of blossoms wafted by the breeze, mark an essential, hypostatic level. While heavenly trees are referred to in the context of perfumed blossoms, gems are mentioned in the lower stratification. Their values are to be treated as interchangeable, whether they are placed hypostatically or hierophantically. When cancelled out vertically, they give homogeneity to the absolute Value, in which gem-beauty and flower-perfumes enter as equal partners, to cause the upsurging billow of mental joy referred to in the last line.

When *śivākāre mañce* is taken to mean that the gods become the legs of the couch of the Devī, there is evidently a challenge staring us in the face. The pictorial representations by Mughal and Rajput schools of painting, printed in the edition of Professor Brown of Harvard, do recognize that the transformation of the gods into the legs of a cot is meant seriously by Śaṅkara, but to this day, no justification of such a transformation has been suggested, at least to the knowledge of the author, by the commentators of this work. We believe, therefore, that only through a protolinguistic, structural approach could such a transformation be even barely understood. A similar image of the gods becoming the legs of the throne of Prajāpati can be found in the *Atharva Veda*.

Structural Analysis

The structural analysis of this verse involves both solid and plane geometric constructions. Three-dimensional solids with conics kept in mind and one normal conic section representing the horizontal reference of work-a-day realistic value has to be inserted between two cones placed base to base for purposes of double reference and correction back to back. These structural and epistemological features have been explained at length in various parts of our previous writings. The colour solid with the chakra with triangles having apexes pointing upwards or downwards is an attempt by the Tantra *śāstra* to schematize protolinguistically the contemplative values and the existent and subsistent factors involved. Ontology counts here above teleology, and it is Śiva and

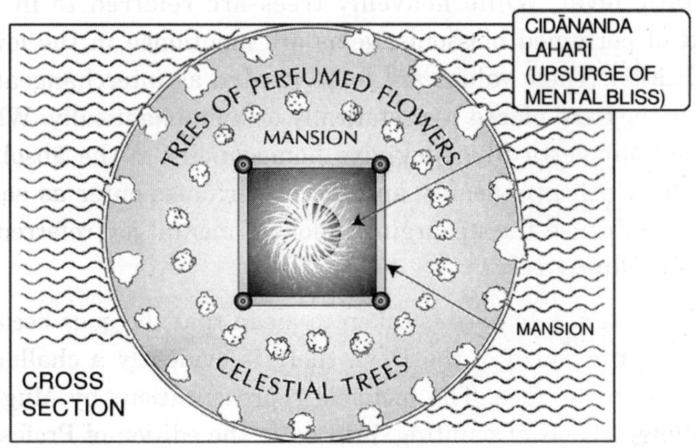

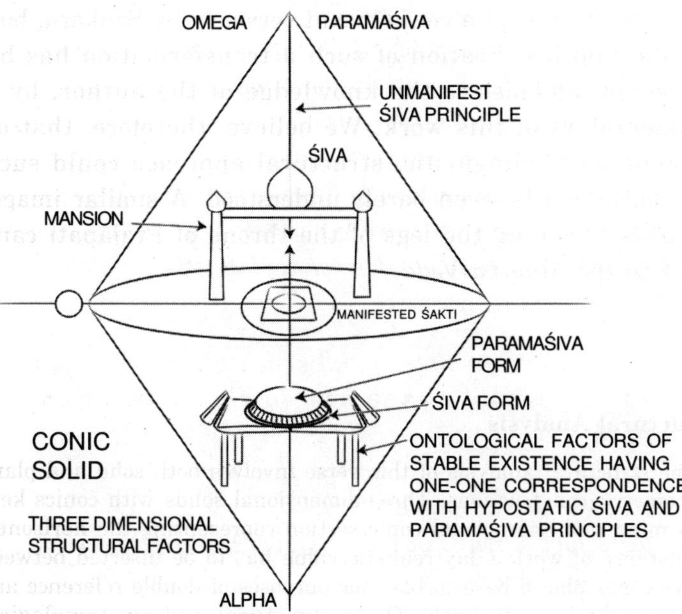

Paramaśiva that have been reduced to the universal concrete status of cushions or cots. The vertical parameter passing through the centre and apexes of the two inverted cones is the non-dual correlating principle integrating physical value factors with metaphysical ones in the structural totality of the Absolute. Other implications in this are clarified in the two figures.

9

महीं मूलाधारे कमपि मणिपूरे हुतवहं
स्थितं स्वाधिष्ठाने हृदि मरुतमाकाशमुपरि ।
मनोऽपि भ्रूमध्ये सकलमपि भित्त्वा कुलपथं
सहस्रारे पद्मे सह रहसि पत्या विहरसे ॥

mahīṁ mūlādhāre kam api maṇipūre hutavahaṁ
sthitaṁ svādhiṣṭhāne hṛdi marutam ākāśam upari ।
mano'pi bhrū madhye sakalam api bhittvā kula pathaṁ
sahasrāre padme saha rahasi patyā viharase ॥

mūlādhāre mahīṁ — the earth placed in the *mūlādhāra*; *maṇipūre* — in the *maṇipūra*; *kam api* — water also; *svādhiṣṭhāne* — in the *svādhiṣṭhāna*; *hutavahaṁ* — the fire principle (receptacle of sacrificial offerings); *hṛdi* — in the heart; *marutam* — the winds; *ākāśam upari* — the sky placed above; *bhrū madhye* — between eyebrows; *manaḥ api* — the mind also; *sthitaṁ* — established; *sakalam kulapathaṁ api bhittvā* — breaking through the whole *kula* path; *sahasrāre padme* — in the thousand-petalled lotus; *rahasi patyā saha viharase* — you do sport with your Lord in secret

The earth placed in the mūlādhāra, *water in the* maṇipūra,
Fire in the svādhiṣṭhāna, *air in the heart, with space above;*
And amid eyebrows placing the mind, and breaking through the whole kula *path,*
You do sport with Your Lord secretly in the thousand-petalled lotus.

After placing the absolute principle of Beauty, presented in the most realistic, universal and concrete form, in her proper position at the core of the total structural set-up in the eighth verse, this verse carries over the same into other grades of stable positions on the vertical parameter, where a natural equilibrium of psycho-physical forces could be expected. As we have pointed out with reference to the classical dancing girl *Kandukavati*, who begins at the proper ontological starting point by respectfully touching the firm earth, before elaborating the graded varieties of her art at more and more perfected levels, which fill the whole field or ground with magenta glory; here also, the most stable ground for an equilibrium to be established between psychophysical forces, introspectively or intuitively understood, is the earth principle, which is the rich ontological basis where the consciousness of the contemplative can naturally find repose and be at ease.

In contemplative literature we know of various grades of value systems, some of which are 'earth earthy', while others are placed in essences at higher, hypostatic levels. The Purāṇas (traditional heroic or epic lore), which are meant for their popular philosophical appeal in the generality of contemplatives, speak of 'twice-seven worlds' of such values, totalling fourteen, seven being above while seven are below. Names are given to each of these value worlds. When we include the subjective Self or the objective Self as an additional point of psychophysical equilibrium, we get eight worlds which are subjective and eight worlds that belong to the non-Self side. The Bhagavadgītā (VII. 4) marks out eight possible stratifications in absolute Consciousness. Buddhism knows of the noble eightfold path, and the Patañjali system of yoga has its eight grades or divisions (*aṣṭāṅga*). In the opening verse of the *Śākuntalaṁ*, Kālidāsa gives importance to this way of dividing the whole of the range covered by the vertical parameter by marking eight points, one set of which is in the descending scale and the other in the ascending, which latter alone figures in the opening verse; the subjective series is omitted evidently for the reason that the onlookers of the play bring to bear on the total situation, by themselves, the subjective side, while the players represent the objective side. The joy of the play results by the interplay of the subjective and objective sides. There is also, in the *Vivekacūḍāmaṇi,* a reference to this graded unit consisting of eight items, there called *puryaṣṭakam* (eight cities) which make up the eight levels describing the subtle body, referred to as *sūkṣma śarīra*. The number eight thus seems to be a normal figure when the whole range of literature is considered, but in this verse there is reference only to six positions.

Śaṅkara, in his commentaries, comes up against this kind of difference between text and text, and votes there in favour of a bigger number, saying that having some extras is always safer than being strictly limited, as in the number of players, for example, in a game. In his *Arivu* (*The Epistemology of Gnosis*), Narayana Guru analyses this same question and comes to a fairly conclusive version of the epistemological problem involved. Knowledge is either of things presented to the senses or of elements experienced from inside oneself, and these two aspects could be broadly divided by putting a horizontal line between the Self and the non-Self, that is, between the knower and what is known. We can go upward in an ascending scale of stable positions, rising gradually into the region of the non-Self; or sink introspectively to the source within, starting with the most stable ontological pole marked by the firm earth. The question of inserting your own Self (*ātman*) as the eighth item on the objective side, to complete the series of eight, could be done last of all (in the manner of 7 + 1, 5 + 3, or 6 + 2).

We are concerned with explaining the problem of only six positions being discussed in the present verse. We could easily add one more below the *mūlādhāra*, which would mark the position of the *kulakuṇḍa* of verse ten, and in this verse itself there is the *sahasrāra* (the thousand-petalled lotus), which does not seem to be included in the six. Thus the puzzle is cleared without us having to suggest some modification of what is stated in this work in very clear terms as the six stable positions (*ādhāra*s). We enumerate them in the ascending series given in this verse:*

1. *mūlādhāra*
2. *maṇipūra*
3. *svādhiṣṭhāna*
4. the heart (*anāhata*: not named here)
5. the space above (*viśuddhi*: not named here)
6. the mind between the eyebrows (*ājñā*: not named here)
7. *Sahasrāra* (thousand-petalled Lotus)

In the Patañjali system, which is based on the dualistic Sāṁkhya philosophy, the dynamism of yoga is in terms of a gradual process of spiritual progress, in eight grades of discipline, ascending to what is marked by the word *kaivalya* (aloneness) at the culminating point. This kind of gradual process of spiritual progress between two points, representing ends and means, is repugnant to the more dynamic unitive view proper to Advaita Vedanta, where no vestige of duality could be tolerated, whether in ends or in means. Ends and means have to be treated together. This is the correct Advaitic approach of the Upaniṣads and the Bhagavadgītā.

The '*kula* path' here is a reference to those who follow the Śakti cult, whether known as Kaulins or Samayins, the latter being considered more respectable than the former. We have explained the difference in our general remarks elsewhere. The words 'breaking through the whole *kula* path' imply the revaluation of those two kinds of esotericism in terms of the more radical or absolutist approach denoting this work. The dynamism of this verse is complemented and completed in the next verse as both an ascent as well as a descent.

---

* Note the change in the order of chakras: *Svādhiṣṭhāna*, the third here is generally placed second while *maṇipura* is generally the third. Some commentators suggest that this may be because Sankara is following the order of the five elements — earth, water, fire, air and ether.

There is a reference to a snake that sleeps in the hollow of the lower limit called *kulakuṇḍa*. This is the much talked about *kuṇḍalinī* snake. *Kuṇḍala* means a hoop or a ring. It is thus sometimes thought of as a circle enclosing an absolute Value ideogram. An improved version of it is when we think of it coiled up like a viper, rather than a cobra, appearing like a spring of three and a half coils, as specifically indicated in the next verse. This snake is not only sleeping in its most easy-going state, but can uncoil itself with a hissing noise, as mentioned in some yogic texts, to become a verticalized and rigid version of the same without coils. By this verticalizing ascent, another hole at the top of the psychophysical set-up is reached, passing through, if possible, what is referred to as an absolute passage situated somewhere below the pituitary gland at the soft palate, behind the uvula. When the head of the snake touches this highest of plexes or points of psychophysical synergism or syndrome, the yogi is supposed to experience an exaltation that makes him, in principle, attain the absolute Vision. These upper and lower limits have to be clearly visualized by us in following the verses nine and ten. Here we are only explaining how 'breaking through the whole *kula* path' is a dynamism to be understood as resembling the sudden increase of electric voltage rather than any slow process as in the case of slow nuclear reactions.

The reference to 'sporting secretly' only means that the yogi's whole dynamism has a public and a private reciprocity in terms of enjoyment. What is private on the minus side is public on the plus side, and vice versa. The secret alluded to here is to be understood as having a reference to the minus side.

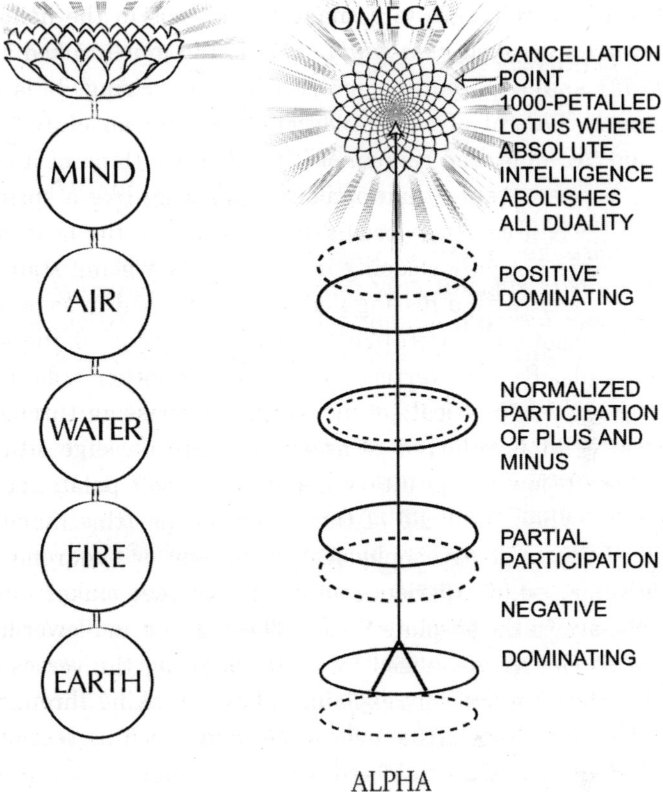

Structural Analysis

The six *ādhāra*s are stable stages or serialized steps of equal epistemological status representing existent, subsistent and value systems. They thus structurally take positions on a vertical parameter, each point compensating, reciprocating or cancelling by neutral absorption. The serial pluralism is only for schematic purposes without intrinsic difference or gradation. The lower chakra absorbs the higher in the ascent that is implied here. Other later verses will stress further structural particularities. There could be ascent as well as descent and normalization at the central points of origin. Numerological indications are also possible.

10

सुधाधारासारैश्चरणयुगलान्तर्विगलितैः
प्रपञ्चं सिञ्चन्ती पुनरपि रसाम्नायमहसः ।
अवाप्य स्वां भूमिं भुजगनिभमध्युष्टवलयं
स्वमात्मानं कृत्वा स्वपिषि कुलकुण्डे कुहरिणि ॥

sudhā dhārā sārais carana yugalāntar vigalitaiḥ
prapañcaṁ siñcantī punar api rasāmnāya mahasaḥ ।
avāpya svāṁ bhūmiṁ bhujagānibham adhyuṣṭa valayaṁ
svam ātmānaṁ kṛtvā svapiṣi kulakuṇḍe kuhariṇi ॥

caraṇa yugala antaḥ vigalitaiḥ — streaming from between your twin feet; *sudhā dhārā sāraiḥ* — streaks of ambrosial essence; *rasa āmnāya mahasaḥ* — from that point of high intelligible (essential) values; *prapañcaṁ siñcantiḥ* — sprinkling blessings over the worlds; *svāṁ bhūmiṁ* — one's proper ground; *punaḥ api avāpya* — and again attaining; *svaṁ ātmānaṁ kṛtvā* — turning Yourself; *bhujaga nibham* — taking serpent likeness; *adhyuṣṭa valayaṁ* — having three and a half coils; *kuhariṇi* — having a small hollow; *kulakuṇḍe* — in the *kulakuṇḍa; svapiṣi* — you sleep

With streaks of ambrosial essence streaming from between Your twin feet,
Sprinkling blessings over the worlds, and again from that point of high intelligible values,
Turning Yourself into a snake-form of three coils and a half,
You sleep in the hollow of the kulakuṇḍa, *Your proper ground attaining.*

We find, by visualizing this work as a whole, that it is tacitly divided into sections of ten, though not strictly in every case. Thus, we can expect this tenth verse to sum up a preliminary section in which all matters of importance are introduced to the reader. They are: the world of paradoxes, the world of particles, the quaternion, the primacy of ontology, the borrowed glory of demiurges, occasionalism, the total structural dynamism, the principle of vertical inversion, and the six stable positions (*ādhāras*). These concepts have all been brought to light to facilitate the understanding of the later verses, before passing on to the *śrī cakra* and its details in the next verse.

Yoga literature is familiar with what is called a *kuṇḍalinī* snake. It is said to be coiled and normally in a dormant, hibernating or sleeping state. By willful disciplines, such as haṭha yoga, yogis are supposed to rouse this sleeping snake which is said to be present within the hollow of consciousness, having its reference at the base of the vertical axis. When thus aroused, it unfolds its coils and raises itself like a spiral spring, reaching higher and higher levels of consciousness, passing through the various chakras where syndromes or synergisms, whether psychologically or physiologically understood, are to be schematically marked out by the yogi for his guidance in meditation. We are familiar also in yogic literature with the three *nāḍī*s: *iḍā* (the left or moon nerve), *piṅgalā* (the right or sun nerve) and *suṣumnā* (the central nerve). The *suṣumnā* marks the central line of nervous facilitation through which the *śakti* or the power called the *kuṇḍalinī* rises upward to transcend the various levels of consciousness. This parameter or line of nervous facilitation is supposed to be a capillary, as thin as one-thousandth of the breadth of a hair, which conducts the ascending vital energy (*ūrdhvaretas*), which, passing through other intermediate plexus, ganglia or synapses — representing various syndromes and synergisms constituting a hierarchy in the nervous system — finally attains the highest position in the centre of the thousand-petalled lotus. The snake is represented conventionally as passing from the left to the right of the central *nāḍī* (*suṣumnā*), the three strands of which, when taken together, perhaps, correspond to the sympathetic nervous system, where the main influx of vital energy is said to ascend by an innate principle of facilitation. Various attempts have been made by physiologists as well as psychophysically-minded experts, as also those who speak in psychosomatic terms, to establish a correct correspondence between this ancient haṭha yogic vision of the ascent of psychic energy and the final attainment of the proper purpose of yoga. All such attempts have been only partial examinations. This is due to the fact that various degrees of abstraction between mind and body factors are possible. It is the philosophy, which accepts dualistic or non-dualistic positions, that determines whether the picture of such a snake presented is to be taken literally or only figuratively.

One sees sometimes in some conventional pictures of this snake that it passes from the right to the left of the central thin and mathematical parameter. Dualistic schools of yoga, such as that of Patañjali, give more importance to the ascent than to the descent of the *kuṇḍalinī* snake. At the final point of the ascent is the *sahasrāra padma*. In other texts, that final point is sometimes called the *brahmarandhra*, an absolutist passage through which consciousness can rise to higher levels than can be envisaged by dualistic thought. The methodology and epistemology of Advaita Vedanta requires that the whole question of the *kuṇḍalinī* snake be viewed from both its positive and negative perspectives, that is, both as ascending beyond the *brahmarandhra* and as descending to sleep again in the cavity at the negative ontological limit of the total psychophysical set-up, within the four limits of which all states of consciousness must necessarily live, move and have their being.

It would not be wrong for us, in the light of these remarks, to attribute to Śaṅkara the intention of presenting here a revised and revalued version of the dynamism of psychophysical states, in which the double movement of the *kuṇḍalinī* snake is presented with its beauty and symmetry as in keeping with his own Advaita Vedanta, rather than according to the philosophy of Patañjali or others vitiated by various degrees of implied dualism.

We have to begin by placing the feet of the Goddess at three different levels, marked by the zero point at the centre and the alpha point and the omega point at the negative and positive limits of the vertical parameter. Between the feet at the centre, viewed from a vertical perspective, the description here is justified, that some ambrosial essences have their origin at that locus, marked by the zero point between the twin feet.

The reference to the blessing of the world by sprinkling ambrosia on all the levels within the limits of the body of the Goddess, necessarily presupposes an upward as well as a downward movement from this point of origin. Thus there are ramified sets of values that resemble the Tree of Porphyry of Western theology, as also an inverted version of the same which could be a reflection of the former. The movement of the *kuṇḍalinī* snake and the levels, both positive and negative that it can attain, thus come to have both a vertical and a horizontal parity or symmetry. The quiet and dormant snake marks the lower limiting point in consciousness when the yogi does not exercise any pressure of psychophysical discipline on himself. When he does exercise such a pressure by what is generally called *tapas* (mystical agony), this hissing snake passing spirally around the central parameter not only attains higher levels by what is marked as the zero point, but touches higher and higher worlds in the domain of the intelligibles. Though all these details are not specifically indicated in the verse itself, we are sufficiently justified in elaborating the purport of this verse in this manner because Śaṅkara does the same in other verses, telescoping into unity many factors which could be elaborated endlessly through didactic verbosity. He is using a non-verbose and necessarily cryptic medium here, which has many aspects to be supplied by the imagination of the reader himself.

The higher levels of the intelligibles attained by the *kuṇḍalinī* snake in its ascent refers to conceptual values, as implied in the phrase *rasāmnāya*, which refers to essence or joy or value described in scriptures such as the Upaniṣads. The term *mahas* (greatness or glory) justifies our position that it is the joy or bliss in experiencing the meaning of the Absolute which is to be kept in mind here. This glory of the Absolute marks the topmost limit in this spiritual ascent, of which the bottom-most limit is known as the *kulakuṇḍa* or the *kuṇḍalinī* which is an inside or hollow rather than an outside. What is lost by the author's avoidance of verbosity has to be supplied by the imagination of the reader, so that this preliminary section of ten verses could effectively round off matters of interest for the student to proceed more normally with his studies beyond this first section.

The reference to three and a half coils of the snake would remind us of a viper rather than a cobra. A viper has a way of coiling in half circles and placing its head at the point where the three and a half coils can be imagined to terminate. Twice three and a half makes seven; thus, we cover all the psychophysical centres in an extended sense when we include factors such as *ahaṁkāra* as we see in the Gītā's enumeration of the hierachy of factors. If we include the *brahmarandhra* and the *kulakuṇḍa*, we could add two more stable positions. If we should add one on the positive side, or the ascent, it would be fair to omit the one on the negative side, or the descent. The 'half' in the 'three and a half' is supposed to indicate this alternate inclusion or exclusion of limits understood dynamically rather than statically. The Yoga Upaniṣads actually speak of ten *ādhāra*s or chakras, six of them real in the cosmological sense while the others could be psychological or theoretical in their status. Śaṅkara elsewhere dismisses such discussions about the actual number, saying that he is unable to settle the difference between text and text, but would prefer a larger number so that nothing, subtle or gross, stands the danger of being overlooked. As in a cricket game, it is always better for a team to have a few extra players along.

Structural Analysis

A double cone placed base to base with the markings of two feet impressed on the bottom or top of each cone, respectively, when, placed in juxtaposition will give us a back to back relation of double correction. The feet could move as a central value for the devotee's meditation of perfect Beauty here intended, upwards or downwards from its normal central position. Raised hypostatically through

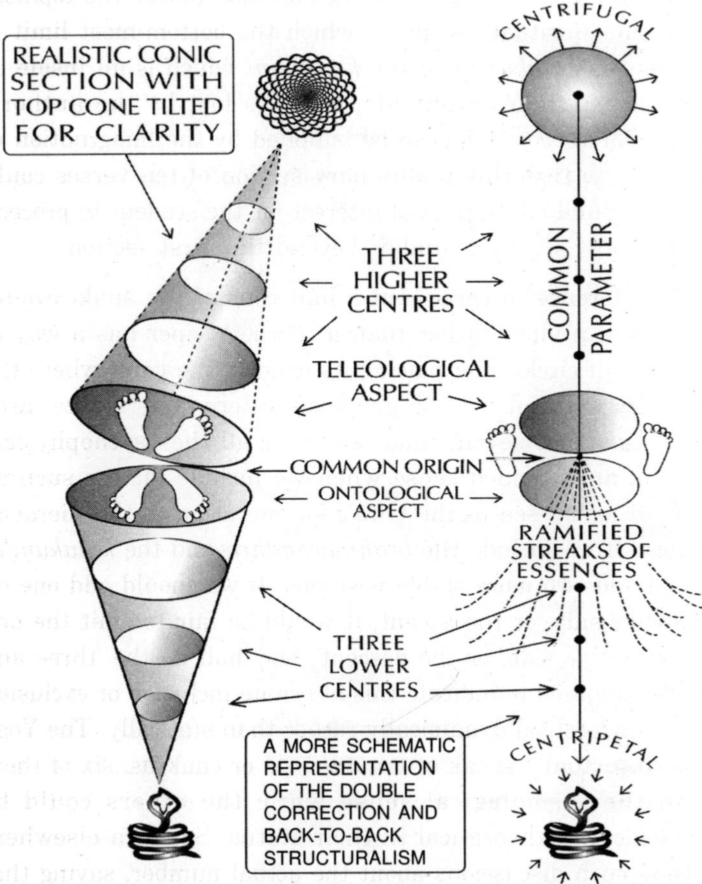

the three higher chakras it will attain the *sahasrāra*, the topmost limit, which is the one-pointed enjoyment of intellectual bliss here under reference. Before this ascent, one has to think of the lower cone as representing the worlds of the perceptibles of physics. The ramified essences sprinkle this world to give it a content-significance in the context of absolute Beauty. They thus gain a revised status under the aegis of the Absolute. This descent is mentioned first in the verse and is of the form of a ramified set of value factors covering the totality of the worlds of physics. The serpent is to be looked upon as representing a parameter for both the ascent and descent of psychic energies or tendencies. Hierophantically viewed, the three-and-a-half coils are justified as already explained.

11

चतुर्भिः श्रीकण्ठैः शिवयुवतिभिः पञ्चभिरपि
प्रभिन्नाभिः शंभोर्नवभिरपि मूलप्रकृतिभिः।
चतुश्चत्वारिंशद्वसुदलकलाश्रत्रिवलय-
त्रिरेखाभिः सार्धं तव शरणकोणाः परिणताः॥

caturbhiḥ srī kaṇṭhaiḥ śiva yuvatibhiḥ pañcabhir api
prabhinnābhiḥ śaṃbhor navabhir api mūla prakṛtibhiḥ ।
catuś catvārimśad vasu dala kalāśra tri valaya
tri rekhābhiḥ sārdhaṁ tava śaraṇa koṇāḥ pariṇatāḥ ॥

śrīkaṇṭhaiḥ caturbhiḥ — with four of Śiva; *śaṁbhoḥ prabhinnābhiḥ* — and severally distinct from those of Śiva; *śiva yuvatibhiḥ pañcabhiḥ* — of Śiva-maid's five; *navabhiḥ mūla prakṛtibhiḥ* — those nine too of prime nature; *tava* — Your; *catuścatvārimśad* — making forty-four (including the *bindu*); *śaraṇa koṇāḥ* — angular refuge; *vasudala kalāśra* — with eight and sixteen petals; *trivalaya trirekhābhiḥ* — with three circles and three lines; *sārdhaṁ* — taken together; *pariṇatāḥ* — are thus complete

With the four of Śiva and of Śiva-maid's five, and
severally distinct from those of Śiva,
Those nine, too, of prime nature, with eight and sixteen
petals,
Three circles and three lines, thus are complete,
The forty-four elements that make up Your finalized
angular refuge.

This verse refers to the well known *śrī cakra*. Chakra suggests a global unit of consciousness. It is represented as a circle for two-dimensional convenience, but is meant to be more than a circle. It consists of triangles with their bases placed conversely, trying to interpenetrate each other from opposite sides. On the plus side, the numerator set of inverted triangles represents the masculine principle of Śiva. The lower set of upright triangles,

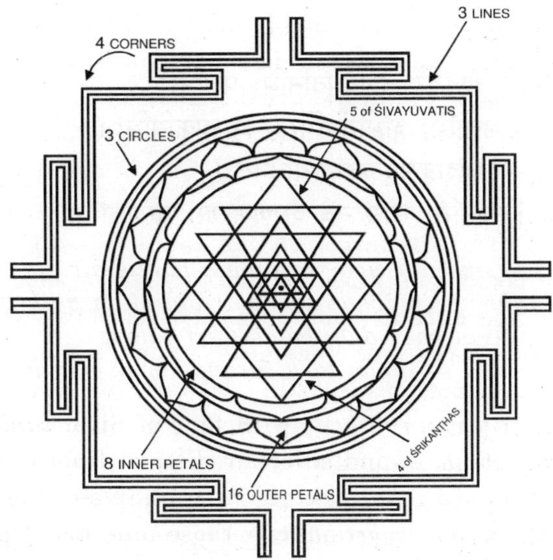

on the denominator side, evidently represents the feminine counterpart of each of the numerator set. A rectangle can be imagined by us to join the apexes of the base angles of the two reciprocal sets of triangles. A circle can be considered as the limit of a polygon of infinite sides; similarly, at the opposite limit, a triangle would be the most elementary polygon. A series of alternating odd and even numbers could be so arranged with four first digits on the first line, one less (i.e., three) on the next, and so on, until we form with these numbers a triangle; thus, polygons and numbers have between them a relationship. If we should consider a polygon with an infinite number of sides as a fully matured form of consciousness, all the other elements, starting from a triangle, could be united as inclusively contained within the two limits of a triangle and a circle. In the fourth line of this verse, the 'finalized angular refuge' suggests the same maturity of finalization that is found in verse seven as the autumnal full-moon face. Between the triangle and the circle, the lower and the upper limits, respectively, could be recognized, and thereafter, the three circles could be treated as three grades of further maturation and abstraction.

The Pythagoreans worshipped *tetraktys,* which is a triangle, numerologically understood. The polygon of infinite sides becomes a circle by maturation of the triangle. In the *śrī cakra*, the triangles are seen to have their apexes on a vertical parameter or axis, some of them in ascending and some in descending order. We can count four such apexes from the top as we descend along the vertical axis; similarly, we can count five apexes in an ascending order. When translated into three-dimensional or four-dimensional space, as in conics and solid geometry, we can see somehow the forty-four elements under reference here. Hilbertian mathematics speaks in terms of *chose mathematique* (mathematical things), which are treated as elements or units, by which the structure of mathematics as a whole is revealed. Within the scope of an endless series of numbers, it is possible to arrange them so as to get all the polygons possible in geometric figures. Adding together the four of Śiva and the five of Śiva-maids' gives us nine apexes which touch the vertical axis. These nine are referred to as of the 'order of prime nature'. Nature (*prakṛti*) is the negative counterpart of spirit (*puruṣa*) of Sāmkhya philosophy, although Advaita Vedanta is against the dualistic treatment of nature and spirit as rival absolutes. Here, for the purposes of distinguishing the function of Śakti from that of Śiva, for the sake of argument at least, the notion of a *mūlaprakṛti* is retained. This is to be treated not as a doctrinal, but as an epistemological and methodological necessity. Thus we have found some *raison d'être* for the apexes and the triangles in the verse.

The base angles in turn, touched by a circumscribing circle there, are to be treated as petals in a flower, or radiation lines of the points of a compass. This circle could be divided into eight divisions of forty-five degrees each. We could further subdivide it into sixteen, because space could be four-dimensional or multi-dimensional, according to the fraction of the right angle that we treat as a unit. If the circle is treated as a cross-section of space, and if we treat the inner circle and the outermost circle as the limits of what is conceptual and what is perceptual within consciousness, and if we put an intermediate circle which participates on both sides, we can roughly see the significance of the three concentric circles. The outermost circle represents the limit of the horizontal maturation of this geometric figure, which combines a horizontal as well as a vertical gradation of elements. If we should now make due allowance for the simplification of the structure attempted here, so as to represent two-dimensionally what is really intended to be multi-dimensional, then the maturation in the form of the outermost circle would mark its limit. Since the two orthogonal axes within the circle are equalized, it would mean that there is a harmony between the two tendencies of horizontalization and verticalization, within which absolute Consciousness with a negative perspective can be said to operate. Vertically viewed, however, we have four against five 'of Siva-maid's where the parity is lost and a handedness seems to prevail instead.

Such are some of the speculations on this verse describing the *śrī cakra*, about which we could not claim any mathematically valid adequacy. Like time and space articulated with each other, we have to imagine something like what Bergson has said, the relevant part of which we quote again here:

> Across the time and space which we had always known to be separate and, for that very reason, structureless, we shall perceive, as through a transparency, an articulated space-time structure. The mathematical notation of these articulations, carried out upon the virtual and brought to its highest level of generality, will give us an unexpected grip on the real. We shall have a powerful means of investigation at hand, a principle of research, which, we can predict, will not henceforth be renounced by the mind of man, even if experiment **should** impose a new form upon the theory of relativity.[1]

1. Henri Bergson, *Duration and Simultaneity*, Bobbs-Merrill, 1922, p. 150

This idea suggests that the Śiva-maids' being 'distinct from those of Śiva' is only to point out that they are positive and negative counterparts, not to be confused together. Prime nature, as in the octave, is composed of 3½ + 3½ = 7, upwards or downwards. Since here the perspective is viewed from the negative side of the Goddess, rather than from the positive side of the God, the five below and the four above can be justified. The finalization is both horizontal and vertical. A circle represents the harmonious integration of vitalistic and pure tendencies in the beauty of the absolute Goddess.

The eight and sixteen petals refer to points of the compass, as we have said. The three circles could be justified in the sense that for an island placed in an ocean there could be a protective rampart placed all around and a trench outside it, with the limit of the open sea touching the island peripherally. Such a picture is found in Kālidāsa's *Raghuvaṁśa*, canto I, verse 5, where the kings of the Raghu dynasty are said to rule over the earth which is bounded by the ocean. Another picture of such a cross-sectional view of consciousness by concentric circles is given in the *Yoga vāsiṣṭha*. In this analogy, we are looking down a well at an ascending bucket from which water is simultaneously descending through a hole in the bucket-bottom.

The word 'refuge' suggests that when the contemplative creates a direct bipolar relationship with this *śrī cakra,* it will make him think of all elements together at one and the same time. Such a complete meditation will be effective as a final refuge, both as a means as well as an end, in his spiritual progress.

There is a far cry between the form of the final good or salvation understood in the prophetic religions prevailing in the West and this way of salvation implied in the meditation of the *śrī cakra* representing the beauty of the Goddess. The gap between the two versions is a difficult one to bridge. While admitting this glaring incompatibility between the prophetic and the pagan ideas of salvation or liberation, it is possible, through a proper interpretation in the light of mathematical structuralism and more modern scientific notions of reality, truth or beauty treated together, to arrive at some way by which the gap could still be bridged. Our comments on individual verses will at least help to reconcile these two standpoints and bring them closer together by abolishing the element of contradiction between them.

To the modern mind, which has now become familiar with the wireless, radio and television, by which families on our planet are put into direct electromagnetic relation with the outermost frontiers of our expanding universe, the task of schematically understanding those waves or pulsations, whether related to light or sound, cannot be considered too hard to imagine, which thus tends to make the whole world into one intimate village. The latest satellite being sent to outer space even contains a gold-plated plaque on which there is, intended to be deciphered by some intelligent being, a kind of universal protolanguage understood in this universal nowhere or elsewhere.

Maxwellian equations and Hertzian conciliations, both of which belong to this electromagnetic universe, give us, in terms of absolute equations and vectors, what can be called the heartbeat of life itself. Both could be fitted into the schema here and unitively understood. Textbooks of physics already contain such figurative representations of electromagnetic pulsation based on the sinus function, on which all energy transmission must depend, independent of distance. The magnetic field is always at right angles to the electrical current. This orthogonality gives us the basis of a quaternion structure, which a unit of harmonic motion would represent by crest as well as trough, both electrically and magnetically understood. Equations verify the geometric figure and vice versa. It is the Pythagorean diagonal, based on logarithms, that is primarily involved here, in addition to the notion of processes in differential calculus, involving both parameters and asymptotic curves which verify equations. Also the machine language of cybernetics could help us to bridge the gap that seems to divide the two rival positions we have referred to above.

A further study of the relational content of the remaining verses would help the reader to arrive at what would at least be a greater degree of unitive understanding, which is the special contribution of the Advaita Vedanta of Śaṅkara to world thought, whether physical or metaphysical, or both. An integrated view of physics and metaphysics would further justify the *śrī cakra.*

Viewed in the perspective of conics and solid geometry, the lotus petals could be considered as representing a just cross-sectional view. The triangles with reversed apex and their plus and minus counterparts could be named more conveniently by numbers. The cones placed base to base tend to be abolished at the omega top of the vertical axis and to be neutral at the zero point. These cones are the most pronounced at the alpha point. In principle they are present at all three levels.

Structural Analysis

This verse itself being fully structurally conceived, it is hardly necessary to add to it any remarks; but as we have already said, the solid geometry of conics and conic sections with a reciprocity, complementarity, compensation and cancellation by one-one correspondence with bilateral parity and symmetry along a vertical parameter with a merging or mixing of aspects sometimes with the torsion of a figure-of-eight or an S-shaped curve, could be read into the ever revolving circulation or dynamism of absolute Beauty as it manifests itself.

12

त्वदीयं सौन्दर्यं तुहिनगिरिकन्ये तुलयितुं
कवीन्द्राः कल्पन्ते कथमपि विरिञ्चिप्रभृतयः।
यदालोकौत्सुक्यादमरललना यान्ति मनसा
तपोभिर्दुष्प्रापामपि गिरिशसायुज्यपदवीम्॥

tvadīyaṁ saundaryaṁ tuhina giri kanye tulayituṁ
kavīndrāḥ kalpante katham api viriñci prabhṛtayaḥ ।
yad ālokautsukyād amara lalanā yānti manasā
tapobhir duṣ prāpām api giriśa sāyujya padavīm ॥

tuhina giri kanye — O daughter of the snowy peak; *tvadīyaṁ saundaryaṁ* — the beauty that is yours; *tulayituṁ* — to estimate the equal of; *kavīndrāḥ* — the best among poets; *katham api* — somehow; *viriñci prabhṛtayaḥ* — Brahmā and others; *kalpante* — exercising their fancy, create; *yat āloka autsukyāt* — which (beauty) eager to see; *amara lalanāḥ* — heavenly damsels; *tapobhiḥ api* — even by asceticism; *duṣprāpām* — hard to attain; *giriśa sāyujya padavīm* — the state of union with Śiva; *manasā yānti* — mentally attain

O Daughter of the Snowy Peak, to estimate the equal of Your beauty,
The best among poets, exercising their fancy, somehow create Brahmā and others;
Eager Your beauty to see, heavenly damsels mentally attain to
What is hard even for ascetics to gain — the state of union with Śiva.

Verse twelve pertains to the subject of the participation of Śiva with Śakti. It takes place at the crossing of the two orthogonal parameters. Above the horizontal parameter there is a conceptual form of beauty which requires the poetic gift of great poets to delineate in any appreciably tangible form. Unable to give a real content to theoretical beauty of this conceptual grade on the upper side of the horizontal axis, great Indian poets like Vyāsa, author of the Vedas, have filled this conceptual aspect of beauty with mythological characters who have their source in their fecund imagination. They have no actuality, but shine by the reflected glory of the indirect conceptual light of reality (*cidābhāsa*).

Ontological richness, on the other hand, resides below the horizontal axis. That is the domain of Nature, represented by the Śiva-maids of verse eleven who feel at home there without any need for exercising austerities or suffering special agonies. Ontological beauty is doubly real, while teleological beauty is arrived at by double negation, by saying 'not this, not this' (*neti neti*). Teleological beauty is an effect, while ontological beauty is the source and the cause, and is nearer to the negative personality of the *śiva kumārī*s. That is why it is said here, in the last line, that ascetics who go to the Himalayas and perform different austerities to gain a glimpse of the Absolute, especially of its positive glories, put themselves under much strain before being able to obtain even a minimum participation with what Śiva represents as a counterpart in the total situation in which Śiva and Śakti are equal partners. Heavenly damsels want to experience in themselves the upsurging bliss of Beauty. They are on the hypostatic side of the situation. The experience of Beauty takes place within the mind, because Beauty is a subtle value within consciousness. These heavenly damsels have only to enter sympathetically with their minds into union with the negative vertical aspect of the goddess of Beauty, to experience the ultimate bliss referred to here. This state of mind is natural and easy for them, while the male ascetics, on the other hand, cannot establish this participation as naturally and easily as the celestial maidens, for whom it is only a question of mental sympathetic adjustment with the absolute Goddess. Both the ascetics and the hypostatic damsels are equally interested in experiencing the same absolute Beauty, but the ascetics have the difficult task of filling the conceptual space with the help of poets or through austerities. The heavenly damsels need no ascetic practice nor poetic imagination if they only know properly how their mistress, the Devī herself, treats her husband as participating with herself, without duality. The two sides thus fuse into one, a comparatively difficult task for the disgruntled and crude ascetics.

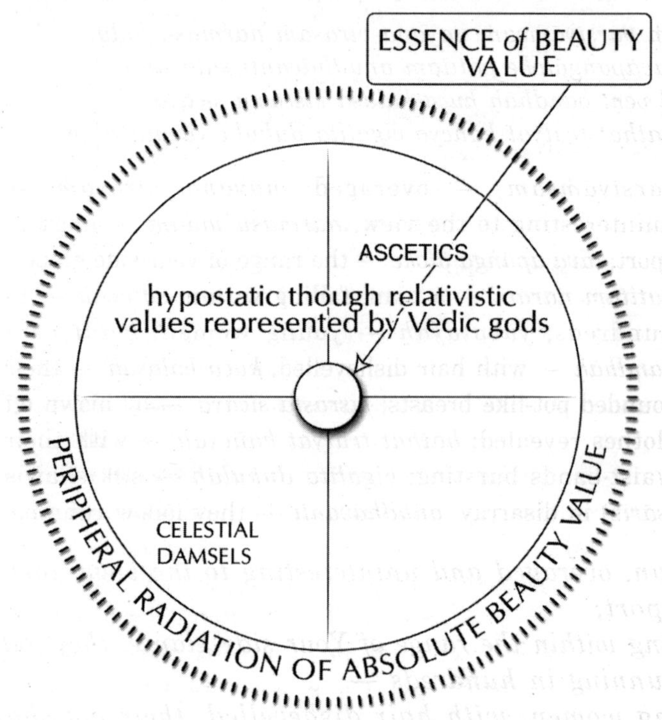

Structural Analysis

The above figure taken together with the comments will suffice for a structural analysis of the content and purpose of this verse. In an overall form the intention of the author is to say that celestial maidens being vertical minus in status understand the value of the goddess by a direct participation, which same the ascetics can have only indirectly.

13

नरं वर्षीयांसं नयनविरसं नर्मसु जडं
तवापाङ्गालोके पतितमनुधावन्ति शतशः ।
गलद्वेणीबन्धाः कुचकलशविस्रस्तसिचया
हठात् त्रुटयत्काञ्च्यो विगलितदुकूला युवतयः ॥

naraṁ varṣīyāṁsaṁ nayana virasaṁ narmasu jaḍaṁ
tavāpāṅgāloke patitam anudhāvanti śataśaḥ ।
galad veṇī bandhāḥ kuca kalaśa visrasta sicayā
haṭhāt truṭyat kāñcyo vigalita dukūlā yuvatayaḥ ॥

varṣīyāṁsaṁ — overaged; *nayana virasaṁ* — uninteresting to the view; *narmasu jaḍaṁ* — inert in sport; *tava apāṅga āloke* — the range of your side glance; *patitam naram* — a man, falling within; *śataśaḥ* — in hundreds; *yuvatayaḥ* — young women; *galat veṇī bandhāḥ* — with hair dishevelled; *kuca kalaśaḥ* — their rounded pot-like breasts; *visrasta sicayā* — by blown off clothes revealed; *haṭhāt truṭyat kāñcyaḥ* — with their waist-bands bursting; *vigalita dukūlāḥ* — silk shawls (*sārīs*) in disarray; *anudhāvanti* — they follow running

A man, overaged and uninteresting to the view, inert in sport;
Falling within the range of Your side glance, they follow, running in hundreds —
Young women, with hair dishevelled, their pot-shaped breasts revealed by blown off clothes,
Their waistbands bursting, and with their silk garments in disarray.

Love affairs can take place under mild circumstances or under the stress of high voltage. Erotic mysticism, as it is to be understood in the *Saundaryalaharī,* is of the high voltage type, which is more conducive to revealing the underlying structure of the absolute ground on which the overwhelming dynamism of the principle of beauty must necessarily operate. In verse twelve, the Śiva-maids have an advantage over the ascetics in the matter of gaining a first glimpse of that exalted value represented by the Goddess. Even an initial participation with what Śiva represents in himself, as the highest of values, is beyond all states of mind known to lesser artificial austerities or disciplines that the usual recluse might practise, to be accomplished only through a lifetime of step-by-step endeavour. In this verse, the dynamic content of erotic mysticism is further accentuated and brought into clear relief. One falls in love suddenly, and expressions like 'love at first sight' reveal the unpremeditated and overwhelming nature of the event called 'falling in love'. The mechanism and dynamism involved in this lightning-like process is critically examined in this verse.

Any girl, when she is full of vitality at the proper age, could experience this sudden onslaught of love within herself, even in respect of a man who has no sex appeal in the ordinary sense. He could be overaged and not a sport at all. The absolute urge of pining for a counterpart, so that her own soul could fulfil itself vertically, at a given moment or occasion in life, is imperative in its demand for satisfaction. Heavenly damsels, like Urvaśī, Menakā and others in Indra's world above, are known to have experienced this wonderful moment in themselves, in which they are suddenly plunged into a state of total abandon. All prudery, coquetry and allied sentiments are thrown to the winds at that moment. Such overwhelming infatuation is found in many romantic and even tragic works of literature, irrespective of the traditional or cultural background. An English novel can be thoroughly enjoyed by an Indian student, because the appeal of love is appreciated universally and enjoyed in its minutest details. Nothing can be hidden. Any student in love understands the state of mind of Marius waiting for Cosette in the Luxembourg Garden in Paris, in Hugo's *Les Miserables*. Instances can be multiplied, but what is relevant to this verse is that we must recognize two complementary sides of the total situation in which absolute Eroticism operates. A well-groomed college student may not be attractive to the most intelligent of girls, while, on the other hand, she is intently watching the face of the grumpy, even ugly, absent-minded, overaged professor, who pays no attention to his appearance at all. A nearer example in India is the figure of Śiva, who takes care to make himself most repulsive to all women by letting his uncombed hair become matted and by wearing live snakes on his body.

The *Kumārasambhava* portrays an incident in the love affair between Śīva and Pārvatī, wherein the god of love is burnt to ashes in the presence of the elaborate Vedic worship that Pārvatī is able to offer to Śiva to propitiate him. It was a terribly negative response that she got, after which she had to be carried home by her father, who appeared as an elephant (representing space). This brutal setback in her initial efforts to attain Śiva does not stop her renewed efforts. She begins to perform different austerities in a Vedantic key, wearing bark garments instead of the silk shawls of rich, elaborate Vedism. Śiva not only becomes favourably disposed by the *tapas* and renunciation in her revised approach, he even takes the trouble to come down from his heights to speak to her personally, taking the disguise of a *deśika* who is a sannyasin. Their conversation reveals that her aspiration is compatible with his own status as a complete absolutist personality. A cancellation between counterparts thus takes place, not in terms of mere dualistic ritualistic propitiation of a lukewarm reciprocity or complementarity between them. It takes place only when, searching for the total experience of beauty, under the full stress of the principle of absolute Eroticism, subject and object are abolished and fused into one overwhelming upsurge.

It is in such a perspective that we must examine the present verse. Instead of referring to the Śiva-maid side, it is the numerator aspect, Śiva himself, who is to be taken as the 'man' who is 'overaged, uninteresting to the view and inert in sport'. The next verse gives us a more verticalized perspective, in which erotic mysticism could have a chance to operate within the span of the three hundred and sixty five days of the year, occurring as a sudden event taking place through the occasionalism of a particular situation. The young women here are not ordinary representatives of their kind. They are similar to the celestial damsels like Urvaśī, although the event here takes place on ordinary natural grounds, yet they are neither too earthy nor too celestial. On the numerator side we have an outwardly uninteresting man, and on the denominator side we have the damsels who, like Śakuntalā, are ready to fall in love at the slightest stimulus.

The references to bursting waistbands, total disarray and confusion, and especially the 'pot-shaped breasts', which are meant to reveal youth at its peak moment of horizontal maturity, altogether make for the cancellability of the denominator value of womanhood against its masculine counterpart, whose beauty is not overt, but innate. That this cancellation must take place under the aegis of the Absolute is insisted upon in the second line. To fall within the aegis of the Absolute, it is not necessary for a man to be fully favoured by the goddess of Beauty; it is enough that a side glance, like a secondary polarizing light beam, should fall upon him from a distance. The neurological law of 'partial stimulus, total response' operates here. A side glance, like the moonlight falling equally on palace and forest as in verse fifty-seven, is all that is required to give an absolutist touch to the personality of the uninteresting man here.

The reference to the women 'running in hundreds' is meant to heighten the aspect of total abandon, and shows that pluralism is permissible on the denominator side, as required by cancellation of the many against the one. The notion of the one cannot be complete without implying the many, because the one and the many are dialectical counterparts, as explained by Parmenides and Plato. According to correct epistemology, the Absolute, by its nature, requires that the many running girls cancel themselves out in respect of the one unique Absolute, represented by the numerator personality here.

We have to note the bursting of the waistbands. Absolutism involves a suddenness or surprise. One enters into the arena with a bang and a crash. Similar expressions are used, in other verses, such as 'startled' eyes of deer (eighteen), 'lightning-streak-body' (twenty-one), and also the 'burst of jingling bells on the waistbelt' seen in verse seven. This bursting or suddenness is necessary to give the overall absolutist touch that lifts this kind of eroticism out of the context of the mundane and conventional love affairs of the ordinary world.

The pointed reference to 'pot-shaped breasts' is to show that this rounded shape has a hypostatic origin. This is confirmed by other references, such as in verse seven, where the frontal knobs of an elephant set the anterior model for the posterior ponderous breasts and in verse nineteen, where the breasts are equated to the cosmological luminaries of the sun and the moon. Such are some of the implications of the erotic dynamism portrayed in this verse.

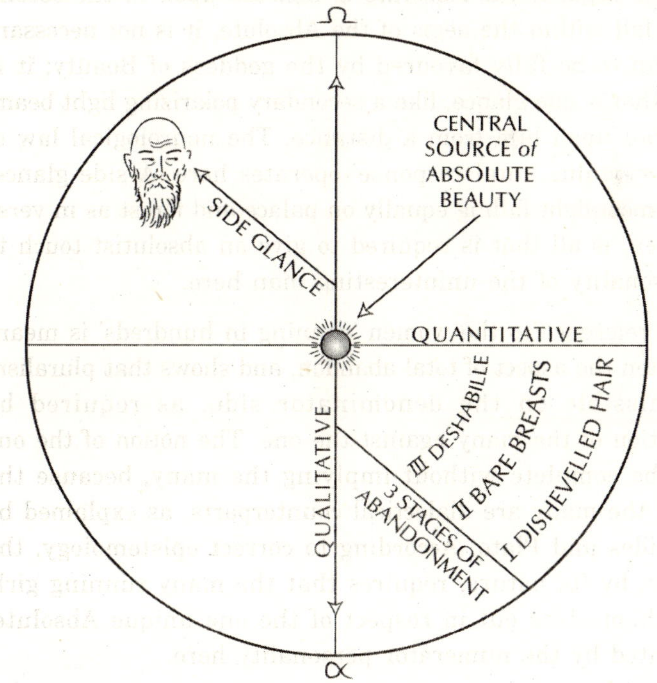

Structural Analysis

There are a number of features of structural import which require clarification in this verse. (1) to come within the scope of the grace in terms of beauty one need not have direct participation in a bipolar fashion with the absolute Value represented by the absolute beauty Goddess here. The side glance suggests indirect recognition. (2) Quality and quantity compensate each other. Hundreds of young women can be balanced by the quality of the Absolute found even in one ugly man. (3) What is denominator beauty can have numerator ugliness as its counterpart. An element of sudden cloudburst-like wonder is implied in the total situation. The women caught in the abandon of absolute wonder of Beauty partially and indirectly implied on the numerator side have between them three grades as suggested first by dishevelled hair, bare breasts and deshabille affecting three stages of womanhood or three aspects of beauty. Partial stimulus on the numerator side is enough for total reaction. Quantity is superseded by the sheer absolute Quality of the beauty even when it is of an indirect or reflected order. Nominalism, schematism and structuralism all cooperate thus protolinguistically to reveal the relational set-up at the core of which the principle of absolute Beauty resides.

14

क्षितौ षट्पञ्चाशद्द्विसमधिकपञ्चाशदुदके
हुताशे द्वाषष्टिश्चतुरधिकपञ्चाशदनिले ।
दिवि द्विःषट्त्रिंशन्मनसि च चतुःषष्टिरिति ये
मयूखास्तेषामप्युपरि तव पादाम्बुजयुगम् ॥

kṣitau ṣaṭ pañcāśad dvi samadhika pañcāśad udake
hustāśe dvā ṣaṣṭiś catur adhika pañcāśad anile ।
divi dviḥ ṣaṭtrimśan manasi ca catuḥ ṣaṣṭir iti ye
mayūkhās teṣām apy upari tava pādāmbuja yugam ॥

kṣitau — for earth, *ṣaḍ pañcāśat* — fifty-six; *udake* — for water, *dvi samadhika pañcāśat* — fifty-two; *hutāśe* — for fire, *dvaṣaṣṭiḥ* — sixty-two; *anile* — for air, *catur adhika pañcāśat* — fifty-four; *divi* — for sky (ether), *dviḥ ṣaṭ trimśat* — seventy-two; *manasi* — for mind, *catuḥ ṣaṣṭi* — sixty-four; *iti ye mayūkhāḥ* — thus what rays there are; *teṣām api upari* — even above all these; *tava* — your; *pādāmbuja yugam* — twin lotus-feet

Fifty-six for earth; for water fifty-two;
Sixty-two for fire; for air fifty-four;
Seventy-two for ether; for mind sixty-four
Are the rays — even beyond these, Your twin feet.

This verse marks a further degree in the abstraction and generalization required before placing oneself in the correct perspective, as it is to be understood in these verses. The overwhelming experience of erotic joy pictured in the previous verse refers to an event that could take place within the span of one day. But there are three hundred and sixty-four other days in the year in which young men and women must live continuously, without having that very occasion repeated the same way each day. It is suggested here that one live through that period by verticalization and generalization, continuing to live three hundred and sixty-five days of the year, but in a dispassionate manner, without looking forward to any overwhelming event that might tend to make any one day different from the rest of the ten thousand years within the context of which, as stated in the *Rubāiyat* of Omar Khayyām, each human being is expected, philosophically, to place oneself.

We found earlier, in verse nine, that the three hundred and sixty-five days of the year could be further subdivided in a vertical ascending series of units that could have reference both to the seasons and to the stable states of mind known to theoretical yoga books. The five elemental principles, treated from the item most earthy to the item most subtle, ether (*ākāsa*), have all to be transcended by a lightning-like meditative vision within the contemplative, so that the principle of absolute Beauty may be realized. Here the feet loom into consciousness, not like a crystal or a flower, nor even as a colour solid with a vague dynamism inside; they are to be visualized at the numerator limit as sending out the rays (*mayūkhāḥ*) directly referred to in the last line. The brilliance of a supernova might be comparable to this hypostatic point, placed beyond all secondary enjoyments derivable from the various seasons, whether rainy or with clear skies. We have to imagine here an hourglass-like crystal, which is at the same time effulgent like a star, marking the omega point of the situation. A logarithmic spiral line traverses the hourglass, beginning at its lower base. The fifty-six, fifty-two, sixty-two, fifty-four, seventy-two and sixty-four are the days of the year, treated as spiralling round the hourglass, ranging from the earthy to the ethereal limits. It is not within these limits that the feet of the absolute Goddess are to be placed, but sufficiently above them so that they could have a status far removed from the contamination of relativistic or hedonistic considerations. absolute Bliss is of an order independent of cheap pleasures, in which one might prefer one season to another or one stable state of meditation (chakra) to another. They are all to be inclusively transcended to attain the final Bliss in the Absolute, which is to be conceived as removed 'oceans apart' from lesser considerations of bliss.

There is to be noted a one-to-one correspondence between the numbers attributed to the states of mind and the elemental manifestations, understood in terms of the mind as a basic reference. The asymmetry and variation in the numbers here can be explained by such astronomical events as the precession of the equinoxes and the solstices, which are all to be understood as coming in a vertical line where light and darkness meet, like the international date line, which is only schematic in status. We can further note that water and air have the lowest number of days to exercise their influence on the mind. The seventy-two of ether and the sixty-four of the mind are longer than the fifty-six of the earth and the fifty-two for water. These asymmetrical factors are to be attributed to ontological density or other astronomical reasons. The numerator side in the light predominates over the denominator side in the darkness. This represents, thus, a perspective which is more hypostatically tilted than that of the colour solid, in which the cones are placed base-to-base at the bottom limit. These structural peculiarities have been discussed previously. We can attain absolute Beauty by ascending, as here, or by descending to the bottom limit, or by placing ourselves correctly at the structural centre for purposes of normalization and renormalization from both limits. Living at the North Pole has its advantages, as does living at the equator. Advantages can also be cancelled out so that one could freely choose to live where one likes. Preference for a particular climate seems to be an unnecessary pleasure that luxury lovers indulge in.

Structural Analysis

It has been suggested by some commentators especially those predisposed to the yoga point of view, that the six chakras are nominalistically or numerologically classed and labelled here as in the figure below. It is easy to see a vase like figure here. A merely mathematical symmetry may be more 'aweful' but less realistic. Formal, sign or symbol languages using figures, numbers or letters are all full of endless possibilities which, when overdone, in esoterics, can defeat the very purpose of wisdom. The real or the

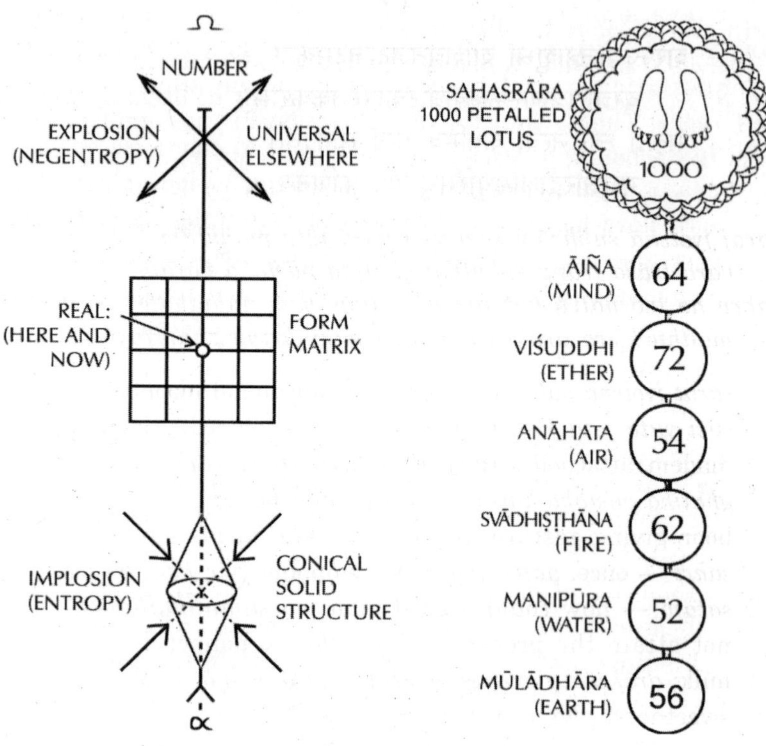

ontologically valid reference must never be lost sight of. This is the strongest point with the Vedanta of Śaṅkara, where the real or the *sat* is never given a secondary place in speculation. Hermeticists and others fall into the error of starting with *a priorism*. Structure, form and number could all be given their legitimate place as in *fig*. a.

In *fig*. b the feet are placed above hypostatically for focusing the attention of the devotee or contemplative. No principle of yoga is violated by placing the feet at any level in the vertical parameter. The bipolarity always cancels out into the unity of the Absolute at whatever level placed. The law of compensation operates.

15

शरज्ज्योत्स्नाशुभ्रां शशियुतजटाजूटमकुटां
वरत्रासत्राणस्फटिकघटिकापुस्तककराम् ।
सकृन्न त्वा नत्वा कथमिव सतां संनिदधते
मधुक्षीरद्राक्षामधुरिमधुरीणा फणितयः ॥

śaraj jyotsnā śubhrāṁ śaśi yuta jaṭā jūṭa makuṭāṁ
vara trāsa trāṇa sphaṭika ghaṭikā pustaka karām ।
sakr̥n na tvā natvā katham iva satāṁ saṁ nidadhate
madhu kṣīra drākṣā madhuri madhurīṇā phaṇitayaḥ ॥

śarat jyotsnā śubhrāṁ — clear as autumnal moonbeams; *śaśi yuta jaṭā jūṭa makuṭāṁ* — with matted-hair-made diadem, attached with crescent; *vara trāsa trāṇa sphaṭika ghaṭikā pustaka karām* — with hands bearing refuge and boon-giving gesture, rosary of crystal beads and book; *sakr̥t* — once; *natvā tvā* — worshipping you; *kathaṁ iva satāṁ* — how could a good man; *na saṁnidadhate* — not attain the presence of; *madhu* — honey; *kṣīra* — milk; *drākṣā* — grapes; *madhurimā dhurīṇā* — pleasing sweetness; *phaṇitayaḥ* — the flow of words

Clear as autumnal moonbeams, with matted-hair-made diadem,
Attached with crescent with hands bearing refuge and boon-giving gesture,
Rosary made of crystal-clear beads and book — how could anyone, worshipping You but once,
Not gain in flow of words, somehow, the pleasing sweetness of honey, milk and grapes?

In this verse we are no longer concerned with the phenomenal aspects of beauty, as we ascend one step higher in the vertical direction. The value here is the gift of poetic expression, which is not to be understood in a religious sense, but in a wholly aesthetic context. One aspires to be a great poet so that he can hold up a mirror to life or to truth. Poetry has sometimes been defined as a critique of life. Social novels reflect the state of contemporary society and all that belongs to it, in the form of criss-cross or rival interests, with heroes and heroines who have problems great and small. Romantic plays, however, like Victor Hugo's *Hernani*, rise higher in the scale where romance and tragedy blend their value systems together. In the plays of Sophocles and Euripides tragedy attains to further heights of the fearful and the pitiable. There is thus a difference of levels represented by the literary works of great poets.

The expert manipulation of phrases is the main task of an author. When word value takes the place of other values, such as the joy implied in the successive seasons as in the previous verse, we naturally come to the Goddess of word-wisdom, like Santa Sophia of Constantinople, to whom a great domed church was once dedicated, although the votaries inside have been, indifferently, Christians or Muslims at different times. Word-wisdom has its value and its consolation to cultured people. On the Indian soil, Sarasvatī represents this value. In the *Śatapatha Brāhmaṇa*, she is represented as sending her arrows in two diametrically opposed directions: one upwards to nominalism through conceptualism, and the other downwards, through earthy expressions, to the very source of the word.

The third line describes such a Sarasvatī with her familiar crystal rosary beads and book. When we look at the first line, though, we find a slight departure from the conventional Sarasvatī, where Śaṅkara applies a dialectical touch to her representation. The brightness of moonbeams still suggests a hypostatic region of highly intelligible values, but the reference to the 'diadem of matted hair' serves as an anticlimax. The word-goddess is here deprived of her jewelled headdress; instead, she is to have her glory expressed through the same matted hair of which her husband is so proud. This anticlimax introduced into the upper limit of the situation is intentionally meant to cancel out against the actual sweetness of 'honey, milk and grapes', referred to in the last line. The matted hair represents renunciation and indifference to sense values, but at the opposite limit the taste of honey, milk and grapes are represented as containing within their existential enjoyability, an essence which is meant to participate with the value represented by the same matted hair.

This third line also says that austerity cannot go with love of grapes, except by people who can understand how to put them together as limiting instances of one and the same value parameter, from the highest to the most factual limit of ontologically significant values. The *laharī* of overwhelming beauty here resides within the mind of a poet who is able to see how the taste of grapes and the matted hair could belong together, when compressed within the one absolute notion of Beauty. Anyone could come to understand how such a cancellation of two aspects is possible for one in terms of spiritual progress forever. The result might be that one decides to be a poet rather than a religious magnate. This does not make any fundamental difference, because a *kavi,* poet, and a *manīṣin*, a spiritually perfected person, are both treated as equal partners in terms of their understanding of absolute Values.

In the second line, the crescent of Śiva is also duplicated as the natural heritage of Pārvatī although her glory has only a negative reference. The ambivalence is transcended when existence and subsistence, or fact and truth, meet and cancel out into the significant value of Beauty, expressed through words here.

The 'hands giving refuge and boon' have been described previously by the author in verse four. His justification for bringing them into the picture again here is, as we pointed out before, a methodological necessity and should not be mixed up with doctrinal conclusions. By the same token, we could now understand this compromise between the conventional Vedic Sarasvatī and a fully ontologically biased Pārvatī, on the grounds that her downright existential aspects, like the taste of honey, milk and grapes, are intended to be cancelled out against essential values at the higher levels. That Pārvatī consents to remove her crown and be satisfied with matted hair like her husband Śiva is already a gesture that heightens her status in a full Vedantically revised context of absolutism. In order to have a one-to-one correspondence with this heightened status implied at the higher limit, the poet takes care to balance it by such factual elements as the joy one gets from tasting honey, milk or grapes. Cancellation thus becomes mathematically adequate and justified. The resultant vision is meant for very highly evolved poets. Others may not get this vision so easily. Moreover, it should be noticed that the sweetness of honey, milk and grapes is to be enjoyed here through literature, and not as a preference of the palate merely. This puts the whole meaning into the core of word-wisdom, which has nothing to do with sense indulgence at all.

It is suggested here that poetry excels when realistic aspects are correctly blended with word-aspects, which are nominalistic only. A perfect sentence or paragraph must contain as many references to fact truths as to truths that are only imaginary. It is the one-to-one correspondence between these bipolar aspects that makes literature pleasing in an absolute sense. This truth has been recognized by Shakespeare when he makes the acts and scenes of a play alternately touch lighter and serious chords in the human heart. Indian jewellers know how to set rubies and diamonds side by side, pearls with coral stone or amber and crystal beads together so that the different qualities of jewels cancel out into a beautiful garland. A book is a natural ornament for Sarasvatī, the word-goddess, while the thin crescent of Śiva represents a pure mathematical function in the domain of reason. She also wishes to possess the same pure reasoning as her husband, represented by the crescent moon. The bright moonbeams of clear autumn nights figure in Sanskrit poetry as a favourite ideogram dear to Indian pundits.

The overwhelming Beauty in this verse is to be located in the reference to the 'matted-hair-made-diadem', which effects a complete cancellation of any negativity that the Devi might represent otherwise. Taken as a whole, this verse might be said to cover the same value ground as what is meant to be covered by the *Logos* (the *verbum*, the Word) in Western theology. The value ground of the word continues up through verse nineteen.

It might further be suggested that there is a gentle touch of sarcasm that a keenly critical eye can discern in this verse. This sarcasm belongs to the same order as in the expression, 'damning with faint praise'. There are numerous places in the Bhagavad-gītā and the Upaniṣads where veiled sarcasm and faint praise blend into something ineffable, beautiful, and harmless. Śaṅkara is not unaware of this subtle literary device. When viewed in such a light, the praise of Sarasvatī here could be still seen to fit correctly into the context of these verses. When we read, in the third line, that it is enough to worship such a Sarasvatī *even once*, the ironical implications present here in a veiled manner would become recognizable and even appreciable.

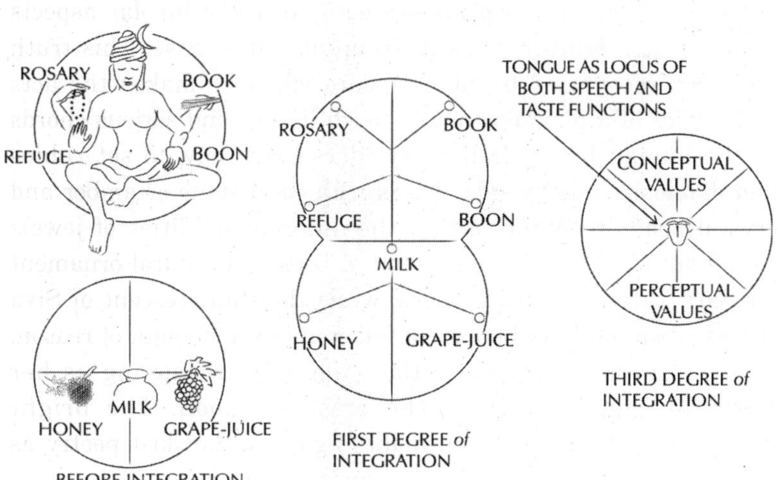

Structural Analysis

Semantic polyvalence and the cancellation of verticalized counterparts at the core of the situation representing generally and abstractly the world of poetics is what we have to recognize here in the structural analysis of this verse. On the numerator side it is not hard to distinguish the quarternion factors by the monomark symbols used, such as the book, the rosary and the boon-giving and protecting gestures of the four hands. On the denominator side we have to put the tongue where both language and its meaningful taste or perceptual flavour have a common origin in a central locus represented by the tongue in each of us. When numerator values and denominator values before their integration by vertical participation is not fully effected we have the two separate globes represented by two circles which, when they are brought into contact, could burst like two soap bubbles and become one. Thus we have roughly the structural figures shown here.

16

कवीन्द्राणां चेतःकमलवनबालातपरुचिं
भजन्ते ये सन्तः कतिचिदरुणामेव भवतीम्।
विरिञ्चिप्रेयस्यास्तरुणतरशृङ्गारलहरी-
गभीराभिर्वाग्भिर्विदधति सतां रञ्जनममी ॥

kavīndrāṇāṁ cetaḥ kamalavana bālātapa ruciṁ
bhajante ye santaḥ kati cid aruṇām eva bhavatīm ।
viriñci preyasyās taruṇatara śṛṅgāralaharī
gabhīrā bhir vāgbhir vidadhati satāṁ rañjanam amī ॥

kavīndrāṇāṁ — of superior poets; *cetaḥ kamala vana bāla ātapa ruciṁ bhajante* — who adore the sweetness of the mental lotus forest, when touched by the tender rays of sunlight; *bhajante ye santaḥ katicit* — such rare good souls who meditate; *aruṇām ēva* — as magenta itself; *bhavatīm* — on you; *viriñciḥ preyasyā* — as one dear to Brahmā; *taruṇa tara śṛṅgāralaharī* — of most tender (yet overwhelming) erotic content; *gabhīrābhiḥ vāgbhiḥ* — by profound words; *vidadhati* — he gives; *satāṁ rañjanam amī* — pleasure to those very good souls

That beauty residing within the minds of superior poets,
Resembling that of a forest of lotuses when touched by the tender light of dawn —
He who can thus adore You, who are so dear to Brahmā as magenta itself;
He, by profound words of most tender, yet overpowering, erotic content, shall please the same select ones.

Here in verse sixteen we have to imagine two sets of persons of perfected aesthetic taste: the creative artist on one side and those who can admire the artists' creation on the other. A good car is not compatible with a bumpy dirt road; nor can a beggar wear satin or silk without making himself ridiculous. Just so, the poet must have a reader sufficiently intelligent, or his high-class writings will not have a market at all. This is why Kālidāsa and other great Sanskrit poets are now going into cold storage for ever. In other words, the reader and composer belong together, in the same context of word-wisdom; they are inseparable counterparts. This justifies the pointed reference to 'superior poets' in the first line. The value called word-beauty applies equally to both of them. It is in the mind where the function of good poetry operates, whether by mind-expansion or by mind-contraction, as the case may be. If champagne contracts the mind, LSD expands it. Champagne makes you feel very comfortable but LSD can make you feel like lying on the ground on Mount Sinai and saying your prayers again and again.

Now, whether expanding or contracting the mind, there is a neutral abstract point where these two opposite tendencies cancel each other out, according to the non-dual approach of these verses. For the purpose of touching with one finger the point where this subtle but overwhelming beauty resides, the author asks you to think of a pond full of lotuses, with mixed short and tall stalks, to resemble a forest. If anyone has entered into a lotus pond and watched magenta lotuses just at the time when the pink light of dawn streams onto the face of each lotus, as the present writer has had occasion to do, he would experience a special overwhelming sense of beauty which does not come from the beauty of the lotus only, but is an emergent factor resulting from the lotus being kissed by the pink rays of the sun. By the blending of the two colours, each having its origin in opposite limbs of the parameter, the amplitude of absolute Beauty can live and move with all its possible intrinsic variations.

We have referred to magenta as the colour of all colours. It is more than just one of the spectral octave, which includes the seven chromatic colours. Magenta of visible light has in it the fusion of the infrared and the ultraviolet. The magenta resulting from the meeting of sunlight and lotus is aptly called '*Aruṇā* herself' or 'magenta itself' in the third line. *Aruṇā* is the Sanskrit word for 'magenta', as well as a name of the Goddess. Although we tend to consider rainbow colours as transient and unreal,

Henri Bergson says that unless somebody proves why a colour is false, he would continue to treat it as real. Śaṅkara here is also justified in calling absolute Beauty 'magenta itself'. Viewed thus correctly, *sub specie aeternitatis*, i.e., 'under the aegis of Absolute', we neither have to add to nor subtract anything from the real Beauty status of this colour. Beauty, not theology, is the central theme of the present work. The famous opening words of Keats' 'Endymion' could be called on here to further support the treatment of absolute Beauty, for itself, by itself and through itself. We can attain it in many ways, and this is one of them. It is as justified as any other.

Two further points can be clarified in this verse which brings in the mythological relation of Sarasvatī to Brahmā. Sarasvatī is sometimes referred to as the daughter of Brahmā, although she is also seen sometimes as his wife. Whether as wife or daughter, the affection is the same when translated into verticalized terms. In this sense, she is dear to the creator as the source of all real values. Colour is a real value, especially when given an absolute status, as with magenta, which participates both with the plus and the minus sides of the colour solid, both vertically and horizontally. Sarasvatī is a mythological personification of an absolute Wiṣdom-value factor. This has something directly to do with the profound words which express with dignity the erotic charm of the Goddess. No artist in Paris could be considered a great master if he has not proved his worth by correctly painting a nude. This shows that at the very core of art, the goddess of Beauty is to be visualized, if not in vulgarized hobo-like terms of a pavement artist in Montmartre, but at least in terms of a Jocunda or Mona Lisa, so highly prized by dilettantes the world over. If love poetry is forbidden, Shakespeare and Kālidāsa would have to resign their jobs. The kind of eroticism described here, being a value which is the main article of trade for master poets anywhere and anytime, is of a noble rather than a vulgar order. That the biographies of many great men of the world show them to be great lovers only heightens their value as individuals, without detracting anything from their greatness.

The noble quality of such an eroticism is indicated by the word *gabhīram*, which taken together with *śṛṅgāram*, denotes a very noble and dignified form of erotic mysticism, far beyond the usual vulgar eroticism.

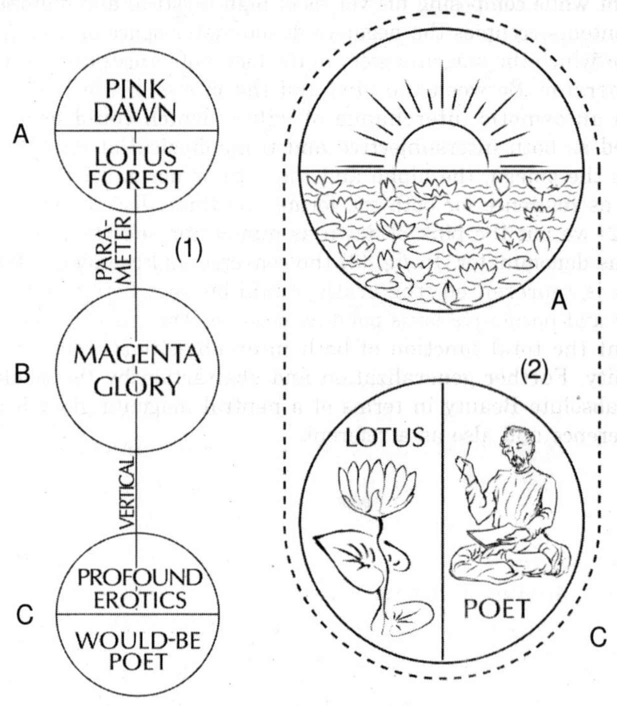

RELATIONS IN B
NORMALIZATION BY ABSTRACTION AND GENERALIZATION IN UNIVERSAL CONCRETE TERMS

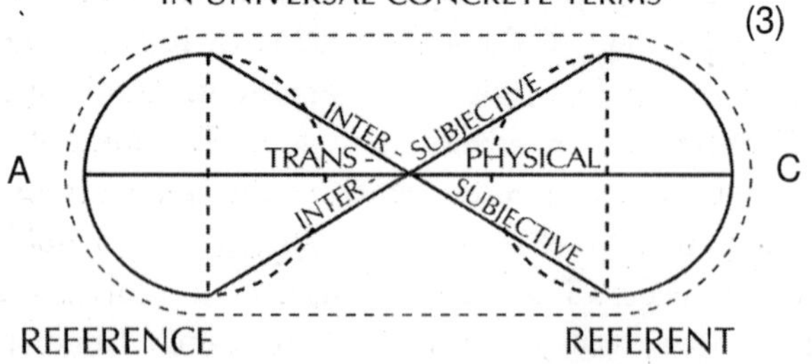

Structural Analysis

The structural analysis here involves the ability on the part of the reader to establish an intersubjective and transphysical pattern of relational strands between poets generally and the poet in the singular spoken of here. The sun-kissed lotus forest of dawn has pink rays of the numerator side blending with the lotus forest of the pond. The singular poet who dips his pen in profound erotic sentiment while composing his verses of high mystical and dignified erotic contents occupies the negative denominator space of a second set up for which the magenta glory of the forest of lotuses constitutes the numerator. Between the plus and the minus of the two sets there is an osmotic interchange of values which could best be described as both intersubjective and transphysical at once. *Fig.* (1) gives the omega, the alpha and the zero or normalized central interest as reference for both the former, as three distinct entities. In *fig.* (2) we put the pink of dawn as numerator and the forest of lotuses as denominator. In *fig.* (3) the converse and complementary position is represented, the erotic would-be poet being vertical negative and normative lotus pond as positive. The crossing arrows represent the total function of both intersubjectivity and transphysicality. Further generalization and abstraction by the reader attains absolute Beauty in terms of a neutral magenta glory both as a reference and also as a referent.

17

सवित्रीभिर्वाचां शशिमणिशिलाभङ्गरुचिभि-
वंशिन्याद्याभिस्त्वां सह जननि संचिन्तयति यः।
स कर्ता काव्यानां भवति महतां भङ्गिरुचिभि-
र्वचोभिर्वाग्देवीवदनकमलामोदमधुरैः॥

savitrībhir vācāṁ śaśi maṇiśilā bhaṅga rucibhir
vaśinyādyābhis tvāṁ saha janani sañcintayati yaḥ ।
sa kartā kāvyānāṁ bhavati mahatāṁ bhaṅgi rucibhir
vacobhir vāgdevī vadana kamalāmoda madhuraiḥ ॥

savitrībhiḥ vācāṁ — those word-bearing elements; *śaśi maṇi śilābhaṅga rucibhiḥ* — of broken moonstone lustre; *vaśiny adyābhiḥ* — with *vaśini*s; *tvāṁ saha* — as associated with you; *janani* — O mother; *yaḥ sañcintayati* — he thus able to contemplate; *saḥ* — he; *kartā kāvyānāṁ* — the author of poetic works; *bhavati* — becomes; *mahatāṁ* — great (poetic works); *bhaṅgirucibhiḥ* — of scintillating sweetness; *vacobhiḥ* — by words; *vāk devī vadana kamala āmoda madhuraiḥ* — adding sweet charm to the lotus face of the Goddess of the Word (sweetened by the fragrance of the lotus face of the Word-Goddess)

He who can contemplate those word-bearing elements of
broken moonstone lustre, with You
Joined with vaśinis, *having an elusively fluid gleam;*
He becomes, O Mother, the author of great poetic works,
Adding sweet charm to the lotus face of the Goddess of
the Word.

In this verse we are again in the domain of semantics. In this branch of study Śaṅkara shows himself, as in his other works, to be an expert rival to his Pūrva Mīmāṁsā critics. The Mīmāṁsakas, as followers of the tradition of Jaimini, rather than that of Bādarāyaṇa, took an anterior position in respect of Vedanta. Modern authorities on semantics, like Bloomfield,

Morris and Karnap, have many theories about how meanings emerge from words. The pragmatics and syntactics of language are the two other aspects of the study of meaning in relation to words. Some authorities, like Ogden, even think in terms of 'the meaning of meanings'. In the days of Śaṅkara, Kumārila Bhaṭṭa, Prabhākara and Vācaspati Miśra, great semantic battles have been fought on the soil of scriptural exegesis, the rumblings of which are heard even to the present day in the domain of advanced punditry or pedantry.

Śaṅkara is content to allude to only two aspects of semantics in this verse: the word-bearing elements of the first line are named *savitrīs*, as opposed to the *vaśinīs* of the second line. The former are 'lustrous as a fragment of broken moonstone', while the latter have a 'fluid gleam'. These two different qualities of precious stones have to be taken into consideration and respected by a master poet who wishes to embellish the beauty of the goddess of the Word, instead of bringing any discredit to her directly or indirectly. The reference to the lustre of broken moonstone is the syntactic aspect of word-meaning content. Bursting into light is a function recognized in Pāṇini's famous grammar as the absolute principle of *sphoṭa*. The word *sphoṭa* is derived from *sphuṭ* (which means to burst into clarity, as in the case of a diamond). The reference is made here to broken moonstone, possibly in the interest of contrasting this way of viewing word-meaning with the kind of homogeneity to be assumed between whole moonstones, which have 'an elusively fluid gleam'. Syntax refers to the mechanical relationship between word and word in a sentence. Each word is considered by the Bhaṭṭa-Prabhākara school to be independent of the total meaning of the sentence and as having a disjunct function of its own. Śaṅkara's followers, however, hold that meaning is an emergent factor resulting from the sentence as a whole and is not to be broken up into bits. Thus the *vaśinī* and the *savitrī* elements of language are treated here as complementary to each other. The *vaśinīs* are to be joined on terms of equality with their counterparts, the individual word elements which generate meaning or *savitrīs*. These latter could be viewed as the cybernetic 'information bits' in digital, binary and analog computers.

Semiosis is a process like the flowing of a liquid, while syntax is a sudden burst into scintillant light, suggesting meaningfulness. As a jeweller might set a ruby and a diamond side by side to enhance the beauty of a circular gold ear-ornament, not unlike the *śrī cakra,* as familiarly worn by Indian women, we could only enhance the beauty of poetry by giving equal importance to syntactic bursting as well as semiotic flowing processes. When an author knows the secret of respecting these subtle semantic requirements, consciously or unconsciously, the beauty of his poetry is enhanced. The whole purpose of writing poetry is to enhance the beauty of the face of the goddess of the Word. It could not be anything else, because no poet wants to defeat his purpose by creating ugliness.

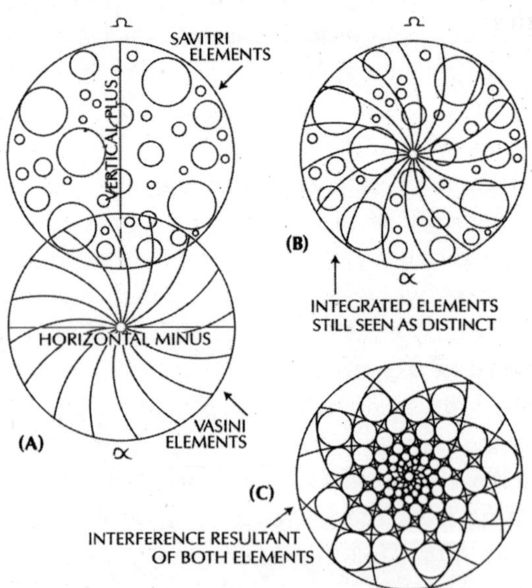

This is one instance only of many and varied emergent patterns resulting from both elements functioning on the same locus.

Structural Analysis

The savitrī (word generating) and the *vaśinī* (the more fluid, vitalistic word-elements) have first to be distinguished as two rival expressions in semantics, the latter being semiotic while the former is only mechanistically or horizontally meaningful. The integration or coordination of these have the Cartesian coordinates implied between them. The resultant is a harmony between a sine function and its reciprocal interfering function placed at 90 degrees of difference. Interfering at right angles thus two sine functions can result in a double figure-of-eight which when placed at the locus of the lotus face of the Goddess of the word here, the face being always structurally equal to the *bindusthāna* spoken of earlier, in respect of the *śrī cakra*, produces the strange effect of giving an absolutist beauty touch to it. Such interference figures could be many and varied and when the secret of the integration of the two elements involved is known to any poet or writer, he comes to have in his hands a rare instrument of fecundity and beauty. Once possessed of such a master secret, all his writings would gain a new absolutist status as has been amply proved at least in the case of Kālidāsa. The stages of the integration of the elements we have spoken of above, could for clarity be decomposed and numbered as in the figures above. The resultant of integration has unlimited and varied possibilities.

18

तनुच्छायाभिस्ते तरुणतरणिश्रीसरणिभि-
र्दिवं सर्वामुर्वीमरुणिमनिमग्नां स्मरति यः ।
भवन्त्यस्य त्रस्यद्वनहरिणशालीननयनाः
सहोर्वश्या वश्याः कति कति न गीर्वाणगणिकाः ॥

tanuc chāyābhis te taruṇa taraṇi śrī saraṇibhir
divaṁ sarvām urvīm aruṇima nimagnāṁ smarati yaḥ ।
bhavanty asya trasyad vana hariṇa śālīna nayanāḥ
sahorvaśyā vaśyāḥ kati kati na gīrvāṇa gaṇikāḥ ॥

taruṇa taraṇi śrī saraṇibhiḥ — having taken the way of the young sun, most tenderly and totally overcovered by the dappled dawn; *te tanucchāyābhiḥ* — with shades of Your bodily form; *sarvaṁ divaṁ urvīm* — the sky as also the whole earth; *aruṇima nimagnāṁ* — as immersed in sheer magenta glory; *yaḥ smarati* — he who contemplates; *asya* — for him; *trasyat vana hariṇa śālīna nayanāḥ* — with startled, gentle wild deer eyes; *urvaśya saha* — together with Urvaśī; *kati kati* — how many, how many; *gīrvāṇa gaṇikāḥ* — celestial courtesans; *na vaśyāḥ bhavanti* — not become won over (attracted)?

With shades of Your bodily form enriched by the tenderly sunlit sky of a dappled dawn,
Submerging the whole earth within its sheer magenta glory —
Able to contemplate You thus, he wins over maids with startled, gentle, wild-deer eyes,
Together with Urvaśī *and how many, many other such celestial damsels.*

Mutual attraction between the sexes is a normal aspiration in the world of erotic life, not only of adolescents of no distinction, but also of beautiful persons, viewed from a neutral point between them, where the prototype of absolute Beauty is to be attributed to the central Goddess of these verses. All manifestations of bodily beauty have to be derived from this central normative model. If we consider this model as real, all other manifestations of bodily beauty are only shadows or reflected images of the same. When we concede these facts in respect of Beauty, and try to fill the total ground or field with beauty of this kind, we get roughly the picture presented here by Śaṅkara.

In verse thirteen the same heavenly damsels of this verse were under reference in respect of their state of infatuation for an overaged ugly man, who had but the side glance of the Goddess embellishing his attractiveness. There the attractiveness was a kind of reflected glory, even a little of which was enough to give him a heightened personal value. This same idea of the mutual heightening of values between men and women of superior or ordinary levels, though in a more wholesale context of overwhelming beauty, is what is again pictured here, in order to view the same subject from a more homogeneously unified viewpoint.

Here it is a devotee within whose consciousness, as he meditates on absolute Beauty, rich patches of shaded magenta are seen. The shade is derived from the earthy side, but the tender dawn contributes its light-pink brilliance. Colours become beautiful by saturation of tint or brilliance. If the brilliance is hypostatic in origin, the tint or shade must have a reference at the lower (heirophantic) limit for origin. Saturation is a quality which depends upon the distance of the colour, which decreases inversely when the patch of colour increases its distance from the centre of the structure. These patches are not essentially different from the forest of lotuses described in verse sixteen. Here the flower form is made to fade impressionistically into the background and the patches take their place with the same overpowering appeal. This is because contemplation here is evidently that of a yogi, also neutrally placed vis-à-vis the model of beauty at the core of his own field of consciousness.

Yoga could be conceived of as a type of union between values, and when this union takes place, the yogi is supposed to see a vision in his inner space, of which this verse is a description. If we suppose for convenience that the yogi is a man, each patch of shaded magenta would represent a beautiful young damsel who is the prototype of the goddess of Beauty. The appeal of beautiful young women to men is to be taken for granted. Here two types of young women are brought into the picture, who have to be carefully distinguished: the 'maids with startled, gentle, wild-deer-eyes', as opposed to 'Urvaśī and the countless other such celestial damsels'. The latter have a hypostatic origin, while the former are evidently ordinary women of tribalistic origin, called *kimpuruṣa*s in Kālidāsa's poetry, who inhabit the slopes of the Himalayas and live among the wild animals, especially wild deer. The patches of magenta light, which invade from the upper limit or those of magenta shade which permeate the scene from the lower limit of reference, represent damsels of one or the other of these two opposite types. The maids with startled deer-eyes may be humbler and more earthy than the celestial beauties, but what they lose by their humble origin, they make up by their extraordinary vitality and alertness, as qualities of inner beauty. A cancellation of inner and outer beauty is thus to be understood here, as intended by the master poet.

The yogi who, while meditating on the Goddess, is able to fill the total ground of his own consciousness with these two kinds of overwhelming magenta patches — which, encroaching from both sides, lending light and shade from opposite poles of the situation so as to immerse the scene into a homogeneous glory of neither light nor shade, neither of heaven nor of earth — has accomplished an important stage in his spiritual progress. The value of such a vision is not to be minimized, and it is indicated here that such an experience of homogeneous and overwhelming beauty is more valuable than the legitimate ambition of all young human beings to be attractive to the other sex. The great number of damsels involved here shows that it is the earthy side that wins the game, while the others are to be counted among the numerous 'runners-up'.

A most important hint is found here in the phrase 'submerging the sky and the whole world in sheer magenta glory'. This describes the full aurora effect that we can sometimes see from either one of the polar regions of the earth. Here, Beauty cancels with its own counterpart, and the resultant is the yogic experience characterized by the absolutist touch.

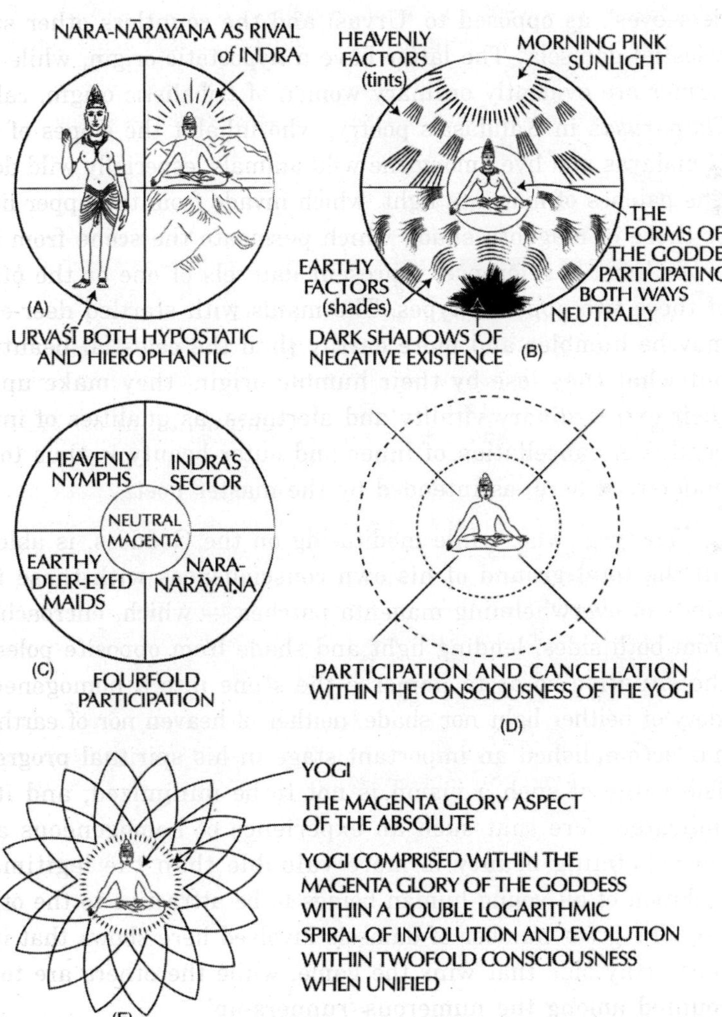

Structural Analysis

The appreciation of the beauty of the absolute Goddess here takes place in this verse at the hypostatic limit and pervades the whole ground downwards. If we should imagine the Goddess to be of a tender lotus pink colour to which is added the magenta glory coming from the just-rising sun, there is created a leaping thrill of exaltation felt, as it were, at the bottom of the heart. The beauty of Urvaśī participating equally with heaven and earth at once, has itself a thrill which corresponds to that of a wild deer that is startled in its tender look. The startled-deerlook is to be cancelled against the thrill of the magenta glory.

When translated into its horizontalized version, the man of contemplation of absolute Beauty gains the status of Nara-Nārāyaṇa, whose penance roused envy of Indra by its total absence of lust and could not be broken by Indra's sending down well-known beauties of heaven. He is able to produce a more perfect nymph of heavenly status from his thigh himself, and so to outwit Indra in the game. Urvaśī's beauty combines the hypostatic and hierophantic elements fused within itself and thus belongs to the Absolute rather than to any hedonistic or relativistic set-up of a Vedic heaven. It is taken for granted in this verse that to be interesting to women in an asset even for a recluse as a qualification for his spirituality, and not as a disqualification in the name of dry-as-dust austerity as might be popularly supposed. The magenta glory as a Value, puts to shade all relatively aesthetic appreciations, thus raising the spiritual status of the aspirant by more understanding to such an extent that he at once becomes endowed with absolute attraction in his own person. Magenta glory as numerator value cancels out correctly with the personal charm of the opposite sex, represented by the Goddess here, in the fourfold set-up. If Urvaśī could be attracted, all other nymphs of heaven are only small change as against the gold coin that she would represent by her more absolutist status. Urvaśī becomes his natural counterpart horizontally, while vertically viewed the startled-deer gentleness of look cancels out the magenta glory which is its own natural numerator factor.

19

मुखं बिन्दुं कृत्वा कुचयुगमधस्तस्य तदधो
हरार्धं ध्यायेद् यो हरमहिषि ते मन्मथकलाम्।
स सद्यः संक्षोभं नयति वनिता इत्यतिलघु
त्रिलोकीमप्याशु भ्रमयति रवीन्दुस्तनयुगाम्॥

mukhaṁ binduṁ kṛtvā kucayugam adhas tasya tadadho
harārdhaṃ dhyāyed yo haramahiṣi te manmatha kalām ।
sa sadyaḥ saṁkṣobhaṁ nayati vanitā ity atilaghu
trilokīm apy āśu bhramayati ravīndu stana yugām ॥

hara mahiṣi — O Consort of Śiva; *mukhaṁ binduṁ kṛtvā* — placing the face at the locus; *tasya adhaḥ* — below that; *kuca yugam* — the two breasts; *tat adhaḥ* — below that; *hara ardhaṁ* — the (better) half of Śiva; *dhyāyed yaḥ* — one who contemplates; *te manmatha kalām* — Your erotic aspect; *saḥ sadyaḥ* — he without delay; *vanitā* — (of) women; *saṁkṣobhaṁ nayati* — can stir the sentiments; *iti ati laghu* — this is but slight; *ravi indu stana yugām* — with sun and moon for her twin breasts; *tri lokīm api* — even Her of the three worlds; *āśu bhramayati* — at once agitates

O Śiva Consort, making Your face the locus, with twin breasts below,
And below still, as the better half of Śiva; meditating on Your erotic aspect,
Without delay he can stir the sentiments of women — this is but slight —
And at once agitate even Her of the three worlds, when sun and moon form Her twin breasts.

The subject of stirring the sentiments of women is continued here. It is not the Advaitic yogi who is to be presupposed here, but evidently a Kaulin or a Vāmācārin. This verse is to be understood in the context of erotic mystical practices prevalent in India at the decadent period, when the rigorous moral standards gave way, in the nooks and corners of temple precincts, to questionable practices which were not always 'above board'. It is known that Śaṅkara lived at this very period, and he must have known many Kaulins, Samayins and Vāmācārins. This verse subjects the practices of such cults to a drastic dialectical revaluation in the light of Śaṅkara's own uncompromising Advaitic position. The intention is unmistakably evident and it gives us the key as to how we should view this whole series of verses: as having nothing to do directly with Śākteya cults as such.

Certain texts that belong to this pre-Advaitic tradition are popular in Bengal even to this day, as is evident from the long passages reproduced by Sir John Woodroffe, who has specialized in this kind of Indian esotericism. The curiosity of certain scholars is guided by lesser motives than the finding of pure wisdom-values. Museum pieces and archives are more interesting to them in their vocation, primarily as scholars, and they place themselves outside the spirituality that they study. It is thus that some of these texts reveal an undertone of disapproval of Śaṅkara's way of giving importance to the eternal female principle. They would rather have him give up his uncompromising love of pure wisdom in favour of a cult in which Śakti is to be considered the last word in philosophy. Woodroffe and Aurobindo Ghose both say that Śaṅkara did not understand the particular aspects of these Śakti cults.

The slightly unilateral point of view prevailing in respect of the absolute principle of Beauty, which is to be brought more correctly under the non-dualistic perspective, gives us a hold on the purpose of this verse. It wants to tell us that in the context of erotic mysticism there are two alternatives in visualizing the Goddess involved, structurally. One could imagine a circle and insert into it the two orthogonal axes. He could even put the face of the Goddess at the zero point of the situation and then proceed, step by step, to fill in items of a vertical series of value factors, in descending order. The verse here enumerates the items thus to be arranged vertically on the denominator side. Śaṅkara wishes to point out here that such a form of meditation could be considered good, as far as it goes, but not good enough. He does not condemn the practice outright by saying that it is to be omitted. In the last two lines he brings out the contrast of the two approaches. It is below the horizontal line alone that the meditation should apply. Advaitic meditation requires a double correction or cancellation between numerator and denominator values. It is with reference to the breasts of a woman, placed hypostatically in the context of the values represented by the sun and the moon, that the cancellation here becomes possible, when the negative approach is replaced by one in which both the sides enter as equal counterparts to be cancelled out against each other.

When this Advaitic approach is borne in mind, all interest in attracting ordinary women in a given locality gives place instead to something noble, by which it is not an eternal female with an earthy reference who is to be won over, but a goddess, whose range of Beauty applies to all the three worlds (*bhūrloka, bhuvarloka* and *svarloka*). The amplitude of the parameter is thus not unilateral but fully absolutist, as indicated in the previous verse where both celestial and tribalistic damsels come under the attraction of a true yogi of a non-dualistic status. Beauty goes beyond the question of attracting the opposite sex, for it could be thought of as illumining the Absolute itself. It is to be noted that Śaṅkara does not discountenance the lower form of the Kaulin cult, but recommends its transcendence through a revised attitude.

Meditation requires a point of locus (*bindu*) where all dimensions converge and from where they emerge, thought of both as the source and the point of reabsorption of all manifestations. This is thus the neutral point (*prabhava pralaya sthānam*) placed between the two processes, which cancel each other out. The face is the index of one's beauty, and Śiva is referred to in verse sixty-seven as looking at the reflection of his own face in a mirror and identifying it as the face of his wife, the Goddess. Thus the *bindu* is both subjective and objective in the revised version of meditation presented here.

The Goddess presiding over the three worlds, referred to in the last line, suggests an absolutist version of the same goddess, though not unilaterally understood, as that of the Kaulins. The revalued Goddess comprises within her scope both hypostatic and heirophantic items of value. Appreciation of value which is of an absolutist order can be said to attract that Goddess who represents in herself the same value. This is based on the law of 'like attracts like'. Attraction becomes synonymous with appreciation here in the context of absolutist devotion.

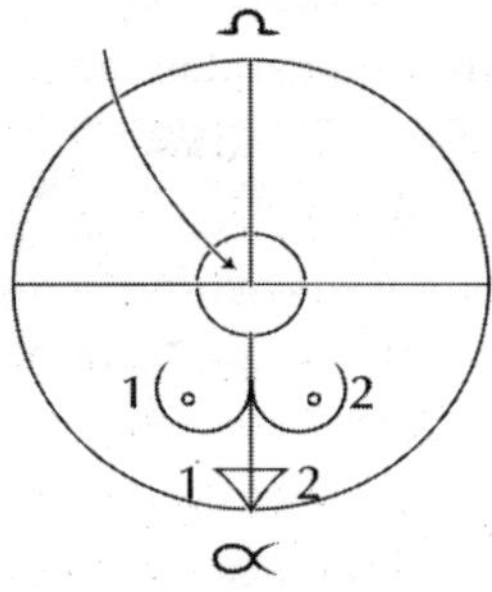

(a)Hypostatic parity at three levels between factors 1 and 2

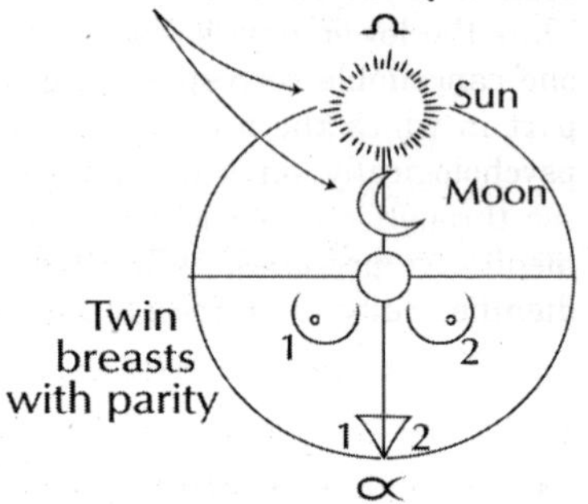

(b) II degree generalization and revision of perspective

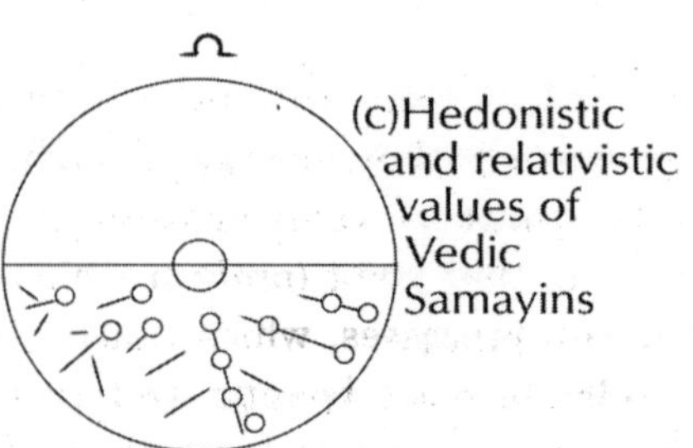

(c)Hedonistic and relativistic values of Vedic Samayins

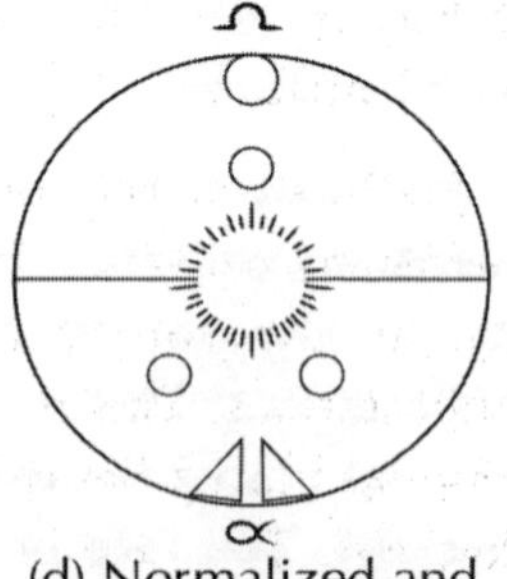

(d) Normalized and Absolutist Beauty

Structural Analysis

The words of this verse bear so directly on the structural aspects involved, that it is hardly necessary for us to labour to reveal it, especially after the complicated structural implications of the previous verse which we have already analysed (*under verse* 18). A central locus is first to be marked within the total field where the absolute function of female beauty can operate. A descending and an ascending line has then to be marked vertically on such a structural plan. The attraction, less in importance to the face, which is to be considered still normally centralized, are the twin breasts. On the lower half of the vertical axis the twin breasts have a horizontal parity. The same parity is to be extended lower down where more concentrated erotic factors reside into the very core of the sex triangle. Even here, however, one should remember that any real joy of sex is equally to be shared between the Śiva and the Śakti factors. Hermaphroditic and androgynous interests have to be made to meet here vertically and not in horizontalized cross-section. Bilateral symmetry is to be replaced by axial symmetry. Thus the lower physical schematic image gets a homogeneous one-one cancellable correspondence within its own numerator counter-part in which the breasts are no more earthy or physiological, but psychologically verticalized and hypostatic. When a yogi is able to see through such structural or theoretical implications to guide his meditative practices, he becomes a yogi of a fully absolutist status, dignified fully to be recognized by the open philosophy of Śaṅkara.

20

किरन्तीमङ्गेभ्यः किरणनिकुरुम्बामृतरसम्
हृदि त्वामाधत्ते हिमकरशिलामूर्तिमिव यः ।
स सर्पाणां दर्पं शमयति शकुन्ताधिप इव
ज्वरप्लुष्टान् दृष्ट्या सुखयति सुधासारसिरया ॥

kirantīm aṅgebhyaḥ kiraṇa nikurumbāmṛta rasam
hṛdi tvām ādhatte himakara śilāmūrtim iva yaḥ ।
sa sarpāṇām darpaṁ śamayati śakuntādhipa iva
jvara pluṣṭān dṛṣṭyā sukhayati sudhāsāra sirayā ॥

aṅgebhyaḥ — out of (your) limbs; *kiraṇa nikurambaḥ amṛta rasam* — the radiating essence of immortal bliss; *kirantīm* — as emanating; *hima kara śilā mūrtim iva* — like a moonstone-made image; *yaḥ hṛdi tvām ādhatte* — he who can bring You into his heart; *saḥ śakuntādhipa iva* — he like the King of Birds; *sarpāṇām darpam śamayati* — quells the pride of serpents; *sudhā dhārā sirayā dṛṣṭyā* — (and) by very look of ambrosial streak; *jvara pluṣṭān* — a fever patient; *sukhayati* — cures

He who can bring You, as emanating nectar out of Your limbs all around,
Into his heart like a moonstone-made statue,
He can quell the pride of serpents like the King of Birds,
And a fever-patient cure by his very look of ambrosial streak.

Verse twenty has to be read with verse ten; between these two limiting verses we have had various perspectives of the dynamism implied between them. Verse ten gives us a picture of the ambrosial essence emanating from between the feet of the Goddess and how a double set of ramified streaks are to be visualized. In the present verse, her image is to be placed at the centre of the heart of the contemplative who is her votary. Thus there are negative and positive attitudes possible in the practice of meditation or adoration of the absolute beauty of the Goddess here. These subjective and objective versions are complementary, reciprocal, or compensatory; and if one is placed at the limit of the Self (the alpha point) the other is placed at the limit of the non-Self, (the omega point). They could even be cancelled out into the neutrality of the Absolute, as indicated in the last verse of this work, where everything is finally abolished.

It is recommended in this verse that the contemplative reduce the Goddess into the semblance of a statue made of moonstone. The gleaming lustre of a moonstone has an interesting subdued tone about it, between brilliance and shade or tint, thus indicating that this statue is to be placed at a neutral point within the consciousness of the yogi, where the transition takes place from the subjective to the objective. This corresponds to what is technically understoood in Patañjali's yoga as *pratyāhāra*, when efferent tendencies are neutralized by afferent tendencies and vice versa. When this neutralization occurs, one experiences an inner psychic richness akin to samādhi.

The emanation of nectar refers to the efferent tendencies of the psyche, while crystallization at the heart-centre into a 'moonstone image' is the cultivation of the opposite (afferent) tendency of centralization at the locus of the heart. When this is accomplished, the yogi's personality, even in the outward sense, comes to have a revised status. His features radiate a confidence and a functional alertness or brilliance. This state has been referred to as *tejas*, and Swāmī Vivekānanda's works, as also his personality, could be cited as evidence of this kind of yogic attainment. The voice is said to become mellowed, the skin becomes more glossy and tender and the metabolism functions in such a balanced and purificatory way that it is said to have the effect of *nāḍī śuddhi* (clarity or transparancy of the blood vessels and lymphatic system).

A yogi in such a state becomes extremely sympathetic to any man, woman or child, who is naturally attracted by him. Jesus was such a healer, always with a multitude of people around him. He becomes 'the cynosure of all eyes' and the focal point of everyone's interest. There are many stories about the psychic feats of certain Tamil saints (*siddhas*); one, especially, was said to make the bones of a dead woman come to life by his songs, when he passed through a village funeral scene. We have to make allowances for natural exaggeration here. Another saint could cure miraculously the chronic stomach ache of a Jain king by sprinkling holy ashes as a treatment.

In the *Yogavāsiṣṭha*, Cūḍāla, the young queen of King Śikhidhvaja, tells her husband how, by practising a yogic and contemplative way of life, she enhances her personal charm and value as a peaceful presence in the palace. Examples of such yogis are found anywhere in the world. They might seem very humble and harmless, but at a given moment they can vomit fire, as it were, if confronted with a proud person who might question the intrinsic positivity coming from pure contemplation only. The sage Kaṇva is described by Kālidāsa, in the *Śākuntalam*, as having this kind of positive power of asserting himself (*tejas*). He says that Kaṇva is like a lens which by itself is cold, but, when confronted with a source of light, can rise to the challenge and vomit its own fire. The mild life of forest dwellers is not to be challenged by forces less intense than those built up within the psyche by austerities.

The Sanskritic literary tradition has created a number of counterparts in the bird or animal world in which the pride of one is cancelled and superseded by the power of another. The lion is the counterpart of the elephant in this respect. The king of birds here, which is a vulture or an eagle, has the power to cancel the pride of a serpent. This is cancellation in the created world of creatures, though the operation of psychic powers need not be confined to this outer world of creation. It could also apply to the inner world of emotions.

The second instance of this verse belongs to this order. A man in a hospital, who is desperate about his own survival, sometimes enters into a negative state of depression, by which he gives up all hope. The doctor in charge can observe that the patient himself does not wish to live. Many instances are known in India of a yogi entering such a sorrowful situation and working a miracle of the kind referred to in this verse by instilling such confidence in the patients that they begin to gain hope instead of losing it. The turning point is as delicate as the retroaction in a thermostat. It can take place with the subtlest of influence in the world of psychophysics or psychosomatic medicine. Sympathetic emotions are contagious and can work wonders between individuals linked together in a bipolar reciprocity. The tears in the eyes of such a yogi will be found to be on the point of bursting out of sympathy. This kind of psychic power is not to be mixed up with other psychic powers, such as atomicity (*aṇimā*) etc., whose status is to be discussed in later verses. This is a global state of sensitivity that is very rich intellectually and emotionally at the same time.

The mode of operation for inducing such a state of yogihood is here explained as residing at the core of the heart of the yogi. That value represented by the Goddess of absolute Beauty cancels out into a fully neutralized state of yogic perfection, by virtue of which, such *siddhi*s, or so-called powers, become natural attributes of the yogically revalued personality. The yogi is always an interesting man to other human beings, especially to women and children.

The stream of nectar in terms of which the psychic powers are to be understood according to this verse, satisfies two requirements at one stroke. Nectar is a perceptual value, while the stream is an intelligible or conceptual value. When fused together, the ambrosial stream represents an emanation which is neither physical nor mental. One hears often of emanations or presences from saints or yogis. Language has conferred on one or the other or both of these aspects, some kind of reality, because it has to refer to either a fact truth or a logic truth. When fact and logic meet, it is a value like beauty that emerges, and combined words like 'thinking substance' or 'ambrosial stream' become permissible in this context. The duality, if it persists, must be countered by unitive understanding to become what is neither a streak of light nor ambrosia, but a central value called Beauty.

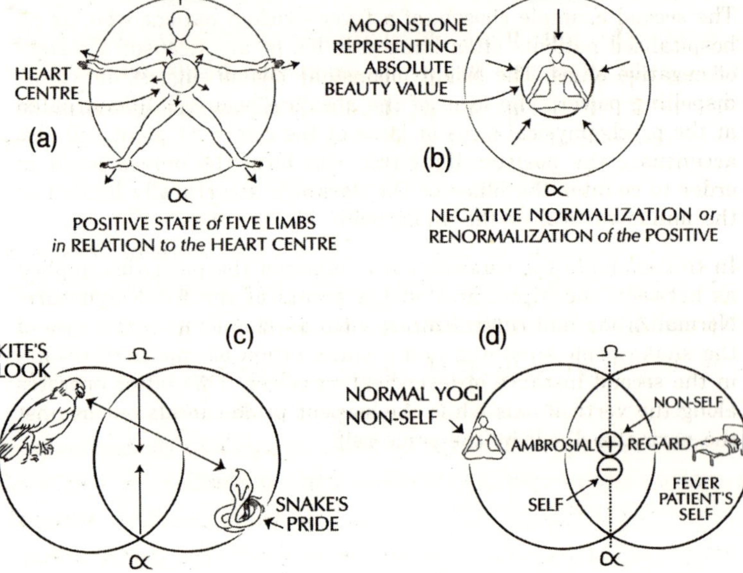

POSITIVE STATE *of* FIVE LIMBS *in* RELATION *to the* HEART CENTRE

NEGATIVE NORMALIZATION *or* RENORMALIZATION *of the* POSITIVE

VERTICAL NORMALIZATION *of the* COUNTERPARTS *of* KITE'S LOOK & SNAKE'S PRIDE

HORIZONTAL RENORMALIZATION *of* MINUS (-) SELF IN TERMS *of* NON-SELF(+): INTERSUBJECTIVE *and* TRANSPHYSICAL NEUTRALIZATION

Structural Analysis

Two sets of images have to be superimposed here. First there is the yogi or contemplative who is able to centralize his whole consciousness and not merely his conceptual mind. Further, this must be inclusive of the full ontological implications of the features of beauty or of joy. When such a bipolar or one-one relation between beauty in the non-self and in the Self gets established, a sublimation of instincts takes place by which the normal or central self approximates in status to the normative and universally concrete self. Such a state of unitive understanding, when allowed to permeate or percolate within the psychophysical libido or system, this harmonized state enhances its quality under the aegis of the dominant eternally absolute Value. By the superimposing of consciousness of the non-self on the Self, finally the former attains to parity or homogeneity with the latter. A subtle cancellation between them can now take place, giving to the new or revalued psyche some secondary powers referred to as *siddhis* elsewhere in Vedantic parlance. Absolute power of which this is only secondary, however, remains normalized and neutralized at the core.

The second example chosen, of a fever-stricken patient who, as all hospitalized patients often happen to be, is one steeped in a state of negative blues. The bright moonstone beams suggest darkness-dispelling power. The form of the absolute beauty Value situated at the psychophysical focus or locus at the centre 'O' point will also accentuate the positive light that can form the omega point in order to counter the blues or the darkness structurally located at the minus vertical or the alpha point.

In this example the cancellation is between the polarities implied as between the alpha and omega points of the total structure. Normalization and centralization yield psychic force in the case of the snake pride-subduing and a cancellation of opposites results in the second instance of fever-healing power. This latter operates along the vertical axis while the serpent pride cancels out against the normalized self by the same self.

21

तटिल्लेखातन्वीं तपनशशिवैश्वानरमयीं
निषण्णां षण्णामप्युपरि कमलानां तव कलाम्।
महापद्माटव्यां मृदितमलमायेन मनसा
महान्तः पश्यन्तो दधति परमाह्लादलहरीम्॥

taṭil lekhā tanvīṁ tapana śaśi vaiśvānara mayīṁ
niṣaṇṇāṁ ṣaṇṇāṁ apy upari kamalānāṁ tavakalām ।
mahā padmāṭavyāṁ mṛdita mala māyena manasā
mahāntaḥ paśyanto dadhati paramāhlāda laharīm ॥

taṭit lekhā tanvīṁ — lightning-streak-bodied; *tapana śaśi vaiśvānara mayīṁ* — made of sun, moon and fire; *ṣaṇṇāṁ kamalānāṁ api upari* — even above the six lotuses; *mahā padma aṭavyāṁ* — in a great lotus forest; *niṣaṇṇāṁ* — as seated; *tava kalām* — such Your aspect; *mahāntaḥ* — great ones; *mṛdita mala māyena manasā* — having mind freed from dross and ignorance; *paśyantaḥ* — seeing this; *parama āhlāda laharīm* — the upsurging billow of ultimate delight; *dadhati* — experience

As lightning-streak-bodied, made of sun, moon and fire,
And as placed even above the six lotuses in a great lotus grove;

Those great ones, as seers of such Your aspect, having mind freed, from dross and ignorance,
They experience the upsurging billow of ultimate delight.

In this verse the thought of verse twenty is carried over, but in terms of a thin streak of lightning, joining the two vertical limits from end to end. We can notice in the first instance that the experience under reference here is one of ascent and not of descent, because it is stated in the second line that the six lotuses are left below. The amplitude of the Kaula cult consists of what is limited to the six bases (*ṣaḍādhāras*), which are to be imagined as six psychophysical levels. The *sahasrāra* and *kulakuṇḍa* are to be added above and below, respectively, to this set of six psychophysical units of beauty-value. They are described here as lotuses in a vertical series.

In the first line, the lightning-streak body of the Goddess consists of abstract light essence, to be distinguished when we descend from the sun to the moon to touch the fire. It is true that the sun is brilliant, the moon subdued, and the fire placed on earth. Although emitting the same light and heat, the fire is weighed down by the weight of the atmosphere. We have to separate mentally the qualitative aspect of light and give to this thin vertical streak its fourth- or multi-dimensional status. This is to be done by a process of reduction, by omitting what is extraneous to the pure essence of light. The *Īśāvāsya Upaniṣad* calls upon the sun to reduce its radiance so that a more auspicious verticalized form of sunlight could be revealed. A flame within a windless room has often been used to describe the state of contemplative intelligence. Even the smoke of burnt incense can be seen to ascend vertically when the atmosphere is not disturbed. Within natural forces themselves, therefore, there is a tendency for a flame to mark out for us a path of spiritual ascent. Some of the Upaniṣads speak of this flame beckoning to the sacrificer to follow its lead upward to various value-worlds. The thinner the streak, the better the absolute quality implied. That is the reason why the lightning-streak body of the Goddess is prominently referred to in the first line. A lightning-flash with thunderclap contains an element of wonder and suddenness which can heighten the meaning of absolute Beauty, which is to be understood qualitatively rather than in its gross quantitative aspects.

It is necessary that the lightning streak body be 'placed even above the six lotuses' for experiencing the ultimate delight referred to in the last line. To the extent that the lightning-streak is thin and rises beyond the reach of lower utilitarian or hedonistic values, it is better for the resultant purity of the light it can induce in terms of an overwhelming experience.

Ontologically it has to be beyond the limit of the velocity of sound to have supersonic effects revealed to the ear. This is also true of light or intelligence. The experience of delight becomes intensified by the height of the intelligence it can attain on the conceptual side. It is in this sense that 'having mind freed from dross and ignorance' is to be understood. The Bhagavadgītā also refers to that positive aspect of the vertical parameter which could be arrived at by putting the sun, moon and fire in a descending order to touch the zero point of our consciousness or of the positive cosmological set-up. The delight itself may be said to ascend from the *mūlādhāra* to the *ājñā cakra*. When these two lights, originating at the two limits, meet a fluorescent light glows as a whole, as in the case of a tube-light, irrespective of the two electrodes. The flow of light represents the essence of the light within consciousness as an overpowering emotional experience; they are inseparable, like the two sides of a coin.

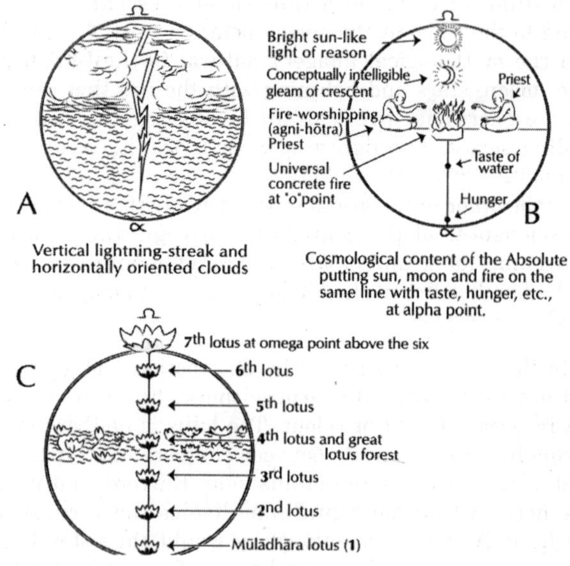

Structural Analysis

The lotus flower ideogram is here used for structural purposes with great advantage by Śaṅkara. A forest of lotus flowers with stems submerged in water and a vertical series of six lotuses are presupposed here to bring into global view the ontologically negative or existential perspective of the Absolute viewed under the caption of a high and significant life-value dear to all mankind. Six such lotuses are required to cover both hierophantic as well as hypostatic levels of absolute Value; three for each. Absolute Value, however, is not to be limited by any conditionings, whether perceptual or conceptual. This is the reason why, in the second line, the reference to the topmost level of a total perspective above all the other six is underlined by the author. What helps us to bring into focal unity for purposes of meditation or the practice of correct *rāja yoga* is the strict separation of the vertical and horizontal aspects of beauty. A streak of lightning, when it cuts electrically across the cloud formation which is one's own consciousness cosmologically and psychologically understood at once, is comparable to the feminine creative principle of beauty, viewed in its pure qualitative glory. The goddess of Beauty has therefore to be first viewed here in pure logical terms like a lightning steak having pure verticalized radiance. When some more concessions are made to this thin lightning streak so as to give it a more cosmological content, we begin to think in terms of a thin silver crescent streak also as belonging to the same at the omega point or crest of Śiva's head, at least in the mythological imagery natural to the Indian peasant. The sun, moon, stars and lightning with the fire that can be lit on earth as a sacrificial fire, can all belong together in a vertical descending series. The lightning reveals the horizontal world of visible realities at night, while the sun, stars, etc., take their turns one after the other in the grand procession whether inside or outside the consciousness of the contemplative yogi. Vaiśvānara is just another name for a universal concrete elemental functioning of which the familiar fire in the kitchen is the commonplace individual localized counterpart.

Absolute Beauty is experienced by abstraction and generalization carried out to its ultimate term without, however, omitting its content in terms of light or colour. The lotus is neither hot nor cold but normally living neutrally between the heat of the plus side and the cold of the water of the minus side. Entropy and negentropy balance here. A thin horizontal line divides the vertical series of lotuses here. A sheer magenta glory would thus stand revealed, with varying degrees, shades and tints of beautiful light, line or colour. Brilliance, fluorescence, scintillation and effulgence are all comprised as varieties of such an experience of inner as well as outer beauty.

22

भवानि त्वं दासे मयि वितर दृष्टिं सकरुणा-
मिति स्तोतुं वाञ्छन् कथयति भवानि त्वमिति यः ।
तदैव त्वं तस्मै दिशसि निजसायुज्यपदवीम्
मुकुन्दब्रह्मेन्द्रस्फुटमकुटनीराजितपदाम् ॥

bhavāni tvaṁ dāse mayi vitara dṛṣṭiṁ sakaruṇām
iti stotuṁ vāñchan kathayati bhavāni tvam iti yaḥ ।
tadaiva tvaṁ tasmai diśasi nija sāyujya padavīm
mukunda brahmendra sphuṭa makuṭa nīrājitapadām ॥

bhavāni tvaṁ — O Goddess wife of Bhava (Śiva) You; *dāse mayi* — on me, Your servant; *sakaruṇām dṛṣṭiṁ* — a look of kindness; *vitara* — bestow; *iti stotuṁ* — thus to praise; *vāñchan yaḥ* — he who desiring; *bhavāni tvaṁ* — 'O Goddess,You'; *iti kathayati* — thus says; *tadā eva* — at that same time, right then; *tasmai* — to him; *mukunda brahmā indra sphuṭa makuṭa nīrājita padām* — the same state as was gained by Viṣṇu, Brahmā and Indra by the waving of bright lights of their diadems; *nija sāyujya padavīṁ* — that state of identity with You; *tvaṁ diśasi* — You grant

'O Goddess, You, on this Your servant, bestow a kind look'
Thus intending to adore, no sooner one begins saying:
'O Goddess, You . . .,' You grant him that state of identity with You —
The same as what Viṣṇu, Brahmā and Indra accomplished by the waving of the bright lights on their diadems.

Prayers can be of different grades of efficacy or word content. Ritual actions of different kinds are also implied in the act of offering adoration or prayers to divinities or gods. An effective prayer is that which establishes the most direct bipolar contact between the supplicant and the god that is being addressed. The gods themselves represent different grades of values, according to the taste or understanding of the seeker. Compatibility between the counterparts of the worshipper and the worshipped, we see here, is the first and foremost condition for efficacy in prayer. Prayer is like an interaction in chemistry, where there is a kind of osmotic interchange of values taking place. It could also be likened to a mathematical equation. There are also many instances of reversible reactions and retroactive processes known in thermodynamic systems or in the context of cybernetics. Semantics and logistics also conform to a system in which there is a reciprocal exchange of meanings taking place interphysically and transsubjectively. Such are some of the subtle structural implications to be kept in mind in order to understand the meaning of this verse.

In the first place, we have to remember that it is not just an ordinary goddess who is the object of adoration here, but it is the ultimate value in the Advaitic context that is being adored. The person fit for such an exalted and pure form of worship must also conform to certain requirements himself. He is not to be treated as a mere *upāsaka* (a worshipper merely paying lip service), who understands a dead letter better than the living word, due to his lukewarm or hidebound attitude, and who lacks wholeheartedness because he is too full of personal outward interests, which keeps his soul from entering the vertical, subtle eye of the needle.

The bipolarity between the worshipper and the worshipped cannot become fully established except on a homogeneous ground where these two counterparts participate on equal terms. This homogeneous ground is called worship. Here the worship is an osmotic interchange between the inner stuff of existential and essential factors. With the Goddess visualised existentially, the supplicant is to be her dialectical counterpart, in terms of the subsistent, with the overall situation of worship itself being the value factor, where the two counterparts cancel out in the glory of the Absolute. The worshipper and the worshipped enter into equal partnership here as interchangeable factors. The thinnest medium through which this participation can take place is where words meet the meanings corresponding to their forms. The cybernetic or thermodynamic equilibrium could also be thought of as taking place in the thinner semantic world, where words and meanings circulate between subject and object, or Self and non-Self. Such an equilibrium is called homeostasis.

In the pure world of non-duality there is reversibilty of reaction, as well as of the validity of an equation expressing the same in algebraic terms. There is also a similar one-to-one correspondence and cancellation in a more subtle domain. Whether in the world of logic or intentionalities, prayers are judged more by the intention implied in them than by the syntactic or pragmatic aspects of the words in which the prayers are clothed. In Advaita Vedanta it is granted that god and man are the same. If a god-like man waves lights to propitiate a god, it is quite natural to reverse the position and say that when such a worthy man humbles himself, the god also decides to wave lights to the personality of the supplicant in return. Thus full cancellation of counterparts occurs.

In the first line, though the prayer is only just begun, the Goddess is already willing to respond to the intention present. It is only for a kind look, and not for any worldly benefit, that the supplicant here prays, because as an Advaitin or sannyasin, he has no other favours to ask for. Not only is the intention readily recognized, but the response is both total and spontaneous, bestowing not just a mere kind look. Partial stimulus produces total reaction of the counterpart, here contained within the word 'You', as between interchangeable counterparts. The Goddess seems to say: 'You are not a mere worshipper, you are myself. There is equality of status and richness of quality between us, because Advaita cannot countenance any shade of duality'.

There is reference in the last line to worship by the three gods, who are supposed to be far superior to human beings as custodians of the three phenomenal functions in the cosmological set-up of the absolute universe. But even if their worship should attain to its fullest benefit or merit, they, the most important agents in the phenomenal context of the universe, are here only given the same marks, when judged finally by effect, as the humble supplicant who stands outside the context of holiness or merit altogether. Vedantic worship is based on understanding rather than on ritualistic merit belonging to mere Vedism.

The reference to the 'lights on the diadems', which are supposed to function here as the flames used in the ritualistic waving of lights in temples to propitiate various gods, is to indicate that Viṣṇu, Brahmā and Indra are doing their best from the standpoints of their own notions and value systems — as far as such values are within their grasp — to honour the absolute Goddess. But in spite of such efforts, they only get pass marks in the final test, while the non-dualistic worshipper not only passes freely beyond such a point of perfection but gets the worship of the Goddess herself. Such is the overwhelming beauty of this situation, to be understood in the overall context of intentionality.

The 'identity with You' is only to be treated as a corollary to any one of the four well-known *mahāvākya*s of the Upaniṣads, each of which is an equation between the Self and the non-Self in the context of absolute Wisdom.

Intentionality counts more than words. We would be justified in thinking that words themselves are finally extraneous to the situation from the last verse of the poem, where Śaṅkara washes off his hands completely of even having taken the trouble of writing these verses, politely excuses himself and withdraws out of the scene of holiness.

Structural Analysis

A horizontal line has first to be put between what the three gods referred to here as Brahmā, Viṣṇu and Indra in this verse represent hypostatically or hierophantically. The former is marked by the sparkling at the tip of their diadems and the latter by the ontological, existential or hierophantic aspects in their elemental states in the animistic or hylozoist sense. After the horizontal

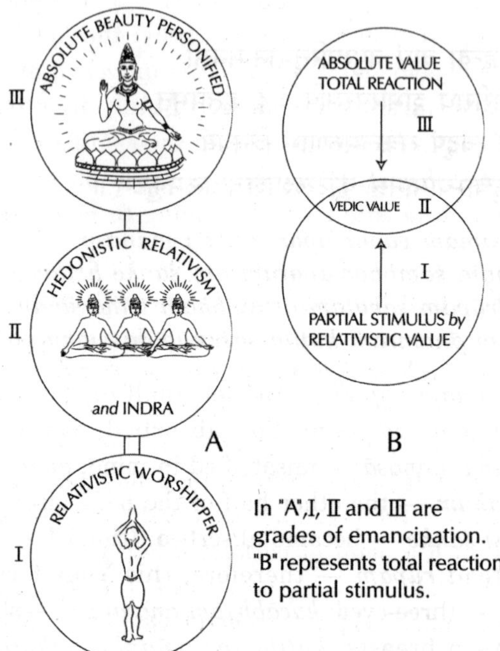

In "A",I, II and III are grades of emancipation. "B" represents total reaction to partial stimulus.

division of absolute beauty Value, one has to place a prayerful devotee on the denominator side. He belongs to the mechanistic world of action and reaction, being equal and opposite. Even when he is unconscious of his relativistic approach, the verticalization of values and the correct bipolarity of his prayerfulness by which he can place himself correctly at the alpha end of the vertical axis, becomes fully effective. The generosity of the Absolute is released even by relativistic intentionality of the devoted who might himself pray incorrectly, unilaterally or partially. If the other experimental conditions of the situation fulfil the structural relational or intentional requirements of the bipolar relation between the two counterparts, one with a horizontal and the other with a vertical reference there will still be produced a more than desired effect. The law of partial stimulus-total response belongs to the vitalistic and absolutist context which is the key to the right understanding of the present verse. The vertical cancels the horizontal values or benefits into the glory of the Value of values called absolute Beauty in this work.

23

त्वया हृत्वा वामं वपुरपरितृप्तेन मनसा
शरीरार्धं शंभोरपरमपि शङ्के हृतमभूत्।
यदेतत् त्वद्रूपं सकलमरुणाभं त्रिनयनं
कुचाभ्यामानम्रं कुटिलशशिचूडालमकुटम्॥

tvayā hṛtvā vāmaṁ vapur aparitṛptena manasā
śarīrārdhaṁ śambhor aparam api śaṅke hṛtam abhūt ।
yad etat tvadrūpaṁ sakalam aruṇābhaṁ trinayanaṁ
kucābhyām ānamraṁ kuṭila śaśi cūḍāla makuṭam ॥

śamboḥ vāmaṁ vapuḥ — the left (half of the) body of Śiva; *tvayā hṛtvā* — by You absorbed, taken over; *aparitṛptena manasā* — unsatisfied in mind; *aparam api śarīra ardhaṁ* — the other half of the body also; *hṛtam abhūt (iti) śaṅke* — became absorbed, (thus) I surmise; *yat etat tvad rūpaṁ* — therefore, this Your form; *tri nayanaṁ* — three-eyed; *kucābhyām ānamraṁ* — slightly bent by twin breasts; *kuṭila śaśi cūḍāla makuṭam* — wearing curved-crescent-bedecked crown; *sakalam aruṇābham* — (became) wholly of magenta glory

Absorbing the left half of the body of Śiva and unsatisfied in mind still,
The other, I surmise, became absorbed also; therefore,
This Your form, having three eyes and bent by twin breasts,
Wearing a curved crescent-bedecked crown, became of magenta glory.

The cancellation of the worshipper and the worshipped is accomplished by virtue of grace between counterparts having different value grades. Each layer is to be removed, one after the other, in a certain epistemological and methodological order, before we can understand how a reality that is beyond the four dimensions could be revealed to view, when shorn of all that is extraneous to the situation.

In this verse Pārvatī, the wife, appears to be devouring her husband alive. When this act of mutual absorption or cancellation attains to its full limit, what remains of Śiva, in vague outline, are the thin crescent moon and three eyes, immersed in the pale magenta halo or glory of the Goddess. On the part of the Goddess, what remains of the eternal feminine principle are the twin breasts, which are so ponderous by the weight of their own responsibility of motherhood that they make her body bent. Her own body is completely dissolved in terms of an all-pervading magenta, dispersed in infinite space, and thus made equally magenta in content everywhere. It is as thin and as tender in consistency, in existential terms, as the mathematical crescent of a subsistential order, against which the vaporous cloud of colour is to be cancelled out. The three eyes are retained as belonging both to the onlooker as well as the one looked upon, interchangeably and indifferently. It is the third eye, through which the thinnest aspect of the vertical parameter is to pass as an eternal inner witness, that is common to both Śiva and Pārvatī.

When scrutinized more closely, these four lines reveal the overall epistemological or cosmological dimensions that even modern physicists are beginning to recognize. The first line promotes us from a one-dimensional to a two-dimensional perspective as a horizontal line that is being cancelled from the right to the left, as when we travel from real to imaginary or positive to negative numbers.

If one goes to a shop and asks for ten oranges and does not pay for five of them, the value of these five oranges is seen to be negative, because one still owes the shopkeeper some money. The five oranges that have been paid for can be eaten with greater satisfaction. Such is the value gradation to be understood here. In the second line, we notice that instead of paying the debt, the Goddess, insists on cancelling it. The 'shopkeeper' who is being refused payment is not a stranger or outside person, but represents her dear husband, Śiva himself, who is being bodily consumed by the wife out of all kindness. The debt is thus being cancelled at the second level, of virtuality.

What remains is the verticalized version of Śiva and Pārvatī, not of the order of mere cancellable equations arithmetically understood, but in terms of a purer three or four-dimensional context of higher mathematics. Such is what we find in integral, differential or infinitesimal calculus, which require higher powers of abstraction and generalization. The operations take place in the form of thinner perimeters or asymptotic curves cutting across the parameter at different levels. Cantor's mathematics also admits of one-to-one correspondence between many grades of infinite sets or ensembles. Points, curves and lines, all thinly visible through a magenta haze — which itself results from ultraviolet and infrared neutralizing each other on the side of real existence — are all meant to give us this finalized picture of the value of absolute Beauty to be shared in common between Śiva and Pārvatī, without any vestige of duality intervening between them.

The bending with breasts is highly suggestive of curves in calculus. The thin crescent would suggest infinitesimal variation. The parameter traverses the total situation, like the streak of lightning in verse twenty-one. The ocean of magenta can also be thought of as encroaching into the total field to obliterate all duality from below, as intended also in verse eighteen. We see that the crown is still retained in the picture. This is merely to mark the omega point of the total situation. The alpha point is to be understood and it will come into evidence when the process of absorption here is reversed and oriented negatively. The culmination is still marked by the magenta glory of the last line, which is not a point, but is meant to fill all space horizontally. The 'crescent-bedecked crown' is more fourth-dimensional or time-like than space-like. The whole picture results from an ascending dialectical process rather than a descending one.

Structural Analysis

The structural implications of this verse are sufficiently patent in the words themselves. First one abolishes the form of the left side of the god Śiva. The left half, when permeated by the negative

A. The plus of the horizontal dimension is first neutralized

B. Parity is bilaterally established between male and female resulting in an androgynous neutrality.

C. Finer negativity pervades upwards

D. Participation becomes complete in an absolute unitive sense when on a magenta glory ground the principle of absolute Beauty triumphs with monomarks both Śiva & Śakti

Absolute Principle becomes a magenta cloud still hanging low and darkening with rain water, making it heavy like the breasts of a mother. The cloud is real though not actual. The real which thus implies the actual or presupposes it, pervades further by gaining absolute parity with the right side which in turn also becomes real, though only virtual in a horizontal perspective. Actuality and virtuality are thus covered by a real magenta which combines dark or bright shades of the same Absolute Glory. From the negative alpha and zero points there is a penetration, percolation or participation neutralizing the positivity of the Absolute by its own negativity to result in the most neutral of all grades of magenta. Even the shade, and tints of greater or lesser saturation or brilliance are harmonized in the maturation of the absolute quality implied in the full magenta. In the third stage of this silent and neutralizing penetration of the basic counterparts within the Absolute, all is absorbed except the most thinly mathematical numerator factors and the most significantly ontological feature represented by the mother's milk. The reference to the recumbent figure shows how necessity, generosity and humility go together. The kind mother is proud only in the name of Śiva but humble and kind in herself.

24

जगत् सूते धाता हरिरवति रुद्रः क्षपयते
तिरस्कुर्वन्नेतत् स्वमपि वपुरीशस्तिरयति ।
सदापूर्वः सर्वं तदिदमनुगृह्णाति च शिव-
स्तवाज्ञामालम्ब्य क्षणचलितयोर्भ्रूलतिकयोः ॥

jagat sūte dhātā harir avati rudraḥ kṣapayate
tiraskurvann etat svam api vapur īśas tirayati ।
sadā pūrvaḥ sarvaṁ tad idam anugṛhṇāti ca śivas
tavājñām ālambya kṣaṇa calitayor bhrūlatikayoḥ ॥

dhātā jagat sūte — Brahmā creates the world; *hariḥ avati* — Viṣṇu preserves; *rudraḥ kṣapayate* — Śiva destroys; *etat tiraskurvan svam vapuḥ api* — negating this and even his own body; *īśaḥ tirayati* — the Lord fades out; *sadā pūrvaḥ* — (he who has) eternity for prefix; *śivaḥ* — Śiva; *tat sarvaṁ idam* — all that (which) is here; *tava kṣaṇa calitayoḥ* — from Your instantly vibrating pair; *bhrū latikayoḥ* — of eyebrow-twigs; *ājñām ālambya* — obeying the order; *anugṛhṇāti ca* — (he) also blesses

Brahmā creates the world, Viṣṇu protects, Śiva destroys,
Negating all this and his own body, the Lord fades out;
Thus what results — Śiva who has eternity for prefix (Sadāśiva),
He blesses too, obeying the order derived from Your instantly vibrating eyebrow-twigs.

This verse, placed in its correct epistemological perspective, views the same process as in the previous verse, but from a partially revised perspective. Here we go from the side of causes to the side of effects. Thus, when we say that Brahmā creates, the reasoning process normally travels from the cause or source of creation, which is below, to a higher level where the effects of creation are more pluralistic or multiple. This function of creation, represented by Brahmā, can be structurally imagined to be like a tree. When this process of creation has gone far enough, the divided multiplicity of entities creates a (horizontal) firm ground for human actions and reactions to operate upon, through which individuals could promote themselves further in the vertical scale of values. This is the Viṣṇu world of graded value stratifications, cutting through which, at right angles, each man or woman attains to life's fulfilment, each according to one's desires or just deserts. In every sentient being capable of aspiring for spiritual progress, one could imagine a vertical parameter cutting through the horizontal, sleeping Viṣṇu-world, to the vertical Śiva-world.

Beyond these Viṣṇu stratifications of graded life-purposes lies the pinnacle point from which Śiva descends, flame in hand, to burn the various value cities, so as to bring balance again between creation and its inevitable opposite. Śiva, conceived as the pinnacle of the situation, is not a mere abstraction, but participates in existence through Pārvatī, with whom he shares his own body as the androgynous god *ardha nārī īśvara* (half-woman-god). Their relation here is one of back-to-back double correction, and not one of mere horizontal importance. Thus, participating with his own counterpart at the zero point and sharing the horizontality, though only through the magenta of the previous verse, he is here represented as being interested in abolishing even this thinnest of absolute substances. This is what is indicated in the second line where Śiva fades out from the third to the fourth dimension. He attains to greater heights of abstraction and generalization, when the term 'Sadāśiva' more aptly applies to him, in his present, more exalted condition, than just Śiva as an agent who destroys the second-dimensional world.

If this process of exaltation of Śiva should be accentuated further, even the various value worlds would stand in danger of being abolished altogether, leaving nothing by which the soul of man could attain its purpose. Life has to be significant, if nothing else. Any philosophy that does not retain this, as the last residue at least, and robs life of all its significance or purpose, becomes a philosophy that is empty of consolation and cancels its own *raison d'être.* Vedanta does not aim at such an ultimate bankruptcy of significance or purpose which other philosophies more thinly speculate, such as lukewarm 'may be/may be not' attitudes — or other speculative systems which do not go beyond paradoxes to purposefulness in life — might claim to do. It is to avoid the total bankruptcy of purpose that the vine-like eyebrows of the Goddess have the all-important role of saving the situation. She does not show her concern in any overtly gross form, but Śiva can see from her vibrating eyebrows that she is highly concerned about the possible destruction of all her progeny in the form of created beings. She, in principle, is in charge of all of them, and she cannot deny her own proper function. The world has to go on as it was in the beginning, now and for ever, without end.

The blessing in the fourth line is to be treated as the combined operation or function of the rays of Śiva and Pārvatī together, with no element of separation, in keeping with Advaita Vedanta.

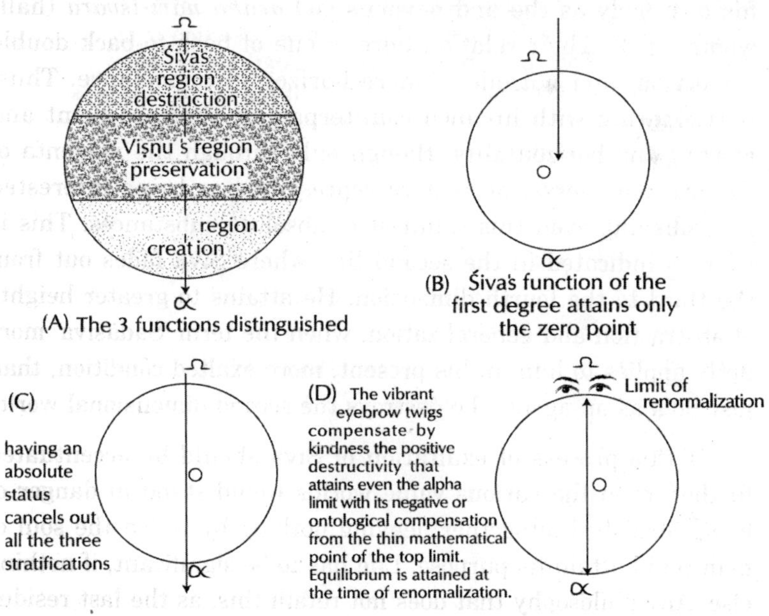

Structural Analysis

In the previous verses the neutralizing process proceeded from the left or the actual side of the total structural ground and encroached into the virtual. Thus it was from an alpha point that normalization proceeded ascendingly till all but the two eyes of Śiva and the middle eye finally, were attained by the normalizing process that pervaded and engulfed all within its scope of a total magenta glory. The mathematically thin crescent moon marked the limit of the omega point where a neutralization was attained, balancing plus and minus vertical factors. Compensation could take place in a reversed order and the destructive positive factor could descend instead of magenta ascending to abolish all but the ultimate limit. When balanced there is complementarity of mutual saturation and a normalization is attained which is one of the many possible or probable instances in abstracted and generalized terms. The real can never be abolished because of its rich ontological content. At the omega point it was the crescent moon and the three eyes that together marked the point of ontological saturation. Here in the next verse, it is the negentropic osmotic process that attains its limit with its feminine maximal limit of the vibrating eyebrows of the absolute value of Beauty. The process of absolute destruction from above must have a limit as thin in its status as the crescent moon. Ontology is negative and teleology as eternal becoming is positive. Double negation has to have double assertion to correct or compensate it. Thus the vibrating eyebrows of the supreme principle of negativity becomes logically adequate for purposes of normalization without which the content of the Absolute can evaporate into empty nothingness.

25

त्रयाणां देवानां त्रिगुणजनितानां तव शिवे
भवेत् पूजा पूजा तव चरणयोर्या विरचिता ।
तथा हि त्वत्पादोद्वहनमणिपीठस्य निकटे
स्थिता ह्येते शश्वन्मुकुलितकरोत्तंसमकुटाः ॥

trayāṇāṁ devānāṁ triguṇa janitānāṁ tava śive
bhavet pūjā pūjā tava caraṇayor yā viracitā ।
tathā hi tvat pādodvahana maṇipīṭhasya nikaṭe
sthitā hy ete śaśvan mukulita karottaṁsa makuṭāḥ ॥

śive — O Consort of Śiva; *tava* — Yours; *triguṇa janitānāṁ* — originated from the three nature-modalities; *trayāṇāṁ devānāṁ* — of the three gods; *yā pūjā viracitā* — which worship is offered; *sā pūjā bhavet* — that alone would be worship; *tava caraṇayoḥ* — of Your twin feet; *tathā hi* — it is indeed so; *ete* — these (gods); *tvat pādodvahana maṇi pīṭhasya nikaṭe* — standing beside Your gem-bedecked footstool; *śaśvat* — eternally; *mukulita karottaṁsa makuṭāḥ* — joining their palms, bud-like, above their crowns; *sthitaḥ hi* — standing indeed

Of the three gods, who are originated from Your three nature-modalities,
Their worship of You, O Consort of Śiva, would alone be worship
Offered to Your twin feet; it is indeed thus when they do so,
Standing eternally beside Your gem-decked footstool, joining bud-like their hands well above their crowns.

There are two alternative grades of worship referred to within the limits of this verse. The three gods Brahmā, Viṣṇu and Śiva are represented in the first half of the verse as worshipping properly, but this is not good enough in the light of the alternative kind of worship mentioned in the second half. When life interests fall within the range or amplitude of hedonistic or relativistic interests, they can be said to be performing proper or correct worship according to Vedic norms. But there is an epistemological, methodological and axiological difference when the same adoration is performed as described in the latter half of the verse, standing around a footstool and raising their worshipful hands to the highest omega point. They are reaching from fully hierophantic levels to the limits of the hypostatic.

The correctness of the puja depends upon the fact that it is performed by representatives of three sets of values, within which life moves within a Vedic frame of reference, and could not be called anything other than a proper puja. But it is not enough if they just get pass marks in the examination. There is still scope for further revision of this correct puja, so as to transcend values limited to the nature modalities recognizable as the three *guṇa*s. It is Vedic ritualism that, limited to the world of relativistic values, comes under the category of hedonistic pleasure. Heaven is filled with such items of value, and heavenly values form a system wherein the three gods are also generated out of the three nature modalities. Thus, in this verse, they are said to be born as effects from the three nature modalities (*triguṇa janitānām*).

Brahmā is the *sāttvik* god of orthodox Vedic values. Viṣṇu represents the action proper to a king or a ruler, which brings up the middle stratum of the set-up, as we have seen in the first and second verses of this poem. As for Śiva, he is known to be an *akula* (a man of no social status) in the context of Vedism. His antagonism to Vedic sacrifices is proved by his not being invited to the sacrifice made by his father-in-law, Dakṣa. Protesting againt this insult, the daughter of Dakṣa, who is Śiva's wife, burns herself in the same sacrificial flames. Śiva thus belongs to the opposite side to that of Brahmā, and his function is also diametrically opposed to the function of creation represented by Brahmā.

To picture the situation in this verse we could imagine a crystal globe within which the crowned figures of these three gods are seen to be bending with a horizontalized elliptical distortion as they are offering their adoration to the central principle of Beauty. This is the proper Vedic attitude, where the hedonistic values of the three *guṇa*s are still operative. Sometimes such a set-up is referred to as *saguṇa brahman* or *apara brahman*, which is the lower, immanent value to be equated with *brahman*.

Vedanta does not think in terms of heavenly values, because the alternating process of samsara does not stop completely by going to heaven. One returns to the same worlds of hedonistic values when he descends again from heaven to live comfortably in a suburbia on earth. This is brought out in many places in the Upaniṣads and the Bhagavadgītā. Vedanta believes in a full dose of absolutism, which will cure one once and for all from a recrudescence or lapse into the same malarial, relativistic love of pleasure, whether in heaven or on earth. Emancipation, without any possibility of relapse, is the model held up by Upaniṣadic teaching; one should not be born again, irrespective of heavenly or earthly values. Such values have to be transcended though not rejected. Nobody should think a comfortable life should be wilfully avoided in favour of austerities that might torture the life within us.

Transcending inclusively without contradiction is the Advaitic doctrine that is being underlined here. The two alternative pictures of worship in this verse are to be comparatively understood. The former represents the Vedic set-up within the scope of the three nature modalities — the pure (*sattva*), the active (*rajas*), and the tragic (*tamas*) — which are still fully operative. The gods themselves, or at least their crowns, as they bend over the Beauty principle at the centre, have generic relationship with the three modalities at the lower point of reference. The crown is the limit of the effect side while their own feet mark the cause or source as stemming out of the three modality principles of nature. The Vedantic alternative to this slightly horizontal version is to be imagined as an ellipse accentuated vertically, like a rugby football held with the narrow end upward. While the Vedic set-up is good enough, this is still better. It is like saying that it is very good to pass the B.A. examination, but it is better to pass the M.A. examination. This justifies the reference to the first kind of devotion being true worship only when it is done as described in the second half of the verse.

The Bhagavadgītā brings out this same idea in Chapter XII where it discusses *saguṇa* (qualified) worship of *brahman*, as against *nirguṇa* worship that transcends the three *guṇa*s, or *triguṇa atīta*. There is a further reference in the Gītā making this point unequivocally clear, when Arjuna is told by Krishna that the Vedas are under the sway of values within the scope of the three *guṇa*s (*traiguṇya viṣayā*). Arjuna is asked to transcend Vedic values in favour of the more correct Advaitic position of the Gītā teaching.

The gods are eternally standing, in the last line, bent in adoration beside the gem-decked footstool at the bottom point. At the same time, with their bud-like hand gestures, they are directing their adoration to the omega point 'well above their crowns'. This is how hedonism and relativism are to be transcended by the full blast of absolutism held up as a model in these verses. The lower form is not excluded, but it is fully, inclusively transcended. One should not purposely choose a bed of nails if a spring cot is available, or live among scorpions and serpents in a forest, if the place could be made less distracting for mediation. *Rājasa tyāga* (willful rejection) is not true renunciation as understood in the correct yogic context of Vedanta. The theory of the three modalities is completely expounded in the Gītā in Chapter XIV, called *guṇatrayavibhāga yoga* (the unitive way of transcending the three nature modalities). The word 'alone' in the second line would seem to suggest that such worship alone would be correct in the context to which all worship belongs, because worship itself becomes extraneous in the context of Vedanta. The difference is as between being dressed properly and being completely unconscious of proper dress convention at all.

The 'twin feet' of the third line could be placed structurally at the centre of the total situation. Passing on to the fourth line, however, the gem-decked footstool would represent the feet, but with greater ontological richness, though this negative aspect is only to be cancelled out against the bud-like folded hands of the gods held above their crowns. The word 'eternally' suggests the heightened absolutist context of the second, Vedantic, alternative recommended here. The reference to gems in the footstool is to raise its value as a hierophantic presence.

Structural Analysis

The absolute Ground is a matrix in which no structural outlines are seen. The three gods representing three functional aspects have to be viewed under two different sets of perspectives. In the first two lines of the verse the horizontalized perspective is presented. This could be said to have a momentary spatialized reference. The element of pure time does not enter therein. One cancels out here horizontally the difference between the source and the term. Something like the law of inverse squares operates here when we are asked to juxtapose the vague matrix of source in the mother principle against the spatialized manifestation of the same with gradations of pure, passionate or dark as represented by each of the gods of the trinity or threefold functional factors. In the second half of the same verse the words 'eternally standing' would at once indicate that there is a pure time reference rather than a spatialized one. The gem-decked footstool has to be placed at the central locus of the *bindusthāna*.

Having done so, one recognizes that by decorating the footstool with gems, the author suggests that the central locus, though a footstool and therefore hierophantic, gets a hypostatic revaluation in status. When thus neutralized, it gets an absolutist status which becomes the fit object of worship by the functional demiurges. This becomes all the more true when they stand before it eternally in bent adoration, holding their palms united like lotus buds above their crowns. They then succeed in cancelling the total absolute Value that they objectively represent against the pure subjective value of the beauty of the Goddess. Outer conflict and inner conflict are thus neutralized and when thus fully nullified by mutual cancellation, one who participates in such a situation himself also attains the Absolute. Total understanding yields wholesale or total result which is no other than realizing the highest value of the ever adorable Absolute.

26

विरिञ्चिः पञ्चत्वं व्रजति हरिराप्नोति विरतिम्
विनाशं कीनाशो भजति धनदो याति निधनम्।
वितन्द्री माहेन्द्री विततिरपि संमीलित दृशा
महासंहारेऽस्मिन् विहरति सति त्वत्पतिरसौ॥

viriñciḥ pañcatvaṁ vrajati harir āpnoti viratiṁ
vināśaṁ kīnāśo bhajati dhanado yāti nidhanam ।
vitandrī māhendrī vitatir api saṁmīlita dṛśā
mahāsaṁhāre'smin viharati sati tvat patir asau ॥

viriñciḥ pañcatvaṁ vrajati — Brahmā regains his (pure) quintuple nature; *hariḥ viratim āpnoti* — Viṣṇu becomes passionless; *kīnāśaḥ vināśaṁ bhajati* — the god of Death meets destruction; *dhanadaḥ nidhanam yāti* — the god of Wealth courts bankruptcy; *vitandrī māhendrī vitatiḥ api* — the great Indra becomes functionless; *saṁmīlita dṛśā* — with half-shut eyes; *asmin mahā saṁhāre* — in this great doom; *sati* — O Constant Spouse; *asau tvat patiḥ* — this Your lord; *viharati* — sports

Brahmā regains his (pure) quintuple nature, Viṣṇu becomes passionless,
The god of Death destruction meets, the god of Wealth becomes bankrupt,
The great Indra becomes functionless with half-shut eyes;
In this great doom, He sports, O Constant Spouse, Your Lord alone.

Between the three verses, twenty-four, twenty-five and twenty-six, there is a two-sided dynamism that we can recognize as pertaining to a world process on a certain kind of world ground, which the philosophy of the Bhagavadgītā (VIII.18) calls *avyakta* (unmanifested). Everything has a vague, amorphous, or mathematical status at a given time anteriorly. It assumes a colourful and real form with different perspectives in a middle stage. In a final stage reabsorption again takes place. Besides the Bhagavadgītā, Cartesian philosophy can also understand a cyclically alternating process with these three phases as taking place between what it calls *res cogitans* and *res extensa*. Thus, we could have the same basic reference in terms of Cartesian correlates instead of by description; *res cogitans* would be a vertical perspective, and *res extensa* the alternative, horizontal version of the same. Bergson would prefer to distinguish them as time-like and space-like counterparts.

Vedanta is familiar with a similar theory, having a double perspective in the manner of viewing the status of the elementals. Professor O. Lacombe describes this theoretical process called *pañcīkaraṇa*, as simply as possible:

> The great elements do not enter as such into the composition of individual realities, but undergo first a sort of shaking-up which is called quintipartition — *pañcīkaraṇa*. Each of them is divided by the creator into two parts, and one of these two halves again into four parts. Each one of these quarters is then mixed with the half that has been left intact of each of the four other elements. It thus results that each element composes itself thereafter as follows: One-half element pure, plus one-eighth of each of the four other elements. It is these composite elements which serve for the constitution of individual things. The dominant proportion of the primary element safeguards its authenticity. But the adjunction of the other element explains the participation of things with all other things and explains certain anomalies of perception.[1]

When the elements remain in their pure self-transparent form, they consist of *tanmātra*s (entities-in-themselves). Manifestation, in realistic terms, takes place when these rays are brought under

1. Lacombe, O. *L' Absolu Selon le Vedanta*, Paris, 1937, our translation.

a perspective by which they attain different degrees of opacity or transparency between themselves.

In the world of light, various interference effects occur when double-polarized light is brought into interplay; depending on the angle of incidence or refraction and due to diffraction or dispersal of light, interesting interference figures are revealed. There is a mesh or lattice which obstructs or permits light waves of different wavelengths to pass through crystals, depending on whether the obstruction is placed at right angles or not. Without entering into the intricacies of such optical phenomena, we shall merely say that Vedanta has long adhered to the theory of *pañcīkaraṇa*. Horizontally perceived, the elements show a heterogeneity between the five of them, but when the *tanmātra*s, as basic elemental units, are rearranged serially and vertically — after being subjected to the process called 'quintuplication' or 'quintipartition' — they attain to a certain homogenized and serial continuity or transparency along the vertical axis. Elementals, when remaining in a crude state, give a horizontal outlook to the world of manifestation. When subjected to quintuplication, they become transparent in themselves. As in television, it is two sets of waves intersecting at right angles, on the basis of an orthogonal matrix or lattice consisting of small rectangular units, that results in the picture effect. Even in chemistry we can either see the elements arranged in a vertical series according to the periodic law, or we could study the properties of chemicals by reactions in the laboratory. The periodic law gives us a verticalized perspective, while the actual properties of chemicals are presented to the senses as a horizontalized reference.

Verse twenty-four is a reference to the positive creative process, but verse twenty-six presents the same picture as a negative process. In verse twenty-four the balancing factor comes from the Devī's vine-like eyebrows, while in verse twenty-six the Devī herself lends her reality to keep her husband continuously alive even as a thin parameter. In verse twenty-five we find a double picture, as seen through two kinds of translucency; one in which the horizontal prevails over the vertical, and the other in which the vertical prevails over the horizontal. Creation and dissolution are brackets facing opposite ways, traversed by the parameter that represents pure becoming, independent of time or space.

With these preliminaries in our mind, we have to understand that the figure of Brahmā, as a member of the Hindu trinity, is the first to be put into the melting pot, because of the quintuplication to which all the elementals are going to be subjected in the negative process that is being presented in this verse. In the case of Viṣṇu, the effect of such a negative process is to make him passionless, because the passions absorb each other without finding horizontal expression. He is subjected to a state of neutralization or normalization at the central stratum, wherein alone he is operative. When we apply the same cancellation of tendencies to the principle of death, we see that the very meaning of death cancels itself out by the double negation involved. Indra is a god at the stratum where hypostatic values prevail. He is also struck by a certain verticalized immobility, by which all his horizontalized tendencies are balanced against their opposites. The result is that he remains immobile, as if in a picture, neither opening his eyes too wide to show any curiosity, nor fully unaware of the interests with which he is surrounded.

This state of dissolution into the original amorphous transparency of the elementals in themselves is called *pralaya* (merging back into pure and primary formless absolutist status). This picture is not unlike the picture of doomsday, except that in the idea of doomsday the dissolution has a futuristic or apocalyptic status. The deluge of doomsday could be treated as complementary to the present image. The prophetic religions give primacy to a doomsday or Day of Judgement, but the antediluvian picture is also a part of the Old Testament. Whatever the theory involved, all that we have to know here is that, in the form of an amorphous matrix, or in the form of crystals once again dissolved, we can get different perspectives, three of which are given in verses twenty-four, twenty-five and twenty-six. Many other perspectives could also be visualized without violating the requirements of the Science of the Absolute. When we take a normalized position, the result is the one stated in the Bhagavadgītā, where Krishna tells Arjuna that the kings and the armies are not there except in *brahman*, and that they are not going to be created thereafter either. This is the prefectly normalized picture, based on which we could get as many varied perspectives as we like, all of which, however, have to be put within the limits indicated here without contradiction. A cryptocrystalline homogenous rock is as good as a rock as a porphyritic one (full of different kinds of well-formed crystals put together). The Absolute is the matrix or mother liquid for all of them.

What we have to note here is whether the process is a positive or a negative one. The status of the Absolute, represented by the vertical parameter, remains unaffected and the same throughout, as in the case of the entropy of the universe tending to be a zero or attaining to a maximum. *Brahman*, the Absolute, as a correlating thread passing through all possible values, is familiar to us in the Gītā (VII. 7) which says that everything in the universe is threaded through by Krishna, the absolute Value of all values. Narayana Guru also identifies the Absolute as God and compares him to the highly mathematical dimension called the depth of the sea, in his *Daivadaśakam* (verse 4). 'Fire cannot burn this (parameter), nor water wet it . . . the sword does not cleave it', as the Gītā says (II. 23, 24). This eternal and changeless parameter or line is what represents the Absolute as nearly as we could think of it in any concrete terms.

We have added the word 'pure' in brackets in the first line to show that it is a negative process that is taking place here, rather than one of positive creation. By saying that the god of Death meets destruction, we are only indulging in a tautology. We neither improve Death nor degrade him in any way. He just marks the zero point by being doubly corrected.

Concerning the reference to the god of wealth becoming bankrupt: wealth functions by getting or spending, which are horizontal processes. Without these two actions the bank becomes sealed against the public, although this does not mean that the bank no longer has any money.

27

जपो जल्पः शिल्पं सकलमपि मुद्राविरचना
गतिः प्रादक्षिण्यक्रमणमशनाद्याहुतिविधिः ।
प्रणामः संवेशः सुखमखिलमात्मार्पणदृशा
सपर्यापर्यायस्तव भवतु यन्मे विलसितम् ॥

japo jalpaḥ śilpaṁ sakalam api mudrā viracanā
gatiḥ prādakṣiṇya kramaṇam aśanādyāhuti vidhiḥ ।
praṇāmaḥ saṁveśaḥ sukham akhilam ātmārpaṇadṛśā
saparyā paryāyas tava bhavatu yanmevilasitam ॥

japaḥ jalpaḥ — incantations, mutterings; *sakalam śilpaṁ api* — all actions done by hands; *mudrā viracanā* — ritual hand gestures; *gatiḥ* — roaming gait; *prādakṣiṇya kramaṇam* — circumambulation; *aśanā ādi āhutividhiḥ* — food, etc. ritualistic fire-sacrifice; *samveśaḥ praṇāmaḥ* — inclination/lying down, prostrations; *sukham akhilam* — all (such) enjoyments; *me yat vilasitam* — what from me might shine forth; *ātmā arpaṇa dṛśā* — treated as coming within the scope of self-surrender; *tava saparyā paryāyaḥ bhavatu* — let them be synonyms for worship of You

Incantations, mutterings; ritual acts, hand gestures; gait,
Circumambulation; food, offerings; inclination, adoration by lying down —
All such enjoyments, as coming within the scope of self-surrender,
And thus synonyms for worship of You, let such be what from me might shine forth.

Worship is a form of self-surrender. Such self-surrender yields joy to the person thus surrendering. Thousands of temples in this world, especially those based on ritualistic idolatry in South India, have various forms of ritualistic activities which could all be thought of as belonging to one ensemble of ritualistic actions, in the same way as Wittgenstein would bring all aspects of logical discourse together under the one reference of 'word games'. Śaṅkara wants to find a synonym which will inclusively cover the whole wide range of possible ritualistic actions that an elaborately trained Tāntric priest might employ before an idol within the sacred sanctum of a temple, under the inclusive reference of *saparyā paryāya*.

The synonym and antonym could then be cancelled ontologically into the joy of self-surrender, which would then be an absolute Value. What shines forth from the supplicant is to be cancelled ontologically against the value significance emanating from the idolatrous presence within the temple. When subjected to this double process, we get a reversible equation or reaction which is to be imagined as taking place between the idol and the worshipper prostrating before the idol. The items that express self-surrender in one form or another could be as varied as the outward forms of expression of devotion. But if we should put a circle around the whole lot of them, amounting to the same joy of self-surrender vis-a-vis the non-Self value of the idol itself — treating the former as an inclusive ensemble representing an experience of joy in the act of worship — a fully cancellable situation results.

The Self is equated with the non-Self and vice versa. Śaṅkara refuses to take any notice of the individual gestures, meaning of *mudrās*, or attitudes, however varied they might be. He, as an Advaitin, is not interested in Tantra for its own sake. He has his own correct methodology, by which he would find the synonymous counterparts capable of reduction logically, semantically, or even mathematically, into terms that could cancel out into the pure value notion represented by the Absolute. In the light of such a cancellation, it is easy to see that the authorship by Śaṅkara of a Tāntric text — which has been treated as questionable even by such scholars as Woodroffe and Brown, not to mention more recent Tāntric commentators of this text — does not present any problem to us at all. Śaṅkara is not interested in Tantra at the expense of Advaita. On the contrary, Tantra is revalued and restated, as is so clearly evident in this verse, to serve the purpose and heighten the doctrine of pure Advaita Vedanta, for which Śaṅkara has always taken a consistently uncompromising stand.

It is because many scholars, both Indian and Western, have failed to see how Śaṅkara's protolinguistic non-verbose approach presented here is fully compatible with the more verbose or metalinguistic version of Advaita found in his commentaries that the whole suspicion about his authorship has arisen. While all the evidence taken as a whole tends to suggest Śaṅkara as the only possible author, punditry and pedantry at present have conspired to call into question such clear indications as presented in this verse because of their own inability to see the same doctrines as that of the *bhāṣya*s, when presented here in a protolinguistic form. The difference between these two forms of expression is ignored by pundits even to this day. The available editions of the *Saundaryalaharī* do not succeed even in giving us a bare gist of the sense of these verses, whether for genuine appreciation or at least in the name of academic or artistic dilettantism. We have said that, as far as the authorship of Śaṅkara is concerned, the allusion 'this Dravidian child' in verse seventy-five leaves no room for vain speculation, except when pseudo-orthodoxy enters into the picture to complicate matters beyond simple recognition. In our comments we have tried to take a simpler view without getting lost in the great forest of words, which Śaṅkara himself takes care to warn us against in his *Vivekacūḍāmaṇi*.

In this verse, then, we can easily see how Śaṅkara takes care to reduce Tantra in terms of an equation between two aspects of the Self, exactly as in the case of the great dicta (*mahāvākya*s), which together constitute the keystone of the doctrine of Advaita Vedanta. The purpose of Śaṅkara in this verse is patently clear, and also puts the question of his authorship beyond all disputes. This is too precious and valuable a work to be lost to the disrespectfulness of pundits and scholars.

28

सुधामप्यास्वाद्य प्रतिभयजरामृत्युहरिणीं
विपद्यन्ते विश्वे विधिशतमखाद्या दिविषदः।
करालं यत् क्ष्वेलं कबलितवतः कालकलना
न शंभोस्तन्मूलं तव जननि ताटङ्कमहिमा ॥

sudhām apy āsvādya pratibhaya jarā mṛtyuhariṇīṁ
vipadyante viśve vidhi śatamakhādyā diviṣadaḥ ।
karālaṁ yat kṣvelaṁ kabalitavataḥ kālakalanā
na śaṃbhos tan mūlaṁ tava janani tāṭaṅka mahimā ॥

pratibhaya jarā mṛtyu hariṇīṁ — so potent against fear, old age, and death; *sudhām āsvādya api* — even on partaking of nectar; *vipadyante* — they reach their doom; *viśve* — all; *vidhi śatamakha ādya* — Brahmā, Indra and others; *diviṣadaḥ* — the gods; *karālaṁ yat kṣvelaṁ* — that fearful poison; *kabalitavataḥ* — even on swallowing; *kāla kalana na (asti)* — time's becoming is not operative; *śambhoḥ* — for Śiva; *tanmūlam* — the root cause of which; *tava janani tāṭaṅka mahimā* — O Mother (is) the glory/power of Your ear ornaments

Even on partaking of nectar, so potent against fear, old age and death,
They reach their doom, all such gods as Brahmā and Indra;
On even swallowing that terrible superpoison, for Śiva, time's function is not operative:
The source here being the power of Your ear ornaments.

Time, or duration, is the central concept on which the status of Śiva is brought into relief as an eternal principle — beyond the reach even of the process of becoming — in his pure personal value, as against other gods who are all subject to phenomenal factors in a graded epistemological order. Magnetic fields operate on lesser levels with other dimensions than that of high voltage electricity. Śiva's function could become still more absolutist, and cancel further vestiges of duality, until immobility and mobility exist together, beyond the taint of the weakness of the human mind to create its own paradoxes. Paradoxes vanish when pure absolutism becomes possible to the human mind, by getting as far removed as possible from relativistic and hedonistic considerations of visible or intelligible values. Śiva represents this high point, where he reigns eternally supreme, for himself, in himself, by himself and through himself. It is this Advaitic doctrine that is intended to be underlined in this verse with the help of the different functionaries or demiurges, who also belong to the same set-up when viewed from a perspective of lesser voltage, as it were, than what applies to Śiva himself.

The first two lines take cognition of Brahmā and Indra, the most flagrantly vitalistic demiurges, to whom good, nourishing food and tonics are very important to make them continue in vitality and normal health. One can become sleek by drinking meat broth, but the next fever might wash down the drain all the health thus gained. Life has within its core a source of energy which can defy doctors' prescriptions, and assert itself in spite of the grave mistakes that doctors may commit. In this sense, we could say that the patient continues to live in spite of the havoc caused by pills or medicines.

Nectar is the natural nourishment of the gods, but Śiva is capable of surviving even a superpoison and remaining in a fully operative form according to his own function, which is a vertical and not a horizontal one. Transporting a lorry-load of building stones from one place to another is an example of horizontal function, while electromagnetic transmission of signals from ship to ship is an example of vertical function. The first must be kept up by crude fuel in the combustion engine, while the other belongs to a fourth-dimensional order. Between these two extremes of horizontal and vertical functionings, we have to postulate the ordinary Śiva, of the same demiurge status as Indra and Brahmā, to understand why the power of the ear ornaments confers the final absolute status on Śiva who would have evaporated had he only represented his usual function as a fourth-dimensional principle of positive becoming. But by a process of double negation, operative at the positive limit, he is not only a 'mover', but an 'unmoved mover', as in the philosophy of Aristotle. The something that counters the exaggeration of the ascent, by making Śiva again descend from his high world of intelligibles to a more normal position at the core of the total value situation, is represented here by the Devī. Normal food would represent negative entropy and this guarantees the neutralization of too rapid a metabolic process which in the case of childbirth, for instance, would kill the mother. Entropy has to counter negentropy to establish equilibrium, as in thermodynamics. In this sense, the entropy of the universe tends to be zero. The total energy of the universe remains a constant according to the law of the conservation of energy. Here physics speaks nearly the same language as this verse. Killing human beings by too rapid a process of change through time is the function of the god of Death, called Kāla, personifying Time with a capital letter. Śiva represents a principle or a parameter cutting across the horizontal principle of death. He is beyond the reach of paradox as an 'unmoved mover'. It is in this sense that Time is non-operative in the case of Śiva.

If becoming is vertically positive, then non-becoming, countering its own mobility, is a function having its reference at the negative vertical limit. Such a negative limit is here the proper domain of the Goddess, although for normative purposes we would locate her position at the central zero point. Just as Śiva can ascend or descend from his norm, Pārvatī can also ascend or descend between the zero point and the alpha point. When Śiva and Pārvatī operate as complementary, compensatory and reciprocal functions, they properly cancel each other out into the value implied in this verse. The power of the ear ornaments, or the marital string placed on the neck of the Goddess has reference to its opposite whose source lies in the kind intention of Śiva, and has a one-to-one correspondence with it. It represents a potent factor of intelligent function, and whether the function is in the head or in the legs is not important. The limits of double negation could be at a level where it could operate both intelligently and effectively. In respect of the Goddess, the lower limit is more intuitive and more effective than the functions that could be attributed to the head of Śiva. The one-to-one correspondence between the two opposite tendencies has to be respected, whether placed in the head or in the feet. Duality is abolished when they are correctly cancelled out against each other. A topsy-turvydom, at first confusing to the beginner in structural language, has already been explained under verse eight.

How Śiva swallowed the superpoison is found in the story of the churning of the milk ocean, wherein also the female form of Mohinī acts as a saving factor. Here it is the ear ornament which is the principle of normalization.

29

किरीटं वैरिञ्चं परिहर पुरः कैटभभिदः
कठोरे कोटीरे स्खलसि जहि जम्भारिमकुटम्।
प्रणम्रेष्वेतेषु प्रसभमुपयातस्य भवनं
भवस्याभ्युत्थाने तव परिजनोक्तिर्विजयते॥

kirīṭaṁ vairiñcaṁ parihara puraḥ kaiṭabhabhidaḥ
kaṭhore koṭīre skhalasi jahi jambhāri makuṭam ।
praṇamreṣv eteṣu prasabham upayātasya bhavanaṃ
bhavasyābhyutthāne tava parijanoktir vijayate ॥

puraḥ vairiñcaṁ kirīṭaṁ parihara — remove Brahmā's crown from before; *kaiṭabha bhidaḥ* — of him who is called Viṣṇu (slayer of the *asura* Kaiṭabha); *kaṭhore koṭīre skhalasi* — you trip/stumble over (his) hard headgear; *jambhāri makuṭam jahi* — bypass Indra's crown; *eteṣu praṇamreṣu* — just as these (gods) remain inclining in front of You; *bhavanaṁ upayātasya* — having come home; *bhavasya* — Śiva's; *prasabham tava abhyutthāne* — on Your sudden rising; *parijana uktiḥ* — the words of (Your) retinue; *vijayate* — they win, reign (supreme)

'Remove Brahmā's crown from before, and of him called Viṣṇu,
You are going to hurt his hard headgear, bypass Indra's crown . . .'
As inclining in front of You, they remain at that very moment, for him on his homecoming,
You are about to rise; such the words of Your retinue, they do reign supreme.

Verses twenty-nine and thirty both represent more normalized versions, before the punctuation between sections of ten verses, and passes over to another aspect of the Absolute as a significant value. We have to imagine here the same beautiful palace with its groves and gardens and flowering trees on a gem-island, first mentioned in verse three and developed further in verse eight, and the Goddess sitting in full imperial glory within a mandala in an architectural motif both circular and square. She sits in the centre, evidently enthroned in all her absolutist Beauty and magnificence. We can put into this same picture all those attending on Śiva, who belong to her personal retinue, on one side of the total situation. On the other side, there are the female attendants who are maidens-in-waiting for the private requirements of the Empress herself. We can also imagine armed guards for her protection, distributed more peripherally within the four walls or even outside. The central room represents the sacred sanctuary where the goddess of Beauty presides, commanding the total and complex set-up of her retinue. We could imagine the three demiurges, who have figured consistently in many previous verses, in the act of inclining, in one of the two alternative manners depicted in verse twenty-five. The vertical version is the one where the three modalities are transcended. The horizontal version is where their crowns are going to be hurt, as the verticalized phase is likely to be induced at any given moment, since it should be imagined that Śiva has just been sighted by the retainers outside as about to visit the Goddess in all her normal glory. Fanfare, trumpets and kettledrums could all be inserted into the picture as we like, according to personal taste, but the essence of the occasional moment is what is to be intuitively caught and understood here.

The first two lines of this verse are to be taken as the words coming from the mouths of the retinue surrounding the Goddess, who are concerned that proper dignity and importance be given to the Devī above all others. It is not the horizontal set-up of the Goddess that counts, but the words that ring above the total physical situation as a warning and important directive, although only intentional in status. The words rise above the totality of the important occasional moment, to be placed in an eternal present.

The three gods wear crowns of different grades of hardness or objectivity, on the side of effects. The conical crown generally has a gem marking its terminus point in the case of each of the gods, whose functions we already know. Viṣṇu's headgear is the hardest to transcend. Brahmā can be asked to take his crown away from where it can come into clash with that of the Devī, who is fully intending to rise but not actually doing so, still anticipating the homecoming of her Lord. The headgear of Indra is to be more lightly bypassed because he has only the status of a demiurge among demiurges. He is not an *īśvara*, but only a *deva*, still steeped in the world of hedonistic values. All these gods can be thought of as bending over the crown of the Devī herself in such a way as to obstruct the vertical path that the Devī's own crown-tip might have to cross. It is her verticality that is to be given primacy on this occasion, and the armed guards are in charge of precautions against possible untoward events. The demiurges might intrude their crowns, representing their pride, and obstruct the free passage of the absolute principle as it passes vertically when she rises to receive Śiva, who descends from the heights of his own mental horizon. The verticality attains its maximum when both are fused together into one parameter touching both the higher and the lower limits on the very occasion or moment of the eternal present, wherein absolute Beauty is about to triumph in its full glory. Intentionality here is as good as accomplished fact, so one should not ask whether the Devī actually rose from her seat or not. This is the perfect picture of absolutist occasionalism in which no brute event really takes place.

30

स्वदेहोद्भूताभिर्घृणिभिरणिमाद्याभिरभितः
निषेव्ये नित्ये त्वामहमिति सदा भावयति यः।
किमाश्चर्यं तस्य त्रिनयनसमृद्धिं तृणयतो
महासंवर्ताग्निर्विरचयति नीराजनविधिम्॥

sva dehodbhūtābhir ghr̥ṇibhir aṇimādyābhir abhitaḥ
niṣevye nitye tvām aham iti sadā bhāvayati yaḥ ।
kimāścaryaṁ tasya trinayana samr̥ddhiṁ tr̥ṇayato
mahā saṃvartāgnir viracayati nīrājana vidhim ॥

sva deha udbhūtābhiḥ — arising out of Your own body; *aṇimā ādyābhiḥ* — psychic powers beginning with atomicity; *ghr̥ṇibhiḥ* — from the rays which are; *abhitaḥ* — veiling, overcovering, surrounding; *niṣevye* — O One worthy of worship; *nitye* — O Eternal One; *tvām aham iti* — You in terms of oneself; *yaḥ sadā bhāvayati* — one who ever contemplates; *trinayana samr̥ddhiṁ tr̥ṇayataḥ* — all benefits from the three-eyed (Śiva) are worthless; *tasya* — for him; *mahā saṁvarta agniḥ* — the fire of doom; *nīrājana vidhim* — the light-waving rite; *viracayati* — performs; *kim āścaryaṁ* — what wonder

Out of the rays arising from Your proper body, representing psychic powers such as atomicity,
Attendant on You, O Eternal One, one who contemplates these in terms of oneself:
What wonder, for him, that all benefits from the three-eyed one should only be worth rejection,
And that the fire of doom should perform for him (*in turn*) *the light-waving rite.*

The ritualistic supplicant of this verse gets a reward which is much more than what he could expect from the standpoint of usual Tantra, when he is able to place himself before the absolute principle of these verses in keeping with the Advaitic attitude, in which the worshipper and the worshipped are treated as interchangeable terms in the context of the Self and the non-Self. The tables are turned unexpectedly and completely in his favour and the worshipper, instead of worshipping, is worshipped himself. Ordinarily, a believer in the efficacy of Tāntric ritualism places himself before an image, which is thought of as a presence. By concentrating on this presence, the worshipper will begin to participate in certain values radiating from the body of the Goddess, represented by the image being worshipped.

Favours are involved in all worship, except the Vedantic one. Such favours could include very base ones, such as praying for the defeat of a particular enemy, or praying for riches, not to speak of attracting women in order to make them obedient to one's wishes. These are lesser benefits which could apply, at best, to one or other of the two schools of Śakti worshippers in the context of Tantra, mantra and yantra. They are the Kaulins and the Samayins, the former being more left-handed (non-vedic) or ordinary than the latter. Even if such worshippers should belong to the most respectable of Śakti cults, we cannot imagine them as aspiring for benefits which only Upaniṣadic wisdom could make them aspire for. Even groups of believers belonging to a very superior and intelligent order could be expected to pray for those psychic powers which emanate from the body of the Goddess worshipped, which are the eight classically enumerated *siddhi*s, starting with *aṇimā* (minuteness or atomicity).

The Nyāya and Vaiśeṣika systems of Indian philosophy begin with the *paramāṇu* (an infinitesimal particle or atom), and not the Absolute, as the first category of significance in their system. We have a series of other values which could be built up in an ascending order with this atomic-particle reality as its starting point. Smallness would suggest at once bigness. *Brahman* is neither big nor small, but both at once. Lightness and heaviness can also be treated as the next pair in this ascending series of benefits known to anterior schools, lesser than what Vedanta represents as the final crowning position among them all, as Śaṅkara establishes elsewhere. The other psychic powers are classically recognized and are mentioned even in the *Amarakośa* lexicon. They are not particular to the Tāntric world but acceptable to Indian philosophy in general.

In the first line of this verse, the Devī's body is represented as the seat from where these psychic powers radiate, as their common source. They are like graded rays of light covering a broad spectrum of benefits which the worshipper can acquire for himself by continued meditation upon her. Such powers are the highest point to which an aspirant who is thinking of some kind of success in this world, which will make him important in the eyes of his fellow men, would normally expect to attain. This would apply to one who has not risen to a consciousness of the need for detachment or renunciation — as is normal to an aspirant for knowledge, and emancipation through it, as proper to the Upaniṣadic ideal — and would lead him into the world of personal benefits, which at best would only apply to some form of success in the public eye. The world beyond would be excluded, and although the gates of heaven might be open to him, the gate of salvation would be closed against him. One has to be able to contemplate values originating from the person of the Goddess, not only of a bodily order, but from a presence that combines and cancels physical and metaphysical values into the unitive terms of one absolute Value. The psychic powers are attendant on the person of the Goddess, biased somewhat on the physical rather than the psychic side of the personality. The prayer is thus for unilateral benefits which are only applicable to life here and not to the hereafter.

The fully instructed Advaita Vedantin, however, is able to take the revised position indicated in the second line. He does not think at all of psychic powers that will enhance his value as a spiritual man in this world. He takes the bolder and more correct stand of Vedanta, which gives primacy to the *ātman*, the Self, rather than to miscellaneous benefits, however rare, such as the *siddhis*. He thinks of establishing an equation with himself as one pole, with the absolute eternal Goddess as its counterpart.

Thus, in terms of the Self (*ātman*) there is established a bipolar participation between its further subdivisions, which are here the Self of the devotee and the non-Self that the Goddess represents. When these attain to homogeneity of status by continued contemplative wisdom disciplines, in keeping with Upaniṣadic teachings, there is no violation of any principle if we should turn the tables to say that the worshipper becomes himself worshippable to his own non-Self counterpart. Any one of the *mahāvākyā*s can do this trick of turning the tables completely in favour of the worshipper. When such a radical change takes place, the Vedantic supplicant would not any more be attracted by benefits for himself, however great, which even Śiva, on the numerator side of the gods, could deign to confer on him. It is not the body, but the positive counterpart, the body of the Goddess represented by Śiva, that can confer other-worldly benefits which are more spiritual than benefits proper to the body of the Goddess herself. These latter concern only the ontological Self, *siddhi*s that apply to life here. There is a corresponding series of psychic gifts of a more spiritual order, which Śiva can confer on behalf of the Devī from his own non-Self side. They have a one-to-one correspondence with the former series, starting with minute particles, which still refer to matter only. The benefits from Śiva can range upward instead of downward. He is interested in conferring salvation and not heaven.

The third line, therefore, rightly underlines that the intelligent Advaitin will not care for anything less than salvation, which is far beyond heaven. If by mistake Śiva should confer a benefit within the scope of heavenly values, the superior and proud Advaitin would naturally reject it, and one should not be surprised if he does so. He prays for no sugar-coated benefits, but wants the last benefit of all, on the positive side at the omega point, which is that intense zone where the powers of doomsday are concentrated, possibly at the top of the crown of Śiva himself. It is that tragic doom that he prays for, not any benefit at all, and, when he takes such an absolute and firm position, the man able to take such a radical decision himself becomes the equal counterpart of what that doom represents. Instead of waving lights to the presence of the Devī, which includes the doom of Śiva — when looked upon as representing her full stature of combined bodily and mental aspects together — the Self of the worshipper attains to such an exalted dignity that the numerator doomsday fire would wave its lights to propitiate the denominator side, represented by the full-fledged Advaita Vedantin supplicant. Self and non-Self, in a word, are interchangeable in the highest context of Advaita.

Annotations

The words 'attended on by' (*niṣevye*) mean that the *siddhis*, or psychic powers, are not intrinsically of the nature of the Goddess, but are of the nature of epiphenomena. This phrase clearly states that the *siddhis* are like servants to the Goddess. The absolute Goddess is not directly interested in conferring *siddhis*. To pray for them is not respectable enough in her eyes.

The reference to the 'Eternal One' is intended to mark the transition from a lower goddess, represented as being within the scope of the three *guṇas*, to one who is more eternal and independent of time and place.

The phrase 'in terms of oneself' (*aham iti*) constitutes the pivot around which the turning of the tables may be said to take place. The Self and the non-Self are involved directly here, without the question of benefits coming to mind at all. The natural pride of a superior Advaitin would make him reject the highest of benefits of a hedonistic order, because without renunciation Self-realization, which is the only benefit of Vedanta, cannot accrue to anyone. The three-eyed Śiva is still a divinity to be propitiated, and not the complete counterpart of the devotee's own Self, when fully abstracted and generalized. Further, it is to be understood here that when subjected to abstraction and generalization, the deity loses his theological status and becomes the counterpart of the Self of the supplicant, who cancels himself out in the totality of the unity of the Absolute.

The reference to the 'fire of doom' (*samvartāgni*) is intended to match the top limit of a numerator value against the bottom limit of a denominator value, as its counterpart, implied in the person of the supplicant himself.

In conclusion, we have shown how the structural and methodological requirements are seen to be fully respected here. Inversion, one-to-one correspondence, Self/non-Self dialectics, theological worship — both in ascending and descending order, also with one-to-one correspondence between them — and above all, how hedonistic values are only worth rejection, are all to be noted here as being conducive to Śaṅkara's task of revaluing Tāntric worship in terms of a full-fledged Advaitic one, which is seen to be clearly undertaken in this and many other verses of this series.

We reproduce here some interesting definitions of *siddhis* from the *Sanskrit-English Dictionary* of Monier Williams:

> *siddhi*: The acquisition of supernatural powers by magical means or the supernatural faculty so acquired (the eight usually enumerated are given in the following *śloka*:
>
> *aṇimā laghimā prāptiḥ prākāmyam mahimā tathā*
> *iśitvaṁ ca vaśitvaṁ ca tathā kāmavaśāyita;*
>
> sometimes 26 are added, e.g., *dūra-śravaṇa*, *sarvajñatva*, *agni-stambha*, & c).
>
> *aṇimā*: the superhuman power of becoming as small as an atom.
>
> *laghimā*: a kind of *siddhi* or supernatural faculty of assuming excessive lightness at will.
>
> *prāpti*: the power of obtaining everything.
>
> *prākāmya*: irresistible will or fiat.

mahimā: the magical power of increasing size at will.

īśitva: superiority, supremacy, one of the eight attributes of Śiva.

vaśitva: the supernatural power of subduing to one's own will, mastery of one's self, self-command.

kāmavaśāyin: the power of suppressing desire (one of the eight supernatural faculties of Śiva).

dūra śravaṇa: hearing from afar

sarvajñatva: omniscience

agni stambha: the (magical) quenching of fire.

31

चतुःषष्ट्या तन्त्रैः सकलमतिसन्धाय भुवनं
स्थितस्तत्तत्सिद्धिप्रसवपरतन्त्रैः पशुपतिः ।
पुनस्त्वन्निर्बन्धादखिलपुरुषार्थैकघटना-
स्वतन्त्रं ते तन्त्रं क्षितितलमवातीतरदिदम् ॥

catuḥ ṣaṣṭyā tantraiḥ sakalam atisandhāya bhuvanaṁ
sthitas tat tat siddhi prasava para tantraiḥ paśupatiḥ ।
punas tvan nirbandhād akhila puruṣārthaika ghaṭanā
svatantraṁ te tantraṁ kṣiti talam avātītarad idam ॥

paśupatiḥ — the Lord of beasts; *tat tat siddhi prasava para tantraiḥ* — each capable of overtly generating its own psychic power; *catuḥ ṣaṣṭyā tantraiḥ* — by sixty-four know-how factors (*tantra*s); *sakalam bhuvanaṁ atisandhāya* — transcending the whole world; *sthitaḥ* — remains immobile; *punaḥ* — again; *tvat nirbandhāt* — by Your insistence; *akhila puruṣārtha eka ghaṭanā* — for the unified fulfilment of all life purposes; *svatantraṁ te tantraṁ* — by that free expertness of Yours; *idam kṣiti talam* — this firm earth; *avātītarat* — caused to be brought down

By sixty-four know-how factors, each capable of generating its own overt psychic power,
Transcending the whole world while remaining immobile,
The Lord of Beasts, again by Your insistence by that free expertness of Yours,
Caused to be brought down this firm earth, for the unified fulfilment of all life purposes.

This verse has given room for much speculation among authorities on Tantra. The edition of Sir John Woodroffe, that of Professor W. Norman Brown of Harvard, and the one by Theosophical scholars S. Subrahmanya Sastri and T.R. Srinivasa Ayyangar, have all been consulted by the present author in order to fix the meaning of the reference here to sixty-four Tantras.

None of these English editions are able to give an adequate explanation of this notion. Neither do the Malayalam editions of orthodox pundits of Kerala — where Tantra has traditionally prevailed — like that of G.S. Srinivasa Iyer of Palghat or that of K. Mahadeva Śastri of South Travancore, shed any light on the obscurity of this reference. Srinivasa Iyer even says that this reference must allude to degenerate schools which are not influenced by the Vedas, but this cannot be taken into consideration by us at all. Various doubtful enumerations of these sixty-four items suggested in other books reveal at first glance that they refer to disreputable benefits which could be considered as subdivisions of the eight main hedonistic items of benefit called the *siddhi*s, with their counterparts, which we learned to recognize in the previous verse. Eight plus eight would make sixteen normally, but it is permitted to think of further ramified subdivisions of the same, such as eight × eight = sixty-four, which could be divided into thirty-two upward and thirty-two downward radiating rays. This division into thirty-two + thirty-two fades away into unimportance if we treat Śiva and Śakti as making up one unit which includes both the plus and the minus aspects. Whatever the content of these sixty-four items, it is enough for us to know that they are either of a positive or of a negative order. The Kaulins, the Samayins and the other schools that think in terms of psychic benefits could fill the content of these sixty-four items as they like, according to the value systems that they are committed to. What is more important for us is to see the structural features and their dynamism in the broadest of outlines, so that, interested as we are in Śaṅkara's revalued version of all Tāntric schools, we can get an idea of what Śaṅkara himself is interested in, rather than what an endless number of anterior Tāntric experts might have left behind in the form of a veritable forest of literature.

Viewed from this revised perspective, we can recognize certain features of the modus operandi of the powers of the mind that could be cultivated by any man, not as ends in themselves, but as coming within the scope of an overall Advaitic understanding of esoteric Tantra, restated in terms as exoteric as possible to reveal to our view the structuralism and dynamism implied, in order to take us to a closer vision of the Absolute. One of the *siddhi*s refers to making a man go to sleep in spite of himself. Ramakrishna Paramahamsa once remarked to a man who claimed to be able to walk across the river Ganges that this particular power only saved him a quarter *anna* (less than a penny) at the ferry. All the trouble he took in gaining the *siddhi* was therefore of negligible worth. The question of *siddhi*s, therefore, is to be bypassed by us.

The third line of this verse reveals the delicacy of the regulating mechanism, which, like a cybernetic retroactive principle, operates at the very core of the set-up in the functioning of these know-how factors (*tantra*s). Śiva here remains the agent for both the *sva Tantra* and *para Tantra* functions of the sixty-four factors which we are concerned with altogether in this verse. *Paratantra* and *svatantra* are technical terms meaning impulses of an ascending or descending order, referred to as 'overt psychic powers' applying to Śiva, and as 'free expertness' applying to the Devī. Although the functions are ambivalent, it is the linking parameter represented by the Śiva principle that is the agent for the world to descend again after its dissolution anteriorly.

Thus, in the alternating process of creation and dissolution that takes place throughout eternity, the regulating principle is of a very subtle cybernetic order within the total mechanism. It keeps on establishing a cybernetic equilibrium between opposing tendencies so that life activities could have a chance to continue unhindered. This offers human beings a terra firma on which to stand and fight their various battles in fulfilment of their life-purposes. The four benefits of human life, called *puruṣārtha*s are — correct life expression (*dharma*), wealth (*artha*), desirable items of fulfilment (*kāma*) and salvation (*mokṣa*).

Cybernetics is familiar with this double-sided regulative principle, from which the very word is derived. This principle is a mechanistic parameter which passes through the details of the complex horizontal mechanistic aspects of the machine itself. The parameter itself does not act but, like a catalytic agent, it causes the subtle conditions favourable to both action and retroaction. Such is the two-sided regulating mechanism to be recognized as belonging to Śiva. Pārvatī has an equally subtle function which is referred to here as insistence only, and not as interference or countering of what her husband has sanctioned in principle. The thermostat, so to speak, automatically changes its phase by the simple insistence of the Goddess, exerted equally subtly on the functioning of the cybernetic parameter, to create retroaction rather than action. If Śiva's action points upward to the dissolution of the universe, then the Devī's retroactive function makes the world descend into existence once again, as if by her magic touch. A split-second activity is to be imagined here, and the resulting universe instantly created and recreated affords humanity a sufficiently firm ground upon which men could fight their battles or fulfil life purposes according to each man's desert or necessity.

The 'unified fulfilment' in the last line cancels the multiplicity of the sixty-four items of intelligence (Tantras) in the first line. *A priori* synthesis and *a posteriori* analysis belong together within the scope of the Absolute. Śiva's function is analytic, while the the Devī's function is synthetic and *a priori*. The analytic function leads through thinner and thinner nominalism to nothingness on the positive side, but, as the Lord of beasts, Śiva does not lose his ontological foothold. It is at this point that the negative principle intervenes, and retroaction succeeds in bringing the nominalistically evaporated world back into reality again for the fulfilment of pragmatic life purposes. When life purposes are treated together they form one bundle at the source of life, like a sheaf of corn tied together. The terms *svatantra* and *paratantra*, which we have translated as 'free expertness' and 'overt psychic power' respectively, bring up the two limits of the amplitude within which cybernetic information circulates, establishing equilibrium, positively or negatively, as required, for the overall benefit of mankind. As parents of the universe, both Śiva and Pārvatī are interested in keeping the game going.

The Sanskrit expression *tat tat siddhi prasava paratantraiḥ*, which we have translated as 'each capable of generating its own overt psychic power', not only clearly states that the psychic powers are the subject matter here, but also suggests, with the word *prasava*, a positive process of becoming. *Paratantra* also points to a transcendental rather than an immanent value. As against this *paratantra*, we have its counterpart in the *svatantra*, which refers to a freedom in itself and for itself and not outside itself, because of the word *sva* (one's own), which has a subjective, immanent import. Each psychic power has its own source or origin on the plus side, where Śiva's Tantra is concerned. Individual expertness of this pluralistic kind does not apply to the domain of the Devī, where it has the status of being bound together into one (*eka ghaṭanā*). All these indications have been carefully taken into account for the corresponding words in English, in which we have avoided being too technical. We prefer a commonsense approach in the name of easy readability, without deflecting from the meaning of the Sanskrit as intended by the author. The expression *avātītarat* (caused to descend) still refers to the function of Śiva. It is to her husband Śiva that the Devī is affiliated, without any dualism in their respective functions. Pārvatī caused the world to come by insistence, but she will not take the initiative. Pluralism tends to refer to the numerator, unity to the denominator. Śiva and Pārvatī are participating in the vertical axis only. As the wife, Pārvatī can function in a zone which is neither his nor her's — nor their's together as a compromise — but as the same.

The Śiva-Pārvatī dialogue (*saṁvāda*) makes a pointed reference to the difference between independent (*svatantra*) and dependent (*paratantra*). She wants for herself the corresponding power which is negative in its essence. The Devī says, 'Tell me something of a relativistic and non-relativistic character representing a Tantra (know-how factor) to counteract all the numerator Tantras attributed to Śiva'. The *Vāmakeśvara Tantra* contains a reference to just this counteracting factor of the parameter of Śiva in terms of the Devī's *svatantra*, which is absolutist in character.

32

शिवः शक्तिः कामः क्षितिरथ रविः शीतकिरणः
स्मरो हंसः शक्रस्तदनु च परामारहरयः।
अमी हृल्लेखाभिस्तिसृभिरवसानेषु घटिताः
भजन्ते वर्णास्ते तव जननि नामावयवताम्॥

śivaḥ śaktiḥ kāmaḥ kṣitir atha raviḥ śītakiraṇaḥ
smaro haṁsaḥ śakras tadanu ca parā māraharayaḥ ।
amī hr̥llekhābhis tisr̥bhir avasāneṣu ghaṭitāḥ
bhajante varṇās te tava janani nāmāvayavatām ॥

janani — O Mother; *śivaḥ śaktiḥ kāmaḥ* — Śiva, Śakti, Eros; *kṣitiḥ* — the Earth; *athaḥ raviḥ* — then the Sun; *śītakiraṇaḥ* — cool-beamed (the Moon); *smaraḥ* — Eros; *haṁsaḥ* — Swan; *śakraḥ* — Indra; *tad anu ca* — after which also; *parā māra harayaḥ* — Parā, Māra and Hari; *amī te varṇāḥ* — these Your letters; *tisr̥bhiḥ hr̥llekhābhiḥ* — with the three heart monomarks; *avasāneṣu ghaṭitāḥ* — joined to their terminals (suffixed); *tava nāmāvayavatām* — (as) naming Your component limbs; *bhajante* — they adore

Śiva, Pārvatī, Eros and Earth; Sun, Moon, God of Love,
Swan and Indra; Parā, Māra and Hari;
With these three sets with their heart-monomarks suffixed,
They adore Your letters, O Mother,
By way of naming Your component limbs.

Some clarifications will be needed before the reader can enter into the spirit and full implications of verses thirty-two through thirty-five. We know that there were two schools of Tantra called the Kaulins and the Samayins. The Kaulins were primarily interested in cultivating a form of absolutist delight or enjoyment through what they understood to be the ontological approach to the absolute Source of all delight. Those who practised this kind of eroticism were not necessarily influenced by the Vedas. They belonged to the ordinary stratum of society. Eating meat, drinking wine of some sort, and having sex were to be taken for granted in their lives. They did not feel any guilt in these matters. The Kaula school had two main subdivisions called 'Pūrva Kaula' and 'Uttara Kaula'. Pūrva Kaulins emphasized ontology more than the Uttara Kaulins. We could imagine further subdivisions between them. In both, an actual girl of a good family was a necessary item in their ritualistic orgies, often conducted secretly in the basements of neglected temples. Although their starting philosophy was something concrete and tangible, they made every effort to rise from yantra to mantra through the medium or means of Tantra.

In the South Indian school of Tantra, there is a convention of distinguishing divinities by certain syllables, such as *ha, sa, ka, la, hrīṁ* and *śrīṁ*, *aim* and *klīṁ*. By convention each of these syllables stands for a *devatā*, which is a divinity with a special function within the structural dynamic set-up of the technique of Tantra, yantra and mantra combined, well-known by the overall, though rather vague, term *Tantra*. In the ritual worship of the Kaulins, letters of the alphabet brought to their minds images of these phenomenal functionaries (*devatā*s) in the universe — theological, cosmological or psychological. The first line of verse thirty-two lists three distinct sets of such divinities. The letter *ka* represents Śiva, *e* represents Śakti, *ī* represents Kāma (the God of Love) and *la* represents *kṣiti* (the Earth). These four form the first group. Then Sun (*ravi*) as *ha*, Moon (*śītakiraṇa*) as *sa*, Smara (the God of Love) as *ka*, Swan (*haṁsa*) as *ha*, and Indra as *la* form the second group. The third group consists of *sa, ka* and *la,* which represent Parā, Māra and Hari respectively. When we suffix the letter *hrīṁ*, which represents the heart centre, to each of these three groups, it is easy to recognize the favourite conventional fifteen-lettered mantra belonging to *śrīvidyā* called the *pañcadaśākṣarī mantra,* which is made of the three sets — *ka, e, ī, la, hrīṁ; ha, sa, ka, ha, la, hrīṁ*; and *sa, ka, la, hrīṁ.* Thus we get a charm of fifteen divinities strung together into an imaginary rosary, and indicated by letters of the Sanskrit alphabet. If the divinities are used as monomarks for purposes of taxonomy, we could also say that the syllables stand for the same divinities understood nominalistically rather than realistically.

It is true that sometimes the sixteen-lettered *ṣoḍaśākṣarī mantra* is also conventionally understood. How the sixteenth letter is to be supplied is supposed to be a secret taught only by a guru, who will give it personally to a disciple. This must be due to its very abstract epistemological status. *Pañcadaśākṣarī mantra* and *ṣoḍaśakṣarī mantra* could be treated together under the same tendency to use letters of the alphabet to stand for *devatā*s or divinities, each of whom has his own function in the total set-up of the absolute divinity or principle of Beauty.

Sometimes a sixteen-lettered charm or mantra is seen to be mentioned in textbooks of Tantra. The sixteenth letter is supposed to be a secret one, summing up or cancelling out into a total value having an absolutist status. This final touch cannot be imparted except by a personal guru, acting as an intermediary. We do not propose to enter into the intricacies of such esoteric technicalities (of which there is no end). The reader is referred to other esoteric books, such as *The Śākta Upaniṣad*s and the *Śivānandalaharī*, both published by the Theosophical Publishing House.

This particular school of Kaulins, by intending to bring into proper perspective the total set-up within the structure of the Absolute, could be said to be travelling from the 'universal concrete', as in an actual girl, to the utmost limit of nominalism by attempting to raise themselves through *akṣara*s. *Akṣara* means values resulting from the fusion of the alpha and omega in the alphabet of any language, *a* being the starting vowel and *kṣa* being the last consonant in Sanskrit. *Akṣa mālā* means a rosary of beads, which, when understood in the context of Rudra (Śiva), is called a *rudrākṣa mālā*. In verse thirty-three also, the same kind of values are strung together in two rosary-like formations, one as an actual rosary of beads and another as a rosary of oblations of clarified butter derived from the celestial cow.

In this verse we can see clearly how Śaṅkara is thinking of the *pañcadaśākṣarī mantra* of the *śrīvidyā*. The tendency of the Kaula Tantra, as we have said, is to ascend from the realistic up towards the nominalistic, with iconographic divinities used as monomarks which have corresponding lettered syllable-combinations, with a one-to-one correspondence between the monomarks and their names more symbolically understood. Evidently the pre-Vedic Kaula school of erotic Tantra is the subject of this verse. The overall purpose that Śaṅkara wants to recognize as the *raison d'être* of this kind of Kaula Tantra is to meditate realistically on the goddess of absolute Beauty, first with monomarks and finally with names applied to each element that might contribute to the beauty significance that the Devī here is meant to represent. It is important to give a name as well as a function to each component element so that the totality might effectively loom into the contemplation of the worshipper, whatever school he might incidentally belong to. Even a wrong kind of worship could be made right by the light of its correct intentionality, according to the Bhagavadgītā (IX.29-31). God accepts everything, according to the calibre of the man. The attitude concerning worship is a catholic one. A man is saved by his intentions only, for his actions in this world may not have amounted to anything due to uncontrollable circumstances.

The three sets of *devatās* in this verse have each to have the syllable *hrīṁ* suffixed. The heart is a centre which is both a monomark and also something that can be understood by a syllable. It is easy to see the need for suffixing the heart monomark, because the heart refers back to the Self at the centre of one's own consciousness, to which all things must refer.

When we add the letter *ṁ* at the end of a syllable, like *hrīṁ*, we are reminded of the syllable *auṁ*, which also ends in *ṁ*. The letter *a* of *auṁ* is an open sound, the letter *u* is a half-open sound, while the letter *ṁ* is fully closed. The syllable composed of these three letters suggests the base, sides and apex of a triangle respectively, within the totality called absolute Beauty, or absolute Value-significance in human life. We are asked in this verse recognize three rosary-like garlands adorning the totality of the structure of the Goddess. Between the open syllable and the closed syllable there is implied a cancellation between horizontal and vertical values. When we are able to properly place the three sets indicated as complete garlands within the total frame of reference represented by the Devī here, we could be expected to have understood her total Value under three main sets of categories, making up fifteen elements, each based on monomarks and spelled out by letters of the alphabet.

33

स्मरं योनिं लक्ष्मीं त्रितयमिदमादौ तव मनो-
निधायैके नित्ये निरवधिमहाभोगरसिकाः ।
भजन्ति त्वां चिन्तामणिगुणनिबद्धाक्षवलयाः
शिवाग्नौ जुह्वन्तः सुरभिघृतधाराहुतिशतैः ॥

smaraṁ yoniṁ lakṣmīṁ tritayam idam ādau tava manor
nidhāyaike nitye niravadhi mahābhoga rasikāḥ ।
bhajanti tvāṁ cintāmaṇi guṇa nibaddhākṣa valayāḥ
śivāgnau juhvantaḥ surabhi ghṛta dhārāhuti śataiḥ ॥

eke nitye — O Lone and Eternal One; *tava manoḥ ādau* — first within Your charm; *smaraṁ yoniṁ lakṣmīṁ* — Eros, Source, Wealth; *idam tritayam* — this triplet; *nidhāya* — placing; *niravadhi mahā bhoga rasikāḥ* — innumerable seekers of great enjoyment; *cintāmaṇi guṇa nibaddha akṣavalayāḥ* — telling rosaries of philosophers' stone; *śiva agnau* — into the fire of Śiva; *surabhi ghṛta dhārā āhuti śataiḥ* — by hundreds of streaks of clarified-butter oblations from the celestial cow (*Surabhi*); *juhvantaḥ* — ever sacrificing; *tvām bhajanti* — they worship You

Eros, Source, Wealth — this triplet placing first within Your charm,
O Lone and Eternal One, innumerable seekers of great enjoyment
Adore You, telling rosary beads of philosopher's stone, ever sacrificing into the fire of Śiva,
By hundreds of streaks of clarified-butter oblations from the celestial cow.

It is not difficult to see that this verse is dealing with the Samayins because there is reference to the sacred cow (*Kāmadhenu*) and the Vedic ritual of the fire-sacrifice (*śivāgni*). We are called upon to make two degrees of abstraction in order to grasp the meaning of the situation described. We have to think of spoonfuls of ghee derived from a celestial cow being poured thousands of times into a fire. In performing this ritual act, the spoon which contains the ghee circulates a thousand times in the hands of the Vedic votary. When abstracted, this circulation will resemble a rosary, but with the ghee as its value factor instead of the usual rosary such as one made of *rudrākṣa* beads which is natural to the context of Śiva worship. The word *akṣa* is made up of the first and last letters of the Sanskrit alphabet. An *akṣa mālā* is a rosary, with the help of which votaries of divinities — whether in India or elsewhere — repeat mystical syllables, each representing a divinity, symbol or monomark. Instead of *a* and *kṣa*, one could think of alpha and omega. *Akṣa mālā*, then, is a rosary consisting of some sacred items of value in the form of a 'universal concrete', but derived from letters or syllables made up of signs of the alphabet. The first and the last, when fused together, would represent a value resulting from the reciprocal cancellation of counterparts.

If verse thirty-two was nominalistic in its intention to name the various limbs of the Goddess in order to understand her both realistically and in an abstract form, then the intention of this verse tends to be hedonistic. Ancient Vedism was characterized by its love of 'the good life'. The drinking of *soma* juice and the sacrificing of calves to propitiate one god or another was a natural form of behaviour to the Aryans. Later Vedism, however, began to eschew the infliction of suffering (*hiṁsā*) and the shedding of blood as impure and unvirtuous. The Buddhist and Jain doctrine of *ahiṁsā* (non-hurting) must have had its share in shaping this revised way of life through the ages. Whatever their historical origin might be, the brahmins of the present day, at least in South India, do not lend support to those items which are distinguished as 'left-handed' (*vāmācāra*) features of Tantra. As a dialectical revaluator, Śaṅkara evidently wishes to recognize the claims of both the Samayins and the Kaulins by treating them as representative rival schools and accepting what is laudable in each of them, so as to present them both without partiality, but in a form slightly revised and restated. By this unitive approach, both these forms of prevailing spirituality can be brought into line with his own fully Advaitic standpoint. The Bhagavadgītā even speaks of the Vedas as being under the sway of the three nature-modalities (II.45).

Hedonism, relativism, ritualism and negativism are not defects in themselves, but they are capable of being revised in the name of a fully unitive absolutist standpoint. Clarified butter and the wish-fulfilling cow of heaven, Kāmadhenu, are natural to the brahminical world of values. Pouring ghee into a 'Śiva fire' instead of into a 'Brahman fire' is to be understood as a slight concession made in this verse to the Śiva-Śakti context of South India, to which Tantra must necessarily belong. There is no Tantra that can be called purely Vedic, and the conflict between Vedism and Tantrism is clearly evident in many parts of pre-Vedic Tāntric literature, as revealed in the writings of Sir John Woodroffe and others. If verse thirty-two represents an ascending movement from the actual or 'universal concrete' to nominalism through conventional syllables applied to divinities used as monomarks, in the interest of taxonomy or nomenclature of the various aspects of the Goddess, then the movement in verse thirty-three is clearly one of descent from the value represented by the celestial cow toward actual benefits here on earth, in the name of *bhoga*, or enjoyment. By clarifying or enhancing the path of hedonism, Śaṅkara here refers to *bhoga* in revised terms as *mahābhoga*, because the word *mahā* (great) lifts its meaning to the status of *sub specie aeternitatis*, 'under the scope of the eternal', thus taking off any stigma that might be attached to *bhoga* as a brute reality in life. In other words, *mahābhoga* is not to be treated as just *bhoga*.

Verses thirty-two through thirty-five, when read together in the structural perspective we are presenting, reveal two opposite movements — between positive and negative counterparts — in the context of the scrutiny, analytic or synthetic, of the same high value of absolute Beauty, which is always the subject matter or object matter of these verses. When we give primacy to effect, as in verse thirty-four, a new novelty is introduced into beauty. When we give primacy to cause, as in verse thirty-five, our reference is to the source of all things, already existing in the past. The reference in the second half of verse thirty-five is to a simple wife of Śiva, although to be understood in the light of the rightful dignity of an eternal feminine principle. We find that the body of Śiva referred to in verse thirty-four has the epithet 'new' applied to it. By this attribute, one has to understand that it refers to the effect side and not to the cause side of the total situation. The double movement implied in these four verses taken together will be progressively abolished in purer epistemological terms of non-dual cancellation. In the coming verses, which refer to the actual chakras such as *ājñā* and so on, we will find the principles of compensation, reciprocity and complementarity (or milder forms of ambivalance and parity), presented in a certain epistemological and methodological sequence by Śaṅkara. Verses thirty-two through thirty-five are meant to reveal the structural dynamism before the same stands revealed in its fully revalued Advaitic form, from verse thirty-six onward.

'Samaya' is the conventional name applied to the Vedic goddess as implied in the revised Tāntric context, while the term 'Kaula' would suggest a more popular approach to the Tantrism of pre-Vedic times. On final analysis, whether we employ an ascending or a descending dialectical approach, it is the same *śrī cakra* that is implied in both the movements, positive and negative. Advaita Vedanta does not admit of any duality between part and whole, cause and effect, substance and attribute. Unitive vision, at whatever level, refers to one and the same *brahman,* and all references to higher or lower *brahman* have to be left behind when the doctrine is to be stated in its finalized form. What is gained on one side is lost on the other, as between transcendental and immanent values, leaving behind a constant always to be understood under the aegis of the same absolute

Selfhood. Neither epistemological, methodological, nor axiological duality is to be allowed to taint, even in the least, the status of the non-dual Absolute. That is the requirement of Śaṅkara's position as an Advaita Vedantin. Narayana Guru endorses this in verse sixty of his *Ātmopadeśa śatakam:*

> Even when knowledge, to egoism is subject, in any predication
> And one is unmindful of the ultimate verity of what is said,
> Yet as with the truth however ultimate, such knowledge
> Can never fall outside the scope of the knowing Self.

The language of abstraction and generalization has various degrees and dimensions, always within the scope of the gross, the subtle, the causal and 'the fourth' (*sthūla*, *sūkṣma*, *kāraṇa*, *turīya*), the four states of consciousness as described in the *Māṇḍūkya Upaniṣad*. Hedonistic motives might be reprehensible ordinarily, but, as we have pointed out already, the qualification *mahā* added to *bhoga rasikāḥ*, which means 'lovers of great delight', absolves the devotee from any charge of hedonism. And when the duality between ends and means is abolished, his worship becomes at least as dignified as the kind of worship envisaged in the previous verse.

In these two verses, thirty-two and thirty-three, Śaṅkara succeeds in revaluing and restating both Kaulin and Samayin ways of worship without detracting anything from either of them, by giving them their full status in the light of the intentionality natural to Advaita Vedanta. If intentions are good, the actions themselves have also to be good necessarily, according to the doctrine of the Bhagavadgītā (IX.31). There Krishna says that the disciple will never perish, because his intentions are good. This doctrine of grace is the most touching thing a god can say to a human being. This is not found in Buddhism. If you are dedicated to the Absolute (*brahman*), ends and means will cancel out by your intention.

34

शरीरं त्वं शंभोः शशिमिहिरवक्षोरुहयुगं
तवात्मानं मन्ये भगवति नवात्मानमनघम्।
अतः शेषः शेषीत्ययमुभयसाधारणतया
स्थितः संबन्धो वां समरसपरानन्दपरयोः॥

śarīraṁ tvaṁ śambhoḥ śaśi mihira vakṣoruhayugaṁ
tavātmānaṁ manye bhagavati navātmānam anagham ।
ataḥ śeṣaḥ śeṣīty ayam ubhaya sādhāraṇatayā
sthitaḥ sambandho vāṁ samarasa parānanda parayoḥ ॥

śaśi mihira vakṣoruha yugaṁ — having sun and moon for twin breasts; *tvaṁ śambhoḥ śarīraṁ* — You are the body of Śiva; *bhagavati tava ātmānaṁ* — Your Self, O beneficent Goddess; *anagham nava ātmānam manye* — as a new and sinless Self, I surmise; *ataḥ* — therefore; *śeṣaḥ śeṣi iti* — thus by mutual complementarity; *ayam sambandhaḥ* — this relation; *sama rasa parānanda parayoḥ* — on equal terms of transcendent bliss; *vāṁ* — between You two; *ubhaya sādhāraṇatayā* — by common reciprocity; *sthitaḥ* — remains, stays

You are the body of Śiva, having sun and moon for twin breasts;
Your Self, I surmise, O Goddess, as a new sinless Self;
Therefore, by mutual complementarity, this relation remains one of common reciprocity
Between You two, participating on equal terms of transcendent bliss.

Verse thirty-four and thirty-five require a special epistemological and methodological approach before they could make normal meaning to the modern reader. It is only in the light of modern phenomenology or of 'intentionality', as understood in the philosophy of Brentano, that we can give even a barely justifiable meaning to these two verses. Phenomenological terms like 'noetic', 'noematic' and 'eidetic' presentiments are the only notions in modern philosophy which resemble the treatment that Śaṅkara adopts here. There are different degrees of abstraction and generalization implied when we represent an object, pronounce a judgement about it, or evaluate it. Śiva, as understood here, is only a thin mathematically understood entity without any concrete or tangible body of his own. The very first verse of this work presupposes this, when it states that Śiva is incapable even of pulsation without being joined with his own counterpart, Śakti. If mathematics has a teleological status, at the positive limit of the vertical parameter, then ontology could be said to mark a point lower down in the vertical scale of intentions or values. Viewed in the light of such a perspective, there is no duplication or conflict between any rival bodies, as between those of Śiva and Pārvatī.

We suggest that verses thirty-four and thirty-five be scrutinized together, because we find a secondary goddess introduced in the latter one. The first goddess, of verse thirty-four, has the status of parity with the numerator value called Śambhu (Śiva), while the secondary goddess, found in verse thirty-five, is not an equal to Śiva in the same sense, but prefers to be his wife in a more negatively feminine manner. In reading both these verses, we have to keep in mind four degrees of abstraction and generalization. Gender might be a 'fact truth,' but it is not a 'logic truth'. Similarly, the relationship between 'Śivahood' and 'Pārvatīhood' could have a parity or ambivalence, a complementarity, a reciprocity, or a compensation, consistent with the four degrees of abstraction and generalization, which we could summarily distinguish as the first, second, third and fourth dimensions, based on the principle of the quaternion. We have had occasion to explain this principle many times elsewhere, as in *The Search for a Norm in Western Thought.*[1] Basically, these four dimensions are not different from the four states of consciousness described in the Upaniṣads. The *Māṇḍūkya*

1. Nataraja Guru, published by the Narayana Gurukula, Varkala. 1986.

Upaniṣad calls them gross (*sthūla*), subtle (*sūkṣma*), causal (*kāraṇa*), and finally the fourth (*turīya*) which has a fully absolutist status. The numerator aspect has to be further distinguished from its own denominator aspect, because there is a tragic line that separates name and form (*nāma rūpa*), which correspond to conception and perception respectively. These epistemological, methodological and axiological considerations have to be remembered together, if some of the major enigmas of these two verses are to be clarified. We could put our finger on each of the ten distinct enigmas in these two verses taken together. The first seven are in verse thirty-four:

1. 'You are the body of Śiva', (*śarīram tvam śambhoḥ*).

   Śiva has only a thin mathematical status, placed as he is at the extreme positive (omega) limit of the total situation to be kept in mind here. Thus, at a lower level, tending to be ontological rather than teleological, we are asked here to think of a goddess who still has a hypostatic or positive dignity attached to her body. Such a body is not to be treated as physical in the ordinary sense, but may be said to belong to the world of intentionality, whether objective or subjective. Such notions are also found in phenomenology as in the terms 'noetic', 'noematic' and 'eidetic' presentiments. The body of Śiva, has, therefore, an epistemological status of its own.

2. 'Sun and moon for twin breasts', (*śaśi mihira vakṣoruha yugam*).

   The sunlight and the moonlight of spring and summer, both have their respective parts to play in making a tree put forth its fresh sprouts or blossoms. How the sun and moon cooperate in such a task has to be intuitively imagined, as when we understand that the twilight periods of both the sun and the moon, rising or setting through the three-hundred-sixty odd days of the year, are likely to have some kind of psychochemical influence in the growth and metabolism of a human being, especially a woman. The breasts of the Goddess represent the source of life for all children born anywhere, anytime. There is, then, nothing too far-fetched implied when it is suggested here that the breasts of the Goddess are derived from the two celestial sources of light that we call the sun and the moon, which weave a logarithmic spiral within the individual mind or psychophysical set-up, contributing to the status of the person of the Goddess.

The sun dominates the active daytime, while the moon is most beautiful in its thinnest crescent-like virtuality, presiding over the subconscious, innate world of dreams and reveries. We have already indicated that if we should abstract and generalize the twilights of the sun and the moon rising or setting together, we could derive a vertical parameter as a reference for the alternating influences of the sun and the moon on the consciousness of the contemplative. When fitted into the overall scheme in terms of a logarithmic descending spiral, it would be possible to justify this reference as implying both a horizontal parity and a vertical reciprocity between them.

It is important for the revised structuralism proper to the value of Beauty, as presented by Śaṅkara after his revaluation of Kaulin and Samayin Tāntric traditions (in verses thirty-two and thirty-three), that the breasts of the Goddess do not have merely an earthy reference. This kind of revaluation was also clearly underlined in verse nineteen.

3. 'A new and sinless Self', (*navātmānam anagham*).

In this verse we are still thinking of the numerator aspect of the personality of the Goddess. If cause is old, effect is new. Causes have a negative, ontological reference and effects have, on the contrary, a positive, hypostatic or teleological reference. To give a very concrete example, a mango tree displays fresh reddish-green sprouts every year in the flowering season. This tender magenta foliage could be compared to the new body rising out of the old body that the tree would otherwise represent. It is the new side, which is an effect in the personality of the Goddess, that is to be understood here. If we now ask what about the old aspect of the same personality which is on the denominator side of the cause and not on the numerator effect side, the answer will be found in the very next verse, which views the same complementary, reciprocal, and compensatory relationship in a revised and more negative perspective.

Sin is always associated with things that are of 'earth earthy'. Concepts cannot be associated with sin because sin can adhere only in the world of percepts. In this sense, the hypostatic aspect of the self of the Goddess, or anybody else, has to be thought of as removed from all taint of sin.

4. 'By mutual complementarity', (*śeṣaḥ śeṣī*).

   The complementarity referred to here could be only between the higher body having a thin mathematical status and the more actual body of Pārvatī though still hypostatic, pure, or celestial. As between any two levels in the vertical parameter, there must be a complementarity between the positivity and the negativity implied between them. But in the next verse there is another complementarity between two denominator aspects of the same principle of absolute Beauty which is neither male nor female, nor both indifferently.

5. 'Relation of common reciprocity', (*ubhaya sādhāraṇata*).

   The original expression in Sanskrit is *ubhaya sādhāraṇatayā. Ubhaya* means 'participating both ways', and *sādhāraṇatayā* means 'by having a common feature'. Our translation thus correctly corresponds to the meaning of the original Sanskrit.

6. 'Participating on equal terms', (*samarasa parayoḥ*).

 The Sanskrit term *samarasa*, meaning 'equality', sufficiently justifies our rendering.

7. 'Transcendent bliss', (*parānanda*).

 Bliss could be either immanent or transcendent. Consistent with the numerator status of the two partners in this verse, we can see how transcendent bliss, *parānanda,* applies more aptly here than immanent bliss, which would properly belong to the context of the next verse.

 The objective of Śaṅkara in verses thirty-four and thirty-five will become all the more evident when we remember that he shuns the technicalities of Tantra and yoga when they are used too conventionally and out of relation with the realities of everyday life. We even find the name of the *anāhata cakra,* which is evidently implied in verse thirty-eight, to be omitted by Śaṅkara. *Anāhata* means 'not struck', and implies a state of nature. It does not, according to Śaṅkara, call for a special technical term to distinguish it among the chakras. For the same reason, we find that Śaṅkara does not have any use for the terms so inevitably used in yogic and Tāntric literature, such as *iḍā*, *piṅgalā* and *suṣumnā*. Esotericism for its own sake, like scholasticism in European thought, only detracts from the scientific status of a work of the kind that Śaṅkara intends this present one to be.

35

मनस्त्वं व्योम त्वं मरुदसि मरुत्सारथिरसि
त्वमापस्त्वं भूमिस्त्वयि परिणतायां न हि परम्।
त्वमेव स्वात्मानं परिणमयितुं विश्ववपुषा
चिदानन्दाकारं शिवयुवति भावेन बिभृषे ॥

manas tvaṁ vyoma tvaṁ marud asi marutsārathir asi
tvam āpas tvaṁ bhūmis tvayi pariṇatāyāṁ na hi param ।
tvam eva svātmānaṁ pariṇamayituṁ viśva vapuṣā
cidānandākāraṁ śiva yuvati bhāvena bibhṛṣe ॥

manaḥ tvaṁ — the mind You are; *vyoma tvaṁ* — You are the sky; *marut asi* — the wind You are; *marut sārathiḥ asi* — the charioteer of the winds (the fire) You are; *tvaṁ āpaḥ* — You are the water; *tvaṁ bhūmiḥ* — You are the earth; *tvayi pariṇatāyām param na hi* — apart from Your manifest form there is naught else indeed; *tvaṁ eva sva ātmānaṁ* — You, indeed, in respect of Your own self; *viśva vapuṣā* — by means of a universal form, body; *pariṇamayituṁ* — in order to make manifest; *cit ānanda ākāraṁ* — of mental bliss substantial; *śiva yuvati bhāvena* — assuming the role of Śiva-bride; *bibhṛṣe* — (and thus) triumphant rule.

The mind You are, the sky, the wind too, also the charioteer of the winds,
You are the water, as well as the earth — apart from Your manifest form, there is naught else indeed!
You, in order to manifest, Your own self, by taking a universal form
Of mental bliss substantial, do assume the role of Śiva-bride, and thus triumphant rule.

Now, as we pass on to verse thirty-five, we have first to notice that there is a descending series of items, not necessarily elemental or physical in the ordinary sense, but tending to be psychophysical categories, to be understood as in the

Bhagavadgītā (VII. 4), where it says that the mental factors participate with the elemental earthy factors in an imperceptible gradation of mutual interpenetration. Advaita cannot recognize any duality between matter and mind. The same vertical parameter has to pass through whatever series is supposed to make up the total personality, whether of a god or of a human being. The verse in the Gītā gives an ascending series, but here it is a descending series with the mind mentioned first. Slight variations in nomenclature or description would be found in the Upaniṣads or other contemplative texts, such as the eight 'cities' of Śaṅkara's *Vivekacūḍāmaṇī* (verse 96). The same kind of series of items can be found in endless variety in literature. What is important for us to note here is that beginning with the mind, which is not physical, we are tracing stable entities or categories which fall along a vertical descending parameter, terminating with a reference to the earth, or terra firma, which is fully horizontal in its status. Here again, a logarithmic spiral between bases and apexes of triangles has to be kept in mind. The six levels are seen to be preserved intact in descending order, starting from the mind and touching the lower limit of the earth. A cancellation is implied at every level, where a stable equilibrium is to be attained between opposing forces. The lowermost limit of final cancellation is marked by the status of young wifehood conferred on the Devī. The Devī could be meditated upon at any level, suiting the temperament of the supplicant or votary concerned. Between the different levels, when properly cancelled out, no vestige of duality is supposed to exist either as the end of or as the means to the correct contemplation of absolute Beauty, which is always the same high value, implied in each of the verses of this work. Whether we call each stable position a wheel (chakra), a basis or foundation (*ādhāra*), a gesture (*mudrā*), or a cancelled out value of Laya yoga, is not important in Advaita Vedanta. Haṭha yoga could be viewed in the light of the same dynamism of cancellation. The principle of cancellation is thus at the basis of each of the verses, as also of this work as a whole. (This is not understood by the Vedantins of the present day who label Śaṅkara as a *māyāvādin* without entering into the full spirit of his uncompromising speculation.) With this principle in mind let us take the remaining three enigmas contained in this verse:

1. 'Apart from your manifest form, there is naught else indeed!' (*tvayi pariṇatāyām na hi param*).

   This finalized description must refer to the various grades of horizontalization involved in the process of creation or becoming. A ripe mango can be said to have reached its final limit in the process of becoming mature, in itself, by itself and through itself. This process of becoming is not to be confused with the process of evolution as between different species of animals, which is another subject altogether. It is to be understood in the same sense that twilight can be seen as a maturation of the light of noontide. As everything has to be comprised within the scope of the two parameters, the vertical and the horizontal, the statement here that there is nothing left out of the picture is quite justified epistemologically.

2. 'Taking a universal form', (*viśva vapuṣā*).

   Horizontal becoming has primacy in this verse over the vertical becoming of verse thirty-four. Pushing abstraction and generalization to its final limit to arrive thus at the notion of the horizontal parameter, always to be understood in just and proportionate relation with its own verticalized relational counterpart, gives us the universal form that is under reference here. Although it is to be understood philosophically, when applied to the personality of the Goddess for purposes of contemplation, it is not repugnant to the spirit of this verse to say that the Goddess became a pleasing and beautiful young wife for the sake of Śiva, whose love must necessarily control and condition the universal form.

3. 'You assume the role of Śiva's young bride', (*śivayuvati bhāvena*).

It is of the essence of womanhood, which is negative in its import, to establish a reciprocity between the eternal feminine principle within herself and the eternal masculine principle, represented here by Śiva at the omega point. This reference, then, to a beautiful young bride triumphantly ruling at the opposite limit from that of Śiva is quite justified.

The overall purpose of Śaṅkara in composing these two verses, which do not refer to orthodox textbooks of Tantra or Yoga, is to prepare the mind of the student for an independent revalued version of these popular esoteric disciplines so as to bring them in line with his own Advaitic doctrine, for which he has stood consistently throughout his great commentaries. The difference between those commentaries and the present work consists in the fact that here Śaṅkara employs a language in which, to use the terms of Marshall McLuhan, the 'medium' and the 'message' belong to the same epistemological order as interchangeable factors. Essence and existence, as the two main components of absolute Reality, could each be understood in terms of the other. When closely juxtaposed, they could verify each other and the resultant would be a normalized value factor which is here called absolute Beauty. When such beauty is experienced within the consciousness of the yogi, it conforms to the relational pattern represented by the *śrī cakra*. Whether we call stable states of contemplative meditation by the name chakra, *ādhāra* or even *mudrā*, it is the same absolute Value, without any taint of duality and resulting from the cancellation of counterparts, that is always implied.

Śaṅkara is evidently preparing the ground in order to bridge the gap between the meditative factors understood in the context of Tantra and the same factors understood in Yoga, to which series we shall arrive in the very next verse beginning with the *ājñā cakra*. The transition from Tāntric factors of contemplation to yogic ones could gain support from authoritative textbooks on Tantra or Yoga. That would be the more conventional way of understanding their significance. But Śaṅkara, being a fully cultured Sanskrit scholar, refuses to lapse into the use of conventional cliches of esoteric textbooks. He prefers instead to rely on literature originating in the Upaniṣads, and passing through ideograms and iconographic monomarks known to poets like Kālidāsa and others before him, so as to bring them into correct and critically valid use in keeping with the Science of the Absolute (*brahma vidyā*). Vedanta becomes a system in his hands, as also a vision within the experience of yogis. We shall see that even in his treatment of the conventional chakras he employs his critical revaluation. His attitude in this work is the same as in the *Brahmasūtras*, where the Sāṁkhya tendency to schematize and categorize is not favoured. Where reality is self-sufficient proof for the Absolute, to resort to schematization and categorization for their own sake only detracts from the realization of the Absolute.

The yogi experiences beauty within himself. The artist gives it an overt representation in outer space. Chakras can belong to Tantra as well as to the world of mantra or yantra. Semiotic and syntactical processes also conform to the same structural dynamism. In the light of such a unified approach, it is possible to see how Śaṅkara ably revalues not only semiotic processes (as in verse seventeen), but also rival Tāntric schools (in verses thirty-two and thirty-three), to bring all these disciplines in line with Yoga, itself understood non-dualistically and without prejudices and hangovers belonging to its Sāṁkhya origin. We have attempted to show that there is a common epistemology, methodology and axiology underlying these disciplines, which all belong to the same structural whole where categories and monomarks which have a relational togetherness of their own are referable to parameters or perimeters, vertical or horizontal.

It is lack of appreciation on the part of pundits and professors of this fully realistic yet non-dualistically valid approach to absolute Beauty that has been responsible for scholars, even of the stature of Professor Norman Brown of Harvard, to doubt the very authorship of this work. It is difficult for them to see how an Advaita philosopher like Śaṅkara could seem to lend support to Tantra. Professor Brown (pp. 28-29) explicitly states this difficulty as follows:

> It does not seem to me possible to reconcile the teaching of the *Saundaryalaharī,* as I have sketched it, with the teaching of Śaṅkara . . . worship is out of harmony with Śaṅkara's teaching.

[This is not a text of worship, as Śaṅkara tries to make clear both in the first and last verses of this work, as revealed in the words 'one of ungained merit' (*akr̥tapuṇyaḥ*) in verse 1, and 'by words Your own' (*tvadīyābhir vāgbhiḥ*) in verse 100.]

We find that after these two verses, thirty-four and thirty-five, where the new body and the wifely body of Pārvatī are referred to, Śaṅkara is able to refer to the conventional chakras one after another, beginning with the *ājñā cakra* in verse thirty-six. In verse thirty-five we see that he steers clear of any technical or conventional approach to the various levels in the psychophysical set-up. The dynamism of a contemplative Yoga, revised by him, is not to be fitted into the context of dualistic Sāṁkhya but of what is proper to a full-fledged Advaitic standpoint of its own.

Introduction to verses 36 through 41

Verses thirty-six through forty-one refer to stable psychophysical states of consciousness, conventionally named chakras in the discipline of yoga. Chakra means 'wheel'. Sometimes we find the same state of synergic equilibrium called *ādhāra*, which would suggest a foundation or a basement. Fixing the psychophysical Self attentively on a certain type of syndrome or synergism, based on the cancellation of reciprocal functions, is also sometimes called *bandha*s, which would suggest a knot or a binding force.

There are *bandhas* of this kind known to yogic practice, such as *mūla bandha* and *uḍyaṇa bandha*. Vital tendencies could be controlled and cancelled out through the regulation of breathing exercises, where again two opposite tendencies are intended to be neutralized. Each chakra or *ādhāra* represents a psychophysical point of equilibrium, attained at various levels of the dynamism between the Self and the non-Self.

The most characteristic description of yoga would be the word *nirodha*, which, in this context, means 'restraint of the outgoing mental processes', which, through chains of natural associations, keep the mind distracted and wandering from one item of interest to another. Patañjali's definition of Yoga is based on this basic concept of restraint (*Yogasūtras*, I.2.). According to Patañjali, there are eight stages (*aṣṭāṅga*) by which a yogi practises the discipline of meditation (II.29). It begins with the lowest physical limit, where control is indicated by the word *yama*, meaning 'inward withdrawal of tendencies'. After *yama* comes *niyama* which applies to a slightly higher level of the personality, and which means 'restraint or control conditioned by rules'. Then comes *āsana* which refers to the correct posture for restraining the mind. *Prāṇāyāma*, the fourth stage in the process, refers to the regulation of the outgoing and incoming breaths, in order to subdue the vital tendencies which are at the basis of the function of breathing so that they do not obstruct the process of meditation (*dhyāna*), which is one of the stages to follow. The fifth stage of Patañjali's Yoga is *pratyāhāra* which is a negative process of withdrawal — from the side of the non-Self to the Self — of the outgoing tendencies. In *dhāraṇa*, sustained concentration or contemplation, a first degree participation is established between the Self and the non-Self. *Dhyāna*, which is given as the seventh stage in the *Yogasūtras*, underlines a sustained state of *dhāraṇa*. Finally, the eighth stage is called samadhi. The word *sama* suggests equality and *dhi* suggests intellect. The intellect is thus expected to attain to a certain equality or equilibrium with itself. The cancellability of the Self and the non-Self is implied here.

When we think of the subject of yoga in the context of Indian spirituality, the most canonical or authoritative textbook, which all correct scholars or practitioners have to keep in mind, is Patañjali's series of aphorisms called the *Yogasūtra*s. Although Patañjali is thus an authority, his yoga, which is sometimes also called Rāja Yoga, is considered defective in the full context of Advaita Vedanta. Patañjali's Yoga is not countenanced with favour in the *Brahmasūtra*s of Bādarāyaṇa, nor in the *Yoga Vāsiṣṭha*, which is perhaps the latest authoritative textbook of yoga. The *Yoga Vāsiṣṭha* contains an explicit disavowal of the *aṣṭāṅga yoga* of Patañjali, where Rāma is asked by his guru Vasiṣṭha, to treat his own teaching as the final authority. Vasiṣṭha speaks in terms of *sapta bhūmika*s, or seven grounds of consciousness, which he defines elaborately in more than one place. The main objection to the Patañjali system of Yoga, by Vedantic texts such as the Bhagavadgītā, is that its epistemology and methodology are necessarily vitiated by their being based on the Sāṁkhya dualism of Kapila. In the thought of Kapila and Patañjali, and their respective schools of Sāṁkhya and Yoga, there still persists a vestige of duality between nature (*prakṛti*) and spirit (*puruṣa*). This duality is essentially the same as that between matter and mind. Advaita, on the other hand, cannot tolerate even the slightest taint of duality between these two factors. The avowed purpose of Advaita is to abolish all duality whether between causes and effects, means and ends or between disciplines and their results. The fourth and fifth chapters of the Bhagavadgītā are specifically directed to the purpose of cancelling the duality between Sāṁkhya and Yoga, and verse 4 of Chapter V goes to the extent of saying that only children think they are distinct disciplines. Patañjali's *Yogasūtra*s itself has been commented upon by Vyāsa in what is known as the *Vyāsa bhāṣya*, which is an attempt to abolish the duality which persisted as an implicit genetic element of error in Patañjali's original approach. The well-known *Bhojavārttika* of Bhojarāja and the *Tattva Vaiśāradī* of Vācaspati Miśra pushed this revaluation still further, and

Advaitic notions of yoga have also been further revised and made up to date in the writings of Śaṅkarācārya and Narayana Guru.

It is true that the *Saundaryalaharī* refers in these six verses to what might seem at first sight to be the six conventional chakras, *ādhāra*s or *mudrā*s, each implying a stable attitude of the psychophysical Self. Ontological aspects, when implied, would justify the term *ādhāra*, while a teleological state of equilibrium would more properly be referred to as a chakra. The term *bandha* might apply to a discipline conceived under haṭha yoga, which refers to a very wilful form of physical control and is only indirectly important to yoga, which should be properly understood from a more neutral standpoint. Some textbooks refer to four kinds of yoga: *mantra, laya, rāja* and *haṭha*. Mantra evidently refers to the muttering of magic syllables, while visualizing ideograms that belong to them. Laya does not depend upon the nominalistic aspects of yoga, but refers to an intimate form of merging the mind so as to dissolve the duality between object and subject. The term *rāja* is used in the Bhagavadgītā to underline a discipline in yoga which is public and experimentally valid, as when we say 'the royal road'. Rāja yoga thus corresponds to a normalized discipline of yoga, neither too esoteric nor too exoteric. We have already indicated the peculiarity of haṭha yoga. Whatever the type of Yoga one might be interested in, there is always a subtle cancellation of counterparts implied, when Yoga is treated as a discipline in the most general terms.

The Frame of Reference Implicit in the Chakras

If Yoga is a discipline that is to be practised at all, it must necessarily have a status that is both physical and psychic at once. Space, whether subjective 'inner space' or objective 'outer space', is necessarily made up of various elements which must have a relational togetherness between them. If we try to think mathematically, this idea of the togetherness of interrelated elements would suggest to us a pattern which could be formally visualized as a 'mathematical object', as Hilbert would call it.

Whether that object is visualized in geometric terms, or merely conceived in terms of algebraic signs, the thing meant in itself cannot be different. The same thing could be viewed conceptually or perceptually. At the negative levels perceptual forms are natural to the mind. At the positive levels conceptual relational togetherness or unity is also equally possible to think of as an idea. Letters of the Greek alphabet can be used to indicate points of intersection between lines. Just as a graph can verify a formula, so geometry can verify algebra. Modern cybernetics is based on this possibility. The machine language can be codified and decodified. Thus we arrive at the possibility of a relational frame of reference for all the yogic meditations, however varied. This is, according to us, what Śaṅkara suggests in his *śrī cakra* of verse eleven, though it is true that there the *śrī cakra* is presented in its statically conceived mathematical form as a ready-made cliche, so repugnant to the philosophy of Bergson. This does not mean, however, that Śaṅkara is not aware of its dynamic version, as revealed in verse seven. Chakras, *ādhāra*s, *bandha*s or *mudrā*s are thus to be understood as stable points of equilibrium that could be established within the amplitude of a parameter that we could postulate as existing between the lower alpha limit and the higher omega limit of a total situation proper to the world of yogic discipline. What is true of yogic discipline could be equally true of Tāntric or semantic discipline by extrapolation or intrapolation, permissible by mathematical convention. The six chakras, having the names *ājñā*, *viśuddhi*, *anāhata* (not mentioned by name here), *maṇipūra, svādhiṣṭhāna* and *mūlādhāra,* conform to the conventionally understood stable centres (synergisms or syndromes) within the total psycho-physical make-up of the individual.

Various textbooks of Yoga define and describe these chakras or *ādhāra*s with endless varieties of subtleties. To enter into these would be to court disaster through 'confusion of tongues' in a verbose forest of words, known as 'Babelization' in biblical language. In order to avoid falling into such a dire predicament, it is recommended that we steer our own speculation clear of the Scylla and Charybdis involved here.

We have already indicated that, as an Advaitin, Śaṅkara could not countenance any dualistically tainted school of yoga theory. Various questionable textbooks on Tantra esoterics refer to the chakras and *ādhāra*s, and describe them in terms of fires, or phalluses, or petals of different colours and numbers, too numerous to enumerate, or even to examine cursorily. The voluminous writings of Sir John Woodroffe give us a sample of such material, to which could be added many others derived from schools of Tantra, whether Bengali, Tibetan, or of the west coast of India, extending from Ujjain down to Kanyakumārī. For a complete list of the available works one is referred to the publication of Harvard University by Professor. W. Norman Brown (pp. 99 ff.) under what he calls 'Critical Apparatus'.

We have carefully avoided entering into the deeper polemical controversies in the present study, in order to salvage this wonderful work from being lost within the ocean of verbosity, whose volume is still increasing as days pass by. In order to settle any controversy on such matters, it has once and for all been recommended in the Bhagavadgītā, in the words of Śrī Krishna himself, that it is the canonical texts (*śāstra*) that are to be treated as authorities (*pramāṇa*s) (XVI, 24). *Guru vākya* (the word of the Guru) and *śāstra pramāṇam* (the authority of canonical scriptures) are the two final touchstones for doctrinal validity or acceptability. For our own part, we have avoided getting lost in the bypaths of Tantrism or textbooks of Yoga, however much each might claim to be more secret or profound than another. Our enquiry would never come to an end were we to follow them.

We have used for reference two Upaniṣads which we have come across, one of which is called the *Saubhāgyalakṣmī* and the other the *Yogarāja* (texts and translations of both these Upaniṣads have been provided in Appendices - I & II respectively).

The very fact that these two texts claim to be Upaniṣads must be sufficient guarantee that they are fully acceptable to Vedantins. What is more, both of them use the word *brahmacakra* or *brahmarandhra*, thus bringing into the picture the notion of the Absolute, which is a sure indication that the context is that of the Absolute and not any other lesser discipline, such as that of Kapila, Kaṇāda, or Gautama. Tantra, which gives primacy to the Goddess, would not normally speak of *brahmarandhra* either.

36

तवाज्ञाचक्रस्थं तपनशशिकोटिद्युतिधरं
परं शंभुं वन्दे परिमिलितपार्श्वं परचिता ।
यमाराध्यन् भक्त्या रविशशिशुचीनामविषये
निरातङ्के लोके निवसति हि भालोकभुवने ॥

tavājñā cakrastharn tapanaśaśikoṭi dyuti dharaṁ
paraṁ śaṁbhuṁ vande parimilita pārśvaṁ paracitā ।
yam ārādhyan bhaktyā ravi śaśi śucīnām aviṣaye
nirātaṅke loke nivasati hi bhāloka bhuvane ॥

tava — Your; *ājñā cakrasthaṁ* — as placed in the willing centre; *tapana śasī koṭi dyuti dharaṁ* — shining with the brilliance of millions of suns and moons; *para citā parimilita pārśvaṁ* — flanks illumined by the light of the intelligibles beyond; *paraṁ śaṁbhuṁ vande* — I adore the transcendant Śiva; *yaṁ bhaktyā ārādhyan* — whom, worshipping with devotion; *ravi śaśi śucīnāṁ aviṣaye* — lifted beyond the reach of sun, moon and fire; *nirātaṅke loke* — in that domain above all need; *bhāloka bhuvane* — in that bright world of light; *nivasati hi* — he dwells indeed

I adore that Śiva ultimate, as placed in Your willing
centre, shining with the brilliance
Of millions of suns and moons, whose flanks are illumined
by the light of the intelligibles beyond;
Whom, worshipping with devotion, lifted beyond the reach
of sun, moon or fire,
In that shining domain above all need, one lives indeed in
that bright world of light.

Hardly any tangible item or aspect of beauty, whether in terms of line, light or colour, is suggested in this verse, which refers to the first and the foremost of chakras, to be placed at the positive limit of the vertical parameter. Boundless light seems to be the only factor that is specially underlined in this verse. There are references to the sun, moon and fire, as also to transcending worldly necessities or evils. Transcendence has unmistakable primacy over immanence here. A fluorescent form of brilliance is referred to, which seems to adorn two sides of the vague and almost mathematically pure figure that is intended to emerge into view after one has read this verse as a whole. The Absolute can be viewed both in its immanent and transcendent glory, at one and the same time. Between immanence and transcendence we could imagine degrees of reciprocity, complementarity or compensation. Even when numerator factors predominate over denominator factors, or vice versa, it is still possible to perform that final operation proper to the highest intuitive faculty of the mind, in which the full cancellation of counterparts could take place. Even the distinction between the lower and the higher *brahman* becomes abolished in the light of such a cancellation. Although incidentally examined here under the aegis of 'the willing centre' (*ājñā*), the content, at whatever centre it might be, has to remain the same. It is always a foregone conclusion in Advaita Vedanta that there should not be any internal or external difference concerning a finalized notion of the Absolute when considered in itself, by itself, for itself and through itself. The lowest chakra, *mūlādhāra*, and the highest, *ājñā* or *sahasrāra*, indicate only incidental attributes of the absolute Substance which remains the same, whatever else might be subject to change. This is an epistemological presupposition fundamental to Advaita Vedanta which the reader should keep in mind as applicable to this or any other chakra to be described hereafter.

1. 'Śiva ultimate', (*param śambhum*).

   Param means 'ultimate'. *Śambhu* is Śiva. Śiva represents an auspicious value, when he is not thought of as mythological divinity of the Hindu pantheon. When the notion is pushed in the direction of the omega point of the vertical parameter, as high as the mind of a votary can reach according to his mental capacities, we attain to the status of a notion of the Absolute, which could be said to mark the thinnest mathematical point of absolute or general possibility to the mind of any man. Such a possibility exists in the human mind. Mathematics as a science could not have been developed without such a faculty being normal to human beings.

2. 'Willing centre', (*ājñā cakra*).

As a convention in yogic literature, a 'willing centre' is generally referred to as being placed between the two eyebrows. The physical need not correspond strictly to the psychological monomark. We have to keep in mind only the overall structural implications here. Some texts might attempt to clarify the content of this centre by using comparisons taken from a biological context, as when they refer to the petals of a lotus flower. Sometimes they use the language of polygons, which could refer to crystals, stars or even snowflakes. The points of the compass, whether four, eight or sixteen, could be referred to as rays or tips of petals, pointing upward or downward. The symbols of the phallus (*liṅgam*) and the womb (*yoni*) are also conventionally used to indicate protolinguistically the content of each centre. The reader is asked to scrutinize the legend and chart in the appendix to verify for himself the component elements that are meant to be included within each of these conventional centres. Also he should note there that the *Saubhāgyalakṣmī Upaniṣad* and the *Yogarāja Upaniṣad* have to be viewed complementarily in their description of the chakras. Whatever the order might be, the result of cancellation, as we have said, is meant to be the same non-dual Absolute represented by the *śrī cakra* in more static terms. It is meant to be merely a frame of reference. Dynamism could be introduced into this static relational pattern according to the intuitive imagination of gifted men of wisdom, whether philosopher (*manīṣin*) or poet (*kavi*).

3. 'Millions of suns and moons', (*tapana śaśi koṭi*).

The reference to innumerable suns and moons is to show that quantity does not count when higher generalities, in terms of points on a parameter, are involved. Zeros added to either side of a unit number, when they exceed six, tend to have a qualitative significance rather than a quantitative one. When the sun is placed at the omega point and fire at the alpha point, it is easy to locate the moon between them on the same parameter. The moon also figures below, in the third line. It has to occupy a real position between what is conceptual and what is perceptual, which would be the zero point.

Multiplication beyond the zero point is qualitative, beyond perceptual grasp. It is lifted to the conceptual side. When children play, they are very intrigued with that. They will defeat the other fellow by this. A child will call another by a degrading name and then say, 'I take it back', which cancels the original harm. His two statements are not of the same order. The first is actual but the second lifts the conversation to a conceptual status.

4. 'Whose sides are illumined', (*parimilita pārśvam*).

At sunset sometimes one can see a cloud that is illumined from the opposite side. The silver lining of a cloud suggests the same kind of bilateral fluorescent light. *Iḍā* and *piṅgalā*, which are the left and right nerve strands running from the lowest to the highest point, represent this aspect of the light of consciousness in yogic literature. Śaṅkara avoids such technicalities, because structuralism itself could become a fetish in the hands of persons who are not adepts in using such language.

5. 'Beyond the reach of the sun, moon or fire', (*ravi śaśi śucīnām aviṣaye*).

The *ājñā cakra* under consideration here is evidently meant to refer to the positive or non-Self side of the Absolute. Pure mathematical concepts cannot be tainted by factors which belong to the necessary side of life. The moon, as we have said, marks here the zero point in the scheme. Being raised beyond the zero point is a sure guarantee that all items of necessity, suffering or sin have been left behind negatively and thus transcended. The reference to the 'world of light' in which the votary lives is thus justified.

37

विशुद्धौ ते शुद्धस्फटिकविशदं व्योमजनकं
शिवं सेवे देवीमपि शिवसमानव्यवसिताम्।
ययोः कान्त्या यान्त्या शशिकिरणसारूप्यसरणेर
विधूतान्तर्ध्वान्ता विलसति चकोरीव जगती ॥

viśuddhau te śūddha sphaṭika viśadaṁ vyoma janakaṁ
śivaṁ seve devīm api śiva samāna vyavasitām ।
yayoḥ kāntyā yāntyā śaśikiraṇa sārūpya saraṇera
vidhūtāntar dhvāntā vilasati cakorīva jagatī ॥

te viśuddhau — In Your *viśuddhi cakra*; *śuddha sphaṭika viśadaṁ* — pure/crystal clear; *vyoma janakaṁ* — sky-generating; *śivaṁ* — Śiva (and); *śiva samāna vyavasitām* — with parity of status with Śiva; *devīm api seve* — the Goddess also, I adore; *yayoḥ yāntyā śaśi kiraṇa sārūpya saraṇeḥ kāntyā* — by whose combined moonbeam-like fluorescence; *vidhūta antaḥ dhvāntā* — with banished inner dross; *cakori iva* — like a female partridge; *jagatī* — the whole world (hereunder); *vilasatī* — it shines

In Your viśuddhi chakra, *crystal clear and sky-generating,*
I adore Śiva, and the Goddess also with a parity of status with Śiva;
By whose combined, streaming, moonbeam-like fluorescence,
With banished inner dross, like a female partridge, the world hereunder shines.

In coming to verse thirty-seven, we first note that it is meant to mark a position intermediate between the omega point and the zero point. The word *viśuddhi*, which means 'purity' or 'clarity', still suggests a transparency of the spirit. A distinction is made here between bursting or scintillating light and fluorescent light like that of moonbeams. Moonlight is supposed to be watery, because its light seems to be flowing vertically down into the lower half. The uniqueness of God at the omega point is now seen to be compromised, and we find that the negative aspect of the situation, which belongs properly to the consciousness of the negative Self, is attributed to the consciousness of the female partridge (*cakora*). Without this peculiar literary device, so cleverly resorted to by Śaṅkara here, it would be impossible to make the sky-generating light cancel out against its counterpart.

1. 'Sky-generating', (*vyoma janakam*).

   The numerator side of understanding refers to hypostatic factors, under which a sky could be legitimately included.

2. 'Parity of status', (*samāna vyavasitām*).

   Two personalities are seen to be introduced at this level. In the text, the phrase *samāna vyavasitām* where *samāna* means 'equal' and *vyavasitām* means 'functioning', justifies our translation as 'parity'.

3. 'Like a female partridge', (*cakorī iva*).

   Śaṅkara resorts to the consciousness of a female partridge in order to make it easy for the reader to think of the counterpart of the bright side of consciousness described in the first half of the verse. It is within consciousness, whether of an animal, a bird or a human being, that we can correctly represent to ourselves that cancellable counterpart of consciousness which the numerator is supposed to represent in hypostatic terms. He takes care even to say that it is a female partridge, to show that negativity is more consistent with feminine consciousness than with masculine consciousness.

4. 'The world hereunder shines', (*jagatī vilasati*).

   The world cannot ordinarily be said to be shining, except in terms of consciousness. Advaita philosophy depends on the cancellation of two selves, the *pratyag ātma*, the negative Self, and the *ātma* which is its own mirror reflection (*cidābhāsa*). Whether it is a concept or a percept which looms, the world has to refer to one or the other of these two aspects of consciousness to have any reality at all, whether existent, subsistent, or both. When moonlight falls on a seaside village with its white walls, the calm and pleasing scene is not the same village as seen under the blazing noonday sun. The female partridge sees the world as if by moonlight. It does not like the sun. What it sees is thus to be distinguished from what this chakra implies on its positive side.

38

समुन्मीलत्संवित्कमलमकरन्दैकरसिकं
भजे हंसद्वन्द्वं किमपि महतां मानसचरम्।
यदालापादष्टादशगुणितविद्यापरिणति-
र्यदादत्ते दोषाद् गुणमखिलमद्भ्यः पय इव॥

samunmīlat saṁvit kamala makarandaika rasikaṁ
bhaje haṁsa dvandvaṁ kimapi mahatāṁ mānasa caram ।
yadālāpād aṣṭādaśa guṇita vidyā pariṇatir
yad ādatte doṣād guṇam akhilam adbhyaḥ paya iva ॥

samunmīlat saṁvit kamala makaranda — the nectar in the lotus blooming within consciousness; *eka rasikaṁ* — intently/solely enjoying; *kim api mahatāṁ* — of certain great ones; *mānasa caram* — moving within the minds; *haṁsa dvandvaṁ bhaje* — I adore the pair of swans; *yat ālāpat* — as a result of whose conversation/elaboration; *aṣṭādaśa guṇita vidyā pariṇatiḥ* — the maturation of the eighteen arts takes place; *yat doṣāt* — they (the swans) from dross; *akhilam guṇaṁ* — all goodness (therefrom); *adbhyaḥ paya iva* — like milk from water; *ādatte* — extracts

I adore those twin swans, intent on enjoying the nectar
Of the lotus blooming within the consciousness of certain great ones,
Moving within whose minds, as a result of their elaboration,
The maturation of the eighteen arts takes place, freed from dross, their goodness extracted as milk from water.

In verse thirty-eight we have the picture of two swans swimming in a lotus pond, having at least one lotus blooming at its centre. The first thing to notice about the overall design of this chakra, besides the fact that its conventional name is omitted, is that there is no value referred to that is especially spiritual. It is, rather, meant to be a normalized version of value, where spirituality and morality meet and cancel out into a picture representing Beauty in a very real form. In parks and gardens anywhere in the world it is possible to see a pair of swans swimming in a pond, and it is not difficult to imagine a lotus flower blooming at its centre. Swans are animals that need food in the ordinary sense, and although water supports vitality in a deeper sense, other food such as milk is required for the sustenance of normal life here. The mind with its two functions having a horizontal parity between them, one of which could be auditory and the other visual in its reference — as with music and dance — could be conceded to be the ground on which beings find some sort of aesthetic pleasure or enjoyment. Mindstuff is here compared to water, while something more nourishing, which contains body-building elements of food, is necessary to make the two swans have their enjoyable active life within the pond.

The classical theory of aesthetics belonging to Sanskrit culture comprises all enjoyable artistic values within the scope of a fanlike expansion or elaboration of the elements of interest that could be normal to human beings. These are supposed to be the nine essences, called *rasa*s. The nine *rasa*s are *śṛṅgāra* (love), *vīra* (heroism), *bībhatsa* (disgust), *raudra* (anger), *hāsya* (mirth), *bhayānaka* (terror), *karuṇa* (pity), *adbhuta* (wonder), and *śānta* (tranquillity). If nine *rasa*s are given to the visual (actual) side, nine *rasa*s must be given to the auditory (virtual) side too. Thus we have, between visible and audible arts, eighteen *rasa*s spread out like a fan, resembling the order of colours in the spectrum. The colour red is always associated with passion, because the conventional language of colour is understood, though vaguely, even in common parlance. The point where horizontal values meet the vertical parameter is to be located exactly at the core of the lotus. The one hundred-eighty degrees above that zero point could be divided into eighteen sectors of ten degrees on the plus and minus sides of the structural whole. The long and beautiful necks of the swans can delve down into the mud to pull out the tender edible roots of the lotus plant, on which they are supposed to thrive. When swans migrate to the Himalayan regions it is conventionally understood that some edible parts of the lotus plant are carried in their beaks, at the tip of their outstretched necks. The swans reach Mānasarovar, the 'mind lake' located somewhere high in the Himalayas, in due course, enabling them to live at a celestial level and on an earthly level alternately. Highly evolved souls are compared in Hindu literature to a central locus of this kind when they are called *paramahaṁsa*s, which means that they are very realistically related to the total context of the absolute Value. The two swans touch and do not touch the lotus, like spirits apart, by participating through subtle verticality only at the zero point.

1. 'The nectar of the lotus', (*kamala makarandam*).

   Nectar is something nourishing and enjoyable, of which milk could be considered a particular instance. Nectar is more than milk by its added enjoyability. The extra elements of enjoyability result from the elaboration of aesthetic interests in the minds of the two swans treated as one.

2. 'Certain great ones', (*kim api mahatām*).

   To the perfected *paramahaṁsa*s the duality between actual or virtual, and hypostatic or hierophantic values have all been normalized.

3. 'The maturation of the eighteen arts', (*aṣṭādaśa guṇita vidyā pariṇatiḥ*).

   There is a central locus in the neutral and absolute Self, which is the source from which all enjoyment must start, whether in visual or auditory arts. Even when the arts are withdrawn, in higher samadhi, these outgoing items of elaboration could be thought of as each being withdrawn into its own source, which is this same central locus. Maturation should not be mixed up with the idea of evolution because of the use of the Sanskrit word *pariṇāma* used here. Maturation here only increases its eidetic content without changing it horizontally, as when we say that twilight matures fully when the sun is four degrees below the horizon. A mango ripens and matures without changing its identity horizontally.

4. 'Goodness extracted as milk from water', (*ādatte guṇam akhilam adbhyaḥ paya iva*).

   Milk has a horizontal value reference which is existential in status. Water, on the other hand, has a vertical reference because of its pure sapidity. Thus, we get the two references in respect of value, within the fanlike amplitude of which we could insert the double spectrum of both auditory and visual arts radiating from a central core which is both a source as well as an epicentre for all manifestations or absorptions.

Concluding Remarks

In this verse the language of conventional cliches has been used in an unobtrusive manner, by which it is possible to see that what is real could be the same as what is ideal, when viewed neutrally and normally, as between perceptual and conceptual values. The yogi has nothing to add or subtract here. The *Brahmasūtra*s recommend such an attitude, in which nothing is to be explained away from life nor added as an idea to embellish reality. One has neither to paint lilies nor gild gold. Vedanta is not a form of idealism. It is fully realistic, as the following verse of Narayana Guru's *Darśanamālā* (X.9), clearly underlines:

Of this (world) there is certainly nothing to be rejected nor accepted;
As for the Self, it is self-luminous.
Having understood (thus), one should withdraw (from all functionings);
Thereafter, function does not repeat (itself).

39

तव स्वाधिष्ठाने हुतवहमधिष्ठाय निरतं
तमीडे संवर्तं जननि महतीं तां च समयाम्।
यदालोके लोकान् दहति महति क्रोधकलिते
दयार्द्रा यादृष्टिः शिशिरमुपचारं रचयति ॥

tava svādhiṣṭhāne hutavaham adhiṣṭhāya niratam̐
tam īḍe sam̐vartam̐ janani mahatīm̐ tām̐ ca samayām ।
yad āloke lokān dahati mahati krodha kalite
dayārdrā yā dr̥ṣṭiḥ śiśiram upacāram̐ racayati ॥

janani — O Mother; *tava svādhiṣṭhāne* — in Your *svādhiṣṭhāna*; *hutavaham* — the sacrificial fire; *adhiṣṭhāya* — placing; *tām̐ sam̐vartam̐* — that fire of doom; *tām̐ mahatīm̐* — as also that great one; *samayām ca* — called Samaya; *niratam īḍe* — unceasingly, deeply ever I adore; *mahati krodha kalite āloke lokān dahati yat* — when, by His look of great rage, the worlds burn; *dayārdrā yā dr̥ṣṭiḥ* — Her mercy-moist regard; *śiśiram upacāram̐* — the cooling touch of early spring; *racayati* — renders (to it)

O Mother, I praise, placing in Your svādhiṣṭhāna *the fire of sacrifice,*
Ever looking upon it as the great fire of doom, and placing there her also
Called Samaya, *so that when the worlds are burning due to His anger,*
Her mercy-moist regard renders to it the cooling touch of early spring.

Water cools and fire burns within the totality of the absolute content of reality, viewed as a phenotype and not as a noumenon. We can think of these two factors, fire and water, as participating from opposite sides of the total situation. When viewed from such an overall perspective, we can appreciate how this chakra called *svādhiṣṭhāna* is also based on the principle of the cancellation of counterparts. On a hot summer day a cool and perfumed breeze can act as an absolute source of consolation, even if it should last only for a few moments. The joy of cancellation does not depend upon the duration of the state of consolation and could be enjoyed for itself in the span of a split second.

1. *'svādhiṣṭhāna'*

   The term *svādhiṣṭhāna* suggests that it is a chakra founded on itself. We have examined the status of the previous verse, which corresponds to the chakra conventionally named *anāhata*, which suggests something like a bell that has not been struck. A bell that is unstruck would represent a neutral position between the possibility of its sound and its own material existence. When we come to the *svādhiṣṭhāna*, we have to put its locus a little lower in the vertical axis, because the basis of the chakra is within itself, not on the numerator side of effects. It has a negative reference, but the numerator against which the cancellation within its scope is to take place has got a highly positive status. Finally, lower and higher are meant to have no differentiating significance between chakras or *ādhāra*s.

2. 'The fire of sacrifice', (*hutavaham*).

   We find two references here to fire, one to the fire of sacrifice and the other to the fire of doom. We have to locate these two fires correctly at their proper structural positions before we can grasp the status of this chakra. The fire of sacrifice could be imagined to be somewhere near the region of the navel, just below the zero point — on the side of existence — because such a fire has to be really capable of burning at least some fuel. This idea of 'the fire of sacrifice' is verified in verse seventy-eight.

3. 'Fire of doom', (*saṁvartaṁ*).

The 'fire of doom' cannot be located in the same position as the fire of sacrifice. Doomsday is always in the future and necessarily has an apocalyptic status. The function of doom is thus to be imagined as having a numerator reference, even when that picture has been produced far beyond the omega point in the possible worlds of prospective values. To balance this exaggerated apocalyptic tendency, there is a need to postulate its counterpart in the form of a feminine elemental factor which has to be existential rather than subsistential. Such a factor is what is meant to be implied by the second goddess, named Samaya.

4. 'Samaya'

We are familiar with this goddess favoured by the Tāntric school of Samayins, whom we discussed in our comments on verse thirty-three. The total overall Goddess, having an absolutist status, cannot be held responsible for any partial or unilateral function. This must be the reason why Śaṅkara resorts to a goddess already known in the context of Mother worship, who is capable here of counteracting the heat implied in the omega point reference to the fire of doom.

5. 'Cooling touch', (*śiśiram upacāram*).

We have already explained that this kind of cooling need not be eternally operating. Cartesian occasionalism permits the notion of cancellation taking place at a given moment and thus revealing the will of the Absolute. Taken in this sense, even in this world of suffering, there are pleasant moments of absolute Joy, which Wordsworth would perhaps call 'intimations of immortality'.

40

तटित्वन्तं शक्त्या तिमिरपरिपन्थिस्फुरणया
स्फुरन्नानारत्नाभरणपरिणद्धेन्द्रधनुषम् ।
तव श्यामं मेघं कमपि मणिपूरैकशरणं
निषेवे वर्षन्तं हरमिहिरतप्तं त्रिभुवनम् ॥

taṭitvantaṁ śaktyā timira paripanthi sphuraṇayā
sphuran nānā ratnābharaṇa pariṇaddhendra dhanuṣam ।
tava śyāmaṁ meghaṁ kam api maṇipūraika śaraṇaṁ
niṣeve varṣantaṁ hara mihira taptaṁ tribhuvanam ॥

kam api tava maṇipūra eka śaraṇaṁ — as found in certain contemplatives who take (full) refuge (solely) in Your *maṇipūra*; *timira paripanthi sphuraṇayā* — darkness banishing and bursting into sparks; *śaktyā taṭitvantaṁ* — as traversed forcefully by flash of lightning; *sphurat nānā ratna ābharaṇa* — with brightly-lit, varied gem-set jewels; *pariṇaddha indra dhanuṣam* — matured into Indra's bow; *tava śyāmaṁ meghaṁ* — Your dark cloud; *hara mihira taptaṁ tribhuvanam* — (over) the three worlds agonized by the heat of Śiva-sun; *varṣantaṁ* — as it pours down, rains; *niṣeve* — I adore

As found in certain contemplatives who take full refuge in Your maṇipūra,
I adore that dark cloud of Yours, as traversed by forceful lightning,
Banishing darkness and shining, bursting into sparks with the varied-gem-decked maturity of Indra's bow,
While over the three worlds, agonized by the heat of Śiva-sun, it sheds its showering waters.

In verse forty, we find a description of a cloudburst in a thunderstorm, so familiar to anybody in any part of the world. The name *maṇipūra* adds only a slight embellishment to the real event pictured here and to the minimum extent required in the name of literary flourish. *Maṇi* means 'precious gem', and *pūra* means 'filling up'. *Maṇipūra* suggests a plenitude of gems. The sky and the stars have been compared to a box of gems by many philosophers, including Kant. The jewel box is the counterpart of the sky, especially when beautiful shining gems are displayed against a dark background which could stand for the box, sometimes described as made of ebony, as in verse ninety-four. A rainbow that could dominate a dark cloud is one of the most beautiful of natural sights. Wordsworth says that such a sight makes the heart of the beholder, young or old, leap up in joy. If we put a circle round such a picture and insert streaks of lightning, accompanied by thunder, we get all the component parts that make up a chakra or *ādhāra* even in the world of natural phenomena. Nothing need be left to the imaginations. Lightning traverses a cloud at right angles as a rule, and, if we treat ramifications in it as incidental, a vertical parameter links lightning and thunder. The dark cloud could be considered the body, while thunder and lightning together constitute the soul. Thunder descends while lightning ascends to meet it, or vice versa. The principle of action and retroaction is implied in this situation. Rain is a double blessing that descends onto the terra firma, and all living beings welcome it with gratitude. Let us examine now the implications of the expressions in this verse.

1. 'Certain contemplatives', (*kam api*).

    This reference is to suggest that not all contemplatives will arrive at the full understanding of this vision of absolute Beauty. Most contemplatives are likely to make a personal fetish of their own approach to the high value of the Absolute, thus having a tendency to remove such a value, by abstraction and generalization, from everyday reality. Śaṅkara is conscious of this tendency to fetishism. He therefore underlines that an actual cloudburst or thunderstorm could contain elements of wonder and overwhelming beauty adequate to give significant content to the notion of the highest of absolutes.

In full-fledged Vedanta nothing real is to be explained away in favour of mathematical or schematic abstractions. There is nothing to be added to or subtracted from the Real, as it is in itself, when it is properly understood in the light of Śaṅkara's Advaita Vedanta.

2. 'Traversed by forceful lightning', (*taṭitvantam śaktyā*).

Lightning traversing a dark cloud suggests at once that it cuts through the cloud at right angles. Thus the vertical parameter and its positive and negative aspects have been inserted into the chakra as an important linking relational feature.

3. 'Varied-gem-decked maturity', (*nānā ratnābharaṇa pariṇatam*).

A rainbow seen in the sky is sometimes faint and sometimes clear. Sometimes above one rainbow a second, fainter, rainbow can be distinguished. The fainter colours of the second rainbow, which are inverted in spectral order by a double refraction, would justify the aptness of the term 'maturity' as employed here. A rainbow could suggest fireworks, especially when we think of the chemical elements, which represent colours of the spectrum according to the periodic law. Stars such as the 'white dwarfs' and the 'red gaints' could be thought of as having their elemental peculiarities, as could the different coloured gems. The implications of the term 'maturity' (*pariṇata*) has been explained previously under verse thirty-eight. The rainbow has been named in the various vernaculars of India by popular agreement as belonging either to Kāma or to Indra. When attributed to Indra it gets a more absolutist status, because Indra is the chief of all gods.

4. 'The three worlds', (*tribhuvanam*).

Physiographically, we cannot think of rain moistening the three worlds, but contemplative cosmology permits three levels of value called *bhūḥ, bhuvaḥ* and *svaḥ* (earth, atmosphere, and heaven). *Bhuvarloka* represents the intermediate world of air between *bhūrloka* and *svarloka*, which represent terrestrial and celestial regions, respectively. Modern cosmology admits of millions of miles of empty space between our own planetary system and that of the truly celestial bodies in the Milky Way or in other galaxies. The principle of heat and the principle of cold prevail not only physiographically but also in the large extended cosmology known to modern physics, which is now beginning to talk of black and white holes, matter and antimatter, etc.

5. 'Śiva-sun', (*hara mihira*).

The sun is the source of energy in our solar system. As a logical consequence it must necessarily have a negative counterpart at an opposite limiting pole, by virtue of which the energy gained is balanced by an equal loss, in order to maintain the equilibrium of the cosmos. 'Śiva-sun' marks the omega point limit of the total situation as a source of positive energy. Modern theoretical terms like 'entropy' and 'negentropy' justify such notions.

41

तवाधारे मूले सह समयया लास्यपरया
नवात्मानं मन्ये नवरसमहाताण्डवनटम्।
उभाभ्यामेताभ्यामुदयविधिमुद्दिश्य दयया
सनाथाभ्यां जज्ञे जनकजननीमज्जगदिदम्॥

tavādhāre mūle saha samayayā lāsya parayā
navātmānaṁ manye nava rasa mahā tāṇḍava naṭam ।
ubhābhyām etābhyām udaya vidhim uddiśya dayayā
sanāthābhyāṁ jajñe janaka jananī majjagad idam ॥

tava mūle ādhāre — in Your *mūlādhāra*; *lāsya parayā* — given to her light-step dance; *samayayā saha* — together with *Samaya*; *nava rasa mahā tāṇḍava naṭam* — that great bold-step dancer giving expression to the nine *rasas*; *nava ātmānaṁ* — new Self; *manye* — I meditate (on); *udaya vidhim uddiśya* — intending the (re)birth (of the world); *dayayā* — by (with) mercy; *sanāthābhyāṁ* — by the joint lordship; *etābhyām ubhābhyāṁ* — of these two; *idam jagat* — this world; *janaka jananī mat* — (the status of) having both father and mother; *jajñe* — is known to have/become

I meditate on Your new self as placed at Your mūlādhāra,
together with Samaya
Given to her light-step dance, as also that great bold-step dancer;
Giving expression thereby to all nine aesthetic interests, thus by their joint lordship,
By mercy intending the rebirth of the world, they confer on it the renewed status of having both father and mother.

Verse forty-one refers by name to the *mūlādhāra cakra*. Already, in verse nine, the same *mūlādhāra* has been referred to as 'earth'. There the chakras were mentioned in an ascending order, starting with the *mūlādhāra* as the lowest, which seems to agree with textbooks of yoga. *Mūlādhāra* evidently has a firm ontological reference in the terra firma itself, so there is no room for ambiguity in the matter of fixing its epistemological status among the chakras.

About the actual number of chakras to be officially admitted into our discussion for the purposes of this work, there are particular uncertainties to be noted. In verse nine, counting the chakras that have been named and structurally located in an ontologically biased phenomenological scheme, we find that the *sahasrāra padma* (thousand-petalled lotus) figures as the upper limiting point, making seven chakras in all. In the structure of the *śrī cakra*, as described in verse eleven, we find nine centres of *prakṛti*, or *mūla prakṛti* (prime nature). If we now ask ourselves if there would be any objection to including a tenth, it becomes a fairly ambiguous matter to decide one way or the other. But for purposes of structural symmetry, it would be neater, mathematically at least, to think of 'five plus five' as making up the totality of the chakras. This is not, however, favoured by Śaṅkara, who cannot be said to be without a sense of neatness in his mathematical abstractions and generalizations. Ten can be arrived at by adding one to nine, or nine by subtracting one from ten. When ascending dialectics is involved adding one to nine would be normal, but in descending dialectics subtracting one from ten would be normal. The demands of mechanistic symmetry are not the same as a truly structural symmetry which respects such factors as reciprocity and complementarity. As in the case of extras accompanying a football team, where the bigger number could be favoured, here the tendency toward numbers greater than the minimum required could not be taken as objectionable. Two extras for a match could accompany the team reasonably, even though they will not necessarily be employed in the match itself. Only one of them may be required in the normal course of events, but in principle the other is also necessary, though he will not usually enter into the game actually. A similar status has to be given to the limiting chakra at the plus or minus ends, depending upon the contingency that might call for their entry into the game. There is an either/or option presented here, whether it is an ascending or a descending series with which we happen to be concerned. The status of the *sahasrāra cakra* in verse nine, which would make seven very tangible chakras, is thus to be treated as an extra when we accept six as the normal basis. The *mūlādhāra cakra* could similarly have a tenth one added to its negative limit. It is not difficult to recognize a certain methodological alternative choice implied in the enumeration of different chakras in different textbooks, for which we too have to make some allowance. We could recognize six basic chakras, referred to ordinarily as the *ṣaḍ ādhāra* or *ṣaḍ-cakra*. When verse nine and the present reference to *mūlādhāra* and five others are considered together (verses thirty-six through forty-one), keeping in our minds the either/or ambiguities involved, it will be possible for us to justify the nine *mūla prakṛtis* represented in the *śrī cakra*. The word *prakṛti* would suggest an ontological perspective rather than a teleological one. This does not mean that a teleological perspective is to be ruled out altogether, for both the ascending and the descending methods are equally permissible. Some have suggested that we could invert the *śri cakra* to obtain the male Śiva chakra, but such an inversion is not called for because Vedanta, at least with Śaṅkara, gives primacy to ontological cause over teleological effect in its methodology. A rope is more real than the idea of a snake superimposed on it. Existence must have primacy over essence, as even modern existentialists claim. Sense data cannot be explained away, and any philosophy that tends to such a form of idealism only discredits itself by having to contradict common sense at every stage of its speculation. Appearance might overcover reality but reality is not abolished thereby. Thus it is that the *śrī cakra* calls the nine centres by the name *mūla prakṛtis*. *Mūla* means 'root' or 'source', and *prakṛti* means 'nature'. The ontological bias here is inevitable and necessary for a fully scientific approach. If a value called absolute Beauty is to come within human experience at all, the eighth chakra or *ādhāra* could be added to or subtracted from the basic seven recognized in verse nine and then it could be named either *brahmacakra* or *brahmarandhra* as seen in the two Upaniṣads that we have used for reference (see appendix). Thus the term *aṣṭabandha* (eight stable positions) sometimes used in connection with installation of temple images could be justified in terms meaning 'eight bonds'.

One more detail remains to be clarified. In verse eleven we have referred to the four of *śrīkaṇṭha*'s, evidently referring to a masculine divinity used as a monomark. Any monomark having a numerator reference could be considered masculine. In the present verse we find a reference to Śiva, as a masculine divinity, dancing with a parity of status with a feminine divinity, although the *mūlādhāra* refers to a lower limit in the total situation. The masculine divinity here still has a numerator reference, just as in verse nine the female divinity is promoted to the seventh chakra, beyond the chakras known to the *kula* path, which has still got a denominator reference. Śiva is here on the denominator side with a numerator reference. 'New' means his reference is on the numerator side, while Samaya's reference is normal.

1. 'Your new self', (*navātmānam*).

   This must have an omega point reference and thus must imply a masculine Śiva, because already the feminine is represented by the other goddess called Samaya, who has a normal status with an ontological reference. Newness only implies that its reference is positive.

2. 'Your *mūlādhāra*'.

   Each chakra represents the totality of the Absolute in a normalized form in the context of beauty as a tangible reality. This reference in the second person singular is therefore justified. The word *mūlādhāra* still refers to the ontological or 'source' side of the situation.

3. 'Samaya'.

The status of the goddess Samaya remains the same. Because the school of Samayins were not aware of the rival cancellable aspects, their approach was unilateral, immanent and within the scope of the three *guṇas*. A similar goddess is under reference in verses thirty-four, thirty-seven and thirty-nine. According to the context we have to give a legitimate status to each of these Samaya goddesses or divinities.

4. 'Her *lāsya* dance . . . that *tāṇḍava* dancer'.

Lāsya and *tāṇḍava* are the two styles of dancing proper to feminine and masculine dancers, respectively. *Tāṇḍava* is characterized by a sinuous curve that is vertical like a frequency, while *lāsya* has got a horizontal reference as in a wavelength. This distinction is well known in the Bharata Nāṭya school of Indian dance.

5. 'All nine aesthetic interests', (*navarasa*).

The nine aesthetic interests could be multiplied by two, as they could pertain to visual or auditory expressions in art. Basically they are nine and belong to both of them.

6. 'Joint lordship', (*sanāthābhyām ubhābhyām*).

A husband is considered the master and the wife the mistress. Thus, there is a kind of lordship, whether masculine or feminine, implied within the parity of the status of the two divinities here. Vertically viewed, they are not husband and wife, but father and mother. It is the grace or the sanction of the absolute Goddess that gives room for all these possibilities or probablities.

7. 'Intending the rebirth of the world', (*udaya vidhim uddiśya*).

The rebirth is intended to be considered as taking place every split second. In verse fifty-five, opening and shutting the eyes represent creation and dissolution. Between the contradiction of the opening and the shutting of the eyes, there is a purer process of becoming which knows no contraries. It has a third or fourth-dimensional staus which should not be mixed up with alternate creation and dissolution.

8. 'Renewed status'.

   Renewed status implies that dissolution took place once, as understood in the idea of the great deluge (*pralaya*). Alternation of creation and dissolution can be viewed in the eternal present or in an eternal moment. Plato's writings justify both these possibilities (cf. *Parmenides* or *Timaeus*).

9. 'Having both father and mother', (*janaka jananīmat*).

   Conferring parenthood implies the idea of having both father and mother, as opposed to being an orphan in respect of one or the other. The correct opposite of double orphanhood, which is anterior to this moment, is what is to be kept in mind here.

Part II
Saundaryalaharī

The Transition from Ānanda to Saundarya

Pundits and professors alike have agreed to put a mark of punctuation between verses forty-one and forty-two, distinguishing what is titled *Ānandalaharī* (verses one through forty-one), from the remainder of the work, entitled *Saundaryalaharī*. This latter title is applicable to the work as a whole. Thus there are two works distinguished within the one work.

The reasons given for making such a division in the very heart of this work vary within a wide range of speculation, and are sometimes not unmixed with imaginary episodes connected with the personal life of the author, Śaṅkara. In verse seventy-five there is a lurking enigmatic reference to a 'Dravidian child' who, on being nourished by the milk of the Goddess, became born as a poet who could write beautiful poetry. Sanskrit is unquestionably the language of the Aryan context, and if a Dravidian poet is to be given the authorship of the latter half of this work, as some surmise, it might be conceded that there seems to be at first sight a change of subject matter or at least a revision in the perspective from which the subject matter is treated after the forty-first verse. The transition, when we come to examine it closely, needs to be effected very carefully, taking into consideration epistemological, methodological, and axiological factors of a very thin speculative order. Evidently this requirement has confused the minds of critics and commentators, both European and Indian, to such an extent that Śaṅkara's authorship of these verses, which belong so beautifully together to the same context of absolute Beauty, is put into question. There is no other author in the field who could even be distantly suggested as a substitute for Śaṅkara.

A discrepancy between the style of the two sections of verses has also been suggested by both pundits and professors. The 'Dravidian child' of verse seventy-five, if an actual product of the Tamil or South Indian context of spirituality, must have been well-versed in the Tantra that was natural to the Śaiva type of *siddhānta* as distinguished from the Vedanta based on the Upaniṣads. Some have even dared to suggest the name of one of the four Tamil saints, Tirujñānasambandhar, in trying to identify this Dravidian child. But it is indeed difficult to explain how that Tamil saint, who has never been credited with any other work in Sanskrit, could have composed a work of such classical finish. The enigmatic nature of the theory of double authorship, put forth so fancifully by a sufficiently respectable group of critics and commentators, is only heightened by their hypothetical proposals and cannot therefore be warranted.

There has even been a legendary incident created to explain this imaginary enigma of double-authorship, in which Śaṅkara comes upon a scene where the supposed real Dravidian author had emblazoned these hundred verses on a wall. As the first forty verses contained deeper secrets of the Śaivite Tantra tradition of proto-Aryan origin, that Dravidian child, at the insistence of the Devī herself, quickly wiped off this first half of the work to guard these secrets from the heterodox Aryan eyes of the Sanskritist Śaṅkara, supposedly a stranger to this ancient Tāntric tradition. In spite of this, however, Śaṅkara is said to have been clever enough to reconstruct from memory these first forty verses, having the gift of remembering words which he had read just once. This highly imaginative episode, even including the Devī as an accomplice in the trick, only proves how natural myth-making is to the human mind. (This story is found in the Malayalam edition of *Saundaryalaharī* by K. Mahadeva Sastri, and in the Theosophical Society edition.

The whole mystery stems from the fact that the schematism and non-verbose language of non-didactic description adopted here by Śaṅkara is something completely new even to his latter-day critics, who tend to dismiss him as a mere *māyāvādin*, that is, a believer in the unreality of the universe, and sometimes even as a *pracchanna bauddha*, a Buddhist in disguise. The theologically biased philosophies that superseded Śaṅkara during the Mughal supremacy in India, and especially those latter forms of philosophy that prevailed after the fall of the Vijayanagar Empire, tended to make Śaṅkara a less important figure on the philosophical scene of the decadent India of recent centuries. A cultural hiatus thus developed — both among Indian pundits and among Western scholars, who came with the East India Company more as curiosity hunters than as genuine scholars belonging to the context proper to the precious cultural expressions such as what we have here before us as a supreme example. The Mysore Wars and the Indian Mutiny could be said to be due mostly to the defects of such a cultural gap or vacuum, which tended to put the graded and orderly development of a sense of cultural values into confusion.

A close scrutiny of verse forty-one will reveal to us that although it refers directly to the *mūlādhāra cakra*, one of the most ontologically biased of all the chakras — even referring to the re-emergence of the world into a more real status from its more amorphous anterior state of flux — this same verse suggests that the personality of the Goddess enjoys only a thin schematic status in terms of absolute Beauty, abstracted and generalized to its possible limit. Thus, while the dance of Śiva and Samaya takes place at the ontological limit of the total situation, the Goddess herself remains unaffected by any rivalry with the pair who are given full freedom to bring the world back into existence, while she remains uninvolved in this phenomenal aspect in an overall and implied sense. The requirements of parity and symmetry are both complied with and transcended at the same time. The climax of normalization in the transition from the perceptual to the conceptual, from the Self to the non-Self, from ontology to teleology, or from physics to metaphysics, has been effected in principle in verse forty-one. The *mūlādhāra* of that verse has nothing earthy about it at all, but represents a world ground, sufficiently fluid and displaying a continuous state of novelty, in which the world gets created and destroyed alternately in split-second terms of momentariness in the eternal present. It is not an inert form of realism that is to be understood here, though the lesser Tāntric schools might tend to imagine that it pertains to their own sets of values. Prejudice in favour of Tantra, as against full-fledged Advaita, implies a gap that is in the minds of critics rather than in the work itself, when properly and more closely examined.

One can see that in verse forty-two Śaṅkara takes care to keep close to the chakra form of meditation, even though he is passing from the limit of ontology (verse forty-one) into the domain of teleology (from verse forty-two onward). In fact, it is hard to discover any abruptness at all in the changeover so harmoniously effected in these transitional verses (forty to forty three) whose sequence is perfect. The world becomes real as the focus of attention is transferred from the feet of the Goddess to her crest jewel, which is made up of twelve suns — for each of the twelve months of the year — fused together and tinged with the twilight colour of magenta, to make them resemble rubies rather than diamonds. Bright diamond would apply more to the midday sun, while red ruby would better represent the twilight sun of morning or evening, or both, when pressed close together and fused into the crest jewel of the revised Goddess, whose cosmological personality is going to be reviewed from head to foot in the remainder of this work. The inside becomes outside in this transition but they retain a unity as if enclosed in circles of consciousness, not unlike the chakras of the section just left behind. We could call these circles 'conceptual chakras', having the same unitive value status, though instead of being placed within the heart of the yogi, they have been put 'over there', as it were, in terms of overt beauty, as in a landscape at sunrise. Thus the gem-set island within consciousness gives place to a Himalayan sunrise. Such is the nature of the transition we have to keep in mind to appreciate the continuity of the same value factor which could be called indifferently *ānanda* or *saundarya*. Whether applicable to life in the Self or in the non-Self, it is the same overwhelming experience of Beauty, viewed from two apparently different perspectives, that we are being treated to by Śaṅkara.

He is conscious of his unrivalled position here, as he pointedly pats himself on the back when he says that this same 'Dravidian child' became an equal to any great poet of antiquity that we could think of. The internal evidence of verse seventy-five is thus, to our eyes at least, overwhelmingly conclusive, and we have no hesitation in brushing aside all rival miscellaneous constructions on this matter. Narayana Guru could be considered a legitimate continuator of this Vedantic tradition. He speaks in the Malayalam language, of Kerala, which is the byproduct of the interaction of the Śiva-worshipping culture of South India and the sun-worshipping culture of the Himalayan regions. The island placed in mid-ocean and the sunlit peaks of the abode of Śiva become interchangeable as absolute Value factors with an inner or outer factor of overwhelming intoxication in terms of Beauty.

42

गतैर्माणिक्यत्वं गगनमणिभिः सान्द्रघटितं
किरीटं ते हैमं हिमगिरिसुते कीर्तयति यः।
स नीडेयच्छायाच्छुरणशबलं चन्द्रशकलं
धनुः शौनासीरं किमिति न निबध्नाति धिषणाम्॥

gatair māṇikyatvaṁ gaganamaṇibhiḥ sāndra ghaṭitaṁ
kirīṭaṁ te haimaṁ himagiri sute kīrtayati yaḥ ।
sa nīḍeyacchāyācchuraṇa śabalaṁ candra śakalaṁ
dhanuḥ śaunāsīraṁ kim iti na nibadhnāti dhiṣaṇām ॥

māṇikyatvaṁ gataiḥ — attained/gone to rubyhood; *gagana maṇibhiḥ* — these sky orbs (twelve); *sāndra ghaṭitaṁ* — pressed close together; *te haimaṁ kirīṭaṁ* — Your golden crown; *himagiri sute* — O daughter of the snow peak; *kīrtayati yaḥ* — he who praises; *saḥ* — he; *nīḍeyacchāyā churaṇa śabalaṁ* — by reflected glory from the gems imbedded (therein); *candra śakalaṁ* — (when) the slender crescent (is produced, seen); *śaunāsīraṁ dhanuḥ* — Indra's bow; *iti dhiṣaṇām* — such impression; *kim na nibadhnāti* — will it not occur?

These sky orbs twelve, attained to rubyhood and pressed close together,
He who can praise thus Your golden crown, O Daughter of the Snowy Peak,
Would he not have then in his mind the impression of the bow of Indra,
When, by reflected glory, a slender crescent is produced by gems imbedded therein.

Verse forty-two can be seen to presuppose the chakra form of visualizing the absolute Beauty-value of the Goddess in the same way as hitherto, through the end of verse forty-one. In verses thirty-nine, forty and forty-one, the transition from inner space to outer space has already been completed. The lower negative limit of the vertical axis has been touched when the split-second world is created once again by the joint dance of the goddess and the god there. It is not an actual terra firma that has been created, but one of an ontologically philosophical order. There is a difference between a clod of earth and a mentally revised version of the same, nor is the clod of earth a mere concept either. The schematic status of a neutrally monistic world — neither material nor mental — was what conferred, by the union of the functions of Śiva and Pārvatī in a combined dance of bliss on equal terms, their joint parenthood on an orphaned universe. Now the *mūlādhāra cakra* stands 'over there', as it were, lifted hypostatically into outer space rather than being located in the inner space of the negative and collective unconsciousness of humanity, which is now awakened to its parenthood, having been hitherto steeped in empty orphanhood. Such are some of the implications of be carried over to the present verse before giving it a treatment which continues to respect the same norms and methodological requirements in the positive series of descending pictures that are going to follow in the remaining verses, beginning at the topmost level of the vertical axis.

The three circles surrounding the *śrī cakra* could still be retained, representing three limits of the upsurging billow of Beauty. It cuts both ways, but here these circles are set in a background of borrowed light called *cidābhāsa,* while in the previous context they glowed with a schematic splendour or 'clear obscurity', still visible to the penetrating intuitive vision of the yogi or contemplative. A peacock's feather seen against the magenta background of a dark cloud would perhaps suggest such a dark-splendid vision of Beauty. The magenta thus participates with the blue sapphire of Indra's world on the one hand, and the ruby with all its brilliant fluorescent luminosity on the other. Such would be the nearest analogy, as indicated by Śaṅkara in the first line of this verse. A lotus shines or looms by virtue of its petals. A crystal radiates colour through its cross-polarized light, emitted, as it were, through a grating, while a supernova sends its beams far and wide. Here the term *mayūkha* (ray of light) would be acceptable to Śaṅkara, while monomarks, lettered or unlettered, could apply to a crystal, and the lotus could speak the language of the *śrī cakra*, using symbols but relying on signs, whether colourful or not. The whole set-up would not be unlike that of a chessboard on which the pieces live and move as in a game.

The 'rubyhood' of this verse has therefore to be understood as belonging to a context of brilliance and not of shade or mere tint. A high degree of saturation, however, need not be ruled out because twelve sky orbs seem to have been pressed together and fused into one large brilliant magenta-coloured ruby here. We can readily guess that the twelve orbs refer to the twilight suns, two for each day, of the twelve months of the year. Imagine such suns at twenty-four sunsets and sunrises, typical of each of the twelve months, blending into twilight redness in the sky to produce this particular shade of magenta. One could even add the more fluorescent inner brilliance of moonsets and moonrises. Locate such a precious stone at the very focal point of your meditation inwardly, where you recognize Beauty to reside in abstract and general terms. This requires some philosophical or contemplative effort, but one could consciously or subconsciously cultivate such an attitude and construct it in absolute Space, in spite of what might actually be experienced through the senses directly in the more overt or quantitative version of the same space. It is thus that the reader can place himself, correctly oriented vis-à-vis the Beauty to be appreciated in the remaining verses.

It is a process of descending dialectics that will now unravel itself step by step before the contemplative, as induced by the poetic suggestions of Śaṅkara, who will present a series of positive chakras instead of the negative ones hitherto presented. The reader has to be fully prepared to appreciate them as they are intended to be, and not as he might wrongly presume under premises unwarranted by a Science of the Absolute. If he should make such a mistake it would be his own fault, and not that of anyone else. A further caution is that the onlooker will not see his visions when he is lying in an easy chair — that is, in a state of passivity — as has been hitherto acceptable. He is now asked to put some constructions on something that is hazily presented to his view at the lower level of sense impressions. The photographer must now adjust his camera and not just take sudden snapshots without minding the glare adjustments. As in a time exposure, the message has to 'sink in' to reveal the superimposition of pictures. The datum of the sense is passive while the higher intelligence constructs its own version of value, by 'doing violence', as Bergson puts it, to the given picture so as to see it related to structural lines which, like holographic ghost-outline pictures of a different kind of wavelength or vibration, will add a stereoscopic structural dimension of light as if superimposed on the original datum more passively given to the eyes.

The creative imagination of a poet is brought into position here. The poet who is capable of such imagination will see in the golden crown of the Goddess another crescent, besides the one that is already to be placed there because the Goddess is the dialectical counterpart of Śiva (as in verse twenty-three). It is normal for the absolute Goddess to retain, at least schematically, a point of participation with the highest and thinnest of vertical points where Śiva, in a purely mathematical context, is placed. The thin crescent represents a numerator limit where such a participation between two absolute values, one belonging to the Devī and the other belonging to Śiva, could meet and abolish themselves mutually into one and the same crescent. There is reference to a second crescent here, said to be that of Indra, who is a demiurge of a lower hypostatic order. The bow of Indra is sometimes spoken of as identical with the rainbow. A rainbow in its jewelled glory belongs more to an ontological than to a teleological order. Wordsworth said that a rainbow in the sky could make his heart leap up within him, in his childhood as well as in his old age. We have in him, therefore, just that poet under reference in this verse, to whom the glory of a rainbow succeeds in producing the echo of an upsurge of absolute Beauty within. Half, at least, of such an experience must be personal or perceptual to him, while the other half could have a conceptual or a mathematical status only. The creative minds of great poets are the common meeting ground of these two grades of crescents. A hypostatic and a hierophantic crescent would thus become legitimately both possible and probable here. In verse forty-six also, there will be two more crescents which are juxtaposed like two brackets at a slightly lower level than the ruby tip of the crown of this verse. The crescent of the Indra context and the mathematically thin crescent already there, which marks the limit of the function of Śivahood, belong to two distinct epistemological orders. The former is phenomenal and the latter is noumenal. If we should think in terms of these two divisions of Kantian philosophy, the two crescents given here could be placed inverted like two brackets enclosing the central value of the big ruby, resulting from the fusion of the twelve twilight orbs of each month. Though not explicitly stated in this verse, when read together with verse forty-six, this bracketing could, in principle at least, be thought permissible in anticipation. This is not, however, necessary to insist upon, because it is within a poet's imagination that we are asked to see the second, Indra-bow. Further, it is the product of something like diffraction and not of reflection or even of many refractions. One has to be a great poet to put it there. Then alone would such a second crescent cancel out correctly against the thinnest of mathematical crescents that is supposed already to belong to Śiva, without being based on any crown of the Goddess. Śaṅkara here only intends to cancel the most delicate of ontological beauty-aspects with the most logically thin ones of intelligible values. The cancellation between them is intended to produce in the mind of the reader that overwhelming upsurge of absolute Beauty called *Saundaryalaharī*.

The beauty of a gem is colourful in its appeal. The beauty

enclosed within the two crescents of verse forty-six is meant to encircle the ambrosial content of a mature moon, which essentially appeals to the sense of taste rather than to mere sight. Such gradation between hierophantic and hypostatic values should not be left unnoticed by the reader who wishes to derive the more finalized lessons of the schematism contained in this composition. The 'reflected glory' of this verse could even be changed into a 'diffracted glory'. The Sanskrit text would bear such a revision, as the word *nīḍe* suggests 'home-ground' and *chāyācchuraṇa śabalam* means to 'become brilliant with the variegated effect of bright shining light', a kind of iridescent brightness.

The second and third lines underline that all this is to be attributed to the fertile mind of the poet. Here this imaginary beauty belongs only to the golden crown of the Goddess and not to the person of the Goddess herself, to which we are coming more directly in verse forty-six. We are still in the domain of a kind of mathematical mysticism here.

The fusion of the twelve luminaries of the twelve months is also an operation that only a mathematician-mystic could easily accomplish when extrapolated and imagined as applicable to any number of years, past or future. We can arrive at a thin vertical parameter, without which the correlation of the various implied chakras of many of these verses would become difficult. It is like the thread of Ariadne meant to guide Theseus back through the labyrinth of the Minotaur so that he would not be lost in that horizontal maze.

43

धुनोतु ध्वान्तं नस्तुलितदलितेन्दीवरवनं
घनस्निग्धश्लक्ष्णं चिकुरनिकुरुम्बं तव शिवे ।
यदीयं सौरभ्यं सहजमुपलब्धुं सुमनसो
वसन्त्यस्मिन् मन्ये वलमथनवाटीविटपिनाम् ॥

dhunotu dhvāntaṁ nas tulita dalitendīvara vanaṁ
ghana snigdhaślaksnam cikura nikurumbaṁ tava śive ।
yadīyaṁ saurabhyaṁ sahajam upalabdhuṁ sumanaso
vasanty asmin manye vala mathana vāṭī viṭapinām ॥

śive — O Śiva Consort; *tulita dalita indīvara vanaṁ* — the blooming blue-lotus forest; *ghana snigdha ślakṣṇaṁ* — thick, glossy and lustrous; *tava cikura nikurumbaṁ* — Your cluster of locks; *naḥ dhvāntaṁ dhunotu* — let it banish the darkness within us; *yadīyaṁ sahajam saurabhyaṁ* — whose natural fragrance; *upalabdhuṁ* — to gain; *vala mathana vāṭi viṭapinām* — of the trees in Indra's garden; *sumanasaḥ* — flowers; *asmin vasanti* — they live here; *manye* — I think/guess

Let the blooming blue-lotus-forest-growth of Your thick,
glossy and lustrous cluster of locks,
O Śiva Consort, banish the darkness within us;
To gain whose natural fragrance those (other) flowers of
the garden of Indra,
As I can guess, take their place within Your tresses.

Whereas in verse forty-six the author involves himself in the first person directly instead of looking with the eyes of a mathematician-mystic at the jewel on the crown (verse forty-two) which does not organically belong to the beauty of the Goddess, in this verse he descends into more direct relation to the *elan vital* within the personality of the Goddess in more living terms. Crystal or gem beauty gives place to flower beauty here, where two sets of flowers are seen to be playfully interlaced. They are rivals; one has a perfume that is natural to the life of the Goddess herself, while the other has a 'borrowed' status in so far as it belongs to an Indra-world of values, which is false to the extent that Indra is only a mythological demiurge and not a real person.

Pārvatī's hair has a natural perfume. The ancient *Śiva Purāṇa* even speaks of a wager on this controversy by two holy figures. One said that a flowery perfume could be natural to the hair of the Goddess; while the other, who said that perfume had to be put there and could not be natural, lost the wager. Thus, the flowers of Indra's garden could have a superior fragrance, but they would vie with her natural perfume only in vain. The dispute, according to Advaita, however, is not to be settled in favour of one or the other. There is a darkness to be banished, independently of the value of the rival perfumes, which is a lesson to be learned, and not a question of giving a prize to one of the rivals in a contest. It is true that, methodologically, ontology is more important, so the prize would legitimately go to the natural perfume of the hair of the Goddess rather than to the derived perfume of the blossoms of Indra's garden. It is the lesson that the doctrine teaches, not the method of arriving at the doctrine that is important for us.

Banishing darkness is the main subject of this verse, but where does this darkness reside? The verse itself replies that it is within all of us. It is not the darkness of individuals, some of whom might be more intelligent than others, but a general darkness applicable to all human beings at all times that is under reference here. An educated man might overcome this darkness and become enlightened, though this accomplishment would only be like a flashlight to him on a misty night. There is a general philosophical darkness in which humanity as a whole could be thought of as being steeped in from the beginning of time. One sparrow cannot make a summer. The blue of the sky is an example of such an ignorance applicable to all humans collectively. Blueness is not really there in the sky, but our error in appraising the blueness which is not there reveals this principle of darkness in a general philosophical sense. It is such a blind or double darkness that is represented here by the glossy dark hair of the Goddess. An intelligent man might direct a flashlight at the face of the Goddess in order to see its bright beauty and to appreciate it, but beyond the range of the flashlight everything is still steeped in a form of primordial double darkness. In this verse the double epithets 'blooming blue-lotus forest' and 'thick, glossy and lustrous' underline the double ignorance with which humanity is collectively cursed, such as in concupiscence, which is not the error or sin of any individual.

By the combined presence of two kinds of flowers, we have tried to distinguish that by double negation Advaitic cancellation would take place, by which even this double darkness of a primordial nature, lodged deep within the collective psyche of mankind, could be abolished (by a kind of 'dive-bombing'). In this verse we have descended from the ruby crown of verse forty-two to the hair, which is not fully within the body limits of the Devī. We descend one step more, hierophantically, when speaking of the face in the next verse. Plant life and animal life have a continuity between them which is like that between hair and face, when placed in a vertical descending series.

44

तनोतु क्षेमं नस्तव वदनसौन्दर्यलहरी-
परीवाहस्रोतः सरणिरिव सीमन्तसरणिः।
वहन्ती सिन्दूरं प्रबलकबरीभारतिमिर-
द्विषां वृन्दैर्बन्दीकृतमिव नवीनार्ककिरणम्॥

tanotu kṣemaṁ nas tava vadana saundarya laharī
parīvāha srotaḥ saraṇir iva sīmanta saraṇiḥ ।
vahantī sindūraṁ prabalakabarī bhāra timira
dviṣāṁ vṛndair bandī kṛtam iva navīnārka kiraṇam ॥

tava — Yours; *vadana saundarya laharī* — the upsurging billow of the beauty of the face; *parīvāha srotaḥ saraṇiḥ iva* — outflowing like a stream; *sīmanta saraṇiḥ* — (your) parted hairline; *prabala kabarī bhāra timira* — strong growth of hair (producing) darkness; *dviṣāṁ vṛndaiḥ* — by groups of enemies; *bandīkṛtam* — (as if) taken in bondage; *navīna arka kiraṇam iva* — like the tender ray of dawn; *sindūraṁ vahantī* — wears (is bedecked with) vermilion; *naḥ* — us; *kṣemaṁ tanotu* — may (it) increase well-being/blessedness

May it bless us, the upsurging billow of the beauty of Your face
Outflowing like unto a stream to resemble Your parted hairline,
With vermilion dust bedecked, keeping apart the strong growth of tresses
As if in bondage, held by anti-darkness gangs, to reveal the tender rays of dawn.

In verse forty-four there is a direct reference to the *saundarya* element, which labels this section definitely, as against the *ānanda* of the previous section. We can read this verse together with verse forty-five, as they are almost identical in their subject matter which is the bright chakra-like face of the Goddess.

While verse forty-three spoke in terms of banishing darkness, here the prayer is for Beauty to bless humanity. It is not a passive picture that is presented here. The last line suggests that there are two groups of people trying hard to keep at least a streak of light visible, while darkness in its turn is trying forcibly to enter into every nook and corner of our consciousness when it is allowed to be lazy. Śiva killed the elephant Gajendra in order to conquer his own mystical heights by an agonizing tragic process, without which horizontal evil or ignorance — represented by the wild elephant gone out of control — would hinder the higher flights of contemplative life. The 'anti-darkness gang' here is clearing the thick forest growth, binding it down on both sides, so as to blaze the trail for higher and higher contemplation to follow vertically upwards. A thin line, if it could be marked to indicate the course of contemplative progress the yogi must follow, would in itself constitute a great gain. The situation suggested is not unlike the one that we could see when the king comes in a procession, in which a gang of policemen are pushing aside the crowds on both sides to keep them from blocking the road in front of the king. The vertical parameter must be clearly visualized by the yogi before the chakra itself could be placed in its proper relational perspective. Darkness is the enemy of light; its invasion is in terms of space encroached from both the sides and not in terms of time, which marks the path of light as it extends from the present towards doomsday itself. Thus, the function of the anti-darkness gang is only to help the yogi to meditate better, which is the object of this verse.

The beauty of the face is not the plain conventional beauty, but something that can burst through barriers or other factors of ignorance, however thick. The mixed metaphor here even allows us to imagine that the face could be a lotus-lake bordering on a forest, touched by the pink rays of the rising sun situated vertically above it. Such a picture was presented in verse sixteen. The water in a lake can break its bounds and create a stream vertically, ending at a vanishing point where the sun's rays stream downward, as in this verse. The parameter would then become complete from both ends, the immanent and the transcendent. The only colour that would suit such a glistening streak of light would be vermilion or ruby or other magenta colours which have brilliance, rather than just a tint or shade. Such a structural version of a vision here is to be referred back to the familiar habit of Indian women to put a streak of vermilion powder (*kumkum*) on the line of their parted hair, plaited on both sides or simply kept bound and apart, as by the efforts of the anti-darkness gang here. The *kumkum* powder used by the Goddess touches that colour where hypostatic beauty cancels against its own hierophantic counterpart.

A thick growth of hair in a woman indicates richness of the vital principle, and there is no harm in thinking that it adds to beauty rather than subtracts from it. It is in this sense perhaps, that *La Gioconda* of Leonardo is an improvement on pale pre-Raphaelite Madonnas.

45

अरालैः स्वाभाव्यादलिकलभसश्रीभिरलकैः
परीतं ते वक्त्रं परिहसति पङ्केरुहरुचिम् ।
दरस्मेरे यस्मिन् दशनरुचिकिञ्जल्करुचिरे
सुगन्धौ माद्यन्ति स्मरदहनचक्षुर्मधुलिहः ॥

arālaiḥ svābhāvyād alikalabha saśribhir alakaiḥ
parītaṁ te vaktraṁ parihasati paṅkeruharucim ।
darasmere yasmin daśana ruci kiñjalka rucire
sugandhau mādyanti smara dahana cakṣur madhulihaḥ ॥

svābhāvyāt — naturally/by nature; *arālaiḥ* — curly; *ali kalabha saśrībhiḥ* — shining with the beauty of young bees; *alakaiḥ parītaṁ* — surrounded by strands of curly hair; *te vaktraṁ* — Your face; *paṅkeruha rucim* — the beauty of the lotus; *parihasati* — mocks/puts to shame; *dara smere* — slightly opened by gentle smile; *daśana ruci kiñjalkaḥ rucire* — having bright teeth for filament; *sugandhau* — exuding perfume; *yasmin* — in this (Your lotus face); *smara dahana cakṣuḥ mādhulihaḥ* — the honeybees that are the eyes of the Eros-burner (Śiva); *mādyanti* — become drunk/revel

Your face, exuding perfume as it gently smiles,
Having Your bright teeth for filament, when surrounded
by Your natural curls,
Like so many revelling, honey-licking bees; each the eye
Of the Eros-burner, puts to shame the beauty of the lotus.

The brightness of the face of a woman has been compared to the beauty of the lotus flower almost to the point of surfeit in Sanskrit poetry. The moon is another favourite analogy. A clear complexion and evidence of an intelligence fully alert or alive, with a touch of pink, rose or magenta, sets off the face in a context otherwise steeped in the double darkness of the tresses. By dark splendour, ignorance might come to its own as a form of tragic wisdom which, when further intensified, could become as good as a plus value, as justified in mathematics, logistics and even linguistics, where a negative multiplied by a negative results in a positive value.

If we consider the face as a chakra it would naturally occupy the *bindusthāna*, that is, the central locus of meditation or interest. There is a favourite way of describing the beauty of the face of a goddess, conventionally developed through classical times by Sanskrit poets, the main ideograms of which are seen to be respected by Śaṅkara in verses forty-three, forty-four and forty-five. It is not just beauty by way of a single assertion that is thus intended to be brought into evidence; it is, rather, a deeper form of beauty which has a radiance in and of itself, whether in terms of double darkness or double assertion. The brightness is meant to be more so, and the darkness is to be doubly underlined. That is the reason why the poet insists on bumble-bees, on the pearly lustre of teeth seen through parted lips, and on the curls that form a dark fringe all around the face to set it off like the moon against the background of a dark cloud. Here nature is distorted and rearranged and not just feebly imitated, as presupposed in the Aristotelian theory of art, where art is just an imitation of nature. To Plato art is an imitation of an imitation, and nature need not be presented with any photographic correctness of detail. Both photographic and holographic versions are to be respected here as laser technique is being introduced into photography. With these correctives in mind, we can see each line of this verse leap into a new depth of meaning.

We note first that the perfume of the flower is not omitted from this picture of beauty, for beauty is a value inseparable from the function of the rest of the senses. Honey sweetness, flower perfume, ruby brilliance, and moonlight glory are all enjoyable aspects of beauty, each lending its depth or other dimensions to the total appeal. The revelling bees, because they are restless and agitated, are suggested as the enjoying factor and natural counterpart of the enjoyment principle. This enjoying factor is carried over to the eye of Śiva, situated above, which enjoys the beauty and looks down to the bees, whose eagerness to drink the honey, when totalled up, would amount to his own intense interest to enjoy the same beauty, even though it might be in the form of a mirror reflection of his own beauty, as suggested in later verses. An ordinary lotus has only a relative beauty belonging to the side of nature, but the beauty seen here by Śiva's eyes is the result of an interaction between two aspects of the Absolute, and that is why it is said to put to shame the unilaterally understood beauty of the lotus. Honey is more deeply situated than the perfume of a lotus. The filaments that represent the teeth here are also deeper than the perfume of the face. The locks of black curls form a fringe. The greedy middle eye of Śiva and the two other eyes are on the side of the enjoyer rather than the side of the enjoyed. There is also a circle of excited honey-licking bees forming the same dark fringe of black hair all around. It is not difficult to see that it is a sort of chakra that the poet is trying to reconstruct — a positive one here, instead of a negative one proper to the *Ānandalaharī* section. While the negative one was proper to that negative context, the philosophical version is superimposed onto the sense version here, while there it was the given experience that was interpreted in terms that resemble an actual vision.

46

ललाटं लावण्यद्युतिविमलमाभाति तव यत्
द्वितीयं तन्मन्ये मकुटघटितं चन्द्रशकलम् ।
विपर्यासन्यासादुभयमपि संभूय च मिथः
सुधालेपस्यूतिः परिणमति राकाहिमकरः ॥

lalāṭaṁ lāvaṇya dyuti vimalam ābhāti tava yat
dvitīyaṁ tan manye makuṭa ghaṭitaṁ candraśakalam ।
viparyāsa nyāsād ubhayam api saṁbhūya ca mithaḥ
sudhālepa syūtiḥ pariṇamati rākā himakaraḥ ॥

tava yat lalāṭam — That forehead of Yours; *lāvaṇya dyuti vimalam ābhāti* — shining with pure radiant beauty; *tat makuṭa ghaṭitam* — to the one fixed to Your crown; *candra śakalam* — frail crescent (a bit of the moon); *dvitīyaṁ manye* — a second (crescent), I take it to be; *ubhayam api* — both together; *viparyāsa nyāsāt* — reversed in position; *mithaḥ śambhūya ca* — both knit one-to-one; *sudhā lepa syūtiḥ* — emanating balmy (soft) ambrosial essence; *rākā himakaraḥ* — a full moon; *pariṇamati* — results/matures in form

I fain would treat Your forehead, shining with a pure beauty,
A second crescent to that other frail one fixed to Your crown,
So that reversed in position, both as knit one-to-one,
Results the form of a fully-matured moon emanating soft ambrosial essence.

Verse forty-six speaks in terms of two inverted crescents. The forehead here could make a crescent with its horns turned downward. The crescent fixed to the crown of Śiva or Pārvatī, as the case may be, has to be turned 180 degrees before the magic intended here could be accomplished. We are familiar with this turning at two right angles in physics and mathematics in varied contexts. For instance, polarized light gives different interference figures when the polarizer and the analyser are placed at angles between 45 degrees and 180 degrees. The magic of the interference of double-polarized lights adds wonder to the beauty of mineral crystals.

In this verse it is a question of being able to see absolute Beauty, and not beauty as a unilateral value. Therefore Śaṅkara indulges in giving detailed instructions to the reader so that the perfect Beauty-value intended here could result from a common-sense vision when fully revised and corrected in the light of Advaitic doctrine. The raw materials and the finished product have to be put together unitively. In the theological context, it is enough to decorate Śiva and Pārvatī with a thin crescent at the omega point. But Vedanta is not limited to theological adoration. It must reveal the plenitude of an absolute Value in the context of immortality and not in the context of the relativistic process of cyclic becoming (*saṁsāra*). It is not enough to worship either Śiva or Pārvatī as exalted divine personalities, abstracted and lifted out of the world of necessity. It is the normalized vision of Plenitude that counts, although one-sided versions might still be dear to religious or theologically-minded persons who want a favourite deity (*iṣṭa devata*) to adore.

47

भ्रुवौ भुग्ने किंञ्चिद् भुवनभयभङ्गव्यसनिनि
त्वदीये नेत्राभ्यां मधुकररुचिभ्यां धृतगुणम्।
धनुर्मन्ये सव्येतरकरगृहीतं रतिपतेः
प्रकोष्ठे मुष्टौ च स्थगयति निगूढान्तरमुमे॥

bhruvau bhugne kiñcid bhuvana bhaya bhaṅga vyasanini
tvadīye netrābhyāṁ madhukara rucibhyāṁ dhṛtaguṇaṁ ।
dhanur manye savyetara kara gṛhītaṁ ratipateḥ
prakoṣṭhe muṣṭau ca sthagayati nigūḍhāntaram ume ॥

ume — O Umā; *bhuvana bhaya bhaṅga vyasanini* — ever pained in concern for banishing the fear of all creatures; *tvadīye* — Your; *kiñcit bhugne* — slightly/somewhat arched; *bhruvau* — eyebrows; *madhukara rucibhyāṁ netrābhyāṁ* — with eyes of bee-like beauty; *dhṛtaguṇaṁ* — bowstring fixed; *prakoṣṭhe muṣṭau ca* — arm and fist; *sthagayati nigūḍhāntaram* — the middle part staying hidden; *savyetara kara gṛhītaṁ* — held by the other (than the right) hand; *rati pateḥ dhanuḥ* — the bow of the god of love; *manye* — I surmise

O Umā, ever pained in concern for banishing the fear of all creatures,
And thus with eyebrows somewhat arched, with eyes of bee-like beauty below,
I do surmise them as making up the bowstring for the bow
Of the lord of love, held by his other hand, his arm and fist hiding the middle part.

We have explained that in this second half of the work, Śaṅkara depends more on constructing and superimposing new imagery on the beauty of the Goddess as given to the senses in a more primary sense. Thus, we have seen that the twelve suns had to be fused into a gem of ruby colour, and Indra's bow was made to dominate such a gem in verse forty-two. In verse forty-three, two sets of flowers had to occupy the same tresses of the Goddess. The parted hairline became the prolongation of the vertical axis in verse forty-four, while a row of honey-licking bees was suggested as a perimeter-like line of reference in verse forty-five. Two crescents were requisitioned again in verse forty-six so that, like brackets turned inversely, they could contain an absolute Value, both real and imaginary at once. This complex metaphor, developed stage by stage, is carried over here into verse forty-seven, and the same structural pattern is to be respected in the remaining verses, the evidence of which will be found explicitly in verses fifty-eight and fifty-nine.

The darts of the god of love that can pierce the hearts of persons involved in an erotic world of love is an image not peculiar to Sanskrit literature only. The celebration of Saint Valentine's Day, as known to the West, uses the same imagery. Eroticism is the natural setting for the appreciation of beauty. A masculine beauty and a feminine beauty belong to the same context of absolute Beauty. Śiva represents the eternal masculine aspect while Pārvatī represents the eternal feminine. The function or operation of love has to have its instruments. Statically viewed, we get only non-living perspectives, as in the case of physiology studied by the dissection of dead bodies. The functioning of the living nerves comes to light only when we examine living bodies. This distinction could be said to be the same as that which could be assumed to exist between psychostatics and psychodynamics. Here the static picture is first to be understood in dim outline on the basis of the given empirically-based picture, and it is for us to superimpose another picture more mathematically understood. There are subtle parameters and perimeters to be kept in mind if we are to visualize absolute Beauty with all its living or dynamic implications. This is a difficult task, and any poet or author who can take up this challenge will have to respect the rules or norms of both mathematics and mysticism at the same time.

One could look at the locomotive of an express train and recognize the cylinder, the piston rod and the big weighted engine wheels, as the train starts or slows down. Instead of watching the engine from the platform, from inside the compartment one could feel the jolting alternating movements in terms of his own life movement. One could sympathize with the movement of the train and his own movement with shut eyes, establishing a bipolar sympathy between the engine and its troubles on one side and his own inconveniences to keep steady in his seat on the other. We have to superimpose on the mechanical picture another structural image representing the dynamic one in which the movement is understood by empathic intuition. Thus we get two pictures which we subjected to a certain degree of subjectivity, without which they would refuse to belong together or make any meaning. These are some of the requirements for understanding this verse and the many that follow. The laws of nature could be treated in the form of propositions or predications, or we could use the language of the graph paper. Every formula has got its corresponding graph; the graph verifies the formula and vice versa.

Śaṅkara is faced with the task of revealing the dynamism of absolute Beauty. In the first half of this verse, we notice that it is not just erotic love that is the basis of the emotional life reflected in the face of the Goddess. Her eyebrows are said to be slightly arched. Because Śiva represents the positive side of the process of universal becoming, the Goddess has to represent the negative counterpart of the same function. If Śiva is the God of the universe, it follows that Pārvatī is in charge of saying that all living creatures on earth get a chance to have a life more abundant. She does not love one creature more than another. This absolute Love at the basis of her eroticism is not a mere preference for her husband. God is good and generous, while being the principle of light or intelligence. The Koran insists on bringing these two aspects of generosity and logical truth together in almost everyone of its verses by the epithets *Rahmān* and

Rahīm, which are to be repeated together before each verse is read. The kindness of God or His goodness could be understood as an adjective or as a noun, as when we say 'God is good' or 'God is goodness itself'. The predicative and nominative aspects belong to the same absolute Value represented by Śiva and Pārvatī thought of as one non-dual life Value, which was our starting postulate even from the very first verse of this work. The duality between the functions of Śiva and Pārvatī, if it comes into evidence here and there in these verses, is meant to be only for purposes of discussion, and the intelligent reader must cancel out these dialectical functions in terms of absolute Beauty, of which the Goddess is a more fitting custodian than the God. However, the same Beauty could be discussed from a perspective more pronounced in favour of Śiva, which has been done by Śaṅkara in the conjugate of this composition, the *Śivānanda-laharī*. The arched eyebrows constitute the perimeter indicating the concern of anxiety of the Goddess. Her beauty is enhanced by such a concern for living beings.

No beauty can be said to exist without somebody to enjoy it. The rows of bees as a bowstring represent a parameter which is related to the perimeter of the bow. The analogy becomes more apt when we know that the bow of Kāma (Eros) is not merely one of wood or metal but consists of all the best flowers of the season. The desire of the bees to drink the honey of such a beautiful rainbow-like festival of flowers, meant for them to enjoy there, develops a vertical tension between the two counterparts, viewed in abstracted and generalized terms. If there is no summer, there is no love-making, and the cuckoos cannot mark the arrows flying between the two sides that represent the highly emotional state of mystical eroticism. We have to imagine in this verse the arrow which the right hand of the god of love is supposed to be secretly fixing onto the bowstring. This part is hidden by the left fist and the forearm with the elbow, which together mark the noseridge and centre of the eyebrows. One can pull the string downward along this line with more or less force, depending upon the tension belonging to the situation. Psychodynamic aspects become revealed in this manner. To try to describe them through definitions or predications would give us only various static cliches instead of the real process with all its vitalistic implications. The bow could be fixed vertically when aimed toward Śiva at the omega point, or it could be aimed horizontally through the side glances of the Goddess, when and if she condescends to grant her grace to some supplicant like Viṣṇu, or Kāma, or even Śaṅkara, all of whom are mentioned as votaries of absolute Beauty in the different verses of this work. In verse seventy-five and again in verse ninety-eight, Śaṅkara himself prays for this kind of horizontal side glance recognition from the Devī. Viṣṇu does the same more directly in verse five, and Kāma triumphs over the world because of the same light falling on his body from the Devī's side glance in verse six. We have to notice also that the eyes of the Goddess are sometimes compared to bees in a row, and sometimes to highly active bees who are agitated because of the absolute Compassion or Love which constitute their motivating function in the context of the Absolute. In verse forty-five, the Devī's eyes were seen to be interchangeable with those of Śiva, because he, as her husband, is the final enjoyer of the beauty of the lotus face of his beloved.

One could ask here how the two eyes could form the string for a bow. The two eyebrows have to be joined together in imagination, and the horizontal movements of the two eyes are to be seen intuitively as the string, completing the picture which poetic convention, as respected by a long line of Sanskrit poets, permits. The line could be hyperbolic or parabolic, an incomplete conic section — like a comet's orbit round the sun — when the bowstring is pulled downward, but it is not necessary to suppose any such intention in the picture presented here. A normalized concern uniformly maintained is all that we have to associate with this picture.

The eyebrows are somewhat arched, but not fully arched. When fully arched, it would mean some conflict or dissention.

As they are only somewhat arched, it is not personal passion with its preferences that is to be supposed, but rather a general state of pity or mercy, called *misericorde* in French.

To understand the phrase 'bee-like beauty' we must understand that a bee has to look at something, because its function is intimately connected with beauty.

The use of the name 'Umā' for the Goddess here means that she has no equal or other persons to rival her. Umā is very superior, the nearest to the *brahman* of Vedanta. She is the one in charge of all life functions, and is not limited to the Tāntric context of falling in love with her beauty, as corrected here by Śaṅkara.

48

अहः सूते सव्यं तव नयनमर्कात्मकतया
त्रियामां वामं ते सृजति रजनीनायकतया ।
तृतीया ते दृष्टिर्दरदलितहेमाम्बुजरुचिः
समाधत्ते सन्ध्यां दिवसनिशयोरन्तरचरीम् ॥

ahaḥ sūte savyaṁ tava nayanam arkātmakatayā
triyāmāṁ vāmaṁ te sr̥jati rajanī nāyakatayā ।
tr̥tīyā te dr̥ṣṭir dara dalita hemāmbuja ruciḥ
samādhatte sandhyāṁ divasa niśayor antara carīm ॥

*tava savyaṁ** *nayanam* — Your right eye; *arkātmakatayā* — in essence the same as the sun; *ahaḥ sūte* — generates daytime; *te vāmaṁ nayanam* — Your left eye; *rajanī nāyakatayā* — presiding over night; *triyāmāṁ sr̥jati* — creates (its) three vigils; *dara dalita hemāmbuja ruciḥ* — bright like a half-open golden lotus bud; *te tr̥tīyā dr̥ṣṭiḥ* — Your third eye; *divasa niśayoḥ* — of day and night; *antara carīm* — moving in between; *sandhyāṁ* — twilight time; *samādhatte* — ushers in

The right eye of Yours, in essence the same as the sun, it generates daytime;
The left one, presiding over night, creates its three vigils;
While the third eye, like a half-open golden lotus bud,
Ushers in the twilight time, moving between day and night.

In verse forty-eight there is a pointed reference to the implications of what we have to understand as a verticalized version of a cosmological process. Under verse forty-two, whether we think of the sun or the moon, or the light of the sacrifical fire placed in front of the votary, there are two rival versions possible for the process to be visualized. Day and night

---

* *savyaṁ*, literally can be either the 'left' or the 'right' (of the body), here clearly it means the 'right'. (*ed.*)

could be treated as mutually exclusive opposites. A second way would be to treat them unitively as alternating to succeed one another in time. Such an alternating process could further be accentuated and subjected to a more fully verticalized dynamism by which we could think of twilights common to twenty-four hours or forty-eight hours merging from both sides to fuse in terms of a continuous twilight. One unit of twilight would take over when the previous one is finished, to guarantee the continuity of their vertical participation day-in and day-out. Such a picture would be as true as any other so-called factual one. The difference is one of orientation only, and not of fact. The contemplative prefers the verticalized version rather than a merely mechanistic one. The life process extends to the beginningless past and to the endless future, so that questions of 'destiny', 'salvation', or 'happiness of humanity' would come more completely into the picture. A piecemeal version of the same tends to be mechanistic and cuts off the Day of Judgement or the source of human life from such a cross-sectional view.

The Devī has two eyes placed horizontally and also a half-open golden lotus bud-like third eye which is meant to see yogic visions rather than mere brute facts. The lotus is a flower that is normally pink, but twilight hours can add a tinge of golden orange to the pink colour. The half-openness of such a third eye resembling the bud of a lotus flower touched by colours of the twilight hour, represents the contemplative state of the yogi's mind as it penetrates deeper into the future from the darkness of previous day/night units fused together in terms of twilight.

The object of this verse is to present a contemplative version of light, applicable to the consciousness of a yogi, irrespective of the event as such, but without contradicting the factual features. Classroom physiography may not tally with the version presented here, but that does not necessarily mean that this version is therefore unscientific. Thermodynamic laws are not seen operating in the laboratory, but still physicists make such generalized statements as 'the entropy of the universe is tending to zero.' A structuralized way of thinking is already treated as permissible in modern physics, which speaks of involution and evolution, implosion and explosion, endosmosis and exosmosis, space and anti-space and 'big bang' and 'steady state', in a world of spectroscopic Doppler effects, referring to expanding or contracting universes based on an overall law of conservation of energy. All this is not usually questioned by orthodox physicists.

In this verse one of the eyes of the Goddess, which need not necessarily be the right eye but should not be identified with the left, derives its essence from the sun. The sun is a positive luminary in the sky, and its function is best recognized at midday. Side by side with this positive status, one has to think of the other celestial orb, which takes charge of the night, which Keats describes as 'that orbed maiden with white fire laiden, whom mortals call the moon'. Shakespeare has called it 'the watery moon'. The sun is hot, while the moon is cold in contemplative physiography. The moon might have phases, but it does not shine during the daytime. Lovers feel happier in moonlight than in sunlight. The gentle beams of the moon are a kind of food for love, but the position could sometimes be reversed when lovers suffer the cruel pangs of separation. In the *Śākuntalam,* Duṣyanta complains that the flowery beams of moonlight become like cutting diamond-pointed arrows when Śakuntalā's favour is not known to him. Erotic poetry and contemplative structuralism both agree in placing these celestial orbs at two opposite vertical limits, or by way of concession, as it were, as two orbs placed in a relation reflecting 'parity' instead of the relation called 'handedness'. These are all structural problems which are far from being finally settled by physicists. The 'fall of parity' has been celebrated more than once in some centres of scientific research. We cannot wait for them to settle their disputes to say that a fourfold structuralism, respecting horizontal 'parity' and vertical 'handedness', is permissible to us to concede to absolute Space. Newton and Kant have stood for such an *a priori* absolute Space, while modern physicists, viewing the same from a relativistic perspective, tend alternately to abolish it and to accept it again in a modified form a decade later. The structure is finally what we put there, taking it from our minds, and also what we find 'over there' independently of our minds. The paradox is not likely to get abolished by itself, as long as one has to think to find the truth. The effort of thought can only dance between two possible alternatives. Unitive understanding alone can cancel out the prejudices proper to the Self or to the non-Self, to take us beyond paradox. Śaṅkara's Vedanta claims to do just this, and this verse can be said to be preparing the ground for such a conclusion. The *a priori* and the *a posteriori* are both acceptable to Advaita Vedanta.

The question might be put: 'Why not the right eye?' This is because even the sun can be transcended when positive luminaries with more powerful light could be substituted for it at higher points in the vertical axis. The moon's position is nearer home to us and thus comparable more definitely to the left eye of the Goddess, because there are no other luminaries between the fire on earth and the light of the moon, which is brought near to everyday life. Our moon and our sun tend to come together the more we descend from the teleological to the ontological limit.

The reference to the three vigils of the night is to show that our consciousness passes through three different kinds of contents when we sleep at night. The early part of the night is generally spent in banishing the fatigue of the day. The second vigil could be described as semi-conscious, though equally restful. The third vigil is when angels begin to sing or the evil spirits decide to depart, as in the case of King Hamlet's ghost. The cock is meant to crow to punctuate the vigils, especially of the morning hours, and the Crucifixion is also connected with such divisions known to literature.

It is the subconscious mind that is influenced by moonlight. Virtuality gets first accentuated, and the negativity of subconscious states of dream or deep sleep takes over as night advances and sleep becomes not merely physical in its function. The horizontal alternation in which celebration is either positively or negatively accentuated could come together without the celebration being accentuated in any pronounced manner. Equally transparent states of mind thus can take charge of consciousness at different nightly vigils, under the influence of the moon rather than the sun.

When the coalescing of these two alternating processes becomes more and more visually transparent to each other, we can imagine a creeper with two branches. When such a creeper bears a contemplative golden lotus-bud between the eyebrows of the yogi, as suggested in this verse, waking and sleeping are both abolished in terms of an ever-wakeful contemplative state which is sometimes referred to as 'the fourth', *turīya*. The dynamism of this fourth state can still move vertically up or down in terms of twilight, rather than of contrasting day and night. The last line here implies this state of mind. Narayana Guru describes a similar picture of contemplation in his *Ātmopadeśa śatakam* (verse 9) thus:

> He who dwells in contemplation beneath a tree
> Whereon climbing, a creeper bears aloft on either side
> The blossoms of the psychic states, mark, such a man
> By inferno unapproached ever remains.

49

विशाला कल्याणी स्फुटरुचिरयोध्या कुवलयैः
कृपाधाराधारा किमपि मधुरा भोगवतिका ।
अवन्ती दृष्टिस्ते बहुनगरविस्तारविजया
ध्रुवं तत्तन्नामव्यवहरणयोग्या विजयते ॥

viśālā kalyāṇī sphuṭa rucir ayodhyā kuvalayaiḥ
kṛpā dhārādhārā kim api madhurā bhogavatikā ।
avantī dṛṣtis te bahu nagara vistāra vijayā
dhruvaṁ tattan nāma vyavaharaṇa yogyā vijayate ॥

te dṛṣṭiḥ — Your regard; *viśālā* — the expansive; *sphuṭa ruciḥ* — of clear taste, pure brilliance; *kalyāṇī* — the auspicious; *kuvalayaiḥ* — by blue lotus bound; *ayodhyā* — the invincible; *kṛpādhārā ādhāra* — on mercy's fountain founded; *kim api madhura* — a certain sweet; *ābhogavatikā* — enjoyment affording; *avantī* — of saving power; *bahu nagara vistāra vijaya* — the many cities of lasting fame; *tat tat nāma vyavahāraṇa yogyā* — each fit to be called by its own name; *dhruvaṁ* — certainly; *vijayate* — reign triumphant

Viśālā *the expansive,* Kalyāṇī *the auspicious;*
Sphuṭaruci *the clear of taste;*
Ayodhyā *the invincible, by blue lotus bound;*
Kṛpādhārādhārā, *on mercy's fountain founded;*
A certain Madhurā, *the sweet;* Avantī, *of saving power;*
Ābhogavatikā, *enjoyment affording;*
All such names of various cities of lasting fame, each fit to be called by its own name,
Within Your total regard they do reign triumphant.

In verse forty-eight we have seen how textbook physiography can be viewed in a verticalized perspective. Plainer geography, as it might apply to a country, could also be viewed from a contemplative standpoint. It is a subjective and axiologically biased view that we have to take of a country which might consist of many famous cities, however varied, whether large or small, which could be brought under eight classes representing human interests in which the enjoyer and the enjoyed could meet, so as to make a beauty-factor emerge into view.

Each city is a state of mind, representing a dominant interest associated with its origin, its present utility, or a future destiny towards which it paves the way for its inhabitants. Thus revised subjectively in value terms, all cities of any country could be thought of individually or collectively together. In the subcontinent of India, many holy places have thus grown up through history, and places of pilgrimage attract travellers in large numbers even today. In contemplative geography of this kind, it is the absolute Beauty-value that counts, under whose aegis the eight varieties of interests, here recognized by the names of eight interesting cities, could be contemplatively reviewed.

The idea of eight cities representing the totality of contemplative consciousness is well known in Vedantic literature. Śaṅkara describes, in his *Vivekacūḍāmaṇi*, the collection of eight cities as constituting the subtle contemplative body that we could arrive at by a certain kind of abstraction and generalization. This is the method we have to apply in all these verses to extract the contemplative version of a given factual situation. In verse fifty and following verses, we must consider further abstractions, such as the nine aesthetic interests that we could distinguish in art or literature. This verse prepares the way for such a generalized treatment by telling us that the regard of the Devī could suggest values which represent psychic states or attitudes, which when put together, could apply to the contemplative votary or to the Goddess herself, at once or alternately, in the world of religious pilgrimage among the holy cities of India. It is the enjoyment that represents the regard, or the eye that recognizes beauty. Happiness or salvation is the overall ground on which beauty can loom into consciousness, in the same way that a bright flower on a lotus plant can enter into the foreground or background of the mind as we meditate upon it, sometimes experiencing clarity of vision and at other times experiencing dim states of mind, having a retrospective or prospective suggestibility. Some kind of happiness relevant to the context of spiritual progress is to be represented by each blossom, interchangeably understood as the regard, or grace, or an eye of the Goddess, having a one-to-one correspondence with the contemplative joy within the consciousness of the yogi.

In the *Ānandalaharī* section, a similar structural analysis was undertaken in verse thirty-two, with the help of other monomarks. Here we are dealing with a more objective and open world, where places of pilgrimage, rather than the world of icons, are proper to the context.

When we think of the relationship of cities to human life, it can be generally said that cities are originally founded, if we trace their history, close to the existence of some source of water supply, which is the most essential value, to attract human life around it. The fountain thus represents the grace or kindness of the Goddess, and such a central interest lends its genetic coloration to any city, even after it has grown through centuries on the basis of the same starting factor. It is a continuous streak or stream of value that makes a city famous.

Scrutinizing the content of this verse, we notice that the first-named famous city is Viśālā, meaning 'the expansive'. Heaven is sometimes referred to as being *viśālam*, as in the Bhagavadgītā, expansiveness being suggestive of the plentifulness of opportunities to make a living. In contrast with this first line, the last line refers to all cities bundled up together and treated as belonging to the total regard of the Devī. The values that all the cities are meant to represent are evident from the root meanings or derivations of the Sanskrit terms contained in their very names. Commentators have also suggested that a beautiful woman could display eight kinds of recognizable attitudes in her changing looks, revealed by her eyes which could be half shut or fully open. Lotus buds and flowers could represent such innate or open attitudes, totalling up to the absolute Beauty that is the subject matter or object matter of these verses.

After the attribute of expansiveness comes auspiciousness, followed by clarity of taste. We can easily place these three in a numerator group. The second line represents values that are to be carefully protected against invasion from the outside. Ayodhyā suggests an invincible city, like a beautiful princess confined to a tower. Knights errant have to fight battles to win such a beauty value.

In the third line, the interest is based on enjoyment. Each city has got its pleasures of daytime and of night-time, as in 'gay Paris'. Mathurā in North India, or Madurai in South India, derive their names from the sweet associations of those places.

The last line of this verse tells us how to put all expansive values, such as that of heaven, together into one big ensemble, and how to view such a treasure of values as pertaining to the total regard or grace of the goddess of Beauty, with whom we are always to be concerned. The heaven of the first line is to be included in the cup of total absolute Value implied in the last line, where it is also suggested that each name is to be treated as a noun as well as having a predicative significance. To extract the central value here requires special effort of abstraction and generalization on the part of the student or contemplative to whom this verse might apply. If he is able to rise to such a requirement, it would be easier for him to follow the thinner line of suggestion and generalization contained in the next section of verses fifty to sixty, in which we could say that the structural way of poetic composition sometimes even excels itself by the elusive thinness of its suggestibility. Nominalism and structuralism can also be seen hand in hand here.

50

कवीनां संदर्भस्तबकमकरन्दैकरसिकं
कटाक्षव्याक्षेपभ्रमरकलभौ कर्णयुगलम्।
अमुञ्चन्तौ दृष्ट्वा तव नवरसास्वादतरला-
वसूयासंसर्गादलिकनयनं किञ्चिदरुणम्॥

kavīnāṁ sandarbha stabaka makarandaika rasikaṁ
kaṭākṣa vyākṣepa bhramara kalabhau karṇa yugalam I
amuñcantau dṛṣṭvā tava nava rasāsvāda taralā
vasūyā saṁsargād alika nayanaṁ kiñcid aruṇam II

kavīnām — of poets; *sandarbha stabaka makaranda eka rasikaṁ* — wholly absorbed in drinking the honey from the spray of blooms of aptness; *tava karṇa yugalam* — Your two ears; *amuñcantau* — without parting from (do not give up); *nava rasa asvāda taralau* — mellowed by the play of the nine aesthetic interests; *kaṭākṣa vyākṣepa bhramara kalabhau* — (Your) pair of baby bumblebee-like eyes which seem to cast side-glances; *dṛṣṭvā* — having seen (seeing); *asūyā saṁsargāt* — touched by jealousy; *alika nayanaṁ* — (Your) mid-forehead eye; *kiñcit aruṇam* — (seems) magenta tinged

Seeing Your baby-bumblebee-like pair of eyes, which,
while seeming to cast side-glances,
Do not give up the bases of Your ears, mellowed by the
play of the nine aesthetic interests,
Remaining like aptness with poets, wholly absorbed in
drinking of the honey within a spray of blossoms;
Your mid-forehead lotus-bud eye, by jealousy touched,
seems magenta tinged.

In verse fifty, the abstraction and generalization applied to value factors of geography or physiography is carried over from the previous verses to an even more thin and elusive domain where poets are engaged in finding apt analogies when they play with the nine aesthetic interests which constitute the stock-in-trade of their art. A vibrating magnetic needle can be imagined as slanting ninety degrees to the right or ninety degrees to the left, according to the aptness of the analogies that the poet might employ in his art. In this way the whole range of the nine interests could be imagined at every ten degrees on either side, thus filling the whole one hundred and eighty degrees above the horizontal straight line. When aptness succeeds, the pointer may be said to stabilize itself with an equilibrium point ranging from left to right, covering all possible points between the limits of minus ninety and plus ninety. In this verse the eyes are compared to young bumble-bees who are very impatient to enjoy the honey within a spray of blossoms. The blossoms could be at the positive end of the horizontal axis, or virtually enjoyable at the negative end as when, through apt analogies, we appreciate good poetry. Both could be equally sweet to the young bumblebees as they actively flit between the actual and the virtual interests in the domain of poetic appreciation. We have also to carry over from verse forty-eight a middle eye as a witness to the playful eroticism in which the other two ordinary eyes are likely to indulge. The ordinary eyes can express their interest normally by coquettish side glances. The serious middle eye does not approve of such fickleness on the part of these younger ones. Such is the background on which the dynamism of the structure here is to be superimposed, playing on the living beauty of the face of the Goddess.

The reference to the base of the ears is justified by the fact that it is in this region that visual imagery transforms itself into auditory imagery of a more virtual order. There is a kind of figure-of-eight circulation taking place where alternating interests, virtual or actual, visual or auditory, change sides and play, as it were, a constant game of hide and seek. Aptness is always the constant factor that constitutes the interest. The highest sense of aptness, however, is ashamed of its own fickleness when viewed from a horizontalized perspective.

The young bumblebees here, which refer to the two eyes,

are said to be highly interested in looking slantingly, with the ear bases as a reference. Eroticism being natural to youth, enjoyment of the honey is all they care for, resulting in the fickle form of a vibrating needle, which stabilizes itself only at the zero point or at the one hundred and eighty degree limits, where the ear bases transform visual into auditory impulses and vice versa.

The central eye, carried over from verse forty-eight, is not golden in colour, as it was in that verse. By resentment of the shameful conduct of the fickle-minded young bees, a red colour invades the central lotus-bud eye. The aptness of the analogy of Śaṅkara here makes this colour correspond to the jealousy which arises from the resentment natural to a more mature and dispassionate person whom we could call the absolute Female, for which principle the Goddess here would stand. She is jealous only in proportion to the restless fickleness of the younger bees, who are excited and therefore incapable of any steady contemplation. Steady contemplation corresponds to the vertical parameter, but fickleness oscillates between the positive and negative horizontal limits. When jealousy is cancelled against fickleness, the resultant is the neutral Absolute represented by the beauty of the face of the Goddess.

The expression 'seeming to cast side glances' would suggest that sometimes side glances could be justified, but not all the time as the young folk might claim or pretend. The ear region is further qualified in the vertical axis as 'mellowed' or made more sensitive by their constant interest in aesthetic enjoyment. This seems to suggest that mere dilettantism cannot produce the same enjoyment as the fully matured taste of a person of artistic appreciation. The young bees refuse to leave the bases of the ears because they are able to appreciate art in its full value or import, and not merely as persons with a passing interest in it. Side glances are respectable and become interchangeable with this end of serious interest in art. Pretension of one for the other thus becomes possible, and the element of pretense found in the text therefore becomes justified. The bees are not conferring grace on anyone with a really serious side glance. They are only enjoying the erotic play of this. The ear bases, which are the centre of aesthetic interest, could be centralized together and the fanwise expansion of the various items of interest, radiating and overlapping both ways, could all be bundled up into one master interest when a contemplative touch confers maturity upon the individual sentiments and inclusively binds them together into an enjoyment with a central interest that knows no duality.

51

शिवे शृङ्गारार्द्रा तदितरजने कुत्सनपरा
सरोषा गङ्गायां गिरिशचरिते विस्मयवती ।
हराहिभ्यो भीता सरसिरुहसौभाग्यजननी
सखीषु स्मेरा ते मयि जननि दृष्टिस्सकरुणा ॥

śive śṛṅgārārdrā tad itara jane kutsana parā
saroṣā gaṅgāyāṁ giriśa carite vismayavatī ।
harāhibhyo bhītā sarasiruhasaubhāgya jananī
sakhīṣu smerā te mayi janani dṛṣṭissakaruṇā ॥

janani — O Mother; *te dṛṣṭiḥ* — Your regard; *śive śṛṅgāra ārdrā* — melting/moist/moved by sentimental love for Śiva; *tat itara jane kutsanaparā* — resentful to any other person; *gaṅgāyāṁ saroṣā* — with anger (of jealousy) towards Ganges; *giriśa carite* — at Śiva's story; *vismayavatī* — with transportations of wonder; *hara ahibhyaḥ* — for the snakes of Hara; *bhītā* — fearful (surprise); *sarasiruha saubhāgya jananī* — as the source of lotus-red grace; *sakhīṣu smerā* — for friends a jestful smile; *mayi* — for me; *sakaruṇā* — one of kindliness

Moved by sentimental love for Śiva, resentful to any other person;
With anger of jealousy towards Ganges, and with transportations of wonder at Śiva's story;
With fearful surprise for the snakes of Hara, and for friends a jestful smile;
As such a source of lotus-red grace, Your regard, O Mother, for me will remain one of kindliness.

Sanskrit poetic convention defines rhetorical literature as being based upon certain classes of interest called *rasas*, which are said to be between eight and ten in number. Two of them can be considered as extras, but when one or the other of these is included with the eight (or excluded from the ten), we get nine *rasas* (*navarasas*). Rhetoric more usually refers to classifications such as lyric, heroic, tragic, romantic and so on. As we explained under verse thirty-eight, the ten basic interests are *śṛṅgāra* (love), *vīra* (heroism), *bībhatsa* (disgust), *raudra* (anger or fury), *hāsya* (mirth), *bhayānaka* (terror), *karuṇa* (pity), *adbhuta* (wonder), *śānta* (tranquillity or peacefulness) and *vātsalya* (paternal fondness). The last two are sometimes omitted and sometimes only one of them is included. Fear and pity are attitudes or states of mind which are supposed to be induced by Greek tragedy.

It is not a question, in this work, of depicting a perfect picture of beauty or goodness. All the attitudes, passions or states of mind are to be included together irrespective of whether they enhance the goodness of the character in question. In this sense, in Western literary criticism it is understood that poetry is a criticism of life, and that it holds up a mirror reflecting life, whether in society or in oneself. The Goddess of beauty of these verses becomes perfect to the extent that she comprises within her personality all the attitudes or states of mind which basically constitute what we know as human life in general. It is in this sense, then, that in this verse all psychic states, whether good or bad, are passed in review in a certain order. It is not hard to recognize in the series of emotions or passions described here that the nine *rasa*s, or interests, are being treated of in the abstract. It is the mood induced within the psyche of the enjoyer and also what is in the subject matter of the poem itself, which when treated together, give to these interests, passions, or attitudes an absolutist status, all to be comprised within the beauty of the same Goddess. Each passion enhances her beauty, instead of detracting from it, in the same way that the facets of a cut diamond can set-off its attractiveness in a more pronounced form.

Jealousy normally cannot be considered as a good quality in a model of perfect beauty, but in this verse we find that the Goddess has a rival in co-wife Gaṅgā (the goddess of the river Ganges), and that she is capable of jealousy of that other personified aspect of beauty. The paradoxical element within the beauty of the Absolute is here confronted without any attempt to explain it away. Absolute beauty is beyond good and bad, it is not just good. This is the reason why we find questionable attitudes being included here as adding to, instead of detracting from, the totality of beauty intended to be revealed. In other words, the Goddess is absolutely beautiful in spite of blameworthy aspects in her nature. It is by transcending good and evil, not just by denying them, that perfection is to be attained. The three modalities of nature (*guṇa*s), as we shall see in the immediately succeeding verses, have also to be similarly transcended. The ontologically biased version of beauty which the Goddess here represents, as the consort of Śiva who is her positive counterpart, would permit the inclusion of all modalities that are real to human nature. Even imperfections are thus included here so that they could be unitively absorbed and transcended by participation with the higher absolute principle that Śiva represents. In this sense, Śiva could be called the 'Absolute of absolutes' while Pārvatī's status could be described as the 'relative Absolute'. Even this duality could be abolished by mutual cancellation.

We notice first that the Goddess is capable of sentimental love toward her husband, as in the case of any other girl. This makes her fully human, and thereby adds to her perfection. We might add here that because her husband represents the most uncompromising absolutism, her sentimental affection receives, by virtue of it, a certain dignity of its own, but basically the sentiment remains just human and nothing more. This revised form of sentimental love has already been referred to in verse sixteen as *gabhīra śṛṅgāra*, a revised form of profound erotic love.

Jealousy in love has been condemned by poets like Tennyson as being incompatible with pure love. Here we find again that the Goddess is disgusted with all persons except Śiva. So the poet has in mind here a certain higher type of jealousy which is one-pointed and exclusive of all others, Śiva being the absolute Value dear to Pārvatī. If one should love one's God with all one's heart, then a certain bipolarity of relationship is insured between the worshipper and the worshipped. The strictness of this bipolarity necessarily implies its corollary — a touch of exclusion of everything extraneous to such a vertical affiliation. It is in this sense that we have to understand the jealousy and disgust of Pārvatī for all personages except Śiva. This is above good and bad; it is 'Goodness'. But rising to be 'good' from being 'bad,' in the common religious sense, is not profound enough.

The jealousy toward her rival, Ganges, which is only to be expected, reveals the relative status of Śiva's two co-wives. While Ganges represents a horizontal value, as a geographical river useful to cultivators around Benares and other cities, Pārvatī represents the very source of water in the sky. River water is as valuable as rain water but the dignity of the rain should not be mixed-up with the earthy touch implied in the river. It is in the recognition of this contrast that the beauty of the Goddess is intended to upsurge and overwhelm the contemplative student of these verses. Perfection by transcending is not the same as trying to merely improve on the already vitiated relativistic set-up.

The next emotion is described as a 'transportations of wonder' at the exploits of Śiva. Śaivite epics, especially of South India, tell of many 'Dionysiac' mysteries in which Śiva works wonders among the common people. All miracles are possible in the context of the Absolute. Nothing is impossible for Dionysus either. The wonder here thus belongs to a heightened transcendental order.

We find in the next line that fear and surprise are bracketed together as one sentiment. The Devī, who is afraid of the snakes coiled around Śiva's body, says, 'How wonderful!' Instead of excluding each other, these sentiments blend with and complement each other.

The condescending smile towards younger rivals, who might be just incidental acquaintances shows that she is not equally resentful towards all her rivals. One has to make friends as well as enemies, but only with those who are worthy of such equality of status with oneself. This rule of reciprocity in friendship is mentioned in the *Pañcatantra*, where it is suggested that friendship should be cultivated only with equals so as to avoid strained relations later.

The last line refers to the lotus-red grace of the eyes of the Goddess, where all these possible varieties of attitudes, sentiments or passions can have their source at one and the same locus.

The pointer of the emotional needle, which is verticalized at the beginning here with tender emotion, deflects to the right or left successively thereafter through the whole gamut of other relational attitudes, finally to descend onto the supplicant. This could be the author himself who highly deserves his own favourite form of recognition, which happens to be only a side glance, but is no less dignified for that reason (as will be explained in verse fifty-seven). Sympathy, compassion, pity, consideration for a servant or dependent, or for a supplicant standing far off out of respect, are all to be imagined to be present in this special kind of regard of the Goddess. The absolutist dignity of the regard does not suffer, although it is expressed only in the form of a side glance which seems to say, 'I've not forgotton you'. It is here that an overwhelming touch of absolute Beauty is to be recognized by the critical student.

Whether all the nine conventional *rasas* are respected by Śaṅkara or not is not important here for us. Chemistry could be studied in an overall manner by scrutinizing the periodic table of elements as well as through details in a textbook. It is the global overall view of Beauty, in which the component parts are still recognizable, that is intended by Śaṅkara to be revealed, particularly with reference to the lower or negative perspective of the Absolute, which is neither transcendent nor immanent, but normalized or renormalized between the two limits.

52

गते कर्णाभ्यर्णं गरुत इव पक्ष्माणि दधती
पुरां भेत्तुश्चित्तप्रशमरसविद्रावणफले ।
इमे नेत्रे गोत्राधरपतिकुलोत्तंसकलिके
तवाकर्णाकृष्टस्मरशरविलासं कलयतः ॥

gate karṇābhyarṇaṁ garuta iva pakṣmāṇi dadhatī
purāṁ bhettuś citta praśama rasa vidrāvaṇa phale ।
ime netre gotrādhara pati kulottaṁsa kalike
tavākarṇākṛṣta smara śara vilāsaṁ kalayataḥ ॥

gotrādhara pati kulottaṁsa kalike — O noblest (highest) bud of the clan of the Mountain King; *tava ime netre* — these Your (two) eyes; *karṇābhyarṇaṁ gate* — gone near the ears; *garuta iva pakṣmāṇi* — lashes like arrow-base feathers; *dadhatī* — wears/bears; *purāṁ bhettuḥ* — the City Burner (Śiva); *citta praśama rasa* — the essence of mental detachment; *vidrāvaṇa phale* — with the effect of disrupting; *ākarṇā akṛṣṭa smara śara vilāsaṁ* — drawn fully to the ear-limits, like the gleaming arrows of Eros; *kalayataḥ* — performs/does

Drawn fully to the ear-limits, like gleaming Eros' arrows, with lashes looking like
Arrow-base feathers, these Your eyes, having the effect
Of disrupting the complacent detachment of the City-Burner,
Make for Your glory as of the highest of the clan of the Mountain King.

Verse fifty-two requires a great deal of manipulation and structural construction or interpretation before it gives up its bare meaning. The gleaming arrows of Smara (Kāma) have first to be placed in the correct position before they can even have a chance of piercing the heart of the superascetic Śiva. Even to think of the possibility of Smara being effective against such a superior target, we have to concede that the person who sends the arrow must himself have a dignity sufficiently rich. These requirements are carefully indicated by Śaṅkara when he underlines in this verse that as the City-Burner, Śiva is normally detached and placed above the reach of interests that belong to the various grades of values ranged between heaven and earth. The three cities which Śiva burned represent three such intermediate levels. As against such superior qualifications of the husband, what is the qualification on the side of Pārvatī, which validates her as the rival counterpart of such an exalted value, raised above all earthy considerations? The answer is that Pārvatī has the glory of being the highest descendent of the clan of the King of Mountains. As the daughter of the Himalayas, she presides over existential values, while Śiva is in charge of corresponding subsistential values.

The main incident in this verse refers to some arrow being aimed in order to be sent with such an intensity and velocity that even the absolute dispassionateness of Śiva will be ruffled. The conditions required for such a smiting arrow to succeed in hitting this difficult target are carefully elaborated here in protolinguistic terms. The analogy of the bow and arrow playing on the face of the Goddess, placed in intriguing positions as if visible yet invisible, has been worked out in sufficient detail already in verse forty-seven. Kāma is well known in Sanskrit poetry. In Kālidāsa's masterpiece of mystical eroticism, *Kumārasambhava*, the roles of Kāma and his wife Rati, as well as those of Śiva and Umā, are described in great detail. The central tragedy in that famous epic is the incident where the attempt of Kāma to ruffle the heart of the City-Burner suffers a signal failure. Instead of succeeding, Kāma is struck down by Śiva's lightning and burnt to cinders. The section entitled *Ratī vilāpa* (lamentations of Rati) reveals some precious structural details meant to show why Śiva was able to burn her husband down. The arrow was not sent correctly and frontally, but from a hidden point of vantage which Kāma slyly selected, with no straightforward intention, and where he stood on one leg, peripherally situated from the place where Śiva sat steeped in deep meditation. The poetic justice of Kālidāsa considers that such punishment was justified. A revised picture is then elaborately developed in the same work. It is only through the side glances of a beautiful woman that the arrows of love can operate on such a superior man as Śiva. The beautiful woman involved in such a game must deserve on her part, by her nobility of origin at least, to send the arrows of Kāma, supported by her side glances — which have to act here as a medium to make them fly most effectively in the direction that would correctly hit the bull's-eye.

We read in the *Kumārasambhava* that in the first part of her penance for propitiating Śiva, Pārvatī followed a ritualism which belonged to the hedonistic and relativistic context of Vedic sacrifice. Having failed by this approach, she lay fainting and was carried away by her father, like a wilted lotus flower carried in the tusks of an elephant. She is taken back to her parental home, horizontally, by the King of Mountains, instead of gaining what she badly wanted: the vertical home of her husband Śiva. But she does not give up her austerities. This time she takes a revised and revalued, Vedantic approach. She abandons luxuries and stands for forty days in water and follows a discipline which has, over and above the one-pointedness of Vedism, that touch of renunciation or sacrifice, which changes the complexion of her approach altogether. We have to keep in mind such details, well known to everyone sufficiently versed in Sanskrit lore, before we are able to reinterpret the meaning and structural implications of this verse.

The first half of this verse suggests something very difficult for us to imagine. We can understand how, when Kāma wants to send an arrow sideways to hit an ordinary target, he could intensify its velocity by drawing the bowstring farther backward, the ear being the limit to which the bowstring can be drawn. It is between the ear and the eye, then, as they jointly operate, that Kāma's arrows in the form of side glances can affect the ordinary level. But it pointedly says here that the arrows leave only a gleam in her eye, and that instead of the eyelashes being spread horizontally, they are all gathered together to resemble a bundle of arrow-base feathers which, we should suppose, are evidently used for giving piercing power and lightness to the arrows themselves which are very tender, being made of flowers. Kāma is sometimes called the five-darted one (*pañcabāṇa*). Each dart is compared to a favourite flower, such as the lotus or the jasmine. The idea is that the five senses cooperate in the appeal for attention that the female principle invites to herself by her own beauty, through the intermediary of these flowers and their respective perfumes, colours or tenderness. Flower-tenderness is the nearest analogy to the existent aspect of beauty. The glance of Śiva on the numerator side is the target to be attained. This target, however, is of a conceptual order. Establishing a participation between the two aspects, the existent and the conceptual, contained within the totality of the occasionalism implied in the Absolute has been examined already in verses five and six.

The suggestion in verse forty-seven that the left forearm hides the fixing of the arrow justifies our structural analysis of this verse as belonging to a third-dimensional epistemological level. The base of the ears, to which limit the bowstring has been drawn backward has to be placed within a conic section with an interior locus, rather than peripherally and horizontally, as in the case of the fusion of many twilights into one verticalized line of light suggested in verses forty-two and forty-eight. We have to think in terms of a revised form of side glance, not only involving the five senses as five flowers — which would normally be sufficient for Kāma to operate — but we have also to place the ear limit of negativity in the subjective consciousness at a deeper locus where the mind, itself sometimes referred to as the sixth sense, is located as an inner organ or organon.

A beautiful woman's side glance becomes most powerful to the extent that this kind of verticalization and centralization, attaining to the sixth organ where concepts and percepts meet, could also come into play. There are superficial and deeper side glances, and Pārvatī's side glance has her own wholehearted mind or personal consciousness behind it, although incidentally it is the same Kāma that is operating the instrument as in every other case of effective eroticism. The arrow-base feathers suggest a gleaming arrow that is fully embedded and vertically poised within the solid conic structure that we are compelled to presuppose here. The feathers mark the negative terminus, and when the gleaming arrow and its terminus are alone visible, the negative appeal of the eternal female for her counterpart may be said to have attained to its maximum effectiveness. By the same token, it becomes competent to disrupt the complacency or detachment of the most positive of transcendental principles, represented by Śiva. The stage is thus set for occasionalism to take place in the context of absolute erotic Beauty.

The expression *ime netre*, being grammatically in the dual case, suggests that the two eyes have to be treated as functioning together in unison, in a horizontal set-up. The positive and negative ends of the arrow have necessarily to point in opposite directions, so the eyes cannot be expected to have the same function of striking the heart of Śiva. This is an additional reason for us to think that the structure has to be subjected here to a revision in terms of at least a three-dimensional solid structure, preferably one which has double-sided conic elements included within its purview. In short, it is only the verticalized version of the arrow and not its horizontal functioning that can fit into such a multidimensional dynamic situation.

We could remark that in the previous verse the aesthetic interests, auditory or visual, could be seen either in double-fanwise expansion horizontally, or in a unitary verticalized version of the same. The two fan-folds are dovetailed or telescoped into a bundle as one vertical master interest in erotic mysticism. This verse only carries over the same structural dynamism, to be imagined in highly vitalistic terms before being cancelled against its own conceptual counterpart. The norm is neither conceptual nor perceptual, neither visible nor invisible, but includes both alternately. Paradox, if it should persist, should abolish itself by a mutual transparency of light, as between existence and subsistence. The resultant would be the absolute Beauty-value which is the central theme throughout this work. The mind plays here between the two focuses of structural beauty and poetic, actual beauty. The structural beauty is superimposed on top of the actual.

We could further note that the various attitudes of the Devī have an organic sequence between them. The two eyes that are sentimentally, though negatively, focused on Śiva must be in a kind of meditation between the eyebrows, making the eyelashes tend to come together at the corners of the eyes. The other sentiments or attitudes would pass through other angles, deflected in different degrees from this vertical starting position and finally end with a side glance of grace alighting with sympathy on a dependent supplicant standing far off at the periphery. It is a horizontal side glance, rather than a frontal regard, that is thus vouchsafed to the devotee. Such a devotee is, in turn, more than satisfied with even this kind of recognition, because his devotion is able to magnify the value to its fullest possible limit. What is lost in quantity is gained in intensity. In effect, the light of the sun's orb and the beams that come out of it are the same. Substance and attribute thus can belong together.

53

विभक्तत्रैवर्ण्यं व्यतिकरितलीलाञ्जनतया
विभाति त्वन्नेत्रत्रितयमिदमीशानदयिते ।
पुनः स्त्रष्टुं देवान् द्रुहिणहरिरुद्रानुपरतान्
रजः सत्वं बिभ्रत् तम इति गुणानां त्रयमिव ॥

vibhakta traivarṇyaṁ vyatikarita līlāñjanatayā
vibhāti tvan netra tritayam idam īśāna dayite ।
punaḥ srasṭuṁ devān druhiṇa hari rudrān uparatān
rajaḥ sattvaṁ bibhrat tama iti guṇānāṁ trayam iva ॥

īśāna dayite — O Beloved of Īśāna (the Lord); *vyatikarita* — mixed well together/contiguous; *līlā añjanatayā* — by playful use of collyrium; *vibhakta traivarṇyaṁ* — presented in clear threefold relief the tricolour/ distinctness; *tvat idam* — Yours these; *netra tritayam* — three eyes; *uparatān* — bereft of passion; *druhiṇa hari rudrān devān* — Brahmā, Viṣṇu and Rudra, (the) gods; *punaḥ srasṭuṁ* — create again/afresh; *rajaḥ sattvaṁ tamaḥ* — *rajas* (active), *sattva* (pure) and *tamas* (dark); *iti guṇānāṁ trayam* — these three nature-modalities (*guṇas*); *bibhrat iva* — as if wearing/would seem to be wearing; *vibhāti* — looms

The tricolour distinctness of Your eyes, O Beloved of Īśāna (the Lord),
Presented in clear threefold relief by the playful use of collyrium,
Would seem to create afresh the gods Brahmā,Viṣṇu and Rudra (Śiva),
Bereft of passion and having the qualities of rajas, sattva *and* tamas.

Verses fifty-three, fifty-four and fifty-five bring us back to the question, though more indirectly, of transcending the three modalities of nature (*guṇas*). These modalities belong to the lower or relativistically qualified version of the Absolute. The non-relativistic version of the same, which is technically referred to as *para brahman*, has only a conceptual content. The modalities of nature cannot be present in the world of concepts in any real sense. There is thus an epistemological turning of the tables, between the immanent and the transcendent versions of the value called Beauty, which we have to recognize as playing around the region of the eyes of the Goddess. In verses twenty-five and twenty-six, the relation between the three modalities and the three gods was employed to bring into dynamic relief the mode of operation of the three *guṇa*s. Here in verse fifty-three, a colour language is employed for describing the three *guṇa*s, where *sattva* (the pure), *rajas* (the passionate), and *tamas* (the inert) correspond to white, red and black respectively. The mythological, the psychological and the colour languages are all brought into interplay in this verse to reveal a kind of mesh-like, criss-cross dynamic frame, through which the tendencies involved have to pass so as to be transcended or sublimated. In verse fifty-four another analogy is employed to describe the three modalities, where there is a confluence of three rivers having the same three colours. Finally, in verse fifty-five, transcending the modalities involves the crossing of a split-second gap between the creation and dissolution of the universe. The purpose of each of these three verses becomes clearer to the reader when the intention of transcending the modalities is kept in mind as the common theme running through all of them.

Here in verse fifty-three, being called the 'beloved of Īśāna' gives the Goddess a position intermediate between the operation of the three *guṇa*s and the transcending of the same. The eyes of the Goddess present three colours: the pupils being black, the corners being red and the sclera, white. The Goddess is pictured here as playfully adding her own eye-pencil markings to enhance the contrast between the three colours. It is then suggested that such an enhancement is able to produce the three gods once again, from a background in which they existed perhaps only in a virtual form. Virtuality and actuality are conferred upon entities, divinities or tendencies, on final analysis, by the meeting of the two references which form between them a kind of matrix or lattice formation, also called a 'grating' in crystallographic interference figures of optical motions. Some such idea seems to be in the mind of Śaṅkara here, whether we take him to know these scientific notions as we know them now, or merely to understand the basic principles implied therein in a more vague, intuitive form.

The last part of this verse qualifies the gods that thus emerge into view as bereft of passion, as the word *uparati* would suggest (*rati* being translatable as 'passion'). Thus there are gods capable of passion and gods who could be created again as passionless versions of themselves. Some commentators have suggested that antediluvian gods were passionate and after the deluge they became passionless at the instance of the Goddess. Such an interpretation would only be adding more mythology to the already vague mythological language. We prefer, therefore, to explain that the gods could function with a horizontal reference, or, sublimated, could have a verticalized reference, being placed in the context of the beauty of the face of Pārvatī. This sublimated state of the Goddess must be the result of the absolute quality of her meditation on her beloved God. The three modalities could have three colours as their monomarks, or three divinities taken from mythology or even three rivers, as in the next verse. What we should try to see in and through these stratifications, tending either to be abstract or concrete, particular or general, is the structural dynamism that is meant to be revealed in the process of transcending from the lower *brahman* to the higher *brahman*. There is, through intentionality, a possible position of participation in which both the vertical and the horizontal references are to be considered equally valid in revealing this structural dynamism underlying the frame of reference. The mythological picture is concrete and real, and can be said to be of the first dimension. The picture with nature-modalities is still vitalistically real and could be referred to as a second-dimensional set-up. When these same factors are referred to in terms of colour, they could be said to belong to a third-dimensional context. The voltage of intentionality could be further increased to abolish even the frame of reference into a fully fourth-dimensional context. When bathing in the confluence of the three rivers, as described in verse fifty-four, the pilgrim attains a sense of holiness or sanctification which is fully subjective, and by verse fifty-five, mythological realism is left far behind, in terms of an eternal present or eternal moment where creation and dissolution come together to participate on the most subtle of grounds, which is neither material nor mental.

The collyrium applied as decoration by the Goddess, out of playful love of enhancing her own beauty, is the numerator factor here, which puts the gods and the *guṇa*s in a new and neutral setting that respects both horizontal and vertical values. How the three *guṇa*s and the three gods are to be treated together has already been clarified in verses twenty-five and twenty-six. The passionless state has also been explicitly referred to in verse twenty-six. So, when previous lessons in the same textbook are fully respected, the validity of the lesson in this verse becomes sufficiently clear. It is by intentionality that one transcends the demands of the three nature modalities. When such an intentionality applies to Śiva himself, as the most positive of values, the sublimation takes place most effectively and correctly. It is the strict bipolar affiliation, to the exclusion of all extraneous interests, that can spell success in the contemplation of the Absolute.

The 'threefold relief' and the eventuality of the creation of the gods bereft of passion could all be understood together if we should admit that the horizontalized version of value modalities of interest is reoriented vertically due to the love of Pārvatī for Śiva. As between the three *guṇa*s themselves, *rajas*, the middle one, is more fully horizontal than the other two. The complex mechanism to which these *guṇa*s are subjected is the subject of the whole of Chapter XIV of the Bhagavadgītā, which could supplement what we have to say here. When *rajas,* the active, becomes bereft of passion, it would have the thinnest mathematical status possible, because essentially *rajas* refers to a horizontal function, and would accord with the function of Viṣṇu in mythological terms.

54

पवित्रीकर्तुं नः पशुपतिपराधीनहृदये
दयामित्रैर्नेत्रैररुणधवलश्यामरुचिभिः ।
नदः शोणो गङ्गा तपनतनयेति ध्रुवममुं
त्रयाणां तीर्थानामुपनयसि संभेदमनघम् ॥

pavitrīkartuṁ naḥ paśupati parādhīna hṛdaye
dayā mitrair netrair aruṇa dhavala śyāma rucibhiḥ ।
nadaḥ śoṇo gaṅgā tapanatanayeti dhruvam amuṁ
trayāṇāṁ tīrthānām upanayasi saṁbhedam anagham ॥

paśupati para adhīna hṛdaye — O One with heart given over to the Lord of Beasts (*paśupati*), Śiva; *aruṇa dhavala śyāma rucibhiḥ* — beautiful with the colours red, white and black; *dayā mitraiḥ netraiḥ* — eyes whose regard is kindly and sympathetic; *śoṇaḥ nadaḥ* — the river Śoṇa; *gaṅgā* — the Ganges; *tapana tanaya* — daughter of the Sun, the river Yamunā; *iti trayāṇāṁ tīrthānāṁ* — the sacred waters of these three (rivers); *amuṁ anagham saṁbhedam* — this sinless confluence; *naḥ pavitrīkartuṁ* — in order to purify us; *upanayasi* — You blend obtain; *dhruvam* — certain (do) indeed

O One of kindly, sympathetic regard,
Your heart being given over to the Lord of Beasts:
Of rivers such as Śoṇa, Gaṅgā *and* Yamunā, *coloured red, white and black:*
Their sacred waters You do blend indeed into sinless confluence for our purification.

In verse fifty-four we can at once recognize how the intensity of intentionality is further accentuated from the previous verse. The three colours of the eyes directed upward and concentrated between the eyebrows, where the third eye of Śiva or Pārvatī could be supposed to exist — because of the high degree of sympathy developed between them — could mark also the point of confluence of the three rivers having differently coloured waters. This apt analogy suggests that the modalities mix and merge, one neutralizing the other by being inclusively comprised under the master modality that comes by affiliation to the Absolute. Just as rivers cross the bar of an estuary, losing their names and forms, the modalities can attain the Absolute. Attaining the Absolute is the same as salvation, which implies in turn the purification from all sin. It is not difficult to see how this complex metaphor, which is more than a mere figure of speech, is carried over with a high degree of suggestibility from verse fifty-three into this verse. The way of transcending instinctive conditionings is the main theme of this verse.

The reference to Śiva as the 'Lord of Beasts' is apt. The transition from the inanimate status of the Himalaya as a mountain, to his status as the father of Pārvatī, via the world of animals, respects the natural hierarchy of values. Śiva is the Lord of Beasts before becoming the City Burner. The former implies ascent, while the latter implies descent.

55

निमेषोन्मेषाभ्यां प्रलयमुदयं याति जगती
तवेत्याहुः सन्तो धरणिधरराजन्यतनये ।
त्वदुन्मेषाज्जातं जगदिदमशेषं प्रलयतः
परित्रातुं शङ्के परिहृतनिमेषास्तव दृशः ॥

nimeṣonmeṣābhyāṁ pralayam udayaṁ yāti jagatī
tavety āhuḥ santo dharaṇi dhararājanya tanaye ।
tvad unmeṣājjātaṁ jagad idam aśeṣaṁ pralayataḥ
paritrātuṁ śaṅke parihṛta nimeṣās tava dṛśaḥ ॥

dharaṇi dhara rājanya tanaye — O Daughter of the earth-supporting Lord; *tava nimeṣa unmeṣābhyāṁ* — by the shutting and opening of your eyes; *jagatī* — the world; *pralayam udayaṁ yāti* — attains dissolution and arising (non-being and being); *iti santaḥ āhuḥ* — thus saints say; *tvat unmeṣāt jātaṁ* — (what) came to be was born as You opened them (eyes); *idam jagat* — this world; *aśeṣaṁ* — without remainder/anything left (over); *pralayataḥ paritrātuṁ* — to save from dissolution; *tava dṛśaḥ* — Your eyes; *parihṛta nimeṣāḥ* — unwinkingly (withdrawn) (have) given up closing ; *iti śaṅke* — thus (I) surmise

With eyes shut or open, You can effect, as saints say,
The being or non-being of the world, O Daughter of the earth-supporting Lord;
What thus came to be as you opened them — this entire world, without anything left —
To save from dissolution, I surmise, You remain now with eyes unwinkingly withdrawn.

In verse fifty-five we are still concerned with attitudes connected with the language of the eyes of the Goddess. The gods of the Hindu heaven supposedly do not wink. Fish, which belong to the subhuman level, do not wink either. The meditative eyes of a Buddha are seen to be introspectively withdrawn into a half-open/half-shut condition. Besides the side glances of the Devī, which can refer to particular interests, the open or shut eyes could refer to a wholesale interest in the whole of creation. When her eyes are open the world presents itself; when they are closed it disappears. The simple act of opening and shutting the eyes thus has two opposite effects. Plato divides reality into two categories: the visibles and the intelligibles. The visible world and the intelligible world can alternate within consciousness in a similar way. We could call them, with equal validity, the observables and the calculables, percepts and concepts or forms and names, according to the particular philosophical context belonging to different historical, geographical or cultural expressions. If visibles have a horizontal reference, then calculables could be said to have a vertical reference.

Cosmologically speaking, there are many theories of creation and destruction found in myths, philosophies and sciences. God as a creator or maker, or as the Great Architect, is a theological, anthropomorphic version of creation. More philosophically biased schools would explain creation in terms dependent co-origination of *vijñānavāda*, the rationalist school belonging to the Buddhist context. Vedanta prefers to adopt the doctrine of *māyāvāda*, where indeterminism finds a place side by side with mere rationalism or empiricism. Evolutionism can colour the same picture and give us an endless variety of theories. There is creative evolution, emergent evolution and parallel evolution, as well as Darwinian and Lamarckian theories, which all differ more or less from one another. Modern physics speaks of creation in terms of the 'big bang' theory as against the 'steady state' theory. It is not necessary for the purpose of this verse to enter into the details of all such theories. As Śaṅkara stands for pure Advaita Vedanta it is our task here to see how far this picture of the Goddess creating and sustaining the worlds tallies with the theories as expounded in his great commentaries. A close scrutiny of this verse reveals that, in spite of resembling the theory of instantaneous creation familiar to us in the Buddhist *vijñānavāda* school, there is always the presence of an absolute Goddess, whose function it is to create, maintain or withdraw at will. Buddhists do not recognize any such linking spiritual principle. The Vedantic view conforms to what is known as *vivartavāda*, that is, reality treated as a phenomenal presentiment. According to Vedanta, evolution applies only to matter, as in the familiar example of milk turning sour. The spirit can know no such change. The world is 'will and presentiment', as Schopenhauer puts it, and is thus comparable to a dream that can come and go without involving material change or decay. Such are some of the considerations with which we have to delimit the functions of the Goddess so as to fit them into the correct context intended here by the author.[1]

The first line indicates that the theory presented in this verse is accepted by saints or wise men (*santaḥ*). It thus belongs to a perennial philosophical context, even anterior to Śaṅkara's own Vedanta. By opening her eyes, the Goddess brings the world into being as an overt reality. When she closes her eyes, the reality disappears and gives place to virtuality. According to Eddington, there could be four distinct chairs: a conceptual chair and a perceptual chair; an actual chair and a virtual chair. Each of these four chairs needs a corresponding man, abstract or concrete; actual or virtual, to sit on it. Such is the full quaternion structure within the polyvalently possible meanings through which the consciousness of everyone circulates, participating successively within these four aspects in a figure-of-eight alternation. A fourfold polyvalence is implied in this verse, where the three states, open, closed, and the middle, are brought into the picture as covering the essence of creation, sustenance and dissolution, which the cosmic process must necessarily imply in any philosophy. The Absolute is a constant beyond the changing face of its own phenomenal functionings. Meanings could

1. For further clarifications, see Ch.1. Cosmology, *An Integrated Science of the Absolute,* by the present commentator, DK Printworld, New Delhi, 2001.

circulate semiotically or syntactically into a deeper 'meaning of meanings'. The final meaning of all meanings attains the Absolute, as is meant to be implied here in the state of mind and appearance of the Goddess. Overtness and innateness could be compared to space and time, and through the transparency of articulated space and time, which are both amorphous, as Bergson would put it, we could see a meaning of lasting interest to humanity, even long after relativity is forgotten. The withdrawn half-shut eyes of the Goddess reveal the same picture as Bergson's, but in Śaṅkara's language. We can still notice a mythological consideration which is retained in this highly philosophical version of creation in the epithet, 'Daughter of the Earth-supporting Lord', which also means to show that the Goddess belongs to the ontological side of the total structural situation.

The expression 'without anything left over' shows that, as counterparts, the perceptual and actual contents have an interchangeability. In the context of the Absolute, nothing can be left over as a remainder. The pluralistic world of relativism, when it includes everything (without remainder) under its scope, attains an equality of status with the unique Absolute of the numerator side. Cancellation is possible only between ensembles of the same status. Only two totalities can be cancelled out. The theory of ensembles in modern mathematics makes this requirement binding.

56

तवापर्णे कर्णेजपनयनपैशून्यचकिताः
निलीयन्ते तोये नियतमनिमेषाः शफरिकाः ।
इयं च श्रीर्बद्धच्छदपुटकवाटं कुवलयं
जहाति प्रत्यूषे निशि च विघटय्य प्रविशति ॥

tavāparṇe karṇejapa nayana paiśūnya cakitāḥ
nilīyante toye niyatam animeṣāḥ śapharikāḥ ।
iyaṁ ca śrīr baddhacchadapuṭa kavāṭaṁ kuvalayaṁ
jahāti pratyūṣe niśi ca vighaṭayya praviśati ॥

aparṇe — O Aparṇā (leafless), Pārvatī; *tava karṇe japa* — carried to Your ear; *nayana paiśūnya cakitaḥ* — afraid of the gossip by the eyes; *śapharikāḥ* — female *śapharika* fish; *animeṣāḥ* — unwinking; *toye nilīyante* — (they) lie submerged in water; *niyatam* — surely; *iyam śrīḥ ca* — this Lakṣmī too; *pratyūṣa* — at dawn; *baddha cchada puṭa kavāṭaṁ* — the closed petal-base-doors; *kuvalayaṁ* — (of) the water lily; *jahāti* — leaves behind; *niśi ca* — at night again; *tat vighaṭayya* — forcing them open; *praviśati* — (she re-)enters (therein)

O Aparṇā, afraid of the gossip carried to Your ear bases by Your lengthened eyes,
Surely they lie merged unwinking in water, the female śapharika *fish;*
This Lakṣmī, too, leaves behind at dawn the closed petal-base-doors of water lilies,
And at dusk, forcing them open, she re-enters therein.

There are two complementary structural and dynamic images put into this verse. The first picture refers to a horizontal dynamism, while the second refers to a figure-of-eight dynamism in which the verticalized version is presented in stronger relief. Both belong to the same background of absolute Beauty.

Breaking the surface sheen of certain placid and gently flowing rivers, one sometimes sees the species of silvery fish that jump into the air and add a lively gleam to the situation. Here we have a case of participation between numerator and denominator across the bounds of a horizontal axis of reference. Kālidāsa, in the *Śākuntalam* speaks of the thin oily gleam remaining on the flat stones of the Kaṇva ashram to indicate the same line of demarcation between the plus and minus sides by a horizontal partition, within the core of the total structure of absolute Beauty or Reality.

The second picture in this verse depicts Lakṣmī finding herself shut out of her chamber at dawn; she is thus obliged to re-enter by forcing the petal doors of the blue water lily, which opens only at dusk, responding to moonlight, rather than to sunlight like the other varieties of the lotus. A bee caught within a lotus at dusk can come out only in the morning. Here the converse is true of Lakṣmī, who is shut out of her apartment to wander and probably to spend the whole of her daytime in the company of merchants and moneymakers in the market place.

So there are two contrasts to be kept in mind in this verse. One is the contemptible frivolity of the *śapharikā* fish, frolicking below the horizontal water level or sometimes above it. Then there is Lakṣmī, the goddess of wealth, who is not sufficiently dignified to make her equal to the absolute Pārvatī. Pārvatī is here called *aparṇā* (leafless), suggestive of an austere attitude of mind analogous to a leafless tree, as in the case of some women who observe fasts at certain periods because of their very austere, contemplative state of mind. The two contrasting figure-of-eight movements, involving two kinds of participation within a fourfold frame of reference within the purview of absolute Beauty, are to be inserted together and dynamically visualized in living terms with all the modalities or phases natural to them both. This structural dynamism has been treated in plainer terms by Narayana Guru in his *Ātmopadeśa śatakam* (verses 33, 54, 56, 68 and 83). There is a common Cartesian correlation to be used here to make these two pictures fit into the same pattern.

The implication is especially to be noted that the *śapharikā* fish behave with great restraint because they are being watched closely by the all-seeing eyes of the absolute Goddess, who, being steeped in austere contemplation of Śiva, cannot tolerate frivolity by the younger handmaidens in her retinue. The transmission of gossip takes place through concepts rather than percepts, and what escapes the direct regard of the Goddess is supplemented by hearsay factors that reach the higher intelligible levels implied in the austere meditation normal to the Goddess. In the last line, Lakṣmī, who is excluded from her own lotus apartment at dawn, is required to use force. A spirit like Lakṣmī cannot enter the negative side if she does not do it sufficiently early. She takes some trouble to open it, not really forcing. Why it does not open by itself and how much force she has to use are left open to question. She has to take some kind of action. There are certain vigils in which spirits wander freely, but they have to return before the cock crows, as was the case with Hamlet's ghost.

There are two operations facing opposite ways — like inverted brackets — in this verse, which is perhaps all that we have to understand by Lakṣmī's act of forcibly re-entering her blue-lotus apartment at dusk. Between the two kinds of lotuses, the common *kamala* that opens in daylight, responding to the sun, and the blue *kuvalaya* or *kumuda* of this verse which opens at night, responding to the moon, there is a certain alternating symmetry or reciprocity, as between the overt and the innate aspects of the beauty-value. The gleaming silvery fish participate across the horizontal axis, just as the personification of the value of wealth does at a more negative level. Both of these pictures conform to the same structural dynamism.

57

दृशा द्राघीयस्या दरदलितनीलोत्पलरुचा
दवीयांसं दीनं स्नपय कृपया मामपि शिवे।
अनेनायं धन्यो भवति न च ते हानिरियता
वने वा हर्म्ये वा समकरनिपातो हिमकरः॥

dṛśā drāghīyasyā daradalita nīlotpala rucā
davīyāṁsaṁ dīnaṁ snapaya kṛpayā mām api śive ।
anenāyaṁ dhanyo bhavati na ca te hānir iyatā
vane vā harmye vā samakara nipāto himakaraḥ ॥

śive — O Śiva Consort/auspicious One; *drāghīyasya* — long-extended; *dara dalita nīlotpala rucā* — having the beauty of blue water lilies just opening; *dṛśā* — by (with Your) regard/look; *davīyāṁsaṁ* — standing far off; *dīnaṁ mām api* — even me, steeped in misery; *kṛpayā snapaya* — (do) bathe with mercy; *anena* — by this; *ayaṁ dhanyaḥ bhavati* — this one, (I) become blessed; *iyatā te hāniḥ na ca* — by this for You no loss either; *himakaraḥ* — cool-beamed (the Moon); *vane vā harmye vā* — on forest or on mansion; *sama kara nipātaḥ* — the rays (beams do) fall with equality

With Your long-extended regard, having the beauty of water lilies just opening,
O Śiva Consort, do bathe with mercy even me steeped in misery far-off;
Thus shall I be blessed, with no loss for You either —
The moonbeams do fall on forest and mansion with equality.

The section referring to the grace of beauty lingering round the region of the eyes of the Goddess seems to be terminating at this verse, perhaps extending to verse fifty-eight, where the ears will get primacy over the eyes. Here we find a tacit reference to the devotee who places himself far off and peripherally, because his supplication does not prompt him to obtrude into the presence of the Goddess except from a great distance. He effaces his own ego completely by this attitude, and is satisfied with retaining the thinnest streak of participation to ensure the bipolarity between himself and the principle of absolute Beauty. We can easily guess that, as in the case of the first and last verses of this work as well as verses seventy-five and ninety-eight, no person other than the author of these verses himself could fit into the context portrayed here. He wishes to efface his own personality to the utmost possible extent, while still keeping what is required as a minimum in a contemplatively devotional context. Such a neutral, soft, pure devotion that does not obtrude anywhere is of a superior quality.

The reference to water lilies indicates that a neutral zero point is applicable to the supplicant, who wishes to keep his neutrality intact. The long-extended regard or glance which reaches those far-off can only refer to beams secondarily given out by the beauty of the blue water lily. The pride natural to such an intelligent philosopher is neutralized in this way. One has to be an Aryan to worship Sarasvatī as a numerator Vedic value. This is for orthodox brahmins. The true Advaitin is neither orthodox nor heterodox, and the humble night water lily suits his purpose even better than the other prouder variety of day water lily called the white lotus. The difference between a Mūkāmbika and a Sarasvatī, is to be remembered here. Misery might be objected to as being a non-Aryan sentiment, as expressed in the Bhagavadgītā (II.2) by the words *anārya juṣṭam asvargyam*, which means 'undignified for an Aryan and not conducive to heaven'. Preference for heaven and for a non-sentimental divinity belongs to the plus side, but Śaṅkara, who refers to himself as a 'Dravidian child' in verse seventy-five, is satisfied in taking a humbler position, where the ego of an Aryan is not allowed to obtrude to spoil the cause of true contemplation. The given empirical world is a transitory abode of suffering (*dukhālayam*), as the Bhagavadgītā (VIII.15) puts it. This might be labelled as oriental pessimism, but sin plays the same role in the occidental, prophetic religions. The fear of Allah is another substitute for the same negative factor in life, without which no question of prayer could arise at all. The whole of this composition is meant to be a prayer and, from the side of the supplicant, would necessarily imply something to be prayed for, of recognizing his need for salvation or happiness. All aspiration presupposes some kind of privation or other. There is a touch of agony always implied in contemplation. Contemplation as an ascent presupposes such a factor.

All that the supplicant here asks for is the faintest form of recognition, as one affiliated to the context of universal motherhood. This could be the humble position of a child, or a student, or a worshipper in a temple or as in this verse, even of a tree in the forest outside a mansion, on which the moonbeams might fall without any personal preference involved in such a blessing. This kind of spontaneous, unpremeditated grace is all that the supplicant expects, without the least touch of egoism, as is clearly indicated in this verse. When bathed in the mercy of the Goddess, the personality of the supplicant is overcome by a sense of blessedness, by itself and for itself. No quantitative loss or gain could be involved in such a pure form of benediction. The arithmetical context of getting and spending is to be completely ruled out here, as impersonal devotion attains to its maximum purity. Unlike the equality between citizen and citizen, the vertical relation between the ruler and the ruled is more like the nature of the benediction conferred on the supplicant in the prayer contained in this verse.

The just-opening water lilies show that they are beginning at dusk to respond to moonlight. This picture is not supposed to be a paradise in heaven, but a corresponding paradise available to all mortals at a point where the earth and heaven meet, at a neutral zero point. The half-open blue water lilies suggest such a neutral beauty, neither too glamorous nor too humble.

We find in the second line a specific reference in the first person. This cannot be treated as incidental. Śaṅkara is obviously putting himself in the place of the typical supplicant.

The reference to the forest and palace and moonlight lifts the worship out of the context of religious holiness altogether. This is in keeping with the attitude cultivated even from the first verse and sustained to the very end. This series of verses is not a text that has to do with holiness or any conventional religiously hidebound belief.

अरालं ते पालीयुगलमगराजन्यतनये
न केषामाधत्ते कुसुमशरकोदण्डकुतुकम् ।
तिरश्चीनो यत्र श्रवणपथमुल्लङ्घ्य विलस-
न्नपाङ्गव्यासङ्गो दिशति शरसंधानधिषणाम् ॥

arālaṁ te pālīyugalam agarājanya tanaye
na keṣām ādhatte kusumaśara kodaṇḍa kutukam ।
tiraścīno yatra śravaṇa patham ullaṅghya vilasan-
āpaṅga vyāsaṅgo diśati śarasandhāna dhiṣaṇām ॥

aga rājanya tanaye — O Daughter of the King of Mountains; *te arālaṁ pālīyugalam* — two sets of curved limiting lines of Yours (between the ears and the eyes); *kusuma śara kodaṇḍa kutukam* — fancy (them) to be the bow of the flower-arrowed one; *keṣām na ādhatte* — who will not have (the fancy); *yatra tiraścīnaḥ* — where, placed obliquely; *āpāṅga vyāsaṅgaḥ* — adhering to Your long-extended side glances; *śravaṇa patham* — the path of hearing; *ullaṅghya* — going beyond; *vilasann* — as it shines; *śara sandhāna dhiṣaṇām* — the impression of the fixing of the arrow; *diśati* — makes/gives

The two sets of curved limiting lines of Yours, O Daughter of the King of Mountains,
Who is it that will not fancy them as the bow of the flower-arrowed one;
Where, placed obliquely, and reaching beyond the path of hearing
As it shines, adhering to Your side glances, it gives the impression of the fixing of the arrow.

As the poet watches the face of the Goddess, he fixes his attention successively on certain regions placed in a descending series of vertical points. As he lingers at one point he tries to describe the enigmatic beauty that plays there. He imagines certain highly suggestive double images where one image is superimposed by mental construction upon the other, which is more ontologically biased. Such two-sided images vie with each other in a paradoxical play. At the heart of the Absolute there is an ambiguity, a paradox, an enigma, a two-sided indeterminism, which is not meant by the author to be abolished. This is but in keeping with the doctrine of impredicability (*anirvacanīya khyāti*), which is the final philosophical position that Advaita Vedanta wants to take. Jainism has also got its *syādvāda* based on 'maybe/maybe not' at one and the same time. Impredicability is not looked upon as a weakness in Vedanta, but rather as a strength. As in the case of Heisenberg's indeterminate science, it does not mean that ambiguity of this kind is to be avoided or overcome by a better philosophy. There are various doctrines (*khyāti*s) referred to as characteristic of different kinds of idealistic philosophies on the Indian soil. This kind of discussion of doctrines (*khyātivāda*) attempts to locate error by fixing the paradox on different grounds or realities. *Ātmakhyāti* attempts to fix error onto the ground of the Self. *Anyathākhyāti* is the position which says that 'something else' is the cause of error. *Akhyāti* is still another variety, in which error has no real ground at all. Abolishing paradox has been the challenge successively taken up by philosophers in India and variously settled by foisting error on the basic ground. The position of Vedanta is like that of the Jains, but goes one step further by locating the principle of ambiguity or error, or the possibility thereof, at the core of the Absolute itself. The Jains and the Buddhists do not postulate any such Absolute. Vedanta postulates an *eka puruṣa*, the one supreme spirit or *brahman*, within whose personality, by a method of double negation and double assertion, ambiguity abolishes itself in terms of a unitive value revealed in a fourth-dimensional context by cancellation. These are doctrinal aspects of Vedanta, and if we should not take care to keep them in mind, an irreducible perplexity would still remain as a residue when we try to fix the meaning of each of the verses that follow, especially here in the middle of the work. Once we know that the author only wants to heighten the paradox and leave it there, instead of abolishing it — and in so doing wants to underline the principle of indeterminism or uncertainty or impredicability as a vestige that can be abolished, at best, in the form of an element of wonder at the core of the Absolute itself — then we shall be able to see his purpose here. It is not, however, an indeterminism without a proper method and theory of knowledge that we should expect to find.

In this verse the subject is again the arrows of the god of love, aimed at his arch-enemy, Śiva, who is seated at the omega point. The beauty of the Goddess is the excuse for Kāma even to be able to operate, and affords him a neutral ground on which he can still try his pranks. The Goddess wants to attract, while the God refuses to be attracted except when the right conditions are perfectly fulfilled. So an invisible war — sometimes cold, sometimes hot — is taking place here between the beauty on the upper part of the face of the Goddess, with its appeal directed vertically, and Śiva, who represents the positive side of the same principle. The interplay is not a brute form of fighting, but is meant to be reduced to thin schematic terms, both visible and invisible at the same time. At one moment we must exercise our intelligence to catch the conflict. At another moment we have to change our perspective to the perceptual side in order to see the progress of the rival forces. Finally, a slight bias on the ontological rather than the teleological side succeeds, and the battle is declared won by the wonder of the beauty on the face of the Goddess. Then the descending retrogression continues downward into still lower focal points or loci, always in a vertical succession. As soon as a locus has been fixed in a certain verse, it is required that we put a limiting set of circles around that locus called the *bindusthāna*, as in the case of the *śrī cakra*.

Such circles may not be explicitly mentioned, but some kind of limiting lines are required, within which the ambiguous play of beauty could live and move. In this particular verse, such limits are the two sets of curved lines marked by the two ears and the two eyebrows. The secret fixing of the arrow of Kāma behind the visible scene has been alluded to in different stages from verse six through verse forty-seven. The enigmatic beauty of the Goddess cannot be brought into relief without a conflict, however subtle, presupposed between Kāma and Śiva. Thus Kāma has to figure in many places. The Goddess is not just beautiful, but enigmatically so; and this makes all the difference. Beauty without a tragic touch becomes insipid.

Physiologically viewed, there might not really be a circle enclosed by these two sets of curved lines, but in a psycho-physically revised version, we could think of the two functions of seeing and hearing as being contained within the limits of the eyebrows and the ears. The arrows fixed by Kāma could have two rival positions at right angles to each other. Kāma, as a rival to Śiva, can be expected to let his arrows fly in an oblique direction. It is only occasionally, when every other condition is favourable, that his arrows can be made to fly vertically. This he cannot do without complying with the side glance of the Goddess and conforming to the same highly verticalized attitude. These differences have been alluded to already, especially in verse fifty-two. In the present verse the object is merely to represent the functioning of Kāma, whose arrows fly horizontally, beyond the limits of the ears, and what is spatialized motion could be treated as changed qualitatively into time-like motion. Here the arrows, when they fly, have to adhere to the direction of the side glances. Kāma is not yet letting the arrows fly, he is only represented here as fixing them on to the obliquely aimed bow as he gets ready to give battle in his normal way. While still in the act of fixing the base of the arrow onto the bowstring, it is permissible for us to think of the two sets of curved lines as marking the limits within which Kāma could operate, at any of the four right angled positions possible to him. As his target is on the plus side of the situation, a ninety degree tilting of the bow is all that we might have to imagine here. If the arrow belongs to a three-dimensional context, the shining lines of the glances of the Goddess could be said to belong to a fourth-dimensional context, where visibility and audibility cancel each other out. Only the wonder of absolute Beauty remains for us to see when the paradox has thus been abolished.

The fixing of an arrow is the only definite event in this verse. The rest consists of glances and sound elements which make up a kind of chakra, composed of lines representing light or sound radiating from and circulating round the central locus. Beauty is to be meditated upon; and when absolute Beauty is the theme, it can produce such contemplative visions based equally on fact and fable.

59

स्फुरद्गण्डाभोगप्रतिफलितताटङ्कयुगलं
चतुश्चक्रं मन्ये तव मुखमिदं मन्मथरथम् ।
यमारुह्य द्रुह्यत्यवनिरथमर्केन्दुचरणं
महावीरो मारः प्रमथपतये सज्जितवते ॥

sphurad gaṇḍābhoga pratiphalita tāṭaṅka yugalaṁ
catuś cakraṁ manye tava mukhaṁ idam manmatha ratham ।
yam āruhya druhyaty avani ratham arkendu caraṇaṁ
mahāvīro māraḥ pramatha pataye sajjitavate ॥

tava idaṁ mukhaṁ — this Your face; *sphurat* — shining; *gaṇḍābhoga* — cheeks; *pratiphalita* — reflected; *tāṭaṅka yugalaṁ* — the pair of earrings; *catuḥ cakraṁ* — (with) four wheels; *manmatha ratham manye* — Kāma's chariot, I consider; *yam āruhya* — surmounting which; *mahā vīraḥ māraḥ* — the great hero Kāma; *arka indu caraṇaṁ* — with sun and moon for wheels/foothold; *avani ratham* — the globe for chariot; *sajjitavate* — fully ready/equipped; *pramatha pataye* — the Lord of Hosts; *druhyati* — assails

This, Your face, I consider Kāma's chariot with four wheels,
As seen when Your ear ornaments are reflected on Your shining cheeks;
Surmounting which, that great hero Kāma assails the Lord of Hosts,
Who, with sun and moon for wheels, mounting the globe for chariot, is fully ready to give him battle.

In this verse we have to distinguish a situation in which the battle is about to start between Kāma and Śiva, who is here named the Lord of Hosts. It is the beautiful face of the Goddess which is the psychophysical basis for the chariot of Kāma, who was fixing his arrows in the previous verse. Now, on closer scrutiny, the chariot, which is more ontological in status, comes into view. Two of the wheels of the chariot are the large wheel-like ear ornaments worn by women of ancient India, which were common even thirty years ago. These supply the physical basis for the illusion of the chariot, while the two other wheels are created by their reflections, one degree removed from the physical reality and therefore nearer to the metaphysical. The beauty of the Goddess is neither physical nor metaphysical, but both. In the same way that an actual chair and a conceptual chair could belong together in consciousness in an integrated view of reality, so these two pairs of wheels complement each other and do not enter into conflict. The reflected wheels, however, have only a horizontal status of parity with the two original ones. They are like mirror reflections and therefore virtual. The reflecting surface is the glossiness of the cheeks of the Goddess. A thin line has to separate the two sets of wheels because the transition from perceptual to conceptual requires a limiting parameter, as in a mirage which reflects sunlight. A layer of hot air can cause a mirage effect when viewed at a certain angle. The glossy cheeks of the Goddess are therefore aptly referred to as producing this illusion of a chariot with four wheels. Such a chariot has already been introduced into the picture more than once. In verse six it was said to consist of the monsoon breeze favourable to the flowery season. Now Kāma takes his position on the completed chariot to let his arrows fly, not only horizontally. The chance of hitting Śiva himself and making him fall in love with the beauty of the face of Pārvatī is a possibility not to be ruled out in this subtle picture of occasionalism.

Having completed the picture of the chariot of Kāma, the poet passes on to the chariot proper to Śiva. Śiva does not require four wheels, because the two celestial orbs, the sun and the moon, could be so manipulated by him that they would perhaps alternately take over the function of the two back wheels. As for the front wheel with the help of which he is supposed to descend along the vertical line, that has to be of an order less hypostatic than the former two. Thus the chariot could be thought of as functioning with a spherical wheel, which could be none other than the globe of the earth itself. The wheels are, anyhow, imaginary and have a highly hypostatic status, so one should not ask why the analogy does not square with cosmological facts. Cosmology and cosmogony have to differ, and contemplative cosmogony must differ still further. When we make these concessions, we can see that Śiva himself is preparing to fight against Kāma. That Kāma is a sufficiently dignified rival for Śiva has already been established in verse six. Kāma cannot always be victorius, but he has to bide his chance as occasionalism dictates. Beauty being an absolutist value, here the side glances of the Goddess can make the arrow of Kāma fly more effectively, even in the vertical direction, by which Śiva could successfully be hit. That is the reason why Śiva is getting ready to meet the threat. A cancellation will take place in which the beauty of the Goddess will triumph. The spiritual progress of the votary of the Goddess thus becomes assured. We have to note that it is readiness for battle, and not actual battle, that is to be imagined here. The moment is in the eternal present, in which the paradox of the Absolute is cancelling itself out.

We have referred to the glossy skin of the cheeks of the Goddess as reflecting the light of the ear ornaments. Many twilights of moonsets and moonrises or sunsets and sunrises could be fused together to influence the outer skin — even of fruits, such as mangoes or peaches. Oranges are said to be 'sun-kissed'. The glossy surface of fruits implies a thin film which separates the beauty that is inside from the beauty that is outside, as between the taste of the orange and the glossiness of its skin. Many twilight dreams of innumerable sunset and sunrise hours must have produced the dappled coloration seen on certain fruits, and even perhaps the brindled patches on certain cows. The varieties of coloured light can produce all kinds of patterns of beauty in nature, and the beauty of the Goddess here is not outside the scope of such an explanation.

60

सरस्वत्याः सूक्तीरमृतलहरीकौशलहरीः
पिबन्त्याः शर्वाणि श्रवणचुलुकाभ्यामविरलम् ।
चमत्कारश्लाघाचलितशिरसः कुण्डलगणो
झणत्कारैस्तारैः प्रतिवचनमाचष्ट इव ते ॥

sarasvatyāḥ sūktīr amṛta laharī kauśala harīḥ
pibantyāḥ śarvāṇi śravaṇaculukābhyām aviralam ।
camatkāra ślāghā calita śirasaḥ kuṇḍala gaṇo
jhaṇatkārais tāraiḥ prativacanam ācaṣṭa iva te ॥

śarvāṇi — O Blessed One; *sarasvatyāḥ* — of Sarasvatī; *amṛta laharī kauśala harī* — exuding nectar-sweetness; *sūktiḥ* — good sayings; *śravaṇa culukābhyām* — by Your ears (like the hollow of a hand cupped to drink, a small vessel); *aviralam pibantyāḥ* — ever absorbing (drinking without break); *te kuṇḍalagaṇaḥ* — Your series of earrings; *camatkāra ślāghā* — appreciating/approving the bright wit; *calita śirasaḥ* — by moving the head/nodding; *tāraiḥ jhaṇatkāraiḥ* — with high-pitched jinglings; *prativacanam ācaṣṭa iva* — seem to applaud/reply each (saying)

The good sayings of Sarasvatī, exuding nectar sweetness,
Ever absorbing with slow interest by Your ears, O Blessed one,
Each bright wit therein, while approving with nods,
Your series of earrings seem to applaud them with their high-pitched jinglings.

In the previous section the arrows of Kāma and the side glances of the Goddess figured in collaboration to present before us two fully developed chakras, one higher and the other lower. The lower chakra implied the three modalities of nature (*guṇa*s) and other aesthetic interests which were sublimated or verticalized in the earlier half of the previous set of ten verses. That section has terminated. In this verse we pass on to the domain proper to the goddess of the Word, Sarasvatī, who presides over poetry. In the Vedic context she is represented as sitting in white robes on a white lotus, telling crystal beads and holding a book. The *Śatapatha Brāhmaṇa* which presents a later Vedic revision of Sarasvatī, speaks of a goddess who sends arrows both ways, that is, toward both the perceptual and conceptual sides at once. Such a Word-Goddess, who presides over both the dictionaries — the conceptual as well as the perceptual — is sometimes referred to as *ubhaya bhāratī* (a double Sarasvatī), and is proper to the temple which is said to have been established by Śaṅkara himself at the Śṛṅgerī Maṭh.

For the purposes of this verse we need more than one goddess. So Śaṅkara gives us the picture of one goddess responding to the words of the other. It is important for us to fix the epistemological status of these two goddesses before trying to understand the dialogue taking place between them. One is represented here as only nodding while the other is acutally speaking. The difference between these two versions of the Word-Goddess is the same as what Marshall McLuhan might distinguish as 'the medium' and the 'message'. If we take a pencil with red-coloured lead and make a line on a paper with it, that could be called a 'medium' language, based on percepts. The red is immediately evident in the medium itself, and the conceptual 'message' or word is not necessary to make the meaning any clearer. Sarasvatī on the other hand, represents the word 'red', when we spell it out with any pencil, not necessarily one with red-coloured lead. The interaction between perceptual realities and conceptual realities is thus a form of agreement or one-to-one correspondence between numerator and denominator aspects of the same word content. We could have the example of 'stop' and a red light put together in a traffic signal, where symbol and sign meet to cancel out into the same meaning.

The situation in this verse is analogous. The absolute Goddess has two aspects that belong together to the same meaning. Structurally analysed, we get an ontologically biased goddess having a communication with her own teleological counterpart. The lower goddess, who is more real, wears real metallic earrings jingling on her ears. She does not speak, but her response is made up of nods which only approve of the verbose statements made by her own higher dialectical counterpart. As goddesses of the Word, both of them are interested in the aptness of analogies that poets might succeed in choosing. When aptness succeeds, it is the success of the perceptual aspects of analogy cancelling out against its own conceptual aspects. The verdict on this matter has to come from the side of perception, because human experience begins with sensations and perceptions, and only then passes over to higher conceptual constructions.

The sayings of Sarasvatī consist of wise proverbs or witticisms. Witty statements have to be short and convincing. When analogies are aptly employed, those who enjoy good literature will surely applaud the genius of the poet concerned. Without being expressed in words, the applause could come from the ontological side, because seeing is always more convincing than hearing. This is why the jingling of the ear ornaments, along with the gesture of nodding, is meant here by the poet to express in non-verbose language the appreciation by the Goddess on hearing wise proverbs expressed in the more verbose language of literature, belonging to the side of Sarasvatī. Nodding is the vertical link connecting the two sides, and the jingling of the ear ornaments participates both in the world of sound as well as in the world of the 'medium'. Thus message and medium meet and cancel out, resulting in a situation that is meant to enhance the beauty-value of the Word Goddess who could be seen as speaking or silent, as required.

61

असौ नासावंशस्तुहिनगिरिवंशध्वजपटि
त्वदीयो नेदीयः फलतु फलमस्माकमुचितम्।
वहत्यन्तर्मुक्ताः शिशिरकरनिश्वासगलितम्
समृद्ध्या यस्तासां बहिरपि च मुक्तामणिधरः॥

asau nāsāvaṁśas tuhina giri vaṁśa dhvaja paṭi
tvadīyo nedīyaḥ phalatu phalam asmākam ucitam ।
vahaty antar muktāḥ śiśirakara niśvāsa galitam
samṛddhyā yas tāsāṁ bahir api ca muktāmaṇi dharaḥ ॥

tuhinagiri vaṁśa dhvajapaṭi — O Banner of the dynasty of the Himālayas; *tvadīyaḥ asau nāsā vaṁśaḥ* — Your noseridge here as (bamboo) flagstaff; *asmākam ucitam phalam* — for us deserving/appropriate fruit; *nedīya* — standing very near/below; *phalatu* — may it ripen; *antaḥ muktāḥ vahati yat saḥ* — that which bears pearls inside (the noseridge flagstaff); *tāsāṁ samṛddhyā* — due to the plenitude of the same (pearls); *bahiḥ api* — outside also; *śiśirakara niśvāsa galitam* — dropped by (Your) cool moonbeam respiration; *muktāmaṇi dharaḥ* — wears pearls

O Banner of the dynasty of the Himalayas, Your noseridge, here as Your clan's flagstaff,
Let it ripen for us, standing so near below You, deserving fruit;
Inwardly wearing pearls as they do, and dropped by cool moonbeam respiration,
It bears, even outside, pearls due to the plenitude of the same.

The centre of interest now passes from the brightness of the face as a whole, to the noseridge, which represents a vertical descending line. In verse forty-seven the left fist and forearm of the god of love were hiding the downward movement of the bowstring as it was being pulled along the vertical line across the face, corresponding to the ridge of the nose. The archer in that position must be one that aims the arrows upward at Śiva. If the hands of the god of love belong to a three-dimensional grade of appearance, here the line of the noseridge could be said to mark the vertical amplitude within which subtle values reside.

A pearl is always used as an analogy for something precious, as when we say 'a pearl of great price'. In Indian philosophy also, the pearl has figured as an analogy very dear to contemplative speculators for the value of Truth. Though the ocean may contain gems which are equally precious, on a more hypostatic level values are more aptly comparable to bright pearls. Iridescent hues that play on its surface give the pearl a silvery gleam, and Vedanta has used this peculiar quality as an analogy to explain the false glamour of vain appearances. The hard nacreous layer of the inner shell, called the 'mother-of-pearl', is where the pearls are formed, but from a chemical standpoint this layer is nothing other than calcium carbonate.

The Vedanta of Śaṅkara, in its methodology, gives primacy to ontology as against higher theoretical values. Here, however, in the context of the beauty of the face of the Goddess, the pearl is compared to a prayer which in turn is comparable to a wish-fulfilling tree called Devadāru, placed very high in the hypostatic scale of values. The corresponding wish-fulfilling factor belonging to the lower limit of existence is often referred to as Kāmadhenu (the cow of plenty). In the face of the Goddess we are still on the side of the numerator values of life, so it is not unjustified here for the poet to use the image of a heavenly tree, at the bottom of which some supplicants can be imagined to be standing, praying for some kind of benefits to be dropped down to them by way of answer to their various prayers. God grants prayers, because there would have been no God in any of the world's literature if the opposite had been true in the experience of mankind.

In fact, any prayer unanswered could be answered by ourselves, because theology admits that the Kingdom of God is within oneself. In Vedanta, this dictum is quite acceptable, because the axiomatic overall dictum of all *mahāvākyas* (great sayings) categorically asserts that 'Thou art That'. One receives what one deserves: 'Whatsover a man soweth, that shall he also reap'. God, in his justice and generosity, cannot violate such overall laws, within the framework of which He himself is placed. No god can exist otherwise than by granting prayers because prayers alone can apply to possible boons or benefits. The axiomatic laws of reciprocity, complementarity, compensation and cancellability in the overall structural context of the Absolute, make such a law binding equally for man and God at once, though only in a subtle absolutist fourth-dimensional sense. It is to this order of values that the beauty of the Goddess belongs, where pearls are items of beauty representing benefits like fruits that could drop down from a heavenly tree for hungry children to pick up and eat. The production of fruit in such superabundance by a tree could not be explained if such a theory were to be discarded as completely fanciful.

The opening epithet, 'banner of the dynasty of the Himalayas', means that since the Himalayas are already the highest of mountains, to erect a flagstaff to make them rise even higher indicates that such attributes as family honour or reputation can be produced, as much as one chooses, along a vertical positive parameter. *Noblesse oblige* (nobility obligates) is the rule: the more noble you are, the more your generosity is heightened. In the previous verse, we were still in the realm of values that belonged to the world of good literature, but here honour is a value that can reach even higher and subtler limits. The flagstaff analogy is thus very apt. In India we are justified in thinking of a bamboo flagstaff, because this verse implies that it must be hollow in order to allow the passage of moonbeams, as well as air, through it. The nose exists for breathing through, up or down. Here, waiting immediately below such a vertical nose, are those who are praying for benefits like fruits to fall down to the horizontal terra firma. The gods confer blessings from above while the denizens of the earth wait to receive them. Such is the overall situation from which we have to extract the beauty-value of the centre of the face of the Goddess. The glory of the flagstaff could refer to the father of Pārvatī at its base, while the flag at the top could be a symbol that glorifies Śiva. Between these two limits, there is an ascent and a descent taking place in terms of cool and pearly moonbeam respiration, in the context of sheer beauty. Such an abstracted respiration is like the alternation between space-like and time-like factors within the Absolute, where space can devour time, and time space, in the eternal cosmic process of alternating phases, just as in human respiration.

Life matures with each act of breathing and fulfils itself in the form of that generosity which is basic to its overall nature. It is not just generosity, but overgenerosity, like that of a gambler who gives even his shirt when only the coat is asked for. Absolute generosity cannot be compatible with the calculative precaution of a hesitant man. Fruit trees in springtime overladen with flowers reflect unquestionably the generosity of nature. In the tropical regions of palm trees and coral reefs, the many small coconuts that drop to the ground during the ripening process surely reveal such a superabundance, within the context of which nature normally operates. In India, mango trees are sometimes so overladen with fruit that their branches are bent down to the ground. Such a picture has touched the hearts of mystics like Narayana Guru, because there is beauty in such superabundant generosity. Because generosity is normally a subjective feeling, the analogy of pearls ripening inside the hollow of the flagstaff and dropping down to the supplicant subjectively, as if through a tube, would be justified. But absolute Generosity in a fully Advaitic sense, knows no limit of inside or outside. It must be with the view of abolishing this distinction between inside and outside, which gets dissolved or abolished by itself as generosity attains to its more absolutist quality, that Śaṅkara resorts to such a far-fetched analogy of pearls covering the outside and filling the inside of the nostrils of the Goddess. Pearl nosescrews worn by Indian women show a cluster of pearls, which look as if they are overflowing from inside the nostrils. Poetry might have guided the jeweller's art here, or vice versa. For us, it is important to derive the lesson that generosity and beauty are inseparable.

Minor Considerations

The opening line refers to the clan of the Goddess. A young woman is proud of her father's clan, but after marriage her loyalties are transferred to her husband. The transition between the two loyalties, one turned retrospectively and the other turned prospectively, is a delicate one, and is sometimes seen to be very touchy in the case of sensitive women who feel easily insulted if a slight slur is cast upon their ancestry. Later on in verse eighty-six, we will see that this kind of touchiness is possible even in the relation between Śiva and Pārvatī. This is good advice for husbands: do not discredit the father-in-law.

The second line underlines the fact that devotees are placed very near to the foot of the flagstaff, and that they get only those benefits which they deserve. Cause and effect are related vertically in a law of reciprocal specificity. Clay is the material cause of the pot and the medium through which cause and effect are linked either way. One cannot make curd without milk, and no wave is possible without water. No illusion is possible without some basis for the illusion. Vedanta respects such a law of reciprocity as categorical or imperative. One cannot pray for something that one does not implicitly or explicitly deserve. A woman can only pray for a husband, not for a wife. We can see that any young woman's prayer for a husband is generally answered sooner or later, the differences being only incidental, making allowances for the accidental joltings in life. It is by the timely answer of prayers that humanity continues to live normally, generation after generation.

In the third line, the cool moonbeams are suggested as favourable to the dropping of ripe fruits from the trees. Wintering is as important for fruits as the heat of the sun for the putting forth of tender leaves and for giving an impetus to flowering.

We see in the mango tree, for instance, that strong sunlight is required to usher in the best season for the fruits. Apples, on the other hand, require heavy winter conditions for the fruits to mature. The dropping of the fruits occurs only after they have first matured by sunlight. In this sense, it is not against nature to think that the cool breezes help to make the fruits drop down. The idea that moonbeams mixed with cool air pass through the cavity of a flagstaff to grant benefits to supplicants might seem far-fetched, but such a style is normal to the whole of this work, where creative imagination and poetic fancy are given the fullest freedom.

Finally, in the last line, where pearls cluster outside as well as inside the nostrils of the Goddess, the function of the poet surpasses itself. The only excuse for doing so is that Śaṅkara thereby justifies his own Advaitic position in treating absolute Beauty as an ultimate value. Internally and externally, as between the selfsame class or as between two classes (*sajātīya* and *vijātīya*), Advaita tolerates no duality or difference. In these verses, which are often mistakenly considered to be merely part of Tantra, such poetic excesses can be justified, according to us, only in the name of that uncompromising unitive stand so characteristic of Śaṅkara's philosophy as a whole.

62

प्रकृत्यारक्तायास्तव सुदति दन्तच्छदरुचेः
प्रवक्ष्ये सादृश्यं जनयतु फलं विद्रुमलता ।
न बिम्बं तद्बिम्बप्रतिफलनरागादरुणितं
तुलामध्यारोढुं कथमिव विलज्जेत कलया ॥

prakṛtyā raktāyās tava sudati dantacchada ruceḥ
pravakṣye sādṛśyaṁ janayatu phalaṁ vidruma latā ।
na bimbaṁ tadbimba pratiphalana rāgād aruṇitaṁ
tulām adhyāroḍhuṁ katham iva vilajjeta kalayā ॥

sudati — O One of goodly teeth; *prakṛtyā āraktāya* — naturally red; *tava danta cchada ruceḥ* — of the beauty of Your parted lips; *sādṛśyaṁ pravakṣye* — I shall declare the similitude; *vidrumalatā* — the coral reef; *phalaṁ janayatu* — let (it) bear fruit; *bimbaṁ na* — not the *biṁba* fruit; *tat biṁba pratiphalana rāgāt* — by reflection from its original model (the lips); *aruṇitaṁ* — reddened; *tulām adhyāroḍhuṁ* — desiring to climb to a state of mid-parity; *katham iva* — somehow (however); *kalayā* — at least by a shade (degree); *na vilajjeta* — not be abashed

O One of goodly teeth, of Your parted lips, naturally red,
I shall declare the similitude:
Let the coral reef bear fruit, not the bimba fruit, but by reflection reddened from its original model,
With which desiring to climb to the point of mid-parity,
However could they (the teeth) avoid being abashed at least by a shade?

In verse sixty-two the *bindusthāna*, or central locus, is to be placed between the parted lips, where the beautiful teeth of the Goddess are revealed. The play of participation between the pearly teeth and the coral-red lips is the central theme of this verse. Sanskrit poets are fond of one analogy in particular for the luscious, rich and fully red lips of a voluptuous maiden, which is the *bimba* fruit (the bright-red fruit of the plant *Momordica monadelpha*), so a beautiful girl is often called 'one of *bimba*-fruit-lips'.

Here the poet steps down from the platform, as it were, to speak intimately with his audience by means of analogies that are most fitting to the beauty of the lips and teeth, which blend their colours both ways to create a non-dual form of absolute Beauty by mutual participation. The teeth are hard like coral, while the lips are naturally soft and supple like the *bimba* fruit. The problem is to establish a parity or one-to-one correspondence between them to fulfil the requirements of a central Advaitic value which should always be the same, at whatever level, inside or outside. The beauty of the Goddess is going to be appreciated by the poet himself here. By stepping down from the platform to talk to the reader, he throws off his formal status, and seems to say that between the reader and the poet an intimate understanding could be established on a certain basis. Both of them are equally interested in finding the nearest analogy to the beauty that emerges at that particular locus where the teeth reveal the bright colour of the parted lips. The object of the poet here is to show that the magenta colour of coral and also that of the *bimba* fruit seem to rival each other in establishing superiority over some other analogy that another poet might suggest.

Thus, the situation is one that involves a subtle intrigue between rival poetic tastes. The solidity of the teeth would make it reasonable for a poet to think that the analogy of hard coral applies more aptly to the teeth than to the *bimba* fruit, which would naturally belong by common-sense standards to the side of the lips. It is clearly stated in the first line that the poet is trying to find the right analogy for the teeth and the lips, and because the teeth are hard and solid, he suggests that if the coral reef could have a fruit, that would establish a parity between the teeth and the lips to reveal the non-dual Beauty that suggests itself in that region. The coral reef does not have fruit, but we could suppose a soft fruit in order to suggest that the redness of the lips permeates into the region of the teeth and thus makes them look like fruit by borrowed light, one degree removed from the suggested analogy. The attributes of solid coral and the attributes that belong to a luscious fruit are meant here to be cancelled out into a state of parity or equality. The teeth, in trying to establish an equality, in respect of a brilliant reddishness, do not fully succeed in doing so. It is even suggested that they shyly hesitate in the attempt. This hesitation implies that at one moment they are equal in beauty to the lips, and at another moment they are not, in the opinion of the teeth themselves.

An element of ambiguity is thus purposely retained by Śaṅkara here in order to underline the doctrinal principle of indeterminism or non-predicability that applies when two conjugates are involved as rival factors to the same absolute Value. The analogy of energy and velocity of particles in quantum mechanics is supposed to represent such a principle of indeterminism. They cannot both be fixed at the same time and place, to give a value that is fully determined. Vedanta accepts this indeterminism as basic to nature itself, when viewed from the side of physics rather than that of metaphysics. Either physics is right or metaphysics is right at a given time. For both to be right at the same time, the Absolute must step in as a normative and a re-normative reference. The shyness and hesitation in the matter of establishing an equality of beauty between the solid teeth, which resemble coral ontologically but which wish to attain an equality of beauty with the luscious fruit-like lips — which are more qualitative or teleological in their status — presents an enigma which refuses to be abolished. The vestige of paradox exists at the core even of the notion of the Absolute, however much we might try to fix its meaning finally. Such a paradoxical element is considered permissible as a last residue, in the Bhagavadgītā. The Absolute is a mystery and a wonder, and it is a rare value within the mind of yogis capable of meditating on it. An alternating figure-of-eight movement belongs to the absolute Value-content, till meditation abolishes even the least duality between the Self and the non-Self aspects of the same content. But the mystery is never to be abolished. Within the core of such a mystery, the stable term is to be marked, if at all, by that finalized experience in which the meditator becomes not other than the object meditated upon, by cancellation. The term of all meditation is thus attained as a supreme yogic experience. Even mind and matter can be said to meet here, as well as ends and means.

It is to bring out this subtle Vedantic position that Śaṅkara leaves the contested equality of beauty between lips and teeth, one shining by the borrowed light of the other, in the form of a rhetorical question in terms of a shyness, where ontology and teleology may be said to be playing a game of hide-and-seek through all time. Such a situation is called *anyonya adhyāsa* (mutual conditioning). The favourite example of conditioning (*adhyāsa*) is that of a clear colourless crystal placed on a piece of red satin. Without becoming red, the crystal is made to look red through and through. The teeth and the luscious fruit complement each other, as do quantity and quality, and the indeterminism that would persist in the form of a hesitation or shyness is itself a value to be equated with the absolute Value and not to be abolished. The two limbs of an equation need not be abolished for a trained mathematician to understand its import. The duality between the limbs of the equation is no drawback to the equation itself.

The final meaning is the message to be sought in the experience of the yogi. It is a form of unitive understanding and nothing more. Pluralism can coexist with the notion of unity, so that the philosopher could cancel them both out into the non-dual Absolute. All propositions must contain terms which it is the task of the logician to resolve into their own middle terms. Such a middle term is the Absolute. To recognize ambiguity between terms so as to abolish them correctly is preferable to just saying, as theologians often do, that one should not believe in many gods. Dialectical methodology would admit both the references of thesis and antithesis for arriving at a final synthesis. Even Hegelianism admits of such a method, of which Engels is only a continuator.

The Guru comes in naturally because people attached to wisdom have an automatic affiliation. Guru and disciple are like the two limbs of an equation. They are equal, in principle, like comrades.

If time and space are conjugates, we can see through their amorphous articulation a being which, like a flame or a dancing Naṭarāja, gives us a figure-of-eight functional picture. This idea is similar to the shyness of the teeth to resemble the lips. One attains the Absolute thus through abstracting rival aspects of beauty. Truth is both a way as well as a fact. Ends and means unite in it into an experience. We must be careful not to bind down with hide the ambiguity of this dancing flame. A 'Lord, Lordism' will result from fixing it down as a doctrine. As the Bhagavadgītā says, 'It is a wonder and a mystery'. That is as far as one can understand it. We must leave it as a value of this kind and not solidify it into a doctrine.

This language of such a high degree of fancifulness is natural to man, and perfectly acceptable to children. If the financial world can speak of the 'dancing pound' or say that the 'dollar is shy', why can Śaṅkara not use such terms in an absolutist context?

The ontological teeth, as cause, lag slightly behind the teleological lips, as effect, in the figure-of-eight participation. This is poetry bent to speak for the philosophy of Vedanta, which Westerners would claim to be unfair. There is a subtle trick played here by Śaṅkara. The interplay here is between quantitative and qualitative aspects of beauty, and the event could be described as intersubjective as well as transphysical.

63

स्मितज्योत्स्नाजालं तव वदनचन्द्रस्य पिबतां
चकोराणामासीदतिरसतया चञ्चुजडिमा ।
अतस्ते शीतांशोरमृतलहरीमाम्लरुचयः
पिबन्ति स्वच्छन्दं निशि निशि भृशं काञ्चिकधिया ॥

smita jyotsnājālaṁ tava vadana candrasya pibatāṁ
cakorāṇām āsīd atirasatayā cañcu jaḍimā ।
atas te śitāṁśor amṛta laharīm āmlarucayaḥ
pibanti svacchandaṁ niśi niśi bhṛśaṁ kāñcika dhiyā ॥

tava vadana candrasya — of Your moon-bright face; *smita jyotsnā jālaṁ* — the smile like a cluster of moonbeams; *pibatāṁ* — drinking; *cakorāṇāṁ* — partridges; *ati rasatayā* — by surfeit of sweetness; *cañcu jaḍimā āsīt* — got numbness of tongue; *ataḥ te āmla rucayaḥ* — therefore, they, desirous of sourness; *śitāṁsoḥ amṛtalaharī* — the nectar flowing from the cool-beamed (moon); *kāñcika dhiyā* — treating it as sour brew; *niśi niśi* — night by night; *svacchandaṁ* — as they please; *bhṛśaṁ pibanti* — eagerly, excessively imbibe

Your smile, like a moonbeam cluster out of Your moon-
bright face,
Partridges, on drinking, by surfeit of sweetness
Numbness of tongue they got; thus presently do they imbibe
eagerly
The nectar from the moon, treating it as sour brew, night
by night.

In verse sixty-three we find a further accentuation of the ambiguous ambivalence implied in the shyness of the previous verse. There is a certain variety of partridge common in India known as *cakora* (Greek partridge), which keeps sleepers awake throughout bright moonlit nights by its repeated noises from trees around homes. Such a partridge is inserted into the context of beauty appreciation in this verse. There are certain aspects of beauty that can produce surfeit, and there are others that are enjoyable in a different, even negative sense. Connoisseurs of wines are aware of this difference, as between sweet and dry wines. Benedictine and Vermouth could be cited as examples. Moonbeams as a numerator value have to be compensated by the taste of the same moonbeams as understood from the inside of a partidge suffering from surfeit. At the beginning of night, the patridges indulge in the positive aspect of sweetness, and when they are fed up with such a sweetness, their power of enjoyment becomes numbed. Their taste is reversed, and they begin to prefer the negative aspect of the same taste.

If the Absolute is enjoyable, it is not in a dull mechanistic sense that we have to understand the enjoyment. The ambivalent aspects of enjoyment have to enter into an alternating interplay, even in the joy of contemplation of the beauty content. It is in this sense that tragedies can be entertaining, and we pay for cinema shows that make us shed tears throughout. Adversities have their sweet uses. Beauty could be one-sided and insipid in the same way. Kālidāsa dwells on this in almost every description of his heroines, as when he says that the beauty of the lotus is enhanced when it is set among mosses. Sweet and savoury items have to alternate at good parties for the same reason referred to in this verse; otherwise tongues would become numb.

The main point is contained in the last line, which says that it is the *cakora*'s attitude of mind that removes the numbness or partly contributes to it, whatever the numerator value in itself might contain, by way of sweetness or sourness. It is an alternation established between the sweet and sour tastes playing between overt and innate factors in a figure-of-eight movement which alone can secure a happiness that can endure through day or night, or early and later moonlight tastes, both of which tend to alternate transsubjectively and interphysically.

We note from the first line that we are still at the locus of the teeth of the Goddess, when they are revealed to view by her sweet smile. If the moon has a sweet brightness, the teeth add to the sweetness as an attribute to the totality of the face. The moon's orb can be sweet, but the smile makes it more specifically or qualitatively sweet. To both these sweetnesses, which coexist on the positive side of the total situation, which we could call absolute Beauty, we have to insert a negative aspect of the same beauty in subjective terms before we could integrate the value of beauty as a totality in which opposites coexist. This requirement is accomplished in the last half of the verse. When put together by abstraction and generalization, absolute Beauty can emerge into view and enter into our own consciousness at one and the same time. Relative or partial beauty thus becomes raised to the status of absolute Beauty by the cancellation of its own positive and negative sides. Surfeit is supposed to be reached at a certain time of the night, whether subjective or objective, where moonlight could be partial or complete. Compensation works both ways: the mind supplies what is not there, and what is there compensates for what the mind hankers after. Thus we get the same constant of absolute Beauty, though placed within the context of night rather than of daytime. The structural and alternating aspects remain the same whatever the conjugates involved, but the conjugates must belong to the same class, context or order, within a phenomenologically understood *epoche* or situation.

The first line suggests a multiplicity of moons within a general moonlight, each bright tooth representing a unit of beauty set within the totality of the beauty of the moon itself. Substance and attribute can belong together, as also unity and multiplicity. The one implies the many and the many can imply the one. Parmenides and Zeno knew of this kind of dialectics, by which duality is finally abolished through a correct methodology and not just doctrinally, as, for example, in monotheism. The eagerness of the last line is meant to balance the surfeit of the second line; they cancel out into a middle state when the equation is understood.

64

अविश्रान्तं पत्युर्गुणगणकथाम्रेडनजपा
    जपापुष्पच्छाया तव जननि जिह्वा जयति सा।
यदग्रासीनायाः स्फटिकदृषदच्छच्छविमयी
    सरस्वत्या मूर्तिः परिणमति माणिक्यवपुषा॥

aviśrāntaṁ patyur guṇagaṇa kathāmreḍana japā
japāpuṣpacchāyā tava janani jihvā jayati sā ।
yad agrāsīnāyāḥ sphaṭikadṛṣad acchacchavimayī
sarasvatyā mūrtiḥ pariṇamati māṇikya vapuṣā ॥

janani — O Mother; *aviśrāntaṁ* — incessant; *patyuḥ* — of (Your) Lord; *guṇa gaṇa kathā āmreḍana japā* — glorifying stories repeated as muttered charms; *tava sā jihvā* — Your (that) tongue; *japāpuṣpa cchāyā* — (of) hibiscus flower-red shade; *jayati* — triumphs; *yat agre āsīnāyāḥ* — seated at the tip of which (tongue); *sarasvatyāḥ* — of Sarasvatī; *sphaṭika dṛsat* — crystal-like; *accha cchavimayī* — pure-clear; *mūrtiḥ* — image/form; *māṇikya vapuṣā* — rubyhood in body; *pariṇamati* — becomes/attains to

By incessant repetition of muttered charm glorifying Your Lord,
As offering, the hibiscus flower red shade of Your tongue triumphs;
The pure, clear-crystal outline-image of Sarasvatī,
While seated at Your tonguetip, O Mother, in turn attains to rubyhood in its bodily form.

Prayers could be said in words or through the throwing of coloured flowers, which is the way in India, the favourite colour being red or magenta. Such is the underlying idea with which we have to understand the meaning of this verse. Whether said in words or in flowers, it is the same absolute devotion that is implied. To put it in another way, we could say that the word-language participates with the flower-language and vice versa.

Words are more on the side of the intelligibles, while coloured flowers represent the perceptibles or the medium aspect of language. There is a thin line of demarcation separating these two aspects of the medium and the message, which it is the purpose of the present verse to treat unitively. It is the tip of the tongue that repeats muttered charms or mantras. In South Indian temples there is the practice of throwing flowers at idols, after dipping them in holy water. Such an action, which is visible, is accompanied by a corresponding muttered charm in the form of a predicative description of the god to be propitiated. Baskets, or sometimes forests, of flowers are offered as 'stainless shrines', and as Sir Edwin Arnold eulogizes for Buddhism, countless millions of lips repeat the formula, 'I take my refuge in Buddha'. Such a flower language is proper to the context of idol worship as practised, especially in South India, to this day. The devotee forgets himself and is never satisfied with the number of times that he repeats such a gesture and its corresponding mutterings.

In this verse the Goddess is worshipping her own husband after the same model. The duality between muttered inward charm and outwardly offered flowers is to be effectively abolished here. The poet finds a rather ingenious way of making the two events, verbal and non-verbal, belong together either as cause or effect to one and the same context. The world of words properly belongs to the goddess Sarasvatī to whom all colour is to be considered extraneous because concepts, as such, are colourless, while percepts could belong to the colourful side of the same situation. If we should think of a small crystal-clear image of Sarasvatī as representing the side of concepts, we could well imagine the tonguetip, where the mantra is articulated an endless number of times, as the ground on which the message could touch the medium. Thus we can see the relevancy of the analogy in this verse which puts the red tip of the tongue of the Goddess at the *bindusthāna*, or locus, around which absolute Beauty is to be visualized.

This series of verses favours the negative or perceptual

perspective of the Absolute as against the merely conceptual one. It is for this reason that this verse proclaims that the red shade is the locus of absolute Beauty. On the tip of such a magenta-red tongue, one has to imagine that somebody has placed a crystal-clear image of the goddess of the Word, Sarasvatī. This image is also to be visualized in all its beauty as a universally concrete clear concept. The form of a concept and the name of a concept cannot be separated from one another. Every name must suggest some form or another, at least as a weakness of the constitution of our own minds. One has to overcome the duality of both visual and conceptual conditioning habits of the mind to be able to transcend both, and to think without name or form at all. The Bhagavadgītā says that such a task of focusing attention on the formless and the nameless is difficult to accomplish. We are embodied human beings, it says, and therefore, anthropomorphism comes as a corollary to our thought forms, especially about God. This is the reason why God is referred to by the third person masculine pronoun 'He' in most scriptures, and it is left unquestioned as a concession to a natural way of thinking, though strictly speaking it is questionable. Anthropomorphism is thus a necessary evil, and therefore can be overlooked. The idolatrous imagery employed here is excusable only on the basis of a similar reasoning. Sarasvatī, the goddess of the Word, has a traditional form known to the conventional Hindu mind. Unless we have some specific reasons to reject it, there can be no objection to the use of such an iconographic representation.

When all these considerations are conceded, it will be seen that this verse does not offer any major difficulty, even for the modern reader. The underlying Advaitic doctrine is all that Śaṅkara is interested in revealing, in a protolinguistic form. This is another example of mutual participation or conditioning. It is on the side of giving primacy to ontology that, if at all, this approach may be said to err. We have to remark here again that it is from a negative perspective that we are examining the content of the Absolute throughout this work, as we have been cautioned even from verse four, where the feet have been given primacy over the hands.

Why the Goddess should indulge in incessant repetition of the name of her Lord, when she herself is of a divine status, might be a relevant question. The answer is that methodological consistency requires that the counterparts have the same homogeneous richness so that they could cancel out against each other. Incessant repetition is needed to give to concepts the same ontological richness that is conferred by nature from the perceptual side. Rubyhood and crystal clarity condition each other at the tip of the tongue, where medium and message meet unitively.

65

रणे जित्वा दैत्यानपहृतशिरस्त्रैः कवचिभि-
निर्वृत्तैश्चण्डांशत्रिपुरहरनिर्माल्यविमुखैः ।
विशाखेन्द्रोपेन्द्रैः शशिविशदकर्पूरशकलाः
विलीयन्ते मातस्तव वदनताम्बूलकबलाः ॥

raṇe jitvā daityān apahṛta śirastraiḥ kavacibhir
nivṛttaiś caṇḍāṁśa tripurahara nirmālya vimukhaiḥ ।
viśākhendropendraiḥ śaśiviśada karpūra śakalāḥ
vilīyante mātas tava vadana tāmbūla kabalāḥ ॥

mātaḥ — O Mother; *raṇe daityān jitvā* — vanquishing the demons in battle; *apahṛta śirastraiḥ* — taking off their headgear; *kavacibhiḥ* — still in their armour; *nivṛttaiḥ* — returning; *caṇḍāṁśaḥ* — the portion meant for Caṇḍa; *tripurahara nirmālya vimukhaiḥ* — discountenancing Śiva's offering; *viśākha indra upendraiḥ* — Skanda, Indra and Upendra (Viṣṇu); *śaśi viśada karpūra śakalāḥ* — moon-bright bits of camphor; *tava vadana tāmbūla kabalāḥ* — the mouthfuls of betel-juice; *vilīyante* — they merge

O Mother, they merge, those mouthfuls of betel-juice of Your face,
As Skanda, Indra *and* Upendra, *returning from vanquishing the demons in battle,*
Taking off their headgear and still in their armour, they discountenance
That Śiva's portion of offering meant for Caṇḍa *which are moon-bright bits of camphor.*

Verse sixty-five seems at first to be a complex jumble of mixed metaphors and mythological imagery superimposed on one another. No wonder, therefore, that most commentaries have gone off the mark in offering even an approximately acceptable meaning for it. We have to place it in its proper context and perspective first, and we should not make the mistake of thinking that what belongs to the canvas belongs also to the painting. There are four epistemological and methodological layers, each implying its own degree of abstraction and generalization. These four possible ways of abstraction were known to Vedantic speculation many centuries before modern physics began to use this same kind of four-dimensional reference.

A mythological reference to three gods who are engaged in some kind of battle is the first film to be separated out from the other deeper layers. Then comes a deeper layer in which the gods (*deva*s) and demons (*asura*s) are arranged on two opposite sides, each representing their own system of life values. This axiological view has a still deeper layer hiding behind it, in which we have to find the reason why Subrahmaṇya (Viśākha) and the other two gods reject some of the holy tokens of offering while accepting others. Still deeper, in fourth-dimensional abstraction, we have to imagine that the whole of this story has its central locus in the mouth of the Goddess, who is engaged in chewing betel-nuts. Camphor is also an ingredient of the mixture that the Goddess is chewing up, and the red juice is swallowed into her own inside each time the mouthful is fully turned to magenta.

We have also to remember that it is in the mind of the contemplative, as he meditates on the betel-chewing mouth, that more peripheral wheels or chakras of thought present themselves, all having the same epicentre or locus, which is the mouth of the Goddess. In its chapter on the vision of the universal principle of Time, the Bhagavadgītā presents a similar picture, where the heads of warriors and kings are being mercilessly crushed like nuts between the teeth of the God (XI.26-27). The idea here is not unlike that vision. It is a war that is being waged between the forces of good and evil, although the Absolute itself is not to be divided into two groups. The evil forces and the good forces have a conflict implied between them to be understood at least schematically, in which a line, however thin, demarcating the two sides is inevitably to be presupposed, at least for the sake of argument. This line is no other than that between the two rows of teeth of the Goddess, where nuts representing the skulls of heroes of one side or the other are being crushed, so that Time could proceed, like the car of Jagannāth in the famous Purī festival, on its destructive onward progression. Time's arrow cannot be reversed except in terms of very pure memory. The forward-flowing breeze of Time could play sometimes on silken sails, but must inevitably imply harsh facts belonging to the stern stuff of duty or historical necessity. The magenta colour, moreover, is highly suggestive of flesh and blood; and if we should add the skulls and armour, it is left to our option to imagine more grades of concreteness or abstraction than the four that we have already mentioned.

The three gods, who appear after giving battle to the evil forces, have removed their headgear out of respect for the presence of the absolute Goddess. They remove only half the accoutrements that make for a warlike situation. The three gods are willing to respect the presence of the Goddess, but they are not willing to negate the function for which they were born. This applies especially to the case of Subrahmaṇya (Viśākha), whose function, by the very circumstances of his birth, consists of teaching a lesson to the denominator factors of evil. He represents the highest possible value within the set-up of the divinities of the Hindu pantheon, Vedic or non-Vedic. Subrahmaṇya is here represented as highly conscious of the function or duty that properly belongs to him. A policeman's duty is to arrest the thieves and not to pardon them.

In the previous verses we have been thinking of the mouth region of the Goddess in various degrees of verticalized value gradations. Here we come to a grade in which retrospective memories as well as prospective imagination enter into the picture with equal force, from both the poles of the total situation. As the contemplative meditates on this picture of the betel-chewing Goddess, associations crowd into his mind, each set having its own epistemological self-consistency. We can even imagine three concentric circles, as in the *śrī cakra*, separating the inner zones from the outer ones. Magenta colour of different saturations, brilliance and shade can distinguish the zones, but historical or mythological events are all to be grounded in the selfsame chakra, which the contemplative constructs, in order to appreciate intelligently the absolute non-dual Beauty of the Goddess.

We could imagine a heroic or epic scene here being acted out within the mouth of the Goddess which could also be seen as a temple or cave in which somebody is offering worship to the absolute Goddess. As it is impolite to wear headgear in pride when approaching a sacred place dedicated to God, the three divinities here are represented as conforming to the requirements of good behaviour by taking off their hats. They retain the rest of their armour, however, with the excuse that they are still in the overall context of battle. Within the temple scene, we could imagine a priest who brings to these three divine supplicants that which they are meant to accept as a token of respect for the supreme principle as they understand it, each from his own standpoint, implying its own frame of value-reference. The absolute Goddess does not take sides, but her son (Subrahmaṇya) cannot deny his own duty, being born historically or mythologically to teach a lesson to the evil forces. The *Kumārasambhava* makes this role very clear, although Subrahmaṇya is not lacking in his knowledge of Vedantic absolutism. He is even said to have taught the meaning of *aum* to his own father, Śiva.

Camphor, especially the soft variety, is an ingredient used to flavour betel-nuts. Camphor is also an integral item among the holy ingredients making up a temple offering to be brought out by the priest after waving of lights before an idol. Camphor is unique in that it is both a solid and (potentially) a flame of light, so it is used as an analogy for the process by which a material substance turns into an intelligent factor, symbolized by the flame. Moon-bright bits of camphor left on the salver brought by the priest for Subrahmaṇya represent a value meant to give a flavour or perfume to betel-chewing. As a solid, it belongs to the side of existence, so in this form, before being lit, it belongs to the denominator context of the demons (*asura*s) and not to the gods (*deva*s) of the numerator context. Like the 'thinking substance', camphor combines within itself substantiality and thought.

Since Subrahmaṇya represents the numerator side, he does not approve of the offered camphor because it is incompatible with his main function of teaching a lesson to the opposite side. He does not wish to pretend to be an absolutist prematurely and inconsistently with his own personality, just as Arjuna is not to leave the battlefield by pretending or claiming prematurely to be a sannyasin. Duty in this sense is sometimes called 'the stern daughter of the voice of God', though this dictum need not be binding on anyone who can claim correctly and completely to be an absolutist. Subrahmaṇya was born as an answer to the prayer of the gods to protect them from the excesses of the demons at that time. His function comes under the category of historical necessity, not in terms of ordinary history, but at least in the order of cosmic evolution, as depicted in the great epics in Indian literature, which are called *itihāsa*s, of which a model in the West could be the *Odyssey* of Homer.

Caṇḍa is another name for a divinity represented by the moon. Śiva himself, representing the numerator aspect of the Absolute, carries moonlight on his head. The camphor bits could, by the same token, be considered as representing the moon principle on the denominator side. Caṇḍa (god of the Moon) and Candra (the Moon) thus become interchangeable as cause or effect aspects of light. As for the three gods portrayed here, who are slightly different from the usual Vedic trinity, the name Upendra can simply denote Viṣṇu or it can also mean 'second in command to Indra'. Viśākha could represent Śiva, because he is born from Śiva's middle eye. Viṣṇu represents lasting enjoyable values. Aryan and Dravidian divinities are thus seen here to be put together in a revised form, without violating their triple principal functions of creation, preservation and destruction.

In the first line the act of swallowing flavoured red-betel juice is represented, with camphor added as a subtly pervasive ingredient. The mouthfuls, when they emerge, could be imagined as permeating upward into the world of prospective or creative imagination, or as merging retrospectively into the totality of memories of past years already contained as a vertical dimension within the presence that the beauty of the Goddess represents. The gods are returning from some past event already accomplished and are seen now to be standing at a neutral point in the present. They could be said to be returning from deeper negative levels of the vertical axis. They do not remove all their warlike accoutrements because they are still within the context of a war situation. Subrahmaṇya could remove his armour only when he goes to his abode nearer to the positive limit of the vertical axis.

66

विपञ्चया गायन्ती विविधमपदानं पुररिपो-
स्त्वयारब्धे वक्तुं चलितशिरसा साधुवचने ।
तदीयैर्माधुर्यैरपलपिततन्त्रीकलरवां
निजां वीणां वाणी निचुलयति चोलेन निभृतम् ॥

vipañcyā gāyantī vividham apadānaṁ puraripos-
tvayārabdhe vaktuṁ calita śirasā sādhu vacane ।
tadīyair mādhuryair apalapita tantrī kalaravāṁ
nijāṁ vīṇāṁ vāṇī niculayati colena nibhṛtam ॥

sādhu vacane — O One of lively/true speech; *pura ripoḥ* — of the City Burner (Śiva); *vividham apadānaṁ* — of the varied exploits; *vipañcyā gāyantī* — singing with Your vina; *vāṇī* — (You as) the goddess of the Word; *calita śirasā* — with movements of the head; *tvayā vaktuṁ ārabdhe* — by you starting to speak (sing); *tadīyaiḥ mādhuryaiḥ* — by the sweetness thereof; *apalapitah* — mocking; *tantrī kalaravāṁ* — the sound of strings; *nijāṁ vīṇāṁ* — Your vina; *colena nibhṛtam* — with cloth to silence; *niculayati* — You cover up

Starting as You do to sing, with Your vina, and with head movements,
Of the varied exploits of the City Burner, (You as) the goddess of the Word,
The one of lively speech, You promptly cover up to silence
Your instrument, as mocking the sweetness thereof by sounds of strings.

In verse sixty-six we are still in a general setting in which the greatness of Śiva is being extolled by Pārvatī. She is starting to sing to the accompaniment of her favourite instrument, the vina, which is seen to be inseparably associated with her wherever she is represented in the traditional style. She and her instrument are to be treated as belonging together to one and the same context. Although she starts to sing accompanied by the vina, she decides soon after starting that its accompaniment does not come up to expectation. This is seen to be an afterthought. Two movements are specifically referred to in this situation, in which there is a vocal as well as an instrumental music starting together. Not long after beginning thus, in fact almost abruptly, the Goddess stops playing her instrument, putting it out of commission. This movement has to be treated together with the other movement of nodding her own head in approval of the music. The voice of the Goddess is here praised as being of a very superior quality.

We are asked to extract whatever meaning we possibly can, given this data, but what we extract must also necessarily enhance the absolute Beauty-value of the Goddess. This is an overall requirement from every verse. It is easy to see that no Tāntric viewpoint or doctrine is meant to be brought into light by the total situation depicted here. Tantra śāstra is not, as we know it, especially interested in music, nor is it a teaching in which a vina is to be silenced in favour of glorifying vocal music, as evidently intended here. The above limitations make it almost inevitable for us to rely on some doctrine of Advaita Vedanta to be the main theme which the Goddess's abrupt change of mind is intended to reveal. We, therefore, surmise that this situation is meant to bring out a double-sided method peculiar to Vedanta when it wishes to abolish, dissolve, or transcend the duality implied in any paradox. Paradox first recognizes two truths. Vedanta abolishes paradox finally, not by recognizing the contradiction, but by absorbing the contradiction into a unitive vision by a higher intuitive way of thinking. We shall not be reading too much into the context here if we say that it is a schematic structural pattern that is to be presupposed as guiding the poetic imagination of Śaṅkara, while, as always, his intention is to underline an Advaitic doctrine conforming to the methodology proper to Vedanta.

Instrumental music from a vina placed horizontally across the figure of the Goddess represents the arithmetic or mechanistic aspect of inert life, while she herself represents the vertical axis. Her nods of approval of her own vocal music represent something like saying 'yes, yes' or a double assertion. Translated into philosophical terms, this would amount to saying, 'What exists thus really exists and can never be abolished'. The horizontal mechanistic world is to be recognized as real enough initially, but when philosophical thought gains ground, it would abolish itself and get absorbed into the vertical axis. The relation between the two parameters or correlates is the same as what Descartes would say exists between *res cogitans* and *res extensa*. The latter is space-like and the former time-like, understood in terms of pure duration.

It is permitted to think, in terms of Cartesian or Bergsonian philosophy, that one attains the Absolute. Śaṅkara's doctrine is not basically different. That which does not exist is abolished by double negation. By double assertion, the picture of the Absolute emerges in terms of a highly significant value, which is the beauty of the Goddess. The more she appreciates the beauty of her own voice, the more it becomes evident to her that the instrument, with its poor twanging imitations by sounds of metallic wires, cannot add anything to the richness that her own voice can give to the music in a fully real sense. Although the instrument is dear to her, she does not hesitate a moment to cover it with a shawl, perhaps one of a dark colour, which is a form of double negation applied to the arithmetical side of the total situation representing the Absolute as a value. Paradox thus stands abolished, dissolved or transcended. Each approving nod of the head of the Goddess describes an implied figure-of-eight, which we can see through the transparency of the total formless space-time situation, reflecting the structure that properly belongs to the content of the Absolute. The change of mind only introduces that dynamic touch to this otherwise static picture, which Bergson would perhaps distinguish by his term *schema moteur*, as against the schema of conceptualists or rationalists like Kant or Descartes. The quickness with which the Goddess covers her vina reflects the dynamism which is *not* meant to be of a gradual or hesitant order. Higher intuition comes, not by instalments, but by split-second understanding.

The overall situation can be summed up in the following words: The goddess of the Word, finding that her speech is superior to its own mechanistic imitation, changes her mind quickly to silence the instrument because the imitation cannot add anything (that is not already there) to the original. Speech is better than just sound, which is included in it already.

We could note also that Kālidāsa, in the *Meghadūta*, has a picture of the wife of a divine being (*yakṣa*) who is separated from her husband and trying to play the vina to pass her unhappy hours in a cavern in the Himalayas, where she is destined to live in loneliness. There the version is similar but slightly different. She is unable to play the vina because of her tears, which come from the richer content of her memories stimulated by the vocally articulated words of music. Here it is a more neutral way of abolishing paradox. In both cases, it is the glory of the husband that is the subject matter of the music. The pangs of separation are not found in the Goddess here, unless slightly reflected in the quickness of the gesture of silencing her instrument. The vina could be thought of as being a dear and inseparable companion, having the effect of consoling her loneliness, like a baby in the arms of a mother.

67

करा‍ग्रेण स्पृष्टं तुहिनगिरिणा वत्सलतया
गिरीशेनोदस्तं मुहुरधरपानाकुलतया ।
करग्राह्यं शंभोर्मुखमुकुरवृन्तं गिरिसुते
कथंकारं ब्रूमस्तव चुबुकमौपम्यरहितम् ॥

karāgreṇa spṛṣṭaṁ tuhinagiriṇā vatsalatayā
girīśenodastaṁ muhur adhara pānākulatayā ।
kara grāhyaṁ śaṁbhor mukhamukura vṛntaṁ girisute
kathaṁ kāraṁ brūmas tava cubukam aupamya rahitam ॥

girisute — O Mountain-daughter; *tuhina giriṇā* — by the Mountain King lit. the snow mountain; *vatsalatayā* — affectionately; *karāgreṇa spṛṣṭaṁ* — touched by the tip of the hand; *girīśena* — by Śiva (the Lord of the Mountain); *adhara pāna ākulatayā* — out of intent desire to drink of the lips; *muhuḥ* — again and again; *udastaṁ* — lifted up; *śaṁbhoḥ* — for Śambhu (Śiva); *karagrāhyaṁ* — to hold by hand; *mukha mukura vṛntaṁ* — the handle for Your face-mirror; *tava cubukam* — Your chin; *aupamya rahitam* — peerless incomparable; *kathaṁ kāraṁ brūmaḥ* — how could we (ever) speak of ?

Affectionately touched by the tip of the hand of the Mountain King,
And lifted again and again by that Śiva out of desire
To drink of the lips thereof, that which makes the handle
For Your face-mirror, how could we ever speak of it, Your peerless chin?

In verse sixty-seven the beauty of the chin of the Goddess is the central locus. This region of the face is a point of common appeal both to the father of Pārvatī as well as to her beloved husband. Her father is referred to here as touching the chin with tender parental affection. The husband, although he is interested in the more erotic act of kissing the Goddess on her lips to enjoy the bliss it can give him, is here referred to as treating the face of the Goddess as a mirror, for which her chin is something like a handle. He lifts this handle so that it could take a verticalized position as he approaches the face, which is only a reflection of his own face in essence. As he looks into it to enjoy the counterpart, as it were, of his own beauty, the reflected version is essentially the same absolute Beauty. The duality of husband and wife is thus seen to be abolished, and herein lies the Advaitic doctrine hidden from superficial view. The lifting of the 'handle of the mirror' gives it a status of equality or parity of subject and object. Only one of these two versions could be real, in keeping with the Advaitic doctrine. The reflection is just an appearance derived from the real. The resultant Beauty, however, is not vitiated by any unilateral consideration of reality, but is the 'Real of reals' as a value, and thus it becomes unique, as stated here in the last words.

The first half of this verse contrasts the ways in which the father and the husband touch the chin of their beloved. We notice that what is lost in actuality is gained in virtuality. The father only touches the daughter with the tip of his fingers. While the actual contact is minimum, there is only figurative contact of the same chin by the husband. What is underlined here is Śiva's intention to drink of the lips. There is no actual contact implied, and even if it had been depicted, it would have been only a contact with the mirror surface intervening between them. Thus the union of Śiva and Pārvatī is fully real but not physical in the factual everyday sense. Dialectical counterparts can operate only on a ground which knows no duality, as between subject and object.

भुजाश्लेषान् नित्यं पुरदमयितुः कण्टकवती
तव ग्रीवा धत्ते मुखकमलनालश्रियमियम्।
स्वतः श्वेता कालागरुबहुलजम्बालमलिना
मृणालीलालित्यं वहति यदधो हारलतिका ॥

bhujāśleṣān nityaṁ pura damayituḥ kaṇṭakavatī
tava grīvā dhatte mukha kamala nāla śriyam iyam ।
svataḥ śvetā kālāgaru bahula jambāla malinā
mṛṇālī lālityam vahati yad adho hāra latikā ॥

pura damayituḥ — of the City Burner; *bhujāśleṣāt* — by being embraced by the arms; *nityaṁ* — eternal/ever (incessantly); *kaṇṭakavatī* — thrilled to thorny bristling; *tava iyam grīvā* — this Your neck; *mukha kamala nāla śriyam* — grace of the stalk of the face-lotus; *dhatte* — bears; *yat adhaḥ* — beneath the same; *svataḥ śvetā* — by itself white; *hāra latikā* — a creeper (garland) of pearls; *kāla agaru bahula jambāla malinā* — smudged by excess of black cosmetic paste; *mṛṇālī lālityam* — the lotus-tendril suppleness; *vahati* — it retains

Incessantly embraced by the arms of the City Burner,
With hair thrilled to thorny bristling, Your neck
Shows the grace of a stalk for Your lotus face, by itself
white, but smudged by excess of dark cosmetic paste,
Retaining a pearly necklace beneath with the suppleness
of a lotus-creeper-tendril.

The erotic advances made by Śiva toward Pārvatī are of a subtle and ineffable order. We have seen even from the second verse that the realism, if any, in these verses has to be understood as belonging to the world of fine particles. Śiva is represented in one of the plays of Kālidāsa (*Mālavikāgnimitra*), in the very opening verse, as having his body intimately mixed-up with that of his wife, Pārvatī, but in spite of such a communion, still remaining the best of ascetics. It is reasonable to expect that

Śaṅkara respects the same Advaitic, Sanskritic tradition. Therefore, it is important for us to extract the meaning of this verse in such a way as not to do violence to any of the tacit conventions respected by Śaṅkara. It is on a very thin schematic as well as conceptual ground, where name and form are just able to participate with each other in clear terms of light, shade and line, with corresponding conceptions which in turn have to belong to a world of discourse rather than of brute fact, that we have to establish the meaning here. Such a neutral ground would fit in with the verses that follow as well as establish a continuity with the previous verses.

In verse sixty-seven we saw that the father and the husband treat the chin of the Goddess with a certain aloofness because of the chin being neither matter nor mind, but something participating both ways. To Śiva it was figurative, while to the father it was existent, though his participation was of a light order. All these details are important for us to remember so that the Advaitic doctrine that is hidden under this living pictorial language could be correctly appreciated.

The incessant embrace described in this verse, which produces horripilation or 'thorny bristling' of the hair on the neck of the Goddess, is to be understood in terms of a thrilling sense of inner bliss, more akin to salvation than to ordinary erotic play. The best eroticism is one in which this kind of two-sided participation is perfectly balanced between subject and object, matter and mind. Unilateral stress on one or the other can only spoil the case of both. We have to place ourselves, therefore, sympathetically on a sort of middle ground and understand that the bristling of the hair only represents the exalted nature of the thrill that the Goddess is able to enjoy. On the side of Śiva, it is to be noted that he is not thinking in terms of an ordinary sex act which might last only a short time, but that he is engaged in an everlasting embrace. This is a revised form of erotic relationship in keeping with mystical eroticism rather than merely sexual eroticism. Kālidāsa's *Kumāra-*

sambhava also describes Śiva, in the last canto, as everlastingly remaining in the bedroom of Pārvatī. Any value could be treated *sub specie aeternitatis* in this manner.

The lotus plant is dear to Sanskrit poets and even to wise philosophers who want to use it as an analogy to reveal all laudable spiritual attributes, especially as seen from an ontological perspective. The colour of the lotus plant, with its tenderness, its purity, its beauty and especially its inner thread-like core (*mr̥ṇāla tantu*) made of vascular bundles forming gleaming supple strands within the stalk — not to speak of its fragrance and the patches of brown and pink when the petals are half open — are the many items offered by the lotus which the Sanskrit poet loves to work upon in his essentially contemplative poetry. In the case of erotic-mystical poetry, the wonder of the lotus plant and its virtues are a source never expended and constantly to be drawn upon age after age, not given up even in the present-day literature of vernaculars based on Sanskrit. The stalk of the lotus has on it the very bristles that are referred to in this verse. They may not be beautiful to an ordinary poet but to a poet like Śaṅkara, to whom good and bad have to reveal the same beauty value, even the thorny hair of the lotus becomes a precious analogy. Eroticism between the God and the Goddess refers to the context of an eternal bliss that can induce samadhi in a votary who can meditate on the subject correctly.

The reference to beauty smudged by dark cosmetic paste reveals another secret. This blemish, instead of detracting from the beauty, only enhances it, according to the Advaitic poet, as we have already explained in a previous verse. Śakuntalā is more beautiful wearing her bark-garment and living in an ashram than if she had been represented as dressed in rustling silks and living in the king's palace. Contrast is at the core of the Absolute, and only when it is cancelled out effectively could the absolute Beauty-value emerge to view. This is the doctrine that should give a key to justify these laboured analogies that would otherwise seem to be artificially pressed into the service of this kind of poetry to make it merely mechanistic and metaphysical in an objectionable sense.

The mud or dross in which the lotus plant has to live gives it a status that belongs to it by natural necessity. Even frailties, when they are fully human, could not be treated finally as frailties at all. Human nature has room for many natural deficiencies, and the totality of all such cancel out in a tragic hero, such as an Othello, to give an absolutist touch to his character, which remains fully human in spite of defects like passion or jealousy. It is when such passions do not cancel out against the overall nobility of the character that the situation can become an anticlimax.

The Absolute is a 'thing-in-itself', but this quality of being 'in itself' implies its dialectical counterpart to set it off in proper relief, without which it cannot be appreciated at all. In the name of such an appreciation of Beauty, the contrast insisted upon here is fully justified. Furthermore, we have to note that the poet is intending to descend step by step into beauty items at the core of the personality of the Goddess, which are not the same as their counterparts at the peripheral limits. The elephant-skin that is supposed to be worn by Śiva, while still remaining the pure universal spirit dancing vertically at the core, contains the same type of ideogram as here. In this verse the thing-in-itself is compared to a pearly necklace which shows through beneath the covering of excess of dark cosmetic paste. Peripherally there is what is extraneous to the thing-in-itself, which is not to be omitted in the complete and realistic picture of Beauty in the context of the Absolute. Evil is not to be explained away, but, it is to be transcended after it has been given its proper place in the total scheme. The pearly necklace reveals a fully verticalized beauty factor, whereas the thorny bristles represent the horizontalized version of the same. The variation is between interiority and peripherality, as also verticality and horizontality. Absolute beauty has to be viewed in fourfold or polyvalent relief to have that overwhelming character which is called *laharī* in this work.

69

गले रेखास्तिस्रो गतिगमकगीतैकनिपुणे
विवाहव्यानद्धप्रगुणगुणसंख्याप्रतिभुवः ।
विराजन्ते नानाविधमधुररागाकरभुवां
त्रयाणां ग्रामाणां स्थितिनियमसीमान इव ते ॥

gale rekhās tisro gatigamaka gītaika nipuṇe
vivāhavyānaddha praguṇaguṇa saṁkhyā pratibhuvaḥ ।
virājante nānāvidha madhura rāgākara bhuvāṁ
trayāṇāṁ grāmāṇāṁ sthiti niyama sīmāna iva te ॥

gati gamaka gīta eka nipuṇe — O One fully expert in time, syncopation and melody; *te gale tisraḥ rekhāḥ* — the three lines on Your neck; *vivāha vyānaddha praguṇa guṇa saṁkhyā* — the string tied at the time of marriage, of strands and substrands; *prati bhuvaḥ* — the counter-ground; *nānā vidhāḥ* — of many kinds/many a; *madhuraḥ rāgāḥ ākara bhuvaḥ* — as the ground wherein sweet melodies are born; *trayāṇām grāmāṇāṁ* — of the three groups of musical keys; *sthiti niyama sīmāna iva* — as factors of position, regulation and limitation; *virājante* — they shine in glory

Those three lines on Your neck, O One fully expert in time, syncopation and melody;
They are the counter-grounds of Your marital thread of strands and substrands;
As they do shine as the ground wherein is born many a melody,
Giving position, regulation and limitation for the three groups of musical keys.

The transition from the delicate lotus-core strands of shining pearl-like vascular bundles to the horizontal lines on the neck of the Goddess gives us a new perspective in verse sixty-nine. We are still in the context of music and words. The nodding head movements of appreciation of her own performance in praise of

Śiva could still be treated as the subject matter of this verse, but we enter here into the domain of musical theory, just as we entered into semantics in verses fifteen through seventeen. The beauty of music depends upon *gati*, *gamaka* and *gīta*, which we have translated as 'time, syncopation and melody'. Indian musical theory might differ from that of the West, and without going into the merits of these items it would be difficult for us to say if these three complete the list. Music has to conform to some rules of the game. Every game has to have two rival sides. Random kicking of a football on a field by boys not divided into two teams cannot interest anybody. Beauty thus has to be an emergent factor when two counterparts enter into intimate interplay.

Here we have to recognize the ceremonial string that husbands tie around the necks of their wives at their weddings. Three strands of such a string could easily be considered permissible even if not always considered obligatory. Śaṅkara gives these three black strands a first-dimensional status in the picture that he is presenting in this verse. Each is here represented as having a corresponding fold of the skin. There are thus three such folds to be recognized on the neck of the Goddess. As she nods to appreciate the beauty of her own song of praise for Śiva these folds could be imagined to become accentuated or lightly marked. Each of the black substrands which make up the marital string comes from the numerator side as a decoration added on to the beauty of the Goddess.

The beating of time refers to the most horizontally factual quality implied in music. It is like a band across a spectrum. The lowest and the most definite of horizontal lines is to be marked first on the neck of the Goddess. Syncopation is a musical device employed by experts in which they can play with the fractional variation in the time beat, to be recovered in the next or successive beats. Time is not so strictly respected in this item of attractiveness in the context of music. When we come to the content in music, called melody, the horizontal reference to time can be relaxed a degree further. An expert singer can take full liberties here so as to reveal to advantage his creative genius, sometimes throwing to the wind cheap conventions which only amateurs are expected to respect to the letter. The three lines, therefore, show three degrees of necessity or freedom, to the requirements of which the creative artist in music should conform.

There are approximately a hundred different keys in Indian music called ragas. Even among such ragas, there are *melakartā*s (chief modes) and *janya*s which are subvarieties belonging to the main ones. This explains the reference to strands and sub-strands in this verse. Good music results when the limiting considerations are respected or transcended, according to the genius of the particular musician. It is possible, as suggested in the third line, to see in visible form the subtle incipient movements which are at the basis of creative musical expression. They have these bright lines for their common locus. In the last line, the *function*, involving the time factor; the *regulation*, which would refer to the syncopation; and the *limitation* of the notes of the particular melody or raga, proper to each creative type of music, which give to each of the three main types of music whatever specific beauty they might possess, are put in a one-to-one correspondence with each other. Thus a complete theory of absolute Beauty in music is covered by Śaṅkara in this verse. Music thus helps us to distinguish further details within the structure of absolute Beauty, which is still within the domain of the word and its meaning. Here again we have to notice how the visible and the intelligible are put together with a one-to-one correspondence between them. Medium and message thus meet and cancel out into sheer musical enjoyability.

We have translated *sthiti* as 'position', *niyama* as 'regulation' and *sīmā* as 'limitation'. There is also reference to the three *grāmā*s (*trayāṇām grāmāṇām*) which we have translated as 'the three groups of musical keys', (major, minor and modal). Each of the keys are limited to certain scales which give them their character.

70

मृणालीमृद्वीनां तव भुजलतानां चतसृणां
चतुर्भिः सौन्दर्यं सरसिजभवः स्तौति वदनैः ।
नखेभ्यः संत्रस्यन् प्रथममथनादन्तकरिपो-
श्चतुर्णां शीर्षाणां सममभयहस्तार्पणधिया ॥

mṛṇālī mṛdvīnāṁ tava bhuja latānāṁ catasṛṇāṁ
caturbhiḥ saundaryaṁ sarasija bhavaḥ stauti vadanaiḥ ।
nakhebhyaḥ saṁtrasyan prathama mathanād antaka ripoś-
caturṇāṁ śīrṣāṇāṁ samam abhaya hastārpaṇadhiyā ॥

mṛṇālī mṛdvīnāṁ — lotus-core tender; *tava catasṛṇāṁ bhuja latānāṁ* — of Your fourfold creeper-like arms; *saundaryaṁ* — beauty; *sarasija bhavaḥ* — the lotus-born (Brahmā); *caturbhiḥ vadanaiḥ* — by means of (all his) four faces; *stauti* — praises; *prathama mathanāt* — (first) once of yore nipped off; *antaka ripoḥ* — of the enemy of Death (Śiva); *nakhebhyaḥ saṁtrasyan* — trembling in fear of (his) nails; *caturṇāṁ śīrṣāṇāṁ samam* — at once, equally for each of the (remaining) four heads; *abhaya hasta arpaṇa dhiyā* — intending to pray for refuge-granting hand-gesture

Of the lotus-core-tender-beauty of Your fourfold creeper-like arms,
He sings the praise, the lotus-born god; trembling the while because of Śiva's nails
That once of yore nipped off his extra head — he, (Brahmā) intending now to pray for
Your refuge-granting hand-gesture for each of his remaining heads.

In verse seventy we are still in the context of the goddess of the Word. Brahmā, the four-headed god of creation, is depicted here as praying for the protective gesture from the four hands of the Goddess. The reason for this prayer is that, according to mythology, he once tried to grow a fifth head facing upward vertically, to attain the glory of hypostatic levels where, as the creator of the universe, he was not deemed fit to encroach on. His proper place is below the horizontal line, but not knowing that it was Śiva to whom any value that was hypostatic and above the horizontal line properly belonged, Brahmā inadvertently made the mistake for which he had to pay the price, by having his fifth head cruelly pinched off by Śiva. Mythologies are not to be taken literally but are generally meant to express some basic spiritual verity which cannot otherwise be made clear. Here Brahmā is seen in a more submissive and humiliated attitude, in which he is singing the praise of his own daughter, Sarasvatī. Her four hands have a certain tenderness or suppleness, comparable to the pearly bright bundle of vascular strands at the core of the lotus stalk, which is the nearest analogy that is meant to express the neutral, though material, status of a 'thinking substance'. Because she is the wife of Śiva, her beauty can have this status. Her four arms can participate both ways because Śiva is not a rival to her but her husband. Brahmā, as mere creator, can at best have the status of very fine pollen, as explained in verse two. Sarasvatī can represent the mixture of ashes and magenta-red *kumkum* powder, not merely pollen, which is only fine creative biological particles.

There are three epistemological gradations strictly dividing each stratum in the total context, which have been clearly demarcated in the second verse and further qualified in some later verses. Brahmā himself is lotus-born and his daughter is born one degree above the lotus' biological reality. The lotus' tendril-like leaves which have fourfold creeper-like arms are meant here to have a status of their own, not merely material, but consisting of a subtler form of 'thinking substance'. Of the four faces of Brahmā, each belongs to one quadrant of a quaternion structure. With all of his four mouths he is engaged in praying for protection from his own daughter who is nearer to the *Logos* or the *nous* than he could aspire to be. The four hands have thus a one-to-one correspondence with the four mouths from which prayers climb upward. This verse is therefore meant to reveal some structural correspondence and necessary stratification between grades of ontological or teleological richness and poverty. What is gained on the side of existence is lost on the side of the absolute Value. When the four hands condescend to offer refuge to the four heads, there would be a cancellation of four against four, resulting in that Absolute intended to be revealed through this structural analysis of the ground of absolute Beauty.

71

नखानामुद्योतैर्नवनलिनरागं विहसतां
करणां ते कान्तिं कथय कथयामः कथमुमे।
कयाचिद्वा साम्यं भजतु कलया हन्त कमलं
यदि क्रीडल्लक्ष्मीचरणतललाक्षारसचणम्॥

nakhānām udyotair nava nalina rāgaṁ vihasatāṁ
karāṇām te kāntiṁ kathaya kathayāmaḥ katham ume ।
kayācid vā sāmyaṁ bhajatu kalayā hanta kamalaṁ
yadi krīḍallakṣmī caraṇatala lākṣā rasa caṇam ॥

ume — O Umā; *nakhānām udyotaiḥ* — by the shining of Your fingernails; *nava nalina rāgaṁ* — the colour of just-opening lotus buds; *vihasatāṁ* — that mock; *te karāṇāṁ* — of Your hands; *kāntiṁ* — the beauty; *katham kathayāmaḥ* — how could I speak of; *kathaya* — you say (granted be); *kamalaṁ kalayā* — if the lotus should at least by a shade; *sāmyaṁ kayā cid vā bhajatu* — equality (parity) have somehow; *hanta* — alas; *yadi krīḍat lakṣmī caraṇa tala* — only when the sole of Lakṣmī as sporting (thereon); *lākṣā rasa caṇam* — with its magenta paste touches it (the lotus)

By the brilliance of Your fingernails that mock the colour
of just-opening lotus buds,
How could we speak of the beauty of Your hands?
Granted be, O Umā, that the lotus could have, somehow,
one shade less of parity with it, if at all,
And that, alas, only when touched by the magenta paste
of the sole of Lakṣmī as she plays thereon.

As in verse sixty-two, a rhetorical question is at the very core of the subject matter of this verse. Umā is being questioned here by the poet who wants to describe the absolute beauty of the Goddess by praising the brilliance of the pink colour of lotus buds touched by sunlight as the flower buds open in the morning. Umā herself has to tell him, because the final reference for the beauty of Umā is her own self or personality, and not what is described by someone else. Absolute beauty has to be in itself, for itself, through itself and by itself. It cannot depend upon anything extraneous to itself. Substance and attribute have both to belong together to the same absolute substance, finally to be understood in terms of the non-dual Self. The fingernails referred to in the first line are part and parcel of the Goddess herself, and hence when compared to the glory of the lotus bud just opening at dawn, the fingernails score advantage over the analogy, which can refer only to the attribute and not to the substantial Self. The poet thus feels perplexed because all the predications about the Absolute do not directly apply to the Absolute itself.

Then he tries an alternative method for successfully giving absolutist status to the beauty of the Goddess. Instead of thinking of the fingertips or the sunlight, which are teleological in import, he descends to the lower ontological limit, where the feet of the Goddess are to be imagined as dancing on the top of a lotus flower. The goddess here is not Sarasvatī, nor Pārvatī, as proper to this series, but Lakṣmī, who is the goddess of wealth and prosperity in this world. She has thus a hierophantic status rather than a hypostatic one, which belongs more properly to Sarasvatī. These structural interrelationships between gods and goddesses will come in for discussion at the end of the work, in verse ninety-nine. In anticipation, we are justified here in saying that Sarasvatī and Lakṣmī are to be considered as partners or counterparts within a totality which properly belongs to Pārvatī, of the Absolute context, to be recognized here as distinct from more relativistic subordinate functionary divinities or presences. In the second half of the verse it is thus Lakṣmī who represents the ontological counterpart of the Absolute, the soles of whose feet are smeared with some kind of magenta paste, as normal to beautiful women who know the use of such decorations round the city of Ujjain, figuring in the poetry of Kālidāsa and others. This magenta paste is a substance meant to enhance the beauty of the whole personality of Lakṣmī. Because it is applied to her feet, we could consider it an attribute to her personality, which would represent the substance. Substance and attribute have to participate in Advaita Vedanta, and the difference between them is to be abolished in the name of the demand of the final oneness of absolute Truth.

Here it is the beauty of the lotus that is being compared to the beauty of the fingernails of the Goddess. There is also the question of whether the lotus on which Lakṣmī dances, with magenta paste on the soles of her feet, is to be considered as glorious as the magenta of the fingernails in the first line. One would expect that on the ontological side the magenta colour conferred by the feet of the Goddess would enhance the beauty of the lotus to such an extent as to make it rival the beauty of the fingernails. But the answer is that this is just a possibility and not a certainty. It is true that ontology scores above teleology in Vedanta, as we have already indicated. This is a doctrine which was underlined by Śaṅkara as early as verse four. A slight difference of degree still remains to be bridged between the notion of absolute Beauty and what even an ontological type of participation can confer on the Absolute. In other words, the poet finds it impossible to praise the Beauty, because absolute Beauty is beyond all predicability. It exists in itself, without any outside reference. The beauty of the Absolute is beyond praise, as is often heard in contemplative literature. Words come back from it without reaching it, as the Upaniṣads put it.

We have to note also that this verse supplies a vertical parameter passing through the quaternion situation pictured in the previous verse. It is therefore meant to make the structuralism complete.

It is also noteworthy that the apellation 'Umā' used here is not an accident. Pārvatī was called 'Umā' (Sanskrit: 'O do not!') by her mother by way of admonishing her against performing austerities to attain Śiva. She being a direct representative of the Absolute, it was supposed by her mother that she needed nothing outside herself, even in the form of austerities, to complete her status. There are other derivations besides this one, found in Kālidāsa's *Kumārasambhava*, which suggest that Umā should not resemble Lakṣmī, but be herself. There is still another derivation which suggests that she considers even Śiva as unnecessary for her happiness, being complete in herself. All these derivations confer upon Umā a self-sufficient and unique status in the overwhelming context of absolute Beauty. It is just this uniqueness that distinguishes mere appreciation of beauty from the *laharī*, the upsurge of beauty, meant to be experienced in these verses.

72

समं देवि स्कन्दद्विपवदनपीतं स्तनयुगं
तवेदं नः खेदं हरतु सततं प्रस्नुतमुखम् ।
यदालोक्याशङ्काकुलितहृदयो हासजनकः
स्वकुम्भौ हेरम्बः परिमृशति हस्तेन झटिति ॥

samaṁ devi skanda dvipavadana pītaṁ stanayugaṁ
tavedaṁ naḥ khedaṁ haratu satataṁ prasnuta mukham ।
yad ālokyāśaṅkākulitahṛdayo hāsajanakaḥ
svakumbhau herambaḥ parimṛśati hastena jhaṭiti ॥

devī — O Goddess; *samaṁ* — equally, at once; *skanda dvipa vadana pītaṁ* — ever being sucked by Skanda and the elephant-faced, Gaṇeśa (*dvipa* = elephant, lit. twice drinking: i.e., both by the trunk and the mouth); *stanayugaṁ* — the twin breasts; *idaṁ tava* — Yours these here; *naḥ khedaṁ* — our misery (paradox); *satataṁ haratu* — for ever let it banish/abolish; *prasnuta mukham* — milk-spouting; *yat ālokya* — which, on seeing; *āśaṅkā ākulitaḥ hṛdayaḥ* — with misgivings in his heart; *hāsa janakaḥ* — causes laughter; *herambaḥ svakumbhau parimṛśati* — as he feels his own front; *hastena jhaṭiti* — with hands, quickly

Let it banish our misery, O Goddess, Your twin breasts,
Ever being sucked equally by Skanda *and* Gaṇeśa*;*
Of which, seeing their milk-spouting fronts, Gaṇeśa causes laughter,
As he feels his own front with misgivings in his mind.

Parity and chilarity (handedness) of the structure of the Absolute are attempted to be put together in this verse, together with a horizontally placed mirror-like reflecting surface separating the counterparts. Gaṇeśa (the elephant-headed god) and Subrahmaṇya (the god who glorifies revalued brāhmiṇical virtues) enter as equal partners into this composite picture, evidently created by Śaṅkara himself and not found in any other mythological story. We have now to put a circle around the breast region of the Goddess and try to visualize the structural relationships that are meant to give an integrated beauty content to the absolute Goddess.

The two breasts being sucked by the two sons of the Mountain Goddess represent in themselves strikingly ambivalent characteristics between them. The elephant-headed god, Gaṇeśa, has a more earthy character than his brother Subrahmaṇya, who is thin and refined and full of heavenly brightness. The difference in their personalities could be traced to the milk that each of them is nourished on, which is from the same mother and cannot be basically different. Peripherally considered, however, the breasts of the Mother could have a slight lack of parity between them; one being derived from the side of sunlight and the other being derived from the side of moonlight. This idea was suggested in verse nineteen. There is a degree of virtuality and of actuality even within the overall status of parity between the breasts, when viewed horizontally. The Absolute is enclosed within an upper limit and a lower limit, and horizontal parity, when tilted ninety degrees, can be absorbed into the vertical axis. Then, instead of parity, we have to think of chilarity. These distinctions are now entering into the discussion of the structure of space in modern science. There is a right-handed spin and a left-handed spin of electrons described in quantum mechanics. Hexagonal crystals of quartz could have their right-handed facets or left-handed facets more developed, presenting a verticalized asymmetry. The complexity of the structure within the Absolute and its dynamism are still the subject of speculation by scientists and philosophers, nor is this question likely to be settled in the near future, unless epistemology and methodology are subjected to drastic revision independently of the one-sided prejudices of either physics or metaphysics. An integrated Science of the Absolute has still to be presented to the world.

After visualizing the two divinites, Gaṇeśa and Subrahmaṇya, sucking the twin breasts of the Goddess on a basis of horizontal parity, it is natural for us to view the same picture later in a more vertically revised perspective at a stage when at least one of these divinities has been weaned out of that early state of childhood, or partially so. This gives us the picture of Gaṇeśa alone confronting the two breasts of the Goddess, so generously spouting milk out of their tips. The suggestion here is that while Pārvatī and Subrahmaṇya are watching Gaṇeśa still engaged in, or just after, sucking the milk of his mother, Gaṇeśa looks round, and gets the strange illusion that the two small tusks that grow on his snout are some sort of duplicates of the ivory-white spouts of milk that he sees coming from the two breasts of the Goddess. This would suggest that there is a reflecting surface between the consciousness of Gaṇeśa and what he is able to visualize in front of him. Gaṇeśa, being a divinity more earthy than Subrahmaṇya, is to be placed below this line of demarcation separating the conceptual from the perceptual.

The situation on the whole occasions humour on the part of everyone except Gaṇeśa himself, who still treats the illusion seriously and wishes to verify the truth experimentally by passing his hands over his face to see if his tusks are real or only a reflection. They could be both; and in this two-sided predicament of doubt, there is an element of the humourous to be recognized by us. Bergson in his well-known work on laughter *Le Rire*, analyses the essence of humour on similar lines. When the mechanistic and the vitalistic worlds interfere with each other, humour emerges.

Now a question remains about the aptness of the prayer of the poet here, that the picture as presented above should banish the misery of humanity. This can only be in the sense that knowledge of the essence of the Absolute, with all its contents, and relations properly understood within its context, would, as the Upaniṣads promise, make a man identical with *brahman* itself, and thus it could confer salvation directly, without any other intervening factor. The word 'ever' in the second line confers an eternal or absolute status on the picture and lifts it out of the context of a mere mythological situation. The last line further underlines that the misgivings of Gaṇeśa take place in his heart, and not really outside. Thus the schematic status of the whole dynamics of the imagery is further assured.

73

अमू ते वक्षोजावमृतरसमाणिक्यकुतुपौ
न संदेहस्पन्दो नगपतिपताके मनसि नः ।
पिबन्तौ तौ यस्मादविदितवधूसंगरसिकौ
कुमारावद्यापि द्विरदवदनक्रौञ्चदलनौ ॥

amū te vakṣojāv amṛta rasa māṇikya kutupau
na sandehaspando nagapati patāke manasi naḥ ।
pibantau tau yasmād avidita vadhūsaṅgarasikau
kumārāvadyāpi dviradavadana krauñca dalanau ॥

naga pati patāke — O Banner of the King of Peaks; *te amū vakṣojau* — these rising out of Your chest (breasts); *amṛta rasa māṇikya kutupau* — are nectar-bearing ruby pots, (indeed); *naḥ manasi* — in our mind; *sandeha spandaḥ na* — without any trace of doubt; *yasmāt* — by reason of it/because of this; *tau pibantau* — drinking (thereof) the two; *dvirada vadana krauñca dalanau* — the elephant-faced (Gaṇeśa) and the mountain-splitting (Skanda); *avidita vadhūsaṅga rasikau* — both innocent of conjugal joy; *kumārau* — infant sons/child-like; *adya api* — even now (they remain)

O Banner of the King of Peaks, these Your breasts,
Are nectar-bearing ruby pots indeed, without any trace of doubt;
These two, Skanda *and* Gaṇeśa, *both innocent of conjugal joy,*
By reason of drinking from them, they remain thus child-like to the present-day.

After outlining in verse seventy-two the broad structural features connected with the breast region of the Goddess, this verse focuses attention on the same breasts when understood from a revised standpoint. They are here spoken of as ruby pots containing nectar instead of nourishing milk. A ruby is also a precious stone. The world of colours and rubies suggests a peak lower than that of Kailās where Śiva with his renunciation reigns supreme among ascetics. Asceticism is to be placed at a higher vertical point in the scale of values, because it transcends all other lesser joys or values, in principle inclusive of them all. The world of luxury is marked by a lesser peak than that where Śiva resides, in which the Lord of wealth, Kubera, reigns supreme.

The difference here is the same as that in the Bible between manna and plain bread which is spoken of as 'the staff of life'. The very first line mentions the banner of the King of Peaks, which combines the nobilities of both her father and her husband in her personality, as already seen in verse sixty-one. Nourishment by manna and nourishment by bread are both life-giving in their effect — but they are placed at different levels: manna being more hypostatic than plain bread. Jesus spoke in terms of plain bread instead of the manna promised by Moses to the chosen people. Advaita respects both these alternatives, and gives each of them a rightful place in a complete scale of values.

Sometimes the breasts are compared to golden pots, as we see elsewhere in Sanskrit literature, as also in verse seventy-seven, where they are not specifically described as golden but as solid and metallic. If we should imagine a series of horizontal lines making up a ladder of values placed in pairs at different levels, we would get a picture of a kind of ladder like the golden ladder of Jacob mentioned in the Bible, where angels go up and down. Goethe, in his *Faust*, has improved on this two-way staircase arrangement by making the angels pour wine into the vases while ascending and descending on this scale. It was suggested in verse seven that the breasts of the Goddess resemble frontal bulges of a calf elephant. In verse nineteen we saw also that it is permitted to think of a pair of breasts below as well as a pair of breasts placed above the face, and to cancel out the two sets thus presented. Wherever the horizontal line crosses the vertical, we could imagine value-centres, not unlike the breasts that feed babies. The higher we go in the scale of the nourishment derived, the more it resembles that of manna than of mere bread or milk. More earthy values like fertility or fecundity can be imagined to be present in corresponding lower psychophysical synergic centres making chakras or *ādhāras*, according to the degree of abstraction or generalization we might be interested in making. The first line further underlines, by the Sanskrit word *vakṣoja* (rising out of the chest), the hypostatic rather than the hierophantic status of these value-nodes, belonging to a series of such.

To explain how Skanda and Gaṇeśa, though nourished on the same divine nourishment, could show between them ambivalent characteristics is another enigma that we have to fit into the dynamism of the scheme presented here. Both of them are free from carnal dispositions which would have made them enter married life quite early. Extroversion and introversion might at first be supposed to be implied in the difference between Gaṇeśa and Subrahmaṇya. If that were so, Gaṇeśa, being an extrovert, could have been married and Subrahmaṇya, being an introverted type, should have been naturally celibate. This, however, is not what is claimed in this verse. We have to suppose, therefore, that there is something in the milk itself, of the same mother, which is capable of accentuating opposite characteristics, as evidenced by the very contrasting bodily structures of Skanda and Gaṇeśa.

Freudian psychology, which gives primacy to sex as influencing the libido and its growth, would perhaps insist that we treat Gaṇeśa as representing horizontally accentuated tendencies and Skanda, his younger brother, as representing more fully verticalized tendencies. Both of these structural features were already put together without conflict, as we have seen in verse seventy-two. Just as the filament of an electric bulb could be visible when the current is weak, but could become effaced when the current is strong, so both these structural features could be thought of as being present alternately or together without contradiction. As always, a fourfold structure is implied, whether visible or invisible.

The ambivalence or polarity between Skanda and Gaṇeśa here could thus in principle be viewed from both perspectives at once, inclusively, or alternatingly as coming under an 'either/or' situation. When the voltage is increased the polarity is also accentuated. Carnal feelings of sexual attraction can apply only to a state of low voltage. Both these divinities happen to be nourished on milk derived from a highly hypostatic point on the vertical scale. For Skanda, being already on the numerator side, this high voltage agrees with the type he already represents. In the case of Gaṇeśa the polarizing effect being equally pronounced, by being nourished from the same milk, has another ambivalent effect, as it were, by double negation and not merely by one-sided absence of electricity. A magnetic needle can be deflected both positively and negatively by virtue of the intensity of the electric current. Electromagnetism follows the same laws as those of light waves and can accommodate parity as well as right- or left-handedness, as some of the latest scientific experiments on this feature have revealed.

Another way of explaining the difference between Gaṇeśa and Subrahmaṇya here could be sought in terms of enzymes found in different balances in both sexes at the same time. Equations are easily reversible here, and bodily growth can depend upon such wonderful elements in chemistry as are everyday being discovered. The predominance of one or the other of these enzymes or hormones could explain these ambivalent types, biologically as well as in the context of electromagnetism. Sex determination itself might be said to be decided by such factors.

The last line would therefore suggest three contingencies: (1) low energy, producing horizontal ambivalence between sexes in which carnality could prevail, (2) a middle state in which intermediate energy is to be presupposed, in which carnality could coexist with more sublimated instincts, and (3) a third stage of high cyclotronic energy in which carnality is abolished and a new kind of dichotomy takes the place of merely biological ambivalence. This applies to deeper regions of abstraction or generalization, of the third or fourth dimension. Predominance of the pituitary or the thyroid without adrenaline entering into the bloodstream, could produce such a state of sex innocence.

74

वहत्यम्ब स्तम्बेरमदनुजकुम्भप्रकृतिभिः
समारब्धां मुक्तामणिभिरमलां हारलतिकाम् ।
कुचाभोगो बिम्बाधररुचिभिरन्तः शबलितां
प्रतापव्यामिश्रां पुरदमयितुः कीर्तिमिव ते ॥

vahaty amba stamberamadanuja kumbha prakṛtibhiḥ
samārabdhāṁ muktāmaṇibhir amalāṁ hāralatikām ।
kucābhogo bimbādhara rucibhir antaḥ śabalitāṁ
pratāpa vyāmiśrāṁ puradamayituḥ kīrtim iva te ॥

amba — O Mother; *te kuchā bhogaḥ* — Your mid-bust region; *stambera madanuja kumbha prakṛtibhiḥ* — derived from the frontal knobs (cranium) of the elephant demon (vanquished by Śiva); *muktā maṇibhiḥ samārabdhāṁ* — pearls well-fabricated; *amalāṁ hāra latikām* — pure and slender (creeper-like) garland; *biṁba adhāra rucibhiḥ* — (with added) redness of lips like the *biṁba* fruit; *antaḥ śabalitāṁ* — with an inner brightness/ made variegated from within; *pura damayituḥ* — of the controller/burner of the cities (Śiva); *pratāpa vyāmiśrāṁ kīrtim iva* — like the reputation mixed with the exploits; *vahati* — it wears

Your mid-bust region, O Mother, wearing a pure and
slender streak of a garland made of pearly beads
Derived and worked out of the frontal knobs of some
elephant-demon vanquished by Śiva,
The semblance bears of his very reputation, mixed with
his exploits; with added redness of lips
And an inner brightness, presenting a variegated
picturesque charm.

Instead of descending another step, we find in verse seventy-four that the chakra refers to even thinner hypostatic factors than the previous verse. There is reference here again to the reputation of Śiva. Reputation (*kīrti*) and fearlessness (*abhaya*)

figure very high in the enumeration of absolute virtues. When such an enumeration of divine or superior positive qualities or virtues is attempted in the Bhagavadgītā, the series begins with *abhaya* (XVI.1). *Kīrti* is the leading item in another series where a woman's absolutism is enumerated in serial order (X.34). Both these factors figure here in the first two lines, which refer to the mid-bust region wearing a pearly garland. The garland is not made of simple pearls, but derived from pearls supposed to be contained within the cranium of an elephant-demon which was a victim to the bravery of Śiva. The elephant represents space and horizontality in the *lingua mystica* of contemplative Sanskrit. Killing the elephant to wear its skin is a mythological way of saying that horizontal values are effectively abolished at a point approximating to the *sahasrāra cakra* (crown of the head) or the *ājñā cakra* (between the eyebrows). Peripherally the elephant is space-like in its evil-portending value status, but within its brow, between the frontal knobs, pearls are said to be hidden, at least by poetic convention. Similarly, the snake is also sometimes said to carry jewels in its hood.[1] This is to show that hypostatic values could be far removed from actual levels of biological life-functions, but still participate with the same vertically bright parameter represented here by the pearly garland. This theory is sufficiently justified by the text when closely scrutinized. Meditation in the middle of the eyebrows represents a superior form of yoga known to experts on the subject. It is supposed to give powers of moving in the sky, in terms of which kind of freedom it is called *khecarī mudrā* ('moving in the sky, sky-moving').[2]

In the third line, besides valour and reputation, we find that a touch of the phenomenal or vitalistic functions of the Goddess as the Mother of the universe is made to condition the sheer

1. Pearls are to be found in clouds, bamboos, oysters and sugarcane, according to certain texts.
2. See *Darśanamālā* of Narayana Guru on the subject of *khecarī mudrā* in the ninth chapter, on yoga.

pearly whiteness of the two other virtues. When blended thus by both positive and negative qualities, the neutralization of the redness of the lips adds vitalism to the otherwise conceptual status of factors like bravery or reputation. The last line further qualifies the vitalism by bringing in the inner factor of self-luminous fluorescence, which is more than mere conceptual brightness. Thus, the language of colour reveals the value gradations within the total amplitude of the vertical parameter marking the mid-bust region of the Goddess.

It is always difficult to relate virtues or qualities with psychophysical levels. Some psychology books have attempted such graded enumerations, which have mostly failed because an overall structural pattern referring to the totality of the psyche has not been seriously attempted. Psychology has been compartmentalized too much into disciplines in which experts alone can operate with intelligence. Freudian psychology introduced many features unknown to brass-instrument dominated experimental psychological disciplines, but it is still considered not quite acceptable to academic psychologists even today. The process of revising what Freud ushered into existence in the world of psychology is still taking place, and such a task is far from being complete even now.

The beads derived from the bone of an elephant first gives place to pearly ones, then they receive a touch of redness at a still lower level and finally an inner fluorescence or iridescence is added; the source being in inner space rather than in outer space. Thus, psyochophysical factors are revealed at all levels possible within the psyche.

75

तव स्तन्यं मन्ये धरणिधरकन्ये हृदयतः
पयःपारावारः परिवहति सारस्वतमिव ।
दयावत्या दत्तं द्रविडशिशुरास्वाद्य तव यत्
कवीनां प्रौढानामजनि कमनीयः कवयिता ॥

tava stanyaṁ manye dharaṇidhara kanye hṛdayataḥ
payaḥ pārāvāraḥ parivahati sārasvatamiva ।
dayāvatyā dattaṁ draviḍaśiśur āsvādya tava yat
kavīnāṁ prauḍhānām ajani kamanīyaḥ kavayitā ॥

dharaṇi dhara kanye — O Maiden born to the Earth-Supporting Lord; *tava stanyaṁ* — Your breastmilk; *hṛdayataḥ* — from the heart; *payaḥ pārāvāraḥ* — as an ocean of nectar; *sārasvatam iva* — as pertaining to word-wisdom; *parivahati* — as flooding out; *manye* — I consider; *dayāvatyā dattaṁ* — as offered by one who is kind; *tava yat* — Yours that (breast-milk); *āsvādya* — having tasted; *draviḍa śiśuḥ* — (this) Dravidian child; *prauḍhānām kavīnāṁ* — amidst superior poets; *kamanīyaḥ kavayitā* — a composer of charming verse; *ajani* — was born (became)

Your breast milk, I consider, O Maiden born to the Earth-supporting Lord,
As if it were word-wisdom's ocean of nectar, flooding out from Your heart,
Offered by one who is kind; which, on tasting,
This Draviḍian *child, amidst superior poets, is born a composer of charming verse.*

Inserted between verses seventy-four and seventy-six we find one that gives a personal reference to the author himself as a Dravidian child, or the product of a proto-Aryan culture. This reference to himself constitutes a kind of signature of the author, which we could also notice in three others: fifty-seven, fifty-nine and ninety-eight.

There is also an implied first-person reference in the first and the last verses, where he disowns his own direct involvement in the content of these verses. The position that this verse occupies between outer and inner aspects of the mind, when correctly balanced and neutrally normalized, justifies the realistic perspective adopted here and the pointed reference to his own cultural affiliation. This reference has got great value for us as unmistakable internal evidence that the author of this work is Śaṅkara (see 'Generalities').

We have to note that it is an ocean of milk on which the would-be poet here is to be nourished. Such an ocean of milk represents a vital or life-giving value. Intelligence cannot thrive when vitality is at a low ebb. Thus, the gift of poetry is based on inspiration from the numerator side as well as nourishment from the side of nature. The second line refers to the ocean of word-wisdom which, being a numerator value, is compared to the more normal level suggested in the first line by the status of Pārvatī as daughter of the earth-supporting Lord. It is not nectar but human breastmilk with which the would-be poet is to be nourished in a real sense. Word-wisdom's ocean is a generalized and abstracted version of common-sense milk, which marks the same difference as between manna and plain bread, as explained under verse seventy-three.

The Dravidian child belongs to the first-dimensional common-sense order. Vedism and proto-Vedism are meant to complement each other and the resultant value, which is just normalized human mother's milk when realistically viewed, is an ocean of wisdom nectar when viewed from a more hypostatic perspective. The kindness referred to in the third line is from the numerator side. The last line refers to superior poets as well as to one who is merely capable of producing charming verses.

Śaṅkara, as a product of South India, is naturally influenced by Śaivite proto-Aryan civilization — to which Tantra also belongs, together with a fully developed structural language which was known to ancient Śaiva cults — where the famous dancing Naṭarāja of Chidambaram and the Eternal Mother principle, Śakti, are understood as representing the two aspects of the Absolute even by the popular mind. The suggestion which is sometimes made that the reference here is to Sambandhar, one of the four Śaivite revivalists, who ruled in Madurai after the defeat of the Jains (a comparatively recent period), cannot be considered tenable, especially because Sambandhar is not known to have composed any poem in Sanskrit. The distinctness of the two personalities is very clear in spite of punditry, which might confuse the two. In our eyes, at least, Śaṅkara was a product of that part of India fed for centuries by the Malaya breeze, which figures so prominently in Sanskrit poetry from the time of Kālidāsa, covering the long richly forested strip extending from the limit of the desert of central India, down to the southern limit marked by the cape at Kanyākumārī. The whole coastal line is dotted with temples to the Devī in this forested region, having an average depth inland toward the east of more than a hundred miles. The Narmadā and the Taptī rivers, Kāladi, as well as Mūkāmbika must have been the regions frequented by Śaṅkara as a pedestrian pilgrim. The most famous of Śaṅkara's institutions is at Śṛṅgerī, also lying within the limits of the same region.

Although Śaṅkara is referred to as belonging to a brahmin, especially a Nambūthiri brahmin family, the well-known fact that his own kinsmen would not cooperate in finding firewood for the funeral of his mother lends enough support to the view that, by his mother's side at least, he was not of brahminic origin at all. Further, he was also often nicknamed by brahmin schools a 'Buddhist in disguise'. This could not have happened if he had belonged already to an orthodox context. The forms of Tantra which we see here revalued by Śaṅkara prevailed in this particular geographical region. Śaṅkara might have been born to an itinerant scholar travelling from North India as a pilgrim to South India, a genius, born, like Leonardo da Vinci, under somewhat questionable circumstances. This theory is here put forward as one at least as believable as some other events attributed to Śaṅkara in the famous work called *Śaṅkara Digvijaya*, many details of which recent research by the Madras University has revealed to be untenable in the light of history, because of a discrepancy of hundreds of years between the personalities with whom Śaṅkara is said to have had arguments or polemic doctrinal duals in his wanderings. (See the short work by Sri Narayana Sastri of Madras University.)

From Ujjain to Kanyākumārī a uniform Sanskritic culture, influencing the lives of the people in this particular coastal area, must have been started about 1200 years ago, which tallies with the number of the Malayalam era and with the age of Śaṅkara himself, who was unmistakably born at Kāladi in the erstwhile North Travancore about AD 800. Śaṅkara did not write any work in Malayalam, probably because the Malayalam language itself came into being after this date by the interaction between an older Malayalam language, resembling Tamil, and Sanskrit, which percolated downwards by the constant contact with pilgrims as they travelled between Ujjain, Śṛṅgerī, Kalyāṇī, Mukāmbika and Kanyākumārī. This pilgrim line must have been a living nerve connecting nerve-centres of cultural and spiritual importance.

Since our main interest in this work is one of salvaging Śaṅkara's precious contribution to Advaita Vedanta, the question of fixing the authorship is only of secondary importance to us. Continuators of the same Tāntric-Vedantic tradition have been found on the same soil of Kerala from time to time, of whom the latest examples are Chattampi Swami and Narayana Guru. These modern gurus have a family resemblance to Śaṅkara's type of spirituality. Their natural affinities belong to those days prior to the infiltration of influences extraneous to that of Śaṅkara on the Kerala soil, from the Muslim supremacy that followed the fall of the Vijayanagar Empire, through the advent of European invaders, terminating on the date of the Indian Mutiny. Revalued spirituality at the hands of these modern continuators bypasses the intervening period to catch up with the anterior epoch, marking the decline of Buddhism and the rise of Advaita Vedanta. The same circumstances also explain why so much suspicion overcovers the clear Advaitic doctrines contained in these verses.

Other mythological explanations of the phrase 'Dravidian child' (*draviḍa śiśu*) arise from: (1) a myth-making instinct where a rational explanation becomes difficult, (2) a failure to appreciate how the first part (verses 1-41) called *Ānandalaharī* and the latter part (verses 42-100) called *Saundaryalaharī* belong together to the same subject of Beauty, the only difference being that they refer to inner and outer spaces, respectively, and (3) a failure to appreciate the deeper structural implications. Such mythological explanations are many and do not deserve our serious attention here.

76

हरक्रोधज्वालावलिभिरवलीढेन वपुषा
गभीरे ते नाभीसरसि कृतसङ्गो मनसिजः ।
समुत्तस्थौ तस्मादचलतनये धूमलतिका
जनस्तां जानीते तव जननि रोमावलिरिति ॥

hara krodhajvālā valibhir avalīḍhena vapuṣā
gabhīre te nābhī sarasi kṛtasaṅgo manasijaḥ ।
samuttasthau tasmād acala tanaye dhūma latikā
janastāṁ jānīte tava janani romāvalir iti ॥

acala tanaye — O Daughter of the Mountain; *manasijaḥ* — the mind-born (god), Eros; *hara krodha jvālāvalibhiḥ* — by the encircling flames of the ire of Śiva; *avalīḍhena vapuṣā* — with body engulfed; *te gabhīre nābhī sarasi* — into Your deep navel-lake; *kṛtaḥ saṅgaḥ* — became merged (dived); *tasmāt* — therefrom (the lake); *dhūma latikā* — the creeper-like streaks of smoke; *samuttasthau* — (thus) raised/emerged; *janani* — O Mother; *tām janaḥ* — that (smoke), the people; *tava romā- valiḥ iti* — as Your rows of hair; *jānīte* — (they) look upon

That mind-born god, once, on his body being engulfed
In the encircling flames of Śiva's ire, into the deep lake of Your navel,
O Mountain Daughter, he dived, and on re-emerging,
The creeper-like streaks of smoke thus raised, the people look upon as Your rows of hair.

From the vitalistic level, which lends a touch of redness to the lowest level marked in verse seventy-four, we pass on now to the transition from the outer to the inner space within the psychophysical structure of the body of the Goddess. The variegated fluorescence that produced a picturesque effect, visible from outside but originating from inside, marked in theoretical terms the lowest point of transition where the participation was equal between outer and inner spaces. In the present verse the mode of operation of this participation is being more closely scrutinized. For the purpose of such a scrutiny it is necessary to think of Kāma as a mind-born divinity or demiurge who could pass from inner space to outer space, as between the two compartments of an hourglass. He is able to dive into inner space when his head has caught fire, and he is also capable of coming back into outer space again. Outer space, representing as it does, conceptual numerator factors not necessarily favourable to life, is comparable to fire rather than to water. In the philosophy of Heraclitus, fire occupies a central place among the elements, while Thales gives importance to water. The Hylozoists or Eleatics give primacy to one elemental principle or another. Here we are concerned with water and fire only, one favourable to life, the other too hot to sustain life. A dividing line passes horizontally at the point of the navel of the Goddess, schematically understood. The mind-born god does not experience discomfort, because eroticism and discomfort cannot go together. Thus, he is said here to move between the plus and minus sides of the vertical parameter, alternately ducking into and re-emerging from the water. When he ducks under the water the smoke will be enclosed within bubbles, if any, in inner space, and when he re-emerges, the smoke could ascend to form a vertical line in the atmosphere, which can be imagined to be motionless and having its own horizontal pressure at the limit of transition between the regions proper to water and fire. The streak of smoke could be like the one that can be seen rising from a burning incense stick in a still room. This streak is compared to the thin streak of hair at the abdominal region of both men and women. Hair growth indicates places where erotic pleasures are likely to be hiding in concentrated form. Secondary sex qualities are indicated by the presence or absence of hair on the surface of the skin. Thus, the absence of hair would indicate negative eroticism and growth of hair would mean positive eroticism. There can be an intermediate region marked by the streak referred to here. Deeper structuralism can thus be revealed by superficial ectodermal features which are secondarily related to sex.

The encircling flames of the second line give place to a streak marked by the growth of hair, represented by smoke at a deeper level. Two inverse logarithmic spirals could be imagined here in terms of the inside and outside of a loop-like structure, according to the principle of the Mobius strip, just at the region where inner space participates with outer space. If Śiva's flames are comparable to his city-burning fervour, the Mountain Daughter's body below her navel can, by contrast, represent the cool kindness of living waters. The mind-born god has been compared by other Sanskrit poets to a limbless magenta ball of light, not unlike the variegated picture presented at the end of verse seventy-four.

77

यदेतत् कालिन्दीतनुतरतरङ्गाकृति शिवे
कृशे मध्ये किञ्चिज्जननि तव यद् भाति सुधियाम् ।
विमर्दादन्योऽन्यं कुचकलशयोरन्तरगतं
तनूभूतं व्योम प्रविशदिव नाभिं कुहरिणीम् ॥

yad etat kālindī tanutara taraṅgākṛti śive
kṛśe madhye kiñcijjanani tava yad bhāti sudhiyām ।
vimardād anyonyaṁ kucakalaśayor antara gataṁ
tanūbhūtaṁ vyoma praviśad iva nābhiṁ kuhariṇīṁ ॥

śive janani — O Auspicious Mother; *tava kṛśe madhye* — at Your slender waist/middle region; *kālindī tanutara taraṅga ākṛti* — having the form of superfine ripples on the river Kālindī; *yat etat kiñcit* — that something which; *anyonyaṁ vimardāt* — by the friction of rubbing against each other; *kuca kalaśayoḥ antara gataṁ* — in between Your pot-like breasts; *tanū bhūtaṁ vyoma* — space reduced to ethereal particles; *kuhariṇīṁ nābhiṁ* — into the cavity of the navel; *praviśat iva* — as if entering; *sudhiyām bhāti* — looms in the minds of contemplatives

O Auspicious Mother, that something revealed at Your slender waist,
Looking like superfine ripples on the surface of the river Kālindī,
Looms in the minds of contemplatives as space reduced to ethereal particles,
Entering into the cavity of Your navel, and produced by the friction of Your pot-like breasts.

Verse seventy-seven presents many enigmatic features which cannot be easily explained. The first is that oft-repeated idea found in many prayers to the Goddess that the waist of the Goddess is so thin that it is falsely put there by the mind (*mithyākalpita*). The second major enigma is the reference to the pot-like breasts, which must be metallically solid, creating waves or vibrations fine enough to reveal the very inner structure of pure space itself. Thirdly, it is stated that such a vision is given to selected devotees called *sudhis*, suggesting that they have to be especially clever, wise, or sensible. We have here translated this word as 'contemplatives'. Even a contemplative has to focus his attention on this region before it can reveal the special kind of wave-effect present on the surface of the river Kālindī when fine ripples play on its placid water. Perhaps this refers to a special light effect which could be described as a glimmering sheen produced by criss-cross effects of ripples of thinly alternating troughs and crests, forming a special pattern made up of spots of light alternately dim or bright.

We have already had a reference to the breasts as ruby pots, in verse seventy-three, which makes them out to be solid instead of supple as in reality. We have also seen that such qualities as applied to the twin breasts could form a whole series, sometimes rich in terms of luxury, sometimes of a consistency that is metallic and solid. Here the pot-like breasts have to be imagined to be made up of a heavy metal, like gold. When two such pots that are floating on water collide with each other, vibrations will be produced, which will send ripples cutting criss-cross against the natural ripples produced by the gentle wind playing on the placid surface of the river. This is a new structural detail that is purposely introduced here by Śaṅkara. The middle waist region of the Goddess round the navel is supposed to present a mystery, into the depth of which only a wise man can penetrate, as it is evidently meant to be understood here.

The structure of absolute Space has been a major headache with modern scientists. Space is said to have a curvature in the context of Einsteinian relativism. There is also non-Euclidian space, solar space, topological space, vectorial space as also the structure of space as understood by Minkowski, Lobachevski and Riemann. We have hitherto kept in mind our own structural pattern of two cones placed base to base. We have elsewhere suggested that these two cones could also be placed apex to apex, when the position of the structure is pushed from the bottom of the vertical scale to the top. We get an ontological, 'universal concrete' here-and-now locus when the cones are placed base to base at the bottom. The converse of the same, where 'universal elsewhere' and 'universal nowhere' meet in an intelligible point of light at the meeting point of the apexes, rather than the bases, of similar cones, could be imagined on the numerator side; instead of a 'universal here-and-now', we would get a 'universal elsewhere' when the perspective is thus changed.

In this verse we are concerned with the middle region of the Goddess. A special kind of magic or mystery is supposed to be hiding here which requires the wise man to see. The ontological basis becomes abolished in favour of a teleological one. When the apex points of two inverted cones come into contact, there is a point of beauty or interest where they participate. This is the central locus to be kept in mind in respect of this verse. This point is what is referred to in the first line as an enigmatic 'something' placed at the centre of the slender waist. The words *yat etat*, 'this something' (which is seen), justify the location of such a point of participation, which could be said to be both invisible and visible to the eyes of a fully informed Advaita philosopher. Thus, the slenderness of the waist and the point of interest at the locus are understood by us from this first line.

The second line refers to superfine ripples, which, read together with the fourth line, are produced by the impact of the solid metallic pot-like breasts and postulated for the purpose of revealing the fine structure applicable to this mid-region where motherhood can freely function. The apellation 'Auspicious Mother' (*śiva jananī*) would indicate that such a sacred idea of motherhood is in the mind of the poet also.

In the fourth line there is reference to *tanūbhūtam vyomam*, which we have translated as 'space reduced to ethereal particles'. Physicists have postulated something like ether as the medium for the propagation of light, but no ponderable ether has been proved by the repeated Michelson-Morley experiment. Ether, thus, remains to us an ambiguity equally relied upon by both physicists and metaphysicians as a kind of absolute substance, both material and mental, within which a measurable velocity of light could be calculated or postulated. We shall not examine the fine epistemological status of this space, but treat it as a kind of neutral medium, both mental and material at once. The collision of the two pots representing the breasts of the Goddess produce vibrations which cut at right angles to the natural ripples produced by the wind on the surface of a river. As the river flows downwards, toward the navel of the Goddess, it is to be imagined as becoming subterranean. The outside world and its space are turned into an inside world, in terms of some kind of negative or pseudospace. Outside can become inside in topological or projective space. Right-angled triangles can become obtuse or acute-angled ones by expansion or contraction of space. Inside can become outside by a Mobius strip inversion. A one-to-one correspondence in relative positions, vectorially or tensorially understood, could still be maintained. Euclidean axioms can give place to revised ones known to modern non-Euclidean geometry. Right and left could be interchanged by torsions or rotations round an axis. The navel of the Goddess is going to be compared to a frozen whirlpool in the next verse.

It thus requires a great deal of what is also known to modern mathematicians to sympathize even barely with what Śaṅkara is saying here. He cannot be easily dismissed as a man of superstitious belief. It must be assumed that contemplation can get certain theoretical intuitions that the physical sciences also get through more positive or demonstrable laboratory-based disciplines. Axiomatic thinking and experimental thinking have to meet in either case. Eddington is known to be a non-experimental physicist. Mathematics is mainly axiomatic in its status as a discipline. Thus, what intuition can guess from one side can meet what laboratory disciplines can reconstruct from the other side. When they meet, as Bertrand Russell would put it, the marriage of these two rival approaches can take place.

On our part, we believe that Śaṅkara, in his own way, understood intuitively long ago what modern scientists are just beginning to understand. There are points of contact between the writings of Eddington and Narayana Guru also.

Without entering into this subject in too much detail, let us think of the 'space reduced to ethereal particles' in the third line. We could easily concede that waves or ripples could be of two kinds. The main waves have a simple harmonic movement, as between crest and trough, which properly measured is called 'wavelength', while 'frequency' is a kind of sinuous movement, vibrating more quickly, where the amplitude and shortness give it an intensity rather than a length. If one is magnetic, the other could be said to be electromagnetic. Maxwell and Fourier have studied the laws of the propagation of waves both of sound and of light; and modern television and the use of the magnetic tape to serve purposes of light or sound propagation have got many secrets, all of which depend upon the uniformity of the laws applicable to the propagation of light and of electromagnetic impulses. An antenna can conduct all these impulses intact and reproduce them thousands of miles away on television screens placed in the drawing rooms of modern houses. Thus, the disappearance of two sets of waves, in the form of ethereal particles, into the cavity of the navel of the Goddess is at least not to be considered merely as a mythological exaggeration.

It is also possible to think of the structure of space as revealed in crystallography, where cross-polarized light can produce strange interference figures, sometimes suggesting the embryonic stages of some simple animals, together with what is called 'optical movements'. Crystals are supposed to have a lattice-like grating in their structural make-up conforming to units of different solid polygons. They are sometimes referred to as 'gratings', through which light is reflected, refracted, or diffracted into variegated coloured patterns, which also seem to be revealed in nuclear structure. We have already said that the surface of some fruits represent light-patterns belonging to outer space. The conversion of outer space into inner space is a magic that takes place at what is referred to here as the navel of the Goddess.

The impact of the metallic breasts finds mention in verse eighty also. The 'universal concrete' can have an accentuated material solidity. Matter is defined as something that occupies space impenetrably. This is a quality of exclusiveness of the extraneous, and thus a highly horizontalized tendency or impetus found at the heart of existence, which can express itself in fluid verticality or solid horizontality. The impact of two solids will produce vertical lines of force resembling ripples. Thus, wavelengths and horizontal free-amplitudes can break up pure space into ethereal particles. Probabilities and possibilities, parameters or perimeters, expressing qualitative or quantitative processes of growth or becoming in the general flux of life, could all be thought of in abstract terms, with the deep navel region of the Goddess treated as the lake in this verse.

78

स्थिरो गङ्गावर्तः स्तनमुकुलरोमावलिलता-
कलावालं कुण्डं कुसुमशरतेजोहुतभुजः।
रतेर्लीलागारं किमपि तव नाभिर्गिरिसुते
बिलद्वारं सिद्धेर्गिरिशनयनानां विजयते॥

sthiro gaṅgāvartaḥ stanamukula romāvali latā-
kalāvālaṁ kuṇḍaṁ kusuma śara tejo huta bhujaḥ ।
rater līlāgāraṁ kim api tava nābhir girisute
biladvāraṁ siddher giriśa nayanānāṁ vijayate ॥

giri sute — O Daughter of the Peak; *tava nābhiḥ* — Your navel; *sthiraḥ gaṅgāvartaḥ* — stilled Gangetic whirlpool; *stana mukula romāvali latā* — for the creeper of hair for which Your breasts are buds; *kalā āvālam* — as the fecund flower bed; *kusumaśara tejaḥ* — of the glory of the fire of Eros; *huta bhujaḥ kuṇḍaṁ* — the sacrificial firepit for offerings; *rateḥ līlāgāraṁ* — for Rati a pleasure bower; *giriśa nayanānāṁ* — to the eyes of Śiva; *bila dvāraṁ siddheḥ* — the cavern mouth for (his) austerities to bear fruit; *kim api* — and what not (in a way impossible to describe); *vijayate* — it reigns supreme

O Daughter of the Peak, your navel reigns supreme as a stilled Gangetic whirlpool,
As the fecund flower bed of Your breast-bud bearing creeper,
As the sacrificial firepit for receiving Kāma's glory, and for Rati as her pleasurebower,
While to the eyes of the Mountain Lord, the cavern mouth for the fruition of his austerities.

Verse seventy-eight further confirms the schematic status of the region marked by the navel. The value or function that it represents or fulfils could be varied, but there is always a substratum that continues to be the same. The latitudes, longitudes or equators marked on a globe are not real, but are only meant to be references. Ships, as they cross the equator, do not cross any black line, which is only found on the map for the guidance of the mariner. Charting only makes the high seas more easily navigable. If the ship's compass works correctly, officers can be trained to pilot the ships to safety with the help of such charted indications. Thus, the schematic markings could be said to be real to the extent that they have a value. A waterfall might keep its shape unaltered through the years, with slight variations permitted for the seasons. Cascades are thus recognizable by name as well as by form, through centuries. The Jog Falls have four such cascades, each named after a lady. When Heraclitus says that one cannot enter into the same river twice, the river is given the paradoxical status of being a flux as well as a reality with a name. It is in this sense that we have to understand what is said in this verse.

The navel of the Goddess need not be only a lake, as described in verse seventy-six. Alternatively, it could be one of the other four analogies enumerated in this verse. The first analogy is of a whirlpool in the Ganges, which is not to be understood as actually petrified or frozen, but simply as a lasting schematic pattern conforming to the shape of a whirlpool. When the analogy is changed to a biological context the navel becomes a hotbed for flowers to grow. The breasts are then compared to the effects that are produced from such a common source. In the structural image proper to Vedic sacrifice the same navel could be compared to the hollow in which the sacrificial fire is lit, receiving offerings of clarified butter into it, which are meant to glorify the function of eroticism for the benefit of the sacrificer, Kāma. But to the wife of Kāma it is a cool bower where, instead of being burnt, she finds the rest and pleasure she needs, as a negative principle of negentropy rather than entropy. The same navel could be compared to a cavern for Śiva, whose only interest in life is to find a quiet place for meditation so that he could get away from it all, while still remaining paradoxically right within the core of the situation. This paradox, which is of the essence of the

Absolute, can be expected to abolish itself when all the polyvalent implications of this central locus, which constitute a profound mystery in themselves, are fully understood as belonging together to a schematic whole. Each component has its own function, whose plus and minus are cancellable against each other, leaving behind the wonder of the Absolute as a supreme value.

The glory of Kāma cannot operate within a vacuum. It must have some kind of locus or receptacle, just as clarified butter must fall within the core of the fire kindled in a hollow. Rati's need is not for a hollow, which she already represents by her negativity, but something that will protect her against the heat normal to the numerator side of the total situation. Hence, to her, the navel becomes a bower affording shade and coolness from the rays, which are likely to be too hot for life, on the positive side of the total situation. When thinking of the analogy it would be helpful to conceive of the orientation of this lake as being within a conic section of solid geometry, instead of the two-dimensional context of the surface of paper normal to the *śrī cakra*. Fire burns upward, water flows horizontally. To turn a lake into a firepit requires a revised orientation so as to fit it into the schema without violating the structure of space known to some kind of geometry or other. All these are left to the imagination of the reader.

The last line would suggest that Śiva's austerities are not unlike an organic process in which one perfection succeeds another form of perfection, as his austerities progress in their eternal course. When the duality of ends and means in austerities is abolished, such a process of becoming amounts to fruition in the eternal present. Thus interpreted, it will not detract even a little from the absolutist quality of the *tapas* or pure austerity proper to Śiva in the context of the positive Absolute, for whom Pārvatī herself is the negative reference. He is always to be given this function, though totally inactive, for, as stated in the very first verse, he is present merely as an 'unmoved mover' or catalyser. Nature cannot operate without this agent, which has only a thin logical status.

79

निसर्गक्षीणस्य स्तनतटभरेण क्लमजुषो
नमन्मूर्तेर्नारीतिलक शनकैस्त्रुटयत इव।
चिरं ते मध्यस्य त्रुटिततटिनीतीरतरुणा
समावस्थास्थेम्नो भवतु कुशलं शैलतनये॥

nisarga kṣīṇasya stana taṭa bhareṇa klamajuṣo ।
naman mūrter nārītilaka śanakais truṭyata iva
ciraṁ te madhyasya truṭita taṭinī tīra taruṇā
samāvasthāsthemno bhavatu kuśalaṁ śailatanaye ॥

nārī tilakaḥ — O Best among women (lit. beauty-spot worn on forehead by women); *nisarga kṣīṇasya* — for what is naturally slim; *stana taṭa bhareṇa* — by weight of bust form; *klama juṣaḥ* — fatigued; *naman murteḥ* — having bent-down figure; *śanakaiḥ truṭyata iva* — slowly, as if about to fall down/on the point of breaking; *truṭita taṭinī tīra* — on a collapsing brook bank; *taruṇā* — (like) a tree; *sama avasthāḥ sthemnaḥ* — holding on to a stable state; *te madhyasya* — for Your waist region; *ciram* — forever; *kuśalam bhavatu* — let there be security; *śaila tanaye* — O Daughter of the Mountain.

For Your waist, O best of women, naturally slim, fatigued
by weight of Your bust form,
With a figure bent down and on the point of breaking,
Equal in state to a tree on a collapsing brook bank;
O Mountain-borne one, let there be security forever.

Verse seventy-nine is addressed to the 'Best of Women', more literally to the 'beauty spot of womanhood'. Śaṅkara has written other verses in which he touchingly says that he cost his mother a lot of emaciation and suffering in the act of giving birth to her child, as is normal to all mothers, through all time, anywhere. Maternity viewed in this way is a form of martyrdom that women have to pass through and deserves, for this reason, the praise and gratitude of all humans born from the mother's womb. The aptness of the apostrophe employed in this verse is therefore perfect, motherhood being the central function of womanhood.

There is reference to the slimness of the waist again here, and also a reference to fatigue due to the weight of the bust. In the second line there is a reference to the disastrous predicament of a possible breaking of the vertical support. A tree standing on the sands next to a deep canyon-like formation cannot maintain its stable and erect position, as the narrow brook below keeps eroding the earth deeper and deeper. Beside the problem of breaking the mid-region of the waist, there is the more seriously precarious position of the whole tree slanting or falling to any side at any moment. The tragedy of incertitude in personal life cannot be portrayed in any more forcible language than that which is adopted here in the name of the status of the pure principle of Motherhood. The reference to the bent figure in the second line underlines the pain and suffering that is involved in childbearing. The canyon-like formation, where the brook flows very deep, is to bring out the profundity of the inner space in which this zone of tragic incertitude is to be located. The reference to the father and the absence of reference to the husband are also to be noticed. We are on the negative side of the situation, where the flagpost and banner proper to verse seventy-three and the reference to Śiva's reputation are seen to be left behind. Here we have a figure, which has already appeared as early as verse seven where the proud *puruṣika* and recumbent motherhood were inserted into the same complex schematic dynamism. The nature of the danger in regard to the middle region snapping is to be brought out in the next verse. The worst trials of motherhood, according to Śaṅkara here, exist in finding some stable ground on which life could thrive with stability and steadiness. It is just these factors that stand in danger where womanhood and its specific functions tend to be most pronounced. The stability of the mountain from whom she is descended is the only feature that can supply what she herself lacks in respect of that function of maternity, for which this region of her body stands.

The central prayer in this verse is the concern of the author for the safety of the middle region of the Goddess. The beauty here could be called a tragic predicament rather than a colourful one, as hitherto presented.

80

कुचौ सद्यःस्विद्यत्तटघटितकूर्पासभिदुरौ
कषन्तौ दोर्मूले कनककलशाभौ कलयता ।
तव त्रातुं भङ्गादलमिति वलग्नं तनुभुवा
त्रिधा नद्धं देवी त्रिवलि लवलीवल्लिभिरिव ॥

kucau sadyaḥ svidyat taṭa ghaṭita kūrpāsa bhidurau
kaṣantau dormūle kanaka kalaśābhau kalayatā ।
tava trātuṁ bhaṅgād alam iti valagnaṁ tanubhuvā
tridhā naddhaṁ devī trivali lavalī vallibhir iva ॥

devī — O Goddess; *sadyaḥ svidyat* — presently perspiring; *taṭa ghaṭita kūrpāsa* — the bodice knotted at the sides; *bhidurau* — bursting; *dormūle kaṣantau* — rubbing at the base of upper arms; *kanaka kalaśābhau* — having the brilliance of twin golden pots; *kucau* — the pair of breasts; *kalayatā* — he who made; *tanubhuvā* — by the god of love; *trivali tava valagnaṁ* — Your threefold mid-region (waist); *bhaṅgāt alam iti* — that it should not break; *trātuṁ* — (wanting) to save; *lavalī vallibhiḥ* — by a wild creeper; *tridhā naddhaṁ* — thrice bound/has bound by threefold strands; *iva* — it would seem

O Goddess, having made Your twin breasts gain the beauty of gold pots,
Rubbing at the upper arms, bursting the bodice and presently perspiring,
The maker whereof, the god of love, now wanting to save your threefold waist
From breaking, saying 'enough', with threefold strands of a wild creeper, he has now bound.

The same predicament found in verse seventy-nine is presented in a slightly more accentuated form in the present verse. Here, the accentuating condition that makes the danger worse is not womanhood in itself, as in the previous verse, but the factor of eroticism personified, called the god of love. Womanly nature in itself is not responsible for exaggerations of certain tendencies at certain times that become accentuated within the scope of the total personality of the Goddess. When a mature mango drops to the ground, that is not considered an advantage from the standpoint of the tree itself. Horizontalization involves an accentuation of certain tendencies at the expense of others. If one should lop off the side branches of a tree, the main branch will gain in strength by the extra sap available for its growth upward. The pruning of fruit trees implies the recognition of such a complementary principle of growth. In cultivating a frail plant, like the tomato, the intelligent gardener often clips away the side branches and retains the main one. When the plant becomes fully laden with fruit, the careful gardener supports the frail stem by binding it to a stick to keep the main stem upright. The heavy weight of the fruitage might tend to snap the vertical stem, and that would spell the disaster implied here.

The function of maternity is directly proportionate to the function of natural eroticism operating within the harmonized system of normal womanhood. Maternity is not a sin because of its libidinous implications. Sex is a sin only in the eyes of an angry god in the garden of Eden, where it is referred to as a 'forbidden fruit'. This does not mean that there is no place for an eroticism that is fully human and natural. The Bhagavadgītā allows for this by saying that when sex does not violate the norms of right conduct and is fully compatible with human nature in its basic tendencies, which it must share with all living beings, it is a kind of *kāma*, or passion, which is to be identified with the principle of the Absolute itself. The principle is represented by Krishna, who says, 'I am myself pure passion of this kind' (VII.11), thus taking away the sense of guilt from eroticism. Although Semitic and prophetic religions have denounced sex, in the *Songs of Solomon* such erotic mysticism is seen to be allowed, as in the *Gīta Govindam* and other works openly based on erotic mysticism in India. Krishna stealing the clothes of female cowherds (*gopīs*) and hiding in the trees is a favourite Rajput theme emblazoned on tapestries which are still admired in modern drawing rooms in the West. Here, beauty is the subject, not sin. Thus, Kāma is admitted as a sufficiently dignified functionary in this work, as we have already seen as early as verses five and six. In fact, there are two rival functions to be recognized here: one in charge of the horizontalizing tendencies, and the other which is normal to womanhood. Eroticism can assert itself strongly or lightly in different types of women, the same way that both Gaṇeśa and Subrahmaṇya could escape the carnal aspect of life. In womanhood especially, the accentuation of vitalistic tendencies can never be considered as a drawback. No cow could be bad because it gives milk as a result of its vitalism. Jesus would not curse a fig tree except for its sterility. What is a virtue with Śiva need not necessarily be a virtue with Pārvatī.

We notice that the god of love is the maker of the horizontalized maturation of the two breasts, which are said to rub against the upper arms because of their fullness. The bursting of the bodice is reminiscent of the nurse Peggotty in Dickens' *David Copperfield*, whose buttons are said to be bursting each time she embraces the boy; so this is an old joke not unknown to English literature. Perspiration is also an indication of an extreme erotic state of mind, as referred to in Kālidāsa's *Śākuntalam*. While on one side Kāma accentuates horizontal sin, on the other side he is much concerned about the danger of the waist snapping when overladen with heavy fruit. The beauty here consists of tragic and comic elements in delicate interplay, neither of which is allowed to predominate and spoil the balance or harmony. Before the last straw enters into the situation, Kāma steps in saying, 'enough, enough!' though he himself induced it horizontally. In order to keep the stem from breaking he props it up and binds it with three strands of a wild creeper, so that it could still stand erect. The three strands represent the three levels through which verticality has to pass to transcend the overaccentuation of any one of them. The way of transcending the three nature modalities (*guṇa*s) has been examined already in verses fifty-three and fifty-four. What applies there at a high level should also apply by extrapolation, below, to the middle region of the waist. The gold pots under reference here are found also in Kālidāsa's poems in the context of watering plants to help their growth. Compared with ruby pots, these might suggest a lower position in the hierarchical scale of values. Here it is not solidity that counts, but the golden coloration or brightness.

81

गुरुत्वं विस्तारं क्षितिधरपतिः पार्वति निजा-
न्नितम्बादाच्छिद्य त्वयि हरणरूपेण निदधे ।
अतस्ते विस्तीर्णो गुरुरयमशेषां वसुमतीं
नितम्बप्राग्भारः स्थगयति लघुत्वं नयति च ॥

gurutvaṁ vistāraṁ kṣitidhara patiḥ pārvatī nijān
nitambād ācchidya tvayi haraṇa rūpeṇa nidadhe ।
ataste vistīrṇo gurur ayam aśeṣāṁ vasumatīṁ
nitamba prāgbhāraḥ sthagayati laghutvaṁ nayati ca ॥

pārvatī — O Mountain Daughter; *kṣiti dhara patiḥ* — the earth-supporting Lord; *nijāt nitambāt*— from his own hips; *gurutvaṁ vistāraṁ* — ponderability and extensiveness; *ācchidya* — cutting (them) off; *tvayi haraṇa rūpeṇa* — on You, as dowry; *nidadhe* — bestowed; *ataḥ* — therefore; *guruḥ vistīrṇaḥ* — which is both weighty and expansive; *te ayam* — Yours this; *nitamba prāgbāraḥ* — hips by prior substantiality; *aśeṣaṁ vasumatīṁ* — the whole earth without remainder; *sthagayati* — cancels out/hides; *laghutvaṁ nayati ca* — and confers lightness (on it too)

Ponderability and extensiveness, O Pārvatī, the earth-
supporting Lord once bestowed on You as dowry,
Cutting them off from his own hips;
Thus, these Yours here, both weighty and expansive,
cancels out the whole world
And by prior substantiality confers lightness on it too.

There are many theories for slimming down known to beauty specialists and physical culturists. Though they are much advertised by those who recommend the regimes or medicaments, there seems to be no agreement about why certain persons are fat and others slim. A certain kind of obesity or fatty degeneracy might result from age. Hormones or enzymes might have their own roles. Sexual dimorphism is noticeable in certain animals.

The queen bee tends to be big while the male is relatively small, and in certain varieties of leeches the male is so small that it can permanently find a place inside the sex organ of the female.

A scrutiny of the contents of this verse reveals that it could not be interpreted meaningfully in the light of any of the contexts suggested above. We notice here that it is the father, who is a mountain personified, that confers on his daughter, who is aptly called Pārvatī (daughter of the mountains), his own 'ponderability and extensiveness' in the form a wedding gift, so that her married life could be easier at a later date. A mountain is both massive and peaked. The peak represents the verticalized aspect, while the massiveness represents the extensive and ponderable aspects. If the former is considered in principle to belong to the numerator side of the situation, then the latter could belong to the same context while representing, in principle again, the denominator side of the same situation. It is suggested in this verse that the father cut off 'ponderability and extensiveness' from himself and made them into a present to constitute a dowry, in the form of a value or wealth, out of concern for his daughter's welfare later in life.

At the end of the verse it is suggested that the Goddess became light and slim again by some kind of personal readjustment, which must have taken place after her marriage with Śiva. The high numerator value that Śiva represents must have helped in accentuating the process of verticalization of the heavy and extensive hips of the Goddess, which were so much so as to equal in epistemological status the whole world, as indicated in the third line. The idea is that ponderability as well as extensiveness could be viewed under two conflicting perspectives, as in the case of conjugates like time and space. Time can devour space and space time, both according to Descartes as well as in the overall context of Einsteinian space-time relationships. *Res cogitans* and *res extensa* are treated by Descartes as correlates which can interact to absorb or abolish each other. Śaṅkara's own philosophy must have had affinities, however vague, with the views which have come into acceptance in the modern world of science. When time is included in the scheme, we get the notion of a continuum in which both time and space enter as equal partners. It would not be reading too much into the meaning of these verses if we should suggest that all the implications of the inertial or gravitational field of the Restricted Theory of Relativity, as well as the fourth-dimensional perspective of the General Theory of Relativity of Einstein are known to Śaṅkara. We have already indicated that axiomatic and experimental disciplines can be expected one day to meet and verify each other. In the case of this particular verse, without being open to the charge of reading more than what is there in the words of Śaṅkara, it would still be quite safe to assert that basically the intuitions involved in the theories originating in the context of Western science and those already present in Vedanta cover at least the same problems, each in its own particular fashion. In fact, there is a growing tendency among modern scientists to suggest a linking bridge between Vedanta, Zen Buddhism or ancient Chinese thought based on the yang and yin. Oppenheimer, Schrödinger and Niels Bohr have indulged in such cross-references from time to time in their writings. Schrödinger even quotes Śaṅkarācārya and suggests that a methodological and epistemological revision must take place if science is to answer such questions as he puts about himself as he watches the alpine glow on Mt. Blanc. He puts the pointed question about his own personal status if his mother had decided to marry a man other than his father. The whole question brings us face to face with the grand process or flux of becoming, in which a personal presence is involved. Time and space, quality and quantity, velocity and energy: all such conjugates begin then to create a world of uncertainty, or maya, as those who have correct visions of it, like Śaṅkara, were able to visualize long ago.

This verse contains a challenge which refuses to be met by any other less wholesale point of view than the one natural to

Advaita Vedanta, which states, as Bergson also does in his philosophy, that the whole of reality is a form of flux in terms of an *elan vital* (vital impetus). The definition of maya by Śaṅkara conforms essentially to the same eternal process of becoming, which is called 'of the form of a beginningless becoming' (*anādi bhāva rūpa*). Heraclitus, whom even Bertrand Russel finds acceptable, also accepts such a flux as the basis of his philosophy. The last two lines of verse seventy-seven underlined the status of the Goddess there finally as conforming to the flux of maya. We have been obliged to make these bold general remarks in order to give at least some kind of consistent meaning to the content of the present verse.

'Ponderability' (*gurutvam*) must refer to the world of inertia or gravitation. 'Extensiveness' (*vistāram*) must refer to the world of space understood in the abstract. The words of the first line suggesting a dowry given in anticipation, and the regaining of lightness of substance suggested by the words 'prior substantiality', which is our translation of *prāg bhāraḥ* (*prāg* means 'anterior', *bhāraḥ* means 'weight'), as applied to the hips of the Goddess here, contain prospective or retrospective elements in reference to the dimension called time. Thus the verse has necessarily to presuppose, in our eyes, a kind of unified field theory, tacitly understood, in broad outline at least, by the penetrating minds of philosophers like Śaṅkara, and which perhaps anticipates some of the further developments and connections likely to take place in the formulation of a unified field theory, which it was the unrealized ambition of Einstein to offer to the scientific world before he died. The same could be said, more or less, of the fate of the great dream of Leibnitz to present a pattern of characteristics based on a universal form or mathematical language. This was another dream of a great genius that was frustrated.

Let us try to go over the actual words of this verse in the light of these general remarks. We could paraphrase the lines as follows: 'Being born of the King of mountains, who possessed the extensiveness of a massive mountain formation, and ponderability (because all matter must have the quality of weight), you must have inherited, at the time of separation from your family to go to the family of your husband, this kind of wealth in a form which could combine both quantitative and qualitative aspects'. The peak represents kinghood as a unique qualitative characteristic, and so the father did not have to depend on more quantitative or inertial aspects of his personality when the daughter went away. This explains the suggestion in the second line that he cut off actual 'ponderability and extensiveness' from the lower levels of his own schematized personality. After marriage, women tend to put on weight especially in anticipation of childbirth, by virtue of which weightiness of the hips and breasts becomes accentuated. Here in verse eighty-one, where we have descended far into the negative ontological side of the totality of what the Goddess represents, it is the ponderability of the hips with which we are more directly concerned. We must think in terms of more quantitative factors like weight, inertia and space. There could be space-like inertia and space-like weighty inertia. When verticalization and horizontalization get neutralized or balanced against each other, the world itself could be treated as consisting of time-like space or space-like time. This could be understood in terms of the Lorentz Transformation and the Fitzgerald Contraction. Thus, when such a revision is applied to the Goddess here, it is quite correct to say that the whole world could be cancelled out by its own counterpart, attributed to the person of the Goddess.

The last line refers to the losing of the weight of what was once heavy. This can be explained by a vertical form of cancellation which can be induced by the influence of the highly austere and pure verticalized principle that Śiva represents, influencing the total situation without being directly involved in it. Vedantic logic would permit prior and posterior substantiality to belong together, as in the context of clay being spoken of as representing the anterior non-existence of the pot. There are four kinds of non-existence acceptable to the Nyāya school of Indian logic, which are: anterior non-existence (*prāg abhāva*), mutual non-existence (*anyonyābhāva*), ultimate non-existence (*atyantābhāva*) and posterior non-existence (*pradhvaṁsābhāva*). All these four forms of non-existence are known in Tantra śāstra as *padārtha* ('word content' or 'substance'). *Abhāva* (non-existence) is one of the seven significant substances (*padārtha*s) categorized by the Nyāya school, negation being considered as real as minus one in mathematics. It is quite real to say that one got five of the ten oranges from a shop on credit, which would not mean that the debt is not real; it is real in a negative sense.

Such are some of the intricacies of Indian logic, tacitly accepted by Vedanta, on the basis of which alone this verse can make cogent meaning at all. The confirmation that we could derive from modern scientific theorization lends support to the same, as we have tried to explain above. Two children in different parts of the world could be seen playing the same game of marbles. This does not mean that one set of boys learned it from the other. We need not, therefore, vainly try to establish any extra credit for one side or the other; to do so would be childish.

82

करीन्द्राणां शुण्डान् कनककदलीकाण्डपटली-
मुभाभ्यामूरुभ्यामुभयमपि निर्जित्य भवती।
सुवृत्ताभ्यां पत्युः प्रणतिकठिनाभ्यां गिरिसुते
विधिज्ञे जानुभ्यां विबुधकरिकुम्भद्वयमपि ॥

karīndrāṇāṁ śuṇḍān kanaka kadalī kāṇḍa paṭalīm-
ubhābhyām ūrubhyāṁ ubhayam api nirjitya bhavatī ।
suvr̥ttābhyāṁ patyuḥ praṇati kaṭhinābhyāṁ giri sute
vidhijñe jānubhyāṁ vibudha kari kumbha dvayam api ॥

girisute — O Mountain Daughter; *karīndrāṇāṁ* — of (great) king elephants; *śuṇḍān* — trunks; *kanaka kadalī kāṇḍapaṭalīm* — (and) groups of golden banana stems; *ubhābhyām ūrubhyāṁ* — by the two thighs; *ubhayam api* — both together; *nirjitya* — having beaten, overcome, defeated; *suvr̥ttābhyāṁ* — well-rounded; *patyuḥ* — to your Lord; *praṇati kaṭhinābhyāṁ* — hardened by prostrations/devotions; *jānubhyāṁ* — by both the knees; *vibudha kari kumbha dvayam* — the twin frontal knobs of the heavenly elephant; *vidhijñe* — O One fully aware of right obligations; *bhavati asi* — You are (outdo)

Beating both the best of elephant trunks and groups of golden banana stems,
By the two thighs and by knees having goodly rounded callosities, due to daily devotions
To Your Lord; even the twin frontal knobs of the heavenly elephant
You outdo, fully aware of right obligations, O Mountain-Daughter triumphant.

In verse eighty-two the locus of beauty, around which we have to put three circles in order to fix the correct perspective by which we are to appreciate the overwhelming beauty factor, consists of the thigh and leg region. It is comparatively easier to describe the beauty of the face or eyes, because we naturally turn to facial features when disposed to admire women. We have now systematically descended from the rubyhood of the gem-set crown of the Goddess, through the parted hair to the forehead, and further descended beyond the navel to now arrive at the region below the hips, but not yet reaching down fully to the feet. The beauty is not of a conceptual order any more. Concepts, if any, have to be put into the beauty by us. Within the domain of experience we have also to find an analogy that will interpret for us the nature of the absolute Beauty which is always arrived at only after transcending the duality or paradox. There is an ascending as well as a descending dialectical approach, which, when employed together, will enable us to dissolve the paradox. Paradox, if allowed to exist, can vitiate the picture through ambivalence and duality, by revealing the fabric to be threadbare throughout, as it were, which is otherwise meant to be of a uniform texture.

The first-dimensional context here has to present us with a sufficiently realistic picture, within the framework of which apparent dualities are permissible for purposes of clarification, in order to bring out the underlying unity later on when deeper abstractions could be allowed in a serial succession. Thus it is that we see a reference in this verse to two familiar organic growths in nature. One of them is the trunk of an elephant, and the other is the banana tree with a very polished and heavy stem that tapers beautifully upward, with a glossy polished golden surface that is also natural to the thighs of a beautiful woman. It is better for a beautiful woman's thighs to err on the side of strength, by which her gait and stability could be made steady and firmly established. Weakness, even in such muscular qualities, cannot be considered anything other than a liability factor in the context of beauty. The suppleness of the elephant's trunk would give it a prehensile form of strength by which it could uproot strongly planted trees. The voluntary and involuntary muscles that cooperate in the making of a firm and beautiful thigh region have thus to be thought of in an ambivalent two-sided fashion. Afferent as well as efferent nervous impluses have to cooperate if the Goddess is to have a dignified and decisive gait. It is not the quality of one elephant trunk or one banana tree that we have to keep in mind here. We have to abstract the two required qualities of beauty from many trees and many elephant trunks. Thus, there will be an outer polish and an inner strength conferring beauty and stability upon this region, which is more existential than theoretical in its value. The mention made of the golden stem is a colourful reference to the complexion, while deeper factors are not omitted.

The second half of the verse adds another and deeper significance to the legs, whose two parts meet at the kneecap. Beauty in the Goddess comes to her not just because she is beautiful physically; her mental dispositions must also contain the same beauty in a sufficiently dignified form. What is such a beauty that could apply to the physical limbs, standing, as it were, on the existential side? The body as a mortal coil is not dignified enough for high philosophical contemplation. What is it good for then, in the context of absolute Beauty, except to somehow contribute to the glorification of a high numerator factor implied in the total value of the Absolute? The Bhagavadgītā mentions that we could practise contemplation by means of the body. In other words, we can press into service an inert lump of flesh called the body, to somehow glorify the Absolute, however low it might be in a scale of spirituality. According to the Bhagavadgītā what one could do with one's body by way of making it subserve spiritual purposes, as best as it can, would be to cultivate straightforwardness or calmness, failing which it could be made to worship wise men or spiritual teachers, including whatever divinities one is capable of revering by prostrations, etc. Otherwise the body would prove itself a hindrance to contemplation. The Goddess here, in the last line, is referred to as being one who is fully aware of inevitable obligations.

A sannyasi might protest against all obligations and say to

himself, 'I am a wise man, and I am above all obligatory duties, which are only meant for less evolved souls than myself'. There is a subtle lacuna or hiatus in this kind of attitude by which necessary forms of action, in which human life is caught, whether one likes it or not, are not given normal importance. Breathing is a necessary function, and even if one has become very wise it would be wrong to forget to breathe. What is necessary cannot be bypassed by mere omission. One has to sublimate one's instinctive dispositions by gradations of normal activities and not by refusing to recognize their presence in one's system. Yoga is a process by which obligations are first recognized as necessary and then transcended by a form of sublimating practice. One cannot live in a vacuum, and the Goddess here is fully aware of this verity, which the Bhagavadgītā makes unequivocally clear throughout its various chapters referring to action and inaction. The last chapter refers to the difference between a *tyāgī* (a relinquisher) and a sannyasi (a man who claims to do without the obligatory ritualism of the Vedas).

The Devī here puts her legs to proper use, according to herself, and is represented as having developed on her knees beautiful circular callosities, which indicate that she must have been kneeling and praying to her Lord, Śiva, secretly everyday for long periods. The callosities here are supposed to be beauty spots, as are the golden pot-like rounded breasts which were referred to earlier. The knees are beautiful, in their own way, at a lower level of human existence, which is steeped in necessities. Between a contingent form of the practice of devotion which can be done, for example, by muttering charms, and the necessary form of the same practice of devotion, there is a subtle form of qualitative difference. A large quantity of small change is required to equal a gold coin. If the post office does not sell a one-dollar stamp, one will be obliged to buy many stamps of a lower count. The thighs of the Goddess would not be performing any contemplative function at all if they were not given some proper work to do. If words have a rich spiritual value, actions have also a value, but with the difference that while understanding is like gold in its value, physical actions are of an inferior grade compared to the gold. They could be said to be of the value of an iron city rather than a golden or silver city, in terms of the three cities of values destroyed by Śiva when he descended from Chidambaram. When the callosities gain, due to the number of times Pārvatī kneels in praise of Śiva as a concept, both the numerator Śiva-value and the value represented by the beauty of the callosities would cancel each other out, revealing a non-dual value, the Absolute. It is in this sense that the frontal knobs of the elephant are outdone by the callosities on the legs of the Goddess. The justification for such a correspondence between the two sets of rounded protuberances has already been suggested as early as verse seven, where the frontal bulges of a calf elephant are referred to as analogously equivalent in beauty to the maidenly breasts of a young damsel. The metaphor might seem to be rather far-fetched and mixed-up, unless it is seen in the light of the importance of recognizing the totality of the value of the Absolute, of which only a structural analysis can reveal the component relational factors.

83

पराजेतुं रुद्रं द्विगुणशरगर्भौ गिरिसुते
निषङ्गौ जङ्घे ते विषमविशिखो बाढमकृत ।
यदग्रे दृश्यन्ते दश शरफलाः पादयुगली-
नखाग्रच्छद्मानः सुरमकुटशाणैकनिशिताः ॥

parājetuṁ rudraṁ dviguṇa śara garbhau girisute
niṣaṅgau jaṅghe te viṣama viśikho bāḍham akr̥ta ।
yad agre dr̥śyante daśa śaraphalāḥ pāda yugaḷī
nakhāgracchadmānaḥ suramakuṭa śāṇaika niśitāḥ ॥

giri sute — O Mountain Daughter; *viṣama viśikhaḥ* — the one of keen arrows (Eros); *parājetuṁ rudraṁ* — to defeat/give battle to Rudra (Śiva); *dviguṇa śara garbhau* — his arrows doubled/duplicated — (twice-five arrows filled); *niṣaṅgau* — (they are) a pair of quivers; *te jaṅghe* — these calves of Your legs; *akr̥ta bāḍham* — he surely made; *yat agre* — at their bases; *pāda yugaḷī nakha agra cchadmānaḥ* — simulating (pretending to be) the toe-nails of the twin feet; *daśa śara phalāḥ* — ten arrowheads; *sura makuṭa śāṇaika niśitāḥ* — sharpened solely on whetstones which are the crowns of gods; *dr̥śyante* — are seen

His quiver duplicating as Your twin legs, (looking like pillars),
Made surely by the god of love for giving battle to Śiva;
They show at their bases ten arrowheads, simulating nails,
Sharpened solely on the whetstones which are the crowns of gods.

This verse marks the close of a descending series started as early as verse forty-two. The next verse contains a tacit signature which has to be added to the four or five others that we have pointed out already (under verse seventy-five). Here the locus of beauty to be kept in mind is the brightness of the nails showing from beneath the feet of the Goddess; and the absolute status of the Beauty of these shining nails emerges just from the fact that they are to be sharpened exclusively on the crowns of the gods who are on the numerator side, whose number could be ten so that one nail could have one crown for its whetstone. A whetstone has to be harder than the instrument it whets, or at least be equal in hardness. One cannot cut glass with a piece of soap. In point of hardness, therefore, there is implied here a one-to-one correspondence between the crowns of the gods and the nails of the toes of the Goddess. When thus cancelled out between head to foot factors of beauty, a certain totality of beauty emerges, with which perspective this series of descending chakras is meant here to touch its natural terminus for the present.

The question might be asked why Kāma sharpens the ten toenails. The answer is contained on the second line: it is to give battle to Śiva. It might again be asked, where do the ten gods range on the numerator side. They are only demiurges, for the toenails representing the arrowheads of Kāma do not require the unique omega point of intensity or hardness to be effectively sharpened. His arrows are not of stern enough stuff to really vanquish Śiva, except on occasion when Śiva might descend somewhat from the height of his own proper omega point. Such an occasion does not take place ordinarily. The crowns of the demiurge-gods are sufficiently hard for making the arrows of Kāma sharp enough for operations within the lesser value system to which he belongs. Below the level of the nails are the soles of the Goddess' feet which are going to be referred to in verse eighty-four. Thus, the one-to-one cancellation for the purposes of this verse is to take place between the sharpness of the toenails as a denominator factor, and the hardness of the whetstones which are the crowns of the gods, representing a numerator factor. Such are some of the overall features which we have to keep in mind before examining the further details of this verse.

In the previous verse the reference came as far down as the legs, to the beautifully rounded knee region. The legs and feet below the knee region are compared here to duplicated pillar-like quivers, within which the arrows stand upside down and not in a position ready to be used directly against Śiva, who is placed at the omega point by us for the sake of structural consistency. This inversion is not due to any oversight. In a magnet, positive lines of force and negative lines of force face contrary directions. The five toes have five arrowheads. This is meant to suggest that there is such a fivefold structure on which the human body is built.

Śaṅkara refers elsewhere to this plan based on two sets of five tiers of duplicated fives, making one hundred, which when thought of as flames or fires, reveals the implied structure of what is referred to as the secret knowledge of the fivefold fires (*pañcāgni vidyā*), which Naciketas is to learn from the god of Death in the *Kaṭha Upaniṣad*, as one of the lesser wisdom-secrets in addition to full-fledged *brahma vidyā*. With this lesser secret-knowledge, the god of Death intends to dissuade Naciketas from asking for the last boon of absolute Wisdom. Śaṅkara builds up an eightfold ensemble of cities built on a fivefold plan, consiting of: five functions such as speech, etc., five functions such as hearing, etc., five vital functions, five chief points of the compass (including the upward one), intelligence with its five subdivisions, the fivefold desires, the corresponding fivefold ignorances and the fivefold tendencies to action — which, when added to the one-hundred already given, gives us the one-hundred and eight syllables of *auṁ*, which are to be repeated when we have to remember gurus, worshippable saints or gods.

Here, when we come to the lower levels of action at least, there is the duplication of the two legs, left and right, which can be abolished if we turn the structure by ninety degrees. The question of whether each arrowhead needs the separate crown of a distinct god could be kept open, because there is not any specific reference to such a duplication on the numerator side.

The first line further refers to a pillar as an apt analogy for the lower part of the legs. Stable support for the body is very important when we think of the chief function of this lower half of the leg. Thus the pillar analogy is quite justified. The pillars are described as 'made by the god of love'. In what sense is eroticism interested in making pillars for the body? Activity means movement, and erotic persons have to seek their mates, male or female, in a place other than the one which they find themselves in. Thus, the organ of locomotion has a direct bearing on the function of eroticism in its most basic sense. But true eroticism is not of this basic kind. It contains verticalized inner principles of attraction and repulsion within the peripheral, or horizontal, outer shell.

It is in the brightness of the nails that the existence of these arrows pointing negatively downward could be guessed or discerned, because they are hardly visible to a superficial view of the legs. The arrowheads are said in the third line to be more real than the nails. The nails are only real in a two-dimensional sense, but the arrowheads are real in a three-dimensional sense and could even attain to a fourth-dimensional, absolutist status when their one-sided brightness is increased by being whetted on their own proper counterparts, the crowns of gods. A three-dimensionally real arrow needs to be whetted upon a more than three-dimensionally hard crown to increase its brilliance and to make it tend, by such a cancellation, towards the absolute Beauty that is to result from this situation. It is true that the nails are hard, but the arrowheads are harder. They can only be whetted on something which is of a greater hardness than the material from which they themselves are made, something tending towards a diamond-hardness, which is at the limit in a scale of hardness that we could think of. All these grades of hardness have to belong to the context of a universal concrete hardness in an absolute overall sense, so as to be fitted without inconsistency into the highly ontologically-biased picture of bright beauty that is still presented in this limiting verse of the series that terminates here.

The second line of our translation underlines the fact that it is the god of love who is responsible for making the two pillars out of the legs of the Goddess. Man is a two-legged animal. Procreation of his kind is for him a basic function, and Kāma is the presiding deity for such a function. He is an absolute in his own domain, as far as it can reach upward, but his arrows cannot always fly high and vertically enough to defeat Śiva. Śiva's heart can be conquered only by the unique and absolute devotion of Pārvatī, who made her way to the water and stood there to practise severe austerities for forty days. God, in trying to create the brightest and most beautiful part of a woman's body, is said by Kālidāsa to have lavished his maximum possible artistic ability on creating that unique heel of Pārvatī, who is depicted as walking to a lake so that she could stand in water for forty days to prove her love for Śiva. In another sense, therefore, we could say that the stability and beauty of the legs of Pārvatī were conferred by the creator of Beauty himself. The heel and the sole do not yet figure in this verse; it must be for that reason that the two pillars and their stability are represented as being the handiwork of the god of love, Kāma. In the next verse we shall pass on to the deeper implications of the feet of the Goddess.

The force of the word 'solely' in the last line of this verse attains a consistency, because the one-to-one correspondence between the arrowheads of Kāma and the rows of gods attains to a self-sufficient cancellability, marking the limits within which erotic tendencies can live and move. A more verticalized version, as in verse eighty-four, would put Kāma out of commission altogether. There, instead of the target of hitting Śiva, we have Śaṅkarācārya as a student of wisdom presented as a supplicant at the alpha point. From verse eighty-four through the end of the work, it is the sole of the feet touching its lower most limit, reaching even into the subhuman world, that comes into the various pictures presented. The wisdom supplicant comes directly under reference in the next verse as well as in verse ninety-eight, while the intervening verses are meant to clarify further structural implications.

84

श्रुतीनां मूर्धानो दधति तव यौ शेखरतया
ममाप्येतौ मातः शिरसि दयया धेहि चरणौ।
ययोः पाद्यं पाथः पशुपतिजटाजूटतटिनी
ययोर्लाक्षालक्ष्मीररुणहरिचूडामणिरुचिः॥

śrutīnāṁ mūrdhāno dadhati tava yau śekharatayā
mamāpyetau mātaḥ śirasi dayayā dhehi caraṇau ।
yayoḥ pādyaṁ pāthaḥ paśupati jaṭā jūṭa taṭinī
yayorlākṣā lakṣmīr aruṇahari cūḍāmaṇi ruciḥ ॥

mātaḥ — O Mother; *tava yau caraṇau* — these Your twin feet; *śrutīnāṁ mūrdhānaḥ* — (mark) the crest-point of scriptural wisdom; *śekharatayā dadhati* — worn as head ornament by You; *etau* — these two (Your feet); *mama api* — mine also; *śirasi dayayā dhehi* — kindly place upon (my) head; *yayoḥ* — for which (feet); *pādyaṁ pāthaḥ* — ablution water; *paśupati jaṭā jūṭa taṭinī* — (is the) brook in Śiva's matted hair; *yayoḥ lākṣā lakṣmīḥ* — the auspicious beauty of their red paste; *aruṇa hari cūḍāmaṇi ruciḥ* — (is) the magenta glory of Viṣṇu's crown

O Mother, Your twin feet, marking as they do the crest-point of scriptural wisdom,
Worn as head ornament by You, as by me, kindly place both upon my head.
Water for their ablution is the brook in Śiva's matted hair,
And the auspicious beauty of their red paste is the magenta glory of Viṣṇu's crown.

In verse eighty-four there is a verticalized transposition of points of value references, all placed in the vertical axis. The limbs of an equation can be transposed from the right to the left or vice versa without changing the value of the truth involved in the equation. Here the feet of the previous verse, which stopped short at the level of the nails within the circle forming the domain proper to Kāma, are further viewed from the bottom and are meant to be transformed vertically upward. Lesser values are interposed, which necessarily must have a vertical dimension, however short, pushed and displaced upward successively, so as to make the soles of the feet correspond either to the top of a crown on the head or still further beyond such an ornamental crown to an even higher level. In other words, the feet could be placed adjustably at whatever level one likes in the vertical scale. In passing from the bottommost limit of the alpha point, wearing the magenta paste on their soles, one could imagine the pair of feet being promoted to the zero point of the total situation, which belongs to the Viṣṇu context (of preservation), as justified in the second verse. It is a magenta glory that represents the value pushed still higher towards the omega point and one passes a jewelled crown representing conventional theological values of the order of the world of Indra, still relativistic and hedonistic in status. The crest-point of scriptural wisdom, referred to in the first line of this verse, is where those values terminate and truly absolutist values prevail, which refer to the highest teachings of the Vedantic wisdom contained in the Upaniṣads, covering both Veda and Vedanta, here referred to as *śruti* (wisdom heard directly from a guru). The value of such wisdom is so high that it is considered worthy of being an ornament to any goddess we could imagine, including the Goddess of this series of verses. Śaṅkara seems to want to place his own head underneath this ornament representing the highest possible watermark of wisdom-values ever. The crest jewel of wisdom could be worn by any real aspirant for wisdom, to which context Śaṅkara here implies that he himself belongs, as well as by any imaginable goddess of a theological context. The short phrase 'as by me' justifies our thinking that Śaṅkara wishes to substitute himself for whatever goddess has been so far dealt with, for puposes of discourse or discussion, in these verses. This shows that a theological deity is not important for him.

The 'both' here refers not to the crown but to the feet transposed in approximation to the omega point. These feet have to be washed by some kind of pure or sacred water that is placed still higher in the scale of values, which here are the little streams originating in the matted hair of Śiva, the source of the heavenly Ganges. From Śaṅkara's use of such water in the present context could be seen, in our eyes, the need for linking the different levels of value, through which the feet have been raised; together in a descending order. The heavenly Ganges is a streak of value, that descends to earth to benefit mortals situated horizontally here below. In mythology it is represented as a thin stream descending out of the matted hair of Śiva. Without the obstruction offered by the matted hair, the flood will be too powerful and would endanger the safety of the world. That is the idea under reference here. Thus after passing the crest jewel of wisdom, the ablution waters derived from the heavenly Ganges could continue to descend, washing against the ruby-coloured crest jewel of the lower Viṣṇu system of values, and finally benefitting mankind in a more humble and earthly sense. The prayer requesting both the feet to be placed on the head of the supplicant gives this verse a touch of intimacy, while respecting ontological realism to its fullest extent. If there is one doctrine which is dear to the teaching of Vedanta as authoritatively contained in the *Brahmasūtras*, it is this respect for the ontological concreteness of the Absolute, which is not to be mixed-up with idealism such as that of Plato or of the Buddhist *vijñānavādin*s. Both the feet are equally real, marking respectively the lower and the higher limits, where ontology begins and teleological axiology ends.

Our guess in the previous verse that the twin feet could be fused into one crown seems to be confirmed by the indication here that the crown represents the twin feet on the numerator side. Twinning represents the last vestige of parity. It is a horizontal structural feature and, when transformed into its own verticalized version with an omega point for reference, it abolishes its own parity in terms of a higher form of axial symmetry instead of bilateral parity. Right-handedness and left-handedness in this axial symmetry could be considered possible, because it is not bilateral anymore. From this verse onward we pass on to other subtler features of nominalism and structuralism treated together, the peculiarities of which we shall presently examine.

85

नमोवाकं ब्रूमो नयनरमणीयाय पदयो-
स्तवास्मै द्वन्द्वाय स्फुटरुचिरसालक्तकवते ।
असूयत्यत्यन्तं यदभिहननाय स्पृहयते
पशूनामीशानः प्रमदवनकङ्केलितरवे ॥

namovākaṁ brūmo nayana ramaṇīyāya padayos-
tavāsmai dvandvāya sphuṭa ruci rasālaktakavate ।
asūyaty atyantaṁ yad abhihananāya spṛhayate
paśūnām īśānaḥ pramadavana kaṅkeḷi tarave ॥

nayana ramaṇīyāya — beauteous to view; *sphuṭaruci rasa ālaktakavate* — smeared over with brilliant magenta paste; *tava padayoḥ asmai dvandvāya* — to these Your twin feet; *namo vākaṁ brūmaḥ* — spoken words of worship we offer; *yat abhihananāya* — to be kicked (by them); *spṛhayate* — (for being) desirous of; *pramada vana kaṅkeli tarave* — towards the *aśoka* tree of (Your) pleasure grove; *paśūnām īśānaḥ* — the Lord of Beasts; *atyantaṁ asūyati* — (is) extremely jealous

Spoken words of worship do we offer to these, Your twin feet,
Beauteous as they are to view, smeared over with paste of brilliant magenta;
Extremely jealous is he, the Lord of Beasts, of that aśoka *tree*
In Your pleasure grove, for desiring to be kicked by them.

The very opening words of this verse seem to underline the importance of 'spoken words', as if there is some difference between spoken and written words, or any other form of representation, such as words that are heard from a radio broadcast. God's words are another possibility. The reason why spoken words are particularly important here must be because the highly nominalistic and schematic status of the contents of the verses from this point onward has to recognize two cancellable counterparts. The beauty of the twin feet of the Goddess is still the subject matter here, but beauty is meant to be treated here in great schematic abstraction. The beautiful form is meant to be abstracted out of other realistic implications, which might complicate our meditations about the absolute beauty-value of the Goddess. Spoken words are tangible, and not just concepts or names in a purely mathematical sense; they are more real. What they are meant to refer to here, so as to give them a visible content, is the colourful beauty of the twin feet of the Goddess. These two counterparts, the nominalistic and formal factors, are meant to be cancelled out, so that the resultant value could attain, as is intended in these verses, to the absolute or overwhelming Value emerging from the equation of the visible with the audible. We can expect the *schematismos* to become thinner and thinner in this section as we proceed step by step towards the culmination of this work where everything is going to be cancelled out, whether into the nothingness or somethingness or both, which the absolute value in terms of Beauty is meant to represent anywhere in this work. Knowing such a plan in advance, it would be easier for us to follow some of the finer subtleties of combining nominalism and structuralism, so as to transcend even these finally. We could pass, thus, not only from realism to what is implied as the meaning lying behind some real pictures, but go one step deeper into the meaning of meanings, delving into the semiotic processes of languages themselves.

After asking the Goddess to place her twin feet on his own head in the previous verse, the author intends to evaluate this relation while standing on still thinner grounds. It is the magenta colour on the soles of the feet that becomes more important than the feet themselves as the locus of beauty. The brilliant magenta describes it, while spoken words meet it from the opposite side, as it were, to enhance its meaning content. This is what might be expected to be happening on the positive or conceptual side of the total situation.

At the same time, there is a more ontological level where the same value called 'the magenta glory' on the soles of the feet is the cause of some disturbance for Śiva, who is here represented as jealous. Jealousy is a negative sentiment and cannot really exist as a virtue in such a high god as Śiva, but even though a negative sentiment, the possibility of jealousy is not to be completely ruled out. It is bad to be hungry but that does not mean that hunger does not exist. Similarly, it is bad to be jealous, but it is seen to be necessarily operative in human life. Godliness cannot thrive in a vacuum, but must have a negative basis on which it can express itself, however faint that negativism might be. In the sense that 'the exception proves the rule', the negative features of the Absolute have to enhance its meaning by demonstrating its capacity to transcend its own negativity. What is a virtue at the head-end has to imply a vice at the tail-end, if absolutism is not to exclude anything from its scope. This follows from the dialectical rule, known to Parmenides and Zeno from ancient times, that 'the one and the many' had to belong together if they were to make any meaning at all.

Śiva is here jealous only of a garden tree and not of any equally worthy person. In other poems, like Kālidāsa's *Mālavikāgnimitra*, the same kind of ideogram is seen to be fully understood by Sanskrit poets. The *aśoka* tree has to be kicked by the decorated soles of a royal personage if its poor soul is to be thrilled sufficiently to stimulate its own kind of erotic mysticism, creating within it a festive marital sense of exaltation natural to its marriage season. In addition to producing new magenta-coloured tender foliage from bottom to top, the stimulus of the kick would be sufficient to thrill the subhuman soul into a kind of exalted mystical state that is supposed to be very enjoyable to the plant. This kind of mixing of human life with the world of mere vegetation, by establishing the unity of life at all levels, underlines the Advaitic attitude which tends to treat life as one, and not as divisible into compartmentalized interests. The jealousy of Śiva in such a context could accommodate a degree of negativity which could be treated, in principle, as already abolishing itself in the context of the totality of the mystical sentiment of life, from which the jealousy itself comes as a byproduct. Kālidāsa's poetry abounds in cancellation of this sort, in which double negation at the tail-end and double assertion of a virtue at the head-end cancel out into a unique form of absolute beauty or virtue. In the second half of this verse, we have to note that Śiva is called Paśupati (the Lord of Beasts), which refers to his overlordship in the world of zoology. The *aśoka* tree belongs to the world of botany; even here there is a correct respect for naming counterparts by which the cancellation could be according to accepted rules and conventions of mathematics. The Goddess here seems to be living in a garden not unlike the pleasure grove of infatuation (*pramadavana*), which figures in almost every play of Kālidāsa. Understanding Śaṅkara, therefore, naturally presupposes understanding Kālidāsa, his forerunner. Śiva has to be jealous of a poor and humble tree in distress, because he cannot find any other rival in the three worlds on whom he could fix his jealousy. This further enhances the verticality of the perspective in which this negative quality is to be cancelled out against itself. Jealousy is a horizontal, negative sentiment which deserves to be abolished, and is in effect abolished in this verse. No judge in a courtroom would take this charge of jealousy very seriously at all.

86

मृषा कृत्वा गोत्रस्खलनमथ वैलक्ष्यनमितं
ललाटे भर्तारं चरणकमले ताडयति ते ।
चिरादन्तःशल्यं दहनकृतमुन्मूलितवता
तुलाकोटिक्वाणैः किलिकिलितमीशानरिपुणा ॥

mṛṣā kṛtvā gotra skhalanam atha vailakṣya namitaṁ
lalāṭe bhartāraṁ caraṇa kamale tāḍayati te ।
cirād antaḥ śalyaṁ dahanakṛtam unmūlitavatā
tulākoṭi kvāṇaiḥ kilikilitam īśāna ripuṇā ॥

mṛṣā gotra skhalanam kṛtvā — having inadvertently defaulted in respect of Your family name; *atha vailakṣya namitaṁ* — then stooping in shame; *bhartāraṁ lalāṭe* — on (Your) husband's forhead; *te caraṇa kamale tāḍayati* — as You kick with Your lotus feet; *cirāt* — (what is) long-standing; *antaḥ śalyaṁ* — rancour; *dahana kṛtam* — caused by the burning (by Śiva); *unmūlitavatā* — having wholly abandoned (plucked out, uprooted); *īśāna ripuṇā* — by the enemy of Śiva (Kāma); *tulā koṭi kvāṇaiḥ* — with the clamour rising from (bells at the end of) anklets; *kilikilitam* — celebrates (his) victory

On having inadvertently defaulted in respect of Your family name,
While stooping in shame, Your husband's forehead as You kicked
With Your lotus feet, that enemy of Śiva, wholly giving up his long-standing rancour, caused by the heat (of Śiva),
His victory celebrates with the clamour of many jingle bells.

In verse eighty-six, the lotus feet are meant to be cancelled out against a mistake made by Śiva in referring to the name of the clan of Pārvatī's father. In short, name and form are meant to be cancelled out to help us to attain the Absolute. There is no

Tāntric secret at all here, as some would try to find in these verses. It is not impossible, however, to see it from a Tāntric perspective if we should so desire. The divinities Śiva, Pārvatī and Kāma enter into the composition of this verse, which might remind us of the Tāntric tradition. The picture of Śiva stooping in shame, also reminiscent of some structural feature belonging to the Tāntric context, has to be seen side by side with the lotus feet, which have to reach the forehead to be able to kick it. This could happen only if the feet are placed in a correspondingly bent position. They could be imagined to be in contiguity within a circle or better still, within the figure-of-eight formation at the core of the total situation. There is a kind of second or third-dimensional loop or circle to be understood here. As we have said in respect of verse seven, solid geometry and conic sections of more than two or three dimensions could be pressed into the service of this structuralism. Pythagorean trigonometry and differential mathematical forms of calculations could be applied also.

The jingle bells have also to be located by us in the total structure, without violating conventions proper to the language of Tantra, mantra or yantra. Evidently they must be treated as the same as the jingle bells of verse seven on the waistbelt of the *puruṣikā*, represented there in the full dynamism of all her possible motions put together into one living form. Here the negative or horizontal feeling, which is not a virtue at all and thus not ornamental even to the god of love, is the element of long-standing rancour which Kāma has been keeping repressed within himself against Śiva, whom he considers to be a rival obstructing his own intentions and free functioning. Śiva stands defeated in this verse, at least for a moment. How does this enhance the beauty of the Goddess to make it attain the Absolute? Here the same argument as in the previous verse should hold good. Every kick on the forehead of Śiva by Pārvatī makes the erotic sentiment circulate more freely. The god of love thus feels that he is not fully useless. Śiva is against him normally, because

Śiva represents the heated or lighted side of reality, with a corresponding cold and dark side to the same. The circulation of erotic values in the core of the Absolute, whether positive or negative, takes place because of a slight mistake in naming the clan to which Pārvatī really belonged. This slight error has had the disastrous consequence of causing eroticism to begin to function, although indirectly, stimulating the sentiments that can bridge the gulf by cancellation of dark against bright instinctive dispositions. The victory belongs directly to the beauty of the Goddess, in whose borrowed light or glory the god of love is also jubilant. It is the occasionalism again that justifies such a temporary defeat and humiliation of Śiva. The beauty of the total picture is not marred by this slight blemish, just as one can prove the opposite by the same token. This way of proving the opposite is a favourite method adopted by wives for arguing with their husbands. It is negative but not false. A knowledge of such a possibility might save many quarrels in everyday life.

87

हिमानीहन्तव्यं हिमगिरिनिवासैकचतुरौ
निशायां निद्राणं निशि चरमभागे च विशदौ ।
वरं लक्ष्मीपात्रं श्रियमतिसृजन्तौ समयिनां
सरोजं त्वत्पादौ जननि जयतश्चित्रमिह किम् ॥

himānī hantavyaṁ himagiri nivāsaika caturau
niśāyāṁ nidrāṇaṁ niśi caramabhāge ca viśadau ।
varaṁ lakṣmī pātraṁ śriyam atisr̥jantau samayināṁ
sarojaṁ tvad pādau janani jayataś citram iha kim ॥

himānī hantavyaṁ — capable of being killed by snow; *hima giri nivāsaika caturau* — fully at home on the snow peak; *niśāyāṁ nidrāṇaṁ* — sleeping at night; *niśi carama bhāge ca viśadau* — in bloom at night and when night ends; *varaṁ lakṣmī pātraṁ* — a desirable seat for Lakṣmī; *śriyam ati sr̥jantau samayināṁ* — overgenerous in gifts to the *samayins*; *tvad pādau* — Your twin feet; *sarojaṁ jayataḥ* — (they) triumph over the lotus; *janani* — O Mother; *citram iha kim* — what wonder herein?

Capable of being killed by snow, and fully at home on the snowpeak;
Sleeping at night, and in bloom both at dawn as after;
A desirable seat for Lakṣmī, *making* Lakṣmī's *bowl overgenerous to Your Vedic worshippers,*
Such the twin lotus of Your feet, it triumphs: O Mother, what wonder herein?

In verse eighty-seven the twin feet are treated together, and not as one plus one. With this secret in mind, we get the intended meaning more easily than if the theory of ensembles involved here is not duly respected at the very start. In order to treat the twin feet as an ensemble consisting of two items of the same class it would be helpful for us to put a circle, or even the three circles of the *śrī cakra*, around them, placed at the central locus of meditation.

There are three sets of lotuses in this verse which have to be arranged in pairs to fulfil the requirements of the correct structuralism intended in these verses. A hierophantic lotus is likely to be killed by snow, but a golden lotus placed at a high hypostatic level would thrive even in a very cold temperature. These two lotuses have thus to be placed in a vertical axis at different levels. There are two other lotuses in the second line which are to be placed horizontally because of the alternation of day and night, and which are not as generalized and abstracted as the first pair of lotuses.

In the third and fourth lines the ensemble represented by the two feet compared to lotuses have no horizontal or vertical duality implied between them. They are compared to the bowl of Lakṣmī, though placed at a lower level, in a more ordinary workaday world, where hedonistic and relativistic interests are still natural and permissible. We have seen that Lakṣmī is the goddess of Wealth, whom those who want to become rich in this life naturally treat as their chosen divinity. Śaṅkara is evidently thinking here of the Tāntric school of the Samayins, who belong to the revised and more respectable Vedic context, as against the Kaulins who connive at certain disreputable practices, though perhaps in a manner more correctly fulfilling the requirements of Tantra in other respects. There is, however, one respect in which the description here does not fit the Samayins. Overgenerousness is an absolutist virtue which cannot strictly apply to a relativistic and hedonistic context such as is actually proper to the Vedic school under reference. This distinction, between just granting prayers and granting more than what is prayed for, has been brought into its correctly revised perspective by Śaṅkara as early as verse four, where the feet of the Goddess alone were considered to be expert in yielding 'more-than-asked-for boon'. This is a touch of revaluation coming from Śaṅkara, of which the Samayins could be taken to be ignorant.

We have to further note that the Sanskrit language has singular, dual and plural numbers, and not merely singular and plural as in most languages. Here the twin feet could be treated as a singular ensemble, or as being dualistic when each foot has got a distinguishable characteristic of its own. Both of these syntactical requirements are meant to be respected in this verse, as we can see by scrutinizing the antecedents of the words *pādau* (twin feet) and *jayataḥ* (they triumph) where the dual verb agrees with a dual noun. Strict syntactical requirements would demand a separate verb to agree with what should be treated in the singular. Amends for this kind of grammatical discrepancy seem to be made quickly by Śaṅkara at the end of the verse, where it says 'what wonder herein!' This is as good as saying that even if there is an impossibility hiding here, the absolutist status intended to be given to the two feet treated together, when understood in all its uniqueness as an ensemble with a unity of meaning in itself and for itself, should not be treated as anything unexpected. In other words, one should not wonder. There is still room for miracles in this world. The Absolute itself is a miracle, and one should not be surprised to find it so.

The reference in the second line to two kinds of lotuses could be treated as referring to a sensitive lotus, like an ordinary lotus, and one that is not sensitive and does not change whether it is day or night. The sensitive lotus would correspond to the virtuality or subjectivity implied in a dream state. Ordinary flowers which have no such sensitivity to light are like the wakeful consciousness, lacking subjectivity altogether. This is a horizontal difference between the positive and negative aspects quantitatively understood, as between plus and minus numbers in the context of Cartesian correlates. They do not refer to the imaginary numbers of incommensurables, which have a deeper and more theoretical transfinite reference. Complex numbers belong together as understood here.

88

पदं ते कीर्तीनां प्रपदमपदं देवि विपदां
कथं नीतं सद्भिः कठिनकमठीकर्परतुलाम्।
कथंवाबाहुभ्यामुपयमनकाले पुरभिदा
यदादाय न्यस्तं दृषदि दयमानेन मनसा॥

padaṁ te kīrtīnāṁ prapadam apadaṁ devi vipadām
kathaṁ nītaṁ sadbhiḥ kaṭhina kamaṭhīkarpara tulām ।
kathaṁ vā bāhubhyām upayamana kāle purabhidā
yad ādāya nyastaṁ dṛṣadi dayamānena manasā ॥

devī - *O Goddess; padaṁ te kīrtīnāṁ prapadaṁ* — Your foot is the supreme seat of good repute; *apadaṁ vipadām kathaṁ nītaṁ* — how then from danger was it led to its denial (with no room for dangers, how did it come to be considered...?) *sadbhiḥ kaṭhina kamaṭhī karpara tulā* — (considered) by the good (poets or writers) as equal in hardness to the tortoise shell; *kathaṁ vā* — however could it have been; *bāhubhyām* — by both hands; *upayamana kāle* — at (his) wedding time; *purabhidā* — by the Destroyer of Cities; *yat ādāya nyastaṁ* — the same was taken and placed; *dṛṣadi* — on the ritual stone (mashing-stone); *dayamānena manasā* — with tender mind (melting with kindness)

Your foot is the supreme seat for good repute, O Goddess;
How then from danger to safety did it come?
The wise treat it as of tortoise-shell hardness; how then was it that Śiva,
At his wedding, could lift it with tender mind to place it on the ritual stone?

In verse eighty-eight the wonder of the previous verse, by which miracles are to be expected as normal, is carried over into the domain of semantic polyvalence. Punning is not considered quite respectable in societies that conform to conventional standards, but Shakespeare indulges in it very frequently. Homer's *Odyssey* contains the story of how Ulysses, along with his fellow travellers, escaped from the cavern of the Cyclops by giving his name as 'No man'. Great poets have such licence, which heightens the quality of their poetry instead of detracting from it. In this verse, Śaṅkara freely indulges in Sanskrit words which seem to contain a mystery based on the interplay of sounds and meanings. In analytic psychology this tendency is looked upon as a low form of association reflecting psychotic states. It is elsewhere understood, however, that poets, madmen and lovers have the same kind of imagination. Viewed in this light, this verse continues the vague background of wonder proper to a devotee whose instincts are stronger than the workings of his intelligence. We have, therefore, not to look for any strict consistency of meaning here. Words and their meanings blend into a beautiful confection, which we are asked to enjoy.

In spite of this, there are vague traces of suggested meaning which we can extract, which, by abolishing paradox, heighten the sense of wonder with reference to the same beautiful pair of feet, which are now again to be put at the focal point or the *bindusthāna* for us to meditate upon. The first two lines, as before, contain a paradox which is of a conceptual, semantic, and semiotic order. The second half of the verse refers to a more realistic paradox in which something rigidly solid is still capable of being treated as something supple. If the former is a metaphysical wonder, taking us beyond paradox, the latter is a physical wonder which heightens the wonder still more than by abolishing paradox altogether. The word *padam* can suggest both 'the feet' and a state sufficiently stable with an idea contained in it, representing an absolute Value. *Padam* (a state) and *apadam* (a non-state) are used interchangeably and figuratively as referring to states of mind.

When thinking of the value represented by the two lotus-feet of the Goddess, two opposite perspectives, belonging to two ambivalent attributes that could be applied to them, could be suggested together to the mind. Normally the feet of a goddess could be treated as the seat of good reputation (*kīrti*). The Bhagavadgītā gives good reputation the first place among absolutist virtues which can embellish the beauty-value of womanhood. As a leading virtue belonging to the bright side of life, good repute could be an attribute applicable to the feet of the Goddess, when viewed from a hypostatic perspective. When the same feet are viewed from the negative standpoint, they could have a dark tragic connotation. These two ambivalent meanings, especially when an element of punning enters into the style, gives this kind of poetry a special appeal. The three words *padam*, *prapadam* and *apadam* employed here are seen to be pressed into service as apt alliterations and as fully artful aids. Epigrammatic pithiness indicates a bright form of literary ability. Nominalism and structuralism are being employed here as if one wants to outdo the other. The first half of the verse suggests that at the lower limit there is a tragic import attached to the feet, which has now been sublimated and cancelled out.

The second half refers to the ritualistic custom in which the husband must make the wife stand on a mashing stone for curry spices and look at one of the small stars, hardly visible to the eye, near the tail-end of the constellation Orion. This is the test of a long and happy married life. Whether the test failed or succeeded, it was adopted because of its ceremonial impressiveness, while relating human destiny with the movements of the stars.

When both of these suggestive representations of polyvalent meaning of meanings are treated together, there is a common characteristic of some value which could be called numinous, as opposed to phenomenal. It is the touch of the numinous that is to heighten the beauty value when the two instances are treated together, as referring to existence and subsistence, to produce a value.

The reference to the wise treating the leg as of tortoise-shell hardness must refer either to some definite mythology somewhere in the eighteen epics in Sanskrit, or in the Tamil epics such as the *Śiva Purāṇa*. As mythologies generally are meant to suggest deeper philosophical truths, we could guess here that the feet of the Goddess is where ontology attains to its maximum richness. In this sense it could be treated as solid matter, rather than anything flexible like a piece of wax. Solidity and liquidity have between them an element of paradox, even in the world of solid existences. That must be the reason why such a reference becomes pertinent here.

Further, we note that the mind of Śiva was in a melted state of kindness or compassion, while the feet of Pārvatī were supposed by the wise to be concrete and rigid. The paradox results from a cross-reference from matter to mind, implying a transfer, or interchangeability of epithets. This is another touch that is meant to heighten the paradox in the domain of semantic polyvalence as applied to the significance of the beauty of the feet of the Goddess.

89

नखैर्नाकस्त्रीणां करकमलसंकोचशशिभि-
स्तरूणां दिव्यानां हसत इव ते चण्डि चरणौ।
फलानि स्वस्थेभ्यः किसलयकराग्रेण ददतां
दरिद्रेभ्यो भद्रां श्रियमनिशमह्नाय ददतौ॥

nakhair nākastrīṇāṁ karakamala saṁkoca śaśibhis-
tarūṇāṁ divyānāṁ hasata iva te caṇḍi caraṇau ।
phalāni svasthebhyaḥ kisalaya karāgreṇa dadatāṁ
daridrebhyo bhadrāṁ śriyam aniśam ahnāya dadatau ॥

caṇḍi — O Tragic One; *kara kamala saṁkoca śaśibhiḥ nakhaiḥ* — moon-like nails that put to shame the lotus hands; *nāka strīṇāṁ* — of celestial damsels; *te caraṇau* — Your feet; *divyānāṁ tarūṇāṁ hasataḥ iva* — seem to mock celestial trees; *svaḥ sthebhyaḥ* — (only) to heaven-dwellers; *phalāni dadatāṁ* — offer fruits; *kisalaya karāgreṇa* — with leaf-tender fingertips; *daridrebhyaḥ* — to the poor; *bhadrāṁ śriyam* — secure riches (auspicious well-being); *aniśam* — incessantly; *ahnāya* — instantly; *dadatau* — they (the feet) offer/bring

**With (toe)nails like moons, putting to shame the lotus hands of celestial damsels,*

O Tragic one, Caṇḍī, *Your feet seem to mock celestial trees*

That offer fruit only to heaven-dwellers, with their leaf-tender fingertips,

(While) they (the twin feet) bring secure riches to the poor, instantly and incessantly.

---

*This is how the verse read in the earlier edition:

With nails like moons, putting to shame the lotus hands of celestial damsels,
And feet that seem to mock celestial trees,
O Tragic One, Caṇḍi, *Your twin feet offer fruit to heaven-dwellers*
And with leaf-tender fingertips, bring secure riches to the poor instantly and incessantly.

A biological analogy is resorted to in verse eighty-nine, rather than a semantic one. States of consciousness were involved in the wonder of verse eighty-seven. The beauty of a tree can be recognized by the magenta-coloured tender shoots which resemble lotus buds. The fingernails could represent the growing points of trees as they unfold the tips of their leaf buds, resembling outstretched hands, trying, as it were, to propitiate heaven by fit offerings from below. The moon is also a biological object in heaven, but it is stated here in the first line that the beauty of moonlight is nothing compared to the beauty of the tender offering of colourful sprouts marking the topmost limit of the structure of a tree. The trees in heaven must have slender stems, corresponding to their refined grade in the scale of hypostatic values. The feet of the Goddess, in such a superfine or superior context, could mock the stems of celestial trees by superior strength or stability, because the Absolute has an equal reference to heaven and earth.

In the second half of this verse, the aspect of the Goddess is seen in a slightly revised perspective. She is no longer a delicate celestial damsel, but is here called Caṇḍi (one with a terrible or tragic touch in her character). Caṇḍi (Kālī) is darker in colour, but what she loses by way of delicacy or refinement, she gains on the side of ontology.

These two polarized perspectives of the same absolute Goddess yield contrasting pictures which are meant to be cancelled out against each other, and not to be treated as permitting any duality to persist between them. One is a horizontalized version of the other, which is the same viewed in a more transparent aspect, where concepts merge instead of being exclusive of each other. The mind participates equally with the two domains, where conflicts could be recognized so that they could be transcended. The feet of the latter Goddess are planted on the earth with full firmness or stability. Here she knows exactly what she wants, because ontology is richer in the content of certitude. The Vedanta of Śaṅkara does not reject the importance of the *pratyakṣa*, that is, what is given to the senses. Experimental evidence is not to be explained away to lift the Absolute out of a workaday context, making it something holy or celestial with an 'ivory tower' isolation or superiority. In this more ontologically biased version the tender leaves are not omitted, but the tragic touch of earthiness is a quality that not only tries to please the heavenly gods, but is sympathetic to the needs of the poorer men on earth. Śaṅkara seems to vote for the latter version, because duality is seen to be more thoroughly abolished in it. This does not mean, however, that heaven-dwellers are to be left starving. The beauty of the Goddess suggested in the first two lines is good enough, but what is suggested in the second half is better. Neither of them is to be rejected, but they are to be fitted correctly into the total context of a non-dual absolute value called Beauty.

The qualifications 'secure riches to the poor instantly and incessantly' makes happiness refer to a here-and-now world, rather than to a promised land which theologians might hold out for believers. Religion is full of promises which may or may not be realized. Politicians also fall under the same category, often without admitting it. The results are instantaneous when ontology is given its full place, and the benefits are more generally applicable. The satisfaction of the needy is more important than the fantasies of the chosen few, who think of going to heaven first before having a life free from scarcity of basic needs here. The dialectics is between the 'good of all' and the 'general good'. In the eyes of Advaita both are equally important. It is not 'either/or' but 'both together' that is to be kept as our aim, hope or idea.

ददाने दीनेभ्यः श्रियमनिशमाशानुसदृशी-
ममन्दं सौन्दर्यप्रकरमकरन्दं विकिरति ।
तवास्मिन् मन्दारस्तबकसुभगे यातु चरणे
निमज्जन् मज्जीवः करणचरणः षट्चरणताम् ॥

dadāne dīnebhyaḥ śriyam aniśam āśānusadṛśīm
amandaṁ saundarya prakara makarnadaṁ vikirati ।
tavāsmin mandāra stabaka subhage yātu caraṇe
nimajjan majjīvaḥ karaṇa caraṇaḥ ṣaṭ caraṇatām ॥

dīnebhyaḥ — to the needy; *āśānu sadṛśīm* — according to desire; *śriyam aniśam* — wealth incessantly; *dadāne* — giving; *saundarya prakara makarandaṁ* — the honey of the celestial blossoms of beauty; *amandaṁ* — plentifully/not slowly; *vikirati* — scattering/distributing all around; *asmin tava caraṇe* — into these Your feet; *mandāra stabaka subhage* — of the beauty of a cluster of celestial blooms; *nimajjan* — immersed (merged); *mat jīvaḥ* — my life; *karaṇa caraṇaḥ* — (with) the inner organs for feet; *ṣaṭ caraṇatām* — into (the state of) six-footed beehood; *yātu* — let (it) attain

Giving riches incessantly to the needy as required, and of the store of honey
Of the celestial blossoms of beauty, distributing plentifully all around;
Into such beauty of the celestial blooms of Your feet,
Let my life go immersed, with limbs and inner organs, into six-footed beehood.

The ninetieth verse brings the two counterparts into closer integration so as to put the seal on them and close the subject, which still refers to the feet of the Goddess. We can see that a certain concession is made in this revised picture in favour of the teleological rather than the ontological, but the unitive character of the values involved is intended to be maintained as a constant, common to the series referring to the twin feet that began with verse eighty-four. The centre of interest can move lower or higher, but the absolute Value-content is still maintained as a constant. The needy people are seen to be satisfied first, but the celestial values are also distributed generously all around without considerations of high or low. The cluster of celestial blooms is inserted, permitting different levels, high or low, within the scope or amplitude of values in the third line, and the ontological aspect has passed from the beauty that is worshipped to the Self of the worshipper, who now compares himself to a six-footed insect, which is the bee that seeks the honey at the core of flower-blossoms. The final term of spirituality is when the non-Self aspect, which is to be objectively enjoyed, and the Self aspect, which is the enjoyer, distinguished as the *bhogya* and the *bhoktā* by Vedantic tradition, are finally cancelled out to accomplish what is called *sāyujya* (union or immersion of the relative into the Absolute). The devotee is so wholehearted in his bipolar affiliation that he goes to the extent of saying that his very life should be abolished, so as to become merged in the absolute Value. The comparison to a bee is a favourite one. The individual personality of an aspirant could have three levels, each with two sides, representing the three *karaṇa*s (inner instruments or organs), which are, *buddhi* (intelligence), *citta* (relational mind) and *ahaṁkāra* (ego sense). *Karaṇa* and *caraṇa* are used together here. *Karaṇa* represents the three instruments which we have just enumerated. *Caraṇa* refers to the feet, such as those of an insect, including the beetle, if it is necessary to think of an alternative. *Ṣaṭcaraṇata* means 'insecthood'.

The feet of an insect are outward organs of action; the three instruments are inner organs of understanding. Action and understanding are guided by the five senses and the mind, which are not mentioned here. This omission must be intentional, because it is the denominator status of the bee that can properly cancel out against the numerator factor of sense alternation, such as colour, smell, et cetera, applicable to the five senses and the mind. By the identity of interest in the content of the flower, the senses and the mind are, in effect, already cancelled, especially when the bee is sitting inside the flower after establishing a wholehearted bipolarity of relationship between the enjoyer and the enjoyed. What remains still to be absorbed or lost into the context of the absolute Value, represented by the beauty of the feet of the Goddess, are the inner organs and the three pairs of feet making six (which is a specific characteristic of the zoological group called *Insecta*).

Insecthood is thus still to be cancelled out against the positive qualities of the flower, which it seeks wholeheartedly to enjoy. The suggested idea is that the aspirant is praying for a wholehearted cancellation between subjective and objective aspects of beauty, so that even life itself could be abolished in favour of what the absolute Value, represented here by the feet, could represent. The limit of a wholehearted affiliation is thus marked by the favourite picture of a bee sucking honey within a flower, having values ranging from celestial to earthly ones without any duality between them. It is permitted here to think of a hierarchy of beautiful feet arranged tier on tier, touching both earthly and heavenly values in an ascending as well as descending order, neutralized at every point of the scale.

91

पदन्यासक्रीडापरिचयमिवारब्धुमनसः
स्खलन्तस्ते खेलं भवनकलहंसा न जहति ।
अतस्तेषां शिक्षां सुभगमणिमञ्जीररणित-
च्छलादाचक्षाणं चरणकमलं चारुचरिते ॥

padanyāsa krīḍā paricayam ivārabdhumanasaḥ
skhalantaste khelaṁ bhavana kalahaṁsā na jahati ।
atasteṣāṁ śikṣāṁ subhaga maṇi mañjira raṇitac-
chalād ācakṣāṇaṁ caraṇa kamalaṁ cāru carite ॥

cāru carite — O One of graceful gait; *pada nyāsa kṛīḍā paricayam* — practising the sportive pose of steps; *ārabdhu manasaḥ* — intending to begin; *bhavana kala haṁsāḥ* — the domesticated cygnets; *skhalantaḥ* — (though) still with faults; *te khelaṁ* — Your lovely gait; *na jahati* — do not give up; *ataḥ caraṇa kamalaṁ* — therefore (Your) lotus feet; *subhaga maṇi mañjīra raṇita* — with auspicious sound of gem-set anklets; *cchalāt* — in the guise of/imitating; *tesāṁ śikṣāṁ* — their instruction; *ācakṣāṇaṁ iva* — as if giving

Your domesticated cygnets, intent on learning from You the sportive pose of steps,
Practising, still with faults, O One of graceful gait, on their not giving up;
With the sound of gem-set anklets imitating,
It would seem now that You are instructing them.

In verse ninety-one the overall context of the scene represented is that of a teacher and many disciples. It is in and around the leg region of the Goddess that the interest still lingers, starting as it did even in verse eighty-two. Beauty is more easily described when it refers to the face than to the feet, but Vedanta insists on giving equal value to both. That is the reason why Śaṅkara seems to take extra trouble to present a picture where the high function of teaching disciples is still the overall theme. Sarasvatī can teach the three gods, who are her admirers or disciples. They are represented in previous verses as bending before her footstool or standing inclined and overcovering it.

Here it is not a question of brahmins, saints, or divinities that are applicants for discipleship. The disciples here consist of little swans, or cygnets, whose attachment to the Goddess is because they want to learn from her the beautiful way in which she poses her steps when she walks, or even dances. Posing of steps correctly is a first lesson when learning to dance, next perhaps to rolling of the eyes and sharp movements of the neck. When legs are properly posed there is the sound of jingle bells fixed to the anklets which can have a firm and united resonance, which is sometimes imitated verbally by dance teachers, when footwork happens to be important. Instead of jingle bells, the anklets themselves are here stated to be filled with gems. If the anklets are made with silver or gold there is a certain firm metallic beauty in the sound.

It is not the sound of the gem-set anklets alone that comes into the picture. The Goddess while teaching, out of consideration even for subhuman disciples, takes the trouble of imitating the sound of the gem-set jewelled anklets as the feet are gracefully planted, as they ought to be, in correct dance poses. Sanskrit literature often describes the gait of a beautiful woman as one that resembles the way a swan walks. This might be a good enough comparison when the feminine features of the body of a woman are meant to be represented naturally and not artificially viewed. The cygnets are nearer to the ideal of the swan-gait, but they themselves are not satisfied with such a maladroit way of walking. Nature has always to be corrected by nurture to complete education, in the same way that decorative embellishments can enhance the beauty of an otherwise crude beauty found in nature. The prostitutes of Ujjain are seen to score in this respect in the writings of Kālidāsa.

When we consider that absolute Beauty involves cancellation of both numerator and denominator, it is not difficult to understand here why the young swans want to add to their natural gait something, for which they are willing to pay the price of learning through great insistence and trouble, so that their beauty could approximate to what might be called absolute Beauty. It might be asked here why Kālidāsa did not give silk garments to increase the beauty of Śakuntalā, and actually said that anything, even a rag or a bark-cloth, could only enhance the superior beauty which is already there in the person of Śakuntalā herself, descended as she was from the celestial damsel Menakā. The prerequisite is therefore not a decoration in itself, or naturalness in itself, but the cancellation of the one against other. The gem-set anklets represent an existent numerator value, but the living voice of the teacher, which imitates the sound of the gem-filled anklets as they are posed gracefully on the ground, adds further numerator accentuation to the beauty that belongs to the plus-side of the situation. When a woman is heavy in her gait and moves slowly along, like a swan when it walks on land, she is described as *vilāsinī* (having accentuated attributes or characteristics of womanhood fully expressed through her beauty). Sanskrit poets revel in such descriptions of womanhood. Here Śaṅkara purposely, it would seem, applies a corrective to this one-sided picture. He accomplishes this by bringing in a gem-filled anklet with a metallic sound, to supply a correct numerator to an otherwise negatively accentuated picture of feminine beauty. The full numerator side becomes added on to the total negative situation when the living voice of the Goddess is represented here as imitating the metallic sound, instead of treating it as inferior, as previously hinted at.

Teacher/pupil relationship is the background on which such a cancellation of counterparts takes place. It is when we remember that it is very difficult to represent beauty when it pertains to the existent side, that this representation of beauty gains a character as overwhelmingly absolutist in its value as the beauty in any other so-called superior context such as that of heavenly blossoms. The domesticated cygnets are treated with as much consideration as the students of the Vedas in a gurukula. The overall dignity of the beauty is thus retained as a constant even here.

There is a reference to the faults that enhance the beauty, rather than spoil it. Birds can be heard in the morning to be repeating some lessons as if to learn them by heart. They can also be heard to hesitate when they can not help making mistakes, on which they stop singing for a while. The lispings of children are beautiful in spite of the errors, and not because they are correct. Imitation of the sound of the anklets is two degrees removed from the actual, in that the sound itself reflects the firmness of the pose of the legs, of which the imitation by the voice of the Goddess is of a second degree.

The process of instruction, and not the actual instruction, is what is to be treated as the essence of the situation here portrayed. This explains the need for the last line, as a finishing touch added to the description.

92

गतास्ते मञ्चत्वं द्रुहिणहरिरुद्रेश्वरभृतः
शिवः स्वच्छच्छायाघटितकपटप्रच्छदपटः ।
त्वदीयानां भासां प्रतिफलनरागारुणतया
शरीरी शृङ्गारो रस इव दृशां दोग्धि कुतुकम् ॥

gatās te mañcatvaṁ druhiṇa hari rudreśvara bhṛtaḥ
śivaḥ svaccha cchāyāghaṭita kapaṭa pracchada paṭaḥ ।
tvadīyānāṁ bhāsāṁ pratiphalana rāgāruṇatayā
śarīrī śṛṅgāro rasa iva dṛśāṁ dogdhi kutukam ॥

gatāḥ te mañcatvaṁ — gone as they are to Your couchhood; *druhiṇa hari rudreśvara bhṛtaḥ* — Brahmā, Viṣṇu, Rudra, Īśvara and others, your servants; *śivaḥ* — Śiva; *svaccha cchāyā ghaṭita kapaṭa pracchada paṭaḥ* — wearing a deceptive canopy derived from His crystal light; *tvadīyānāṁ bhāsāṁ* — (by) Your radiance projected; *pratiphalana rāga aruṇatayā* — turning (it) into a magenta shade; *śṛṅgāra rasaḥ* — (of) erotic bliss; *śarīrī iva* — as if the embodiment; *dṛśāṁ* — the view; *kutukam dogdhi* — (He) charms (lit. milks)

Gone as they are to Your couchhood, Brahmā, Viṣṇu, Rudra, Īśvara and others —
Śiva, wearing a deceptive canopy derived from his crystal light;
By Your radiance projected on to it and turned to a magenta shade,
As the very embodiment of erotic bliss, He charms the view.

In verse ninety-two the reference to the beauty of the legs is finally abandoned in favour of the legs of a couch on which the Goddess is sitting. We had in verse eight, almost symmetrically situated with the present one, a reference to the actual picture of a goddess seated on a couch which represented a metamorphosis of the person of Śiva himself. In the context of

Hermetic philosophy this is known as the principle of correspondence, shown by the tarot card of the man hanging head downward. There is a subtle inversion, what Bergson would call 'a back to back relation', or a correlation between the world of concepts and the world of percepts. Bergson even goes to the extent of saying that 'we happen to accidents' and not the other way about, as we might think. An epistemology and methodology proper to such a view, which we have to learn to understand as a possible philosophical perspective, is quite in keeping with Vedanta and the structure of the Absolute known to it. We cannot enter into the discussion of such a viewpoint here.

Śiva, as a crystal-clear value placed at the omega point in the vertical axis, can lend his own teleological reality to natural objects such as the couch, which is here referred to in the first line as being comprised of his sub-functionaries within the Absolute, who are divinities placed at a lower level. When reflected on the side of percepts, they could in principle lend support to the ontological stability or firmness of the couch on which the Goddess, occupying the neutral point between the two extremes, is to be located or seated. The Śiva principle is not expended by the secondary functions that he sanctions from his own higher position. His crystal-clear pure principle, of a conceptual order, can take the deceptive form of a canopy which could have at first, before he descends too low towards the couch, a clearer complexion or colour participating more closely with the numerator than with the central magenta of the mid-region occupied by the Goddess. Such a clear canopy, however, as it descends toward the centre from above, could have a borrowed magenta colour playing on it.

Thus the canopy would, by its revised and more ontological conditioning with reference to the central magenta glory that the Goddess always represents, appear to be magenta, while really being crystal clear in colour. The real can be conditioned by the false, and vice versa. The resultant indeterminism or ambiguity belongs to maya. Eroticism is proper to the negative side, but it looks as if the positive side is also conditioned by the same quality. This is another example of mutual participation/ conditioning (*anyonya adhyāsa*), of which we have had more delicate instances, as in the description of the lips and the teeth in verse sixty-two, and in other verses. Eroticism, as the last line makes clear, is meant here only to charm the view, and add to the beauty value of the situation represented here.

93

अराला केशेषु प्रकृतिसरला मन्दहसिते
शिरीषाभा चित्ते दृषदुपलशोभा कुचतटे ।
भृशं तन्वी मध्ये पृथुरुरसिजारोहविषये
जगत् त्रातुं शंभोर्जयति करुणा काचिदरुणा ॥

arālā keśeṣu prakṛti saralā mandahasite
śirīṣābhā citte dṛṣad upalaśobhā kucataṭe ।
bhṛśaṁ tanvī madhye pṛthur urasijāroha viṣaye
jagat trātuṁ śaṁbhor jayati karuṇā kācid aruṇā ॥

arālā keśeṣu — curly of hair; *prakṛti saralā manda hasite* — with smile of natural simplicity; *śirīṣābhā citte* — with mind having magenta flower-supple glory (of the *Acacia sirisa*); *dṛṣat upala śobhā kuca taṭe* — at the bust region like a (kitchen) mashing-stone; *bhṛśaṁ tanvī madhye* — extremely slender of waist; *urasija āroha viṣaye pṛthuḥ* — in the matter of shoulders and hips solid/heavy; *jagat trātuṁ* — to save the world; *jayati* — she triumphs/reigns supreme; *śaṁbhoḥ karuṇā kācid* — a certain kindliness of Śiva; *aruṇā* — (called) magenta

Curly in hair and with a smile of natural simplicity, with a magenta flower-supple mind,
Bust firm like a (kitchen) mashing-stone, extremely slender at waist,
With solid shoulders and hips, thus the world to save,
She reigns supreme, a certain kindliness of Śiva called magenta.

In verse ninety-three we have the picture of a common girl whose beauty is of a plain and straightforward kind with nothing glamorous about it. This does not, however, detract from the absolute quality that belongs to it, which we have to try to discern in and through the common earthy touches with which her beauty is here painted in straightforward simplicity. Great painters sometimes produce pictures of a simple girl holding an apple or a rose in her hand. Great masters can succeed in giving just those touches which will make such paintings have an eternal value to those who can genuinely appreciate the value of art. Good art requires people to appreciate it.

The bust is here seen to be compared to a kitchen utensil instead of any heavenly lotus. Her hips and shoulders are firm because she must be a kind of peasant girl used to hard work. The simplicity of her mind is transparently revealed by her smile. She is capable of being extremely sympathetic, having, as it is stated here, 'a magenta flower-supple mind'. Her function, as stated in the third line, is no less than the most important one that we could ever think of: that is, of saving what Śiva would otherwise destroy. Thus she represents in herself a concentrated negative value capable of supplying an adequate denominator to the positive forces of destruction that might put the whole world in danger at a given moment. The common touch in her looks is therefore not to be despised. She is not represented as wearing any jewels or decorations, but her matter-of-fact plainness is of sufficient beauty to her in itself, the value of which she never doubts for a moment.

The only embellishment is the colour magenta, which uniformly overcovers and pervades her personality. Magenta being an absolute Colour among all colours (by addition or subtraction from which any other tint, shade or brilliance — whether of chromatic or achromatic colours — is derivable, as known to the modern colour-film technique), she needs no further coatings of paint or thinning of what already is there. Inner brilliance, fully saturating the colour effect from inside, could be presupposed by us, because in the last line she is said to reign supreme as the very personification of Kindliness, expressed through her mere magenta presence, sufficient unto itself.

Kindliness as a quality can be thought of as having a capital letter, raising it fully to the status of an absolute value at least as dignified as what Śiva, from his own theoretical side, could represent in his person when looked upon as distinct from the

Devī. Separating the two principles, however, is not correct. One has rather to say that the beauty of the Goddess is the same as that of Śiva and vice versa. The slightly ontological bias of Vedantic methodology can, however, be permitted to tilt the delicate balance involved here, in the present series at least, in favour of the Goddess, instead of the God. This is only a methodological necessity. Doctrinally, the same Advaita remains valid.

94

कलङ्कः कस्तूरी रजनिकरबिम्बं जलमयं
कलाभिः कर्पूरैर्मरतककरण्डं निबिडितम्।
अतस्त्वद्भोगेन प्रतिदिनमिदं रिक्तकुहरं
विधिर्भूयो भूयो निबिडयति नूनं तव कृते॥

kaḷaṅkaḥ kastūrī rajanikara bimbaṁ jalamayaṁ
kalābhiḥ karpūrair marataka karandaṁ nibiditaṁ ।
atas tvad bhogena pratidinam idaṁ rikta kuharaṁ
vidhir bhūyo bhūyo nibidayati nūnaṁ tava kr̥te ॥

kaḷaṅkaḥ — the dark zone; *kastūrī* — (is) musk; *rajanikara bimbaṁ jala mayaṁ* — the orb of the moon is watery; *kalābhiḥ karpūraiḥ* — the phases of the moon are camphor (bits); *nibiḍitaṁ* — filled/packed (into); *marataka karaṇḍaṁ* — box/casket (made) of ebony; *pratidinam* — daily; *tvat bhogena* — by Your joys; *idaṁ rikta kuharaṁ* — this (which is) emptied; *ataḥ* — therefore; *vidhiḥ* — Brahmā; *bhūyaḥ bhūyaḥ* — again and again; *tava kr̥te* — for Your sake; *nibiḍayati nūnaṁ* — fills up indeed

The dark zone of the moon is musk; the orb of the moon is watery;
The moon's phases are camphor bits filling a box of ebony,
Which, when emptied daily by Your joys,
For Your sake, Brahmā fills up again and again

In verse ninety-four we come to a very complex structural content, representing beauty which is placed within the context of darkness or night, here referred to as a black box of ebony. The box is suggestive of a real, existent object. We see that cosmological, psychological and theological entities are meant to create this picture of the negative aspect of beauty, which is of the nature of existence rather than of essence. Musk and camphor are favourite examples of objects which can change into more pervious essences in spite of being existent objects.

The duality between existence and essence has been the cause of much philosophical controversy from scholastic times to the present day. Indian philosophy tends to speak in terms of existence, as when the Bhagavadgītā refers to the sapidity of the waters as a *rasa*, or taste, and identifies it with the absolute personality of Krishna himself who says, 'I am the sapidity of the waters' (VII.8).

The composite picture presented in this verse brings existence and essence into relief as items that are contained in a black box belonging to the Goddess, who is supposed to expend them in the form of the joys that she might have during the course of each day. The moon is the presiding orb during the night, and it is in the context of the night that enjoyments of a negative order become operative, thus tending to make the essences either disappear by permeation into the air, or by being changed into heat and light, as in the cases of musk and camphor respectively. Musk is a negative existent form of matter that spreads its perfume subtly throughout an enclosed room. The beauty of the night sky is compared to a jewel box by philosophers like Kant and poets like Shelley.

We have here to think of a living room of the Goddess, who is placed within a cosmological context of the alternating waxing and waning of moonlight. It is not the bright side of the moon with which we are directly concerned here, but rather with the negative or dark side of moonlight. As in Shakespeare's reference to the 'watery moon', even from ancient times the affinities of the moon have been proverbially understood as belonging to the side of water rather than to the side of fire. The moon's phases have already been compared to camphor bits in verse sixty-five. These have to be replaced after a fortnight, but if we think of what is expended instead of what is gained, the light that is lost each day can be said to need replacement after each night's enjoyment of erotic pleasures on the part of the Goddess. Thus, in the last line it is stated that Brahmā, the creator, whose function is connected with eternal regeneration, fills the dark ebony box with what has been lost each day. There is a compensatory metabolism in terms of existences and essences in the combined context of cosmology, psychology and theology evident here. The overall perspective, however, still remains negative, as it is the contents of the black ebony box that occupy the focus of interest in this verse. Beauty seen from the dark side, rather than from the bright side, as subjected to daily increase or decrease is the overall theme. We know that in an ordinary physical metabolism food is transformed into caloric units of energy to be spent by the mechanistic activities of each day. This verse attains to the same kind of diurnally alternating metabolism, connected not with any physiological system, but to an aspect of personal life where subtler enjoyments are involved. Instead of getting exhausted by such enjoyments, it is to be seen that every time enjoyment expends the existent essences involved, they are to be replenished by the god of creation himself. Thus, life goes on eternally in the form of a perpetual alternating motion, as between the getting and spending of existential essences. In spite of this alternating process, what emerges out of the total situation is a form of dark-splendid beauty more proper to a Kālī than to a Sarasvatī. Even in this late verse it is ontology that has primacy over teleology. This viewpoint is underlined by the analogy of the ebony box. Śyāmala, 'the Dark One', is an epithet that is applied to this kind of absolute Goddess, seen from the negative perspective.

95

पुरारातेरन्तःपुरमसि ततस्त्वच्चरणयोः
सपर्यामर्यादा तरलकरणानामसुलभा।
तथा ह्येते नीताः शतमखमुखाः सिद्धिमतुलां
तव द्वारोपान्तस्थितिभिरणिमाद्याभिरमराः ॥

purārāter antaḥpuram asi tatas tvac caraṇayoḥ
saparyā maryādā tarala karaṇānām asulabhā ।
tathā hyete nītāḥ śatamakhamukhāḥ siddhim atulāṁ
tava dvāropānta sthitibhir aṇimādyābhir amarāḥ ॥

(tvam — You); *purārāteḥ* — of the City Burner (Śiva); *antaḥ puram asi* — are the consort (living in the inner apartments); *tataḥ* — by reason of this; *tvat caraṇayoḥ* — as applied to Your feet; *saparyā maryādā* — the equivalent of the way of worship; *tarala karaṇānām* — for those with unstable inner faculties; *asulabhā* — not easy to gain; *tathā hi* — this is surely (why); *śatamakha mukhāḥ ete amarāḥ* — these divinities with Indra as their chief (might have had); *siddhim atulāṁ* — limitless gains/unequalled psychic powers; *aṇimādyābhiḥ* — such as atomicity etc.; *tava* — (from) Your; *dvāropānta sthitibhiḥ* — standing just outside Your door; *nītāḥ* — they got (them)

You being the consort of Śiva, it is difficult indeed
For unsettled minds to attain to the equivalent of the way of Your worship;
Whatever limitless gains they, the divinities such as Indra and others might have had,
Those psychic powers such as aṇimā, *from just outside Your door they got them.*

In verse ninety-five Śaṅkara intends to sound a warning applicable to what he has been so far trying to hold up to view as a superior example of absolute Beauty. He says now that there could be a majority of people for whom this way of looking at beauty, from a feminine and negative standpoint, might be prejudicial to their spiritual progress. Most human beings are interested in gaining some kind of advantage for themselves while they continue to live here on earth. Transcendental values can interest only rare individuals whose minds have been first established in the context of the true contemplation of the Absolute, in which salvation, and not any other hedonistic or relativistic advantage, is to be gained. This is because most people are likely to forget that the Goddess is to be treated as the correct counterpart of Śiva, who is well known to be the greatest of austere personages. He is a model ascetic, so the Goddess, as his consort, cannot be like any other woman. In order to be in love with an ascetic of the superior quality of Śiva, there must be the same complementary quality present in the Goddess as a counterpart of such asceticism. This would mean that the worshipper of such a Goddess could not think in terms of gaining any advantage belonging to the three worlds of earth, heaven or the interspace.

Vedanta discountenances psychic powers (*siddhi*s), such as *aṇimā* (the power to become very tiny) and so on, which we have reviewed under verses thirty and thirty-one. Even Patañjali, though only belonging to the context of Sāṁkhya philosophy, in his *Yogasūtra*s (III.37) clearly states that interest in psychic powers (*siddhi*s) has a counter-effect on the progressive establishment of absorption (*samādhi*). The Bhagavadgītā also disdains *siddhi*s as being obstructions to the right path (*paripanthinau*).

In the second half of the present verse these *siddhi*s are brought into relation with the absolute Goddess. Does the Goddess grant *siddhi*s to votaries that might propitiate her, or is she altogether outside such an inferior context? To such a pointed question, this verse answers that such *siddhi*s are not primarily within the proper scope of the kind of benefit to be prayed for in respect of the absolute Goddess, who, as the wife of Śiva, is not interested in granting *siddhi*s that would only be advantageous in a hedonistic set-up. She would only treat the granting of such psychic powers as incidental and not as her main function. Even Vedic gods, like Indra and others, like to have some advantages in the form of *siddhi*s, with which they could dominate those who do not have such powers. Thus the Goddess here neither grants *siddhi*s nor refuses to grant them. She leaves them outside the door of her temple for those who badly need them. The gods may thus serve themselves freely with them if they should so insist, not knowing that *siddhi*s are really detrimental to the fullest spiritual progress in the correct absolutist context of Vedanta as distinct from the Vedas. The Vedic gods themselves have been beneficiaries in this matter and have been helping themselves to the available *siddhi*s which they could pick up from what was discarded by the Goddess outside her temple door.

Most persons, who are referred to as being of unsettled minds and incapable of the proper way of worship of the absolute Goddess, could belong to the three kinds of Devī worshippers, which are: the Pūrva Kaulins, the Uttara Kaulins, and the Samayins. All of these, like the hedonistic gods of the Vedas themselves, are motivated not by the desire for full emancipation, from a Goddess who is the true wife of Śiva, but for relativistic benefits from various surrogate divinities who are substitutes for the same Goddess. The wifehood of Śiva confers that absolute status, without which true salvation will not be guaranteed to supplicants. The whole of this picture in verse ninety-five refers to the context of a temple worshipper whose interest in the Absolute has not yet attained the 'white heat' of absolutism which alone can insure that full emancipation that Śiva and Śakti united together can confer by the combination of their mutually cancellable functions.

96

कलत्रं वैधात्रं कति कति भजन्ते न कवयः
श्रियो देव्याः को वा न भवति पतिः कैरपि धनैः ।
महादेवं हित्वा तव सति सतीनामचरमे
कुचाभ्यामासङ्गः कुरवकतरोरप्यसुलभः ॥

kalatraṁ vaidhātraṁ kati kati bhajante na kavayaḥ
śriyo devyāḥ ko vā na bhavati patiḥ kairapi dhanaiḥ ।
mahādevaṁ hitvā tava sati satīnāmacarame
kucābhyām āsaṅgaḥ kuravaka taror apy asulabhaḥ ॥

kalatraṁ vaidhātraṁ — wifehood in the context of Brahmā; *kati kati bhajante na kavayaḥ* — how many poets do not pray for; *śriyo devyāḥ ko vā na bhavati patiḥ* — who is it that cannot become the husband of the goddess of wealth (*śrī* = wealth); *kaiḥ dhanaiḥ api* — by having some sort of wealth; *mahā devaṁ hitvā* — outside/other than Śiva; *tava* — Your; *sati* — O true wife; *satīnām acarame* — ultimate meaning of constancy; *kucābhyām āsaṅgaḥ* — the contact with the breasts; *kuravaka taroḥ api* — even for the Aśoka tree; *asulabhaḥ* — not easy to gain

The wife of Brahmā, how many, how many poets do not woo?
Or by having some wealth, whoever is it that cannot claim to be husband to Lakṣmi?
O Constant Wife — of the term 'constancy' the ultimate meaning; outside Śiva
The contact with Your breasts is hard to gain even for an ordinary garden tree.

In verse ninety-six Sarasvatī, Lakṣmī, and Pārvatī are discussed together to underline that the former two, who belong to the context of relativism and hedonism, cannot be of the same order as Pārvatī in her relation with Śiva. Vedic learning and wealth are still mundane considerations, tending to have a horizontal reference. Only in the case of Pārvatī and Śiva is the relation of a pure and disinterested vertical order. Even though their relationship is fully verticalized, fulfilling the requirements of constancy between husband and wife as understood in the human context, the last line wishes to underline the unique superiority of Pārvatī's constancy, to the exclusion not only of rivals to Śiva, but even of anything extraneous to the wholehearted self-sufficiency of their intimate union, in which they are looked upon as being in each other's arms. One could suggest that when sitting in her garden, Pārvatī might have some kind of innocent pleasure in embracing her favourite garden tree. However, even this kind of innocent pleasure does not come to her mind, because the bipolarity involved in her relation with Śiva is so intense that it cannot tolerate any extraneous factor which does not strictly belong to the same level of bipolarity. The union of Śiva and Pārvatī has to exclude, in order to be fully absolute, all duality — as between two classes which are different, two classes which belong to the same side, or between two levels within the same class but of different levels — without violation of parity or identity, horizontally or vertically. The reference to the tree here is to underline the wholehearted nature of the absolute union of Śiva and Pārvatī, with perfect parity between them.

The Absolute is without difference: as between two of the same class, as between two classes and as between itself and another aspect of itself (*sajātiya vijātīya svagata bheda śūnyatā*). The reference in the last line to a tree is to underline the last-mentioned requirement, that is, for any value to be treated as the Absolute. Pārvatī is a constant wife not only in the human sense but in a sense more ultimate and comprehensive, by which the constancy is totally self-sufficient. It is a constancy for itself, by itself, through itself and in itself. Thus, as specifically indicated here, the ultimate meaning of constancy is recognized and complied with by Pārvatī in this verse.

97

गिरामाहुर्देवीं द्रुहिणगृहिणीमागमविदो
हरेः पत्नीं पद्मां हरसहचरीमद्रितनयाम्।
तुरीया कापि त्वं दुरधिगम निस्सीममहिमा
महामाया विश्वं भ्रमयसि परब्रह्ममहिषी ॥

girām āhur devīṁ druhiṇa gr̥hinīm āgama vido
hareḥ patnīṁ padmāṁ harasahacarīm adritanayām ।
turīyā kāpi tvaṁ duradhigama nissīma mahimā
mahāmāyā viśvaṁ bhramayasi parabrahma mahiṣī ॥

girām āhuḥ devīṁ — as the Goddess of the Word; *druhiṇa gr̥hiṇīm* — as Brahmā's wife; *āgama vidaḥ* — the knowers of Vedic wisdom; *hareḥ patnīṁ padmāṁ* — as Viṣṇu's wedded one (Lakṣmī); *hara saha carim adri tanayām* — the consort of Śiva, daughter of the high peak; *turīyā kāpi duradhigama niḥsīma mahimā* — some as the fourth state of boundless greatness, difficult to attain; *mahā māyā* — (as) the great Maya; *tvam viśvaṁ bhramayasi* — You turn the world around; *para brahma mahiṣī* — as Queen of the Ultimate Absolute

As the Goddess of the Word, Veda-knowers speak of You as Brahmā's wife,
Lakṣmī is Viṣṇu's wedded one, and the Mountain Daughter is Śiva's consort;
Certain others, as the unattainable and boundless fourth state, refer to You;
While You remain as the great Maya, making the universe go round,
As the Queen of the Ultimate Absolute.

Sarasvatī, Lakṣmī and Pārvatī again figure in verse ninety-seven, as the consorts of Brahmā, Viṣṇu and Śiva. This is the conventional way of treating the three goddesses. There are philosophically-minded people also referred to who do not resort to mythological language, but understand the Goddess as representing the *turīya*, or the 'fourth state' of consciousness, as clearly distinguished in the *Māṇḍūkya Upaniṣad*. Śaṅkara is not in favour of any of these four possible alternatives, although he mentions them here in a preliminary fashion as representing the opinions of others. He prefers to call the Goddess a principle of indeterminism in the most comprehensive and overall sense, as understood in the context of *brahma vidyā* (the Science of the Absolute), to which the notion of maya is a normal corollary.

We could easily see why the mythological or theological view of the Goddess here does not please Śaṅkara. However, as Śaṅkara is a philosopher attached to the view contained in the *Māṇḍūkya Upaniṣad*, one would expect the above reference to *turīya* to be compatible with his philosophy, and thus deserve his approval. Even this is not so, as Śaṅkara himself states clearly in the last line. The Goddess is not an idealized transcendental picture presented in too abstract and generalized a form, as the notion of *turīya*, though such a picture would not come into conflict with the true nature of the Absolute in a more positive sense. In the context of the present work, where it is the negative perspective of the same *brahman* that can reveal the significant content of Beauty, in relation to which (as a central norm of reference at least) these verses have been composed, consistency would require that we view the status of the Goddess here in a perspective that is more ontologically than teleologically biased.

The 'fourth state' would apply more aptly to Śiva whose status, being conceptual, tends to be less real. The content of the Absolute would evaporate into nothingness if mathematical conceptualism were allowed to have primacy over the perceptualistic outlook, which is here retained in the name of a residue of the beauty-value in the Absolute. If even this slight prejudice in favour of the conditioned *brahman* should be abolished, the poetic function, which is at the basis of these verses, would be stifled and made altogether ineffective. Bergson also prefers to treat the world as a flux, rather than as a mathematical absolute, which is just a conceptual cliche empty of any real content according to him.

On closer analysis, the difference between the two absolutes, called higher or lower *brahman*, is only one of methodological or epistemological convention. When we mark the ends of electric wires with green or red colour for the guidance of the electrician, this does not mean that there are two electricities. In the colloquy of the three gods in the *Kena Upaniṣad* we read that Beauty as a value, in the form of Umā, the daughter of the Himalayas, is made to occupy the same space that had belonged a moment before to the higher Absolute (*para brahman*). Maya and *brahman* are thus interchangeable limbs of the same equation.

98

कदा काले मातः कथय कलितालक्तकरसं
पिबेयं विद्यार्थी तव चरणनिर्णेजनजलम् ।
प्रकृत्या मूकानामपि च कविताकारणतया
कदाधत्ते वाणीमुखकमलताम्बूलरसताम् ॥

kadā kāle mātaḥ kathaya kalitālaktakarasaṁ
pibeyaṁ vidyārthī tava caraṇa nirṇejanajalam ।
prakṛtyā mūkānām api ca kavitā kāraṇatayā
kadādhatte vāṇī mukha kamala tāmbūla rasatām ॥

kadā kāle mātaḥ — when O Mother; *kathaya* — tell me; *kalita ālaktaka rasaṁ* — mixed with magenta sap; *pibeyaṁ vidyārthī* — shall I, this wisdom seeker, drink; *tava caraṇa nirṇejana jalaṁ* — the ablution water of Your foot; *prakṛtyā mūkānām api ca* — even for one born dumb; *kavitā kāraṇatayā* — as the cause of poetry, becoming a poet; *kadā dhatte* — when will I wear (enjoy); *vāṇī mukha kamala tāmbūla rasatām* — the flavour of the betel juice in the lotus mouth of the Word Goddess

When, O Mother, tell me, shall this Your wisdom seeker drink
Of the ablution water of Your magenta-sap-smeared feet,
Causing even one dumb-born to be a poet?
When will I enjoy within, the flavour of the betel juice in the lotus mouth of the Word Goddess?

The black box referred to in verse ninety-four was meant to be a summing up of the factors that have been used in something that resembles a game of chess, where various grades of chessmen have been put in the game to play their specific parts. The blackness of the ebony box marked the dark or negative perspective in which we were allowed to have a peep at the absolute beauty of the Goddess. The celestial bodies belonging to the world of Brahmā, as the creator, were treated as if placed in a jewelled casket, with the dark side more relevant to the context than the bright side of the chessboard. Now the negative perspective has been left behind and we have further crossed over an intervening three verses in which the game-pieces, representing divinities, are again reshuffled and rearranged in different ways so as to reveal the overall togetherness or interrelatedness between them. All psychic perfections have been placed outside the door of the temple of the Goddess in verse ninety-five. The union of Śiva and Pārvatī has been made most self-sufficient in verse ninety-seven. The remaining three verses of this work are meant to help the reader now gather up the loose threads from the anterior parts of this work which has unravelled itself in all its grandeur of overwhelming Beauty.

The dialogue in this verse between the Goddess and the supplicant primarily belongs to the context of the Word-wisdom that she represents. To be a poet, instead of being dumb, as naturally everyone is at birth, is the evident aspiration that motivates him. This is not essentially an aspiration of a religious order, where holiness and sacred merits from obligatory works enter into the picture. The reference in the first person to such an aspirant, who is here addressing the Mother, cannot be to anyone other than Śaṅkara himself. Even from the beginning he has taken care to disengage himself from the merely religious and hidebound context of merit, holiness and works. He maintains this detached attitude right through to the very end, where he is seen to wash his hands finally of all involvement, even disclaiming any direct responsibility for composing these verses. As if by way of preparing the ground for such a culminating attitude of detachment or neutrality, he is seen in the present verse to think in terms of becoming a good poet only.

It is as the goddess of the Word, not merely as understood conventionally when we speak of the Vedic Sarasvatī, but with a whole series of inner beauty-factors added to her total stock-in-trade, as it were, that we have here to think of the Devī. Her function does not pertain only to the numerator side of the poetic genius, which might merely consist of clever manipulation of words and phrases. The poetic genius here covers the whole range of inner and outer endowments that could enrich the consciousness of a man, from being born without words at all, to the positive culmination of the role of a poet at its final limit, taking the genius beyond the zero point to the heights of the perfected Word, located at the omega point. Poetic genius is an inner endowment and an outer accomplishment, referring to the Self and the non-Self respectively, when understood in terms of an inner reference linking both of them by a parameter that passes from the head to the feet of the two-sided personality of the Devī, which we have always to keep in mind.

We have further to notice that it is only under the sole of the feet that evidence of this lengthy parameter of reference could be seen by the eye, because poetic genius cannot be seen from the outside looks of the poet. We have agreed with the author that the beauty of these feet could be placed at the highest point in a scale of values or could be brought down to touch the limits of the black ebony box in which items of essential or existential beauty are enclosed. At whatever level the beauty of the twin feet might be placed, the magenta paste is the link and the indicator of the absolute value of Beauty that traverses the whole positive or negative gamut of possible aesthetic values, on whose basis poetic genius must live, move and have its being.

When ablution further purifies the beauty of the magenta-sap-smeared feet, the water would become the same colour. Why does the supplicant want to drink this impotable water containing paste or incidental dirt? Further, he also intends to enjoy the flavour of the betel juice in the mouth of the Goddess. It is repugnant to think that he wishes to swallow the spit of the Goddess, as some commentaries suggest. Moreover, there is the difficulty of mixed metaphors in different verses. In verse eighty-four it was water that was given importance, in verse seventy-five it was the ocean of milk and in verse sixty-five it was the betel juice in the mouth. Now all these figures of speech seem to have been gathered up and treated together. Śaṅkara, as a philosopher of Advaita, is able to substitute himself for the absolute goddess of Beauty, to the extent of being identical with her, by complete affiliation to what she represents. Even the subject and object duality can be cancelled out, as has been suggested in previous verses, such as verse thirty, where doomsday fire itself performs the light-waving rite. The non-Self and the Self as counterparts, whether as two individuals or fused into one, are to be treated as mathematically interchangeable terms, as in the limbs of an equation or in the cancellation of numerator against denominator.

Although betel chewing and its resultant magenta coloured saliva goes inside the Goddess, because of its containing bits of soft camphor, the essential flavour could spread upward as well as downward into regions of memory or imagination within the body of the Goddess. The act of swallowing a liquid, not excluding one's own saliva, is an activity taking place, as it were, at the very core of our functional consciousness. The child sucks milk even in sleep, and a thirsty man can dream of drinking cool clear water even when the water is not there. Clear water can be coloured magenta to make it participate with the beauty element of the betel juice of the mouth. The lotus plant can have a magenta colour added to its beauty coming either from the earth or from the tender sunlight playing upon it. We have to keep all these possibilities in our mind, especially as they have been justified already at different stages of the development of this composition. Magenta is the element of beauty which could mix with water or milk to inspire the genius of a dumb or inarticulate poet as his career develops from birth to death. From such a wholesale and global perspective we can see the relevancy and aptness of this concluding prayer, where Śaṅkara inserts himself directly in the first person, before he rounds up in the next two verses the whole subject by way of a final conclusion.

Śaṅkara is a wisdom seeker still, because wisdom has never-ending possibilities. One could never say that he has attained to a stage where he does not wish to learn any more. The analogy in verse ninety of the six-footed bee lost in lotus blooms seems to suggest that one is always involved in a process of absorption, at least till life itself is gone. Even then, the six legs cannot be absorbed into the honey of the lotus. They have to drop out of the flower. Even the wisest man is in a process of absorption, and not in any finalized form of absorption. All are thus pilgrims in the path of the Absolute, some possibly superior to others, but none are to be considered statically superior, once and for all. Spirituality is an aspiration in the world of intentions, and is not to be treated as something to be accomplished in fact. This justifies the anticipation contained in the question 'when shall I?' underlined twice in this verse. Magenta pervades and permeates through all the levels of the various chakras, whether of the first part or the second part of this work. The submissiveness and humility of Śaṅkara here adds a touching dimension to the whole situation and sets off the whole work as something which can ennoble any other intelligent man like him.

99

सरस्वत्या लक्ष्म्या विधिहरिसपत्नो विहरते
रतेः पातिव्रत्यं शिथिलयति रम्येण वपुषा।
चिरं जीवन्नेव क्षपितपशुपाशव्यतिकरः
परानन्दाभिख्यं रसयति रसं त्वद्भजनवान्॥

sarasvatyā lakṣmyā vidhi hari sapatno viharate
rateḥ pātivratyaṁ śithilayati ramyeṇa vapuṣā ।
ciraṁ jīvanneva kṣapita paśupāśa vyatikaraḥ
parānandābhikhyaṁ rasayati rasaṁ tvadbhajanavān ॥

sarasvatyā lakṣmyā — in the company of Sarasvatī and Lakṣmī; *vidhi hari sapatnaḥ* — co-consort with Brahmā and Viṣṇu; *viharate* — sports; *rateḥ pātivratyaṁ śithilayati* — (he) disrupts the constancy of Rati to her lord; *ramyeṇa vapuṣā* — by a pleasing body; *ciraṁ jīvan iva* — living long thus; *kṣapita paśu pāśa vyatikaraḥ* — with banished animality and bondage; *parā ānanda abhikhyaṁ* — of what is known as ultimate bliss; *rasayati* — (he) enjoys; *rasaṁ* — taste; *tvat bhajanavān* — Your worshipper

Sporting with Sarasvatī and with Lakṣmī, as co-consort with Brahmā and with Viṣṇu,
While disrupting with his charming body the constancy of Rati to her Lord,
With banished animality and bondage, living long,
He enjoys the taste of what is known as ultimate bliss, your supplicant.

The ultimate Bliss referred to at the end of this verse is nothing other than what is known by various other names such as salvation, emancipation, freedom, self-realization, nirvana and samadhi. Extreme ultimate felicity resides within the space of this verse. The main chessmen of this game are brought into close-knit interplay. That it is a game that is implied here is revealed by the very first word, 'sporting', for which the Sanskrit is *vihāra* (pleasing or recreative activity). Here the goddesses are seen with the husbands that properly belong to each. They are not after the husbands of others, so they are within the limits of good behaviour. Everything is in perfect order and no rule or convention seems to be violated here, except in the second line where it is implied that somebody is spoiling the game that is natural between Kāma and his wife Rati. There is a whole passage called *Rativilāpa* (the wailing of Rati) in the *Kumārasambhava* of Kālidāsa, which could be read here to clarify the implications of 'disrupting the constancy of Rati to her lord'. However undignified Rati might appear to be as the wife of a mere demiurge like Kāma, who can only attain to an absolutist status when everything else is favourable to him on rare occasions, justice would require that nobody should disrupt her right for conjugal enjoyment with her husband. Kālidāsa makes provisions in the passage describing the wailing of Rati for poetic justice in the matter. Vasanta (the Flowery Season), a friend of the husband Kāma, to whom this wailing is addressed, responds consolingly, and some kind of justification is made by way of mending the injustice under reference here. Śaṅkara does not go into such details because he is not writing lengthy poems of the kind that Kālidāsa undertook. The last line suggests that there is some beneficiary of the wisdom taught in this work. The previous verse has already hinted at who this person could be. It is not important who that person is in actuality. This verse just wants to say that there is a beneficiary and that the benefits could apply to anybody, including the reader, who could hope for a long life, without being subjected to animal instincts which could spell suffering and bondage. Such a man, by the peace of mind and harmony that he enjoys, and the normalcy of even his physiological metabolism, could come to have a beautiful body. Yogis are seen to have such bodies, always with clear complexions and voices. When he becomes charming in such a sense, the prolongation of his life will follow as a natural consequence. Life's chief fulfilments, which are referred to as being four in Sanskrit, namely, *dharma* (action according to necessary laws of nature), *artha* (wealth or benefits, such as endowments), *kāma* (right aspirations or desires) and *mokṣa* (salvation or ultimate happiness), are seen thus to be included in the scope of this verse by way of rounding off the contents before the grand conclusion that is to follow. We can easily see that it is not intended as a mere work on Tantra which, although it does not exclude salvation, gives lesser perfections a greater importance than this work does.

In the reference to co-consorts, 'consort' is meant to be treated as a partner independent of the sex. It could apply to a man or woman reader, or to a philosopher like Śaṅkara. Abstraction and generalization, even in respect of the author or the beneficiary of this work, has been pushed to its ultimate possible limit here. Such abstraction and generalization can attain the Absolute irrespective of the reader, or the author or even the Goddess of this work. Śaṅkara is thus able to treat the gods of the Hindu pantheon with a great deal of freedom.

प्रदीपज्वालाभिर्दिवसकरनीराजनविधिः
सुधासूतेश्चन्द्रोपलजललवैरर्घ्यरचना।
स्वकीयैरम्भोभिः सलिलनिधिसौहित्यकरणं
त्वदीयाभिर्वाग्भिस्तव जननि वाचां स्तुतिरियम्॥

pradīpa jvālābhir divasa kara nīrājana vidhiḥ
sudhāsūtes candropala jalalavair arghya racanā ।
svakīyair ambhobhiḥ salilanidhi sauhitya karaṇaṁ
tvadīyābhir vāgbhis tava janani vācāṁ stutir iyam ॥

pradīpa jvālābhiḥ — with the flames of a small lamp; *divasakara* — (of) the sun; *nīrājana vidhiḥ* — ritual propitiation by waving of lights; *sudhā sūteḥ* — to the source of nectar, ambrosia (the moon); *candropala jalalavaiḥ* — with droplets of water from the moonstone; *arghya racanā* — ritual water-offering; *svakīyaiḥ* — one's (its) own; *aṁbhobhih* — with water; *salilanidhi* — the ocean (water-treasure); *sauhitya karaṇaṁ* — satisfying with offerings; *janani* — O Mother; *tvadīyābhiḥ* — Your own; *vāgbhiḥ* — with words; *tava* — your; *iyam* — this; *vācām* — of words; *stutiḥ* — praise

To carry out the ritual propitiation of the sun by waving of lighted flames,
To offer oblations to the moon, the source of nectar, by particles of moonstone water,
To appease the deep with offerings of water its own —
Such, O Mother, is this wordy praise with words Your own.

The sun, the moon and the sea are seen to figure here prominently in the final verse. We are born into a world presided over by these three items. When treated comprehensively, equating oneself correctly with his own natural human environment is all that a man can be expected to do even if he should be wise or clever. When correctly equated, with a one-to-one correspondence, in a spiritually or contemplatively revised orientation, these items cancel out against their counterparts. Even if the light of one candle flame cannot cancel out the bright sunlight, an infinite number of them could be thought of as establishing a correct cancellation of counterparts. 'The one and the many' could thus belong together to a supreme or absolute Value. Nothing would then remain to be said, or all would have been said when this much has been said. Thus we arrive at the grand terminating culmination of this work.

Watery oblations apply to the moon, while light flames apply to the sun, and the water of the ocean is returned by rains and rivers. Thus the overall situation remains 'as it was in the beginning, is now and ever shall be, world without end', forever.

Appendix I

सौभाग्यलक्ष्मी उपनिषत्

अथ हैनं देवा ऊचुर्नवचक्रविवेकक्रमं अनुब्रूहीति
तथेति स होवाच
आधारे ब्रह्मचक्रं त्रिरावृतं भगमण्डलाकारम्
तत्र मूलकन्दे शक्तिः पावकाकारं ध्यायेत्
तत्रैव कामरूपपीठं सर्वकामप्रदं भवति
इत्याधारचक्रम्

द्वितीयं स्वाधिष्ठानचक्रं षड्दलम्
तन्मध्ये पश्चिमाभिमुखं लिङ्गं प्रवालाङ्कुरसदृशं ध्यायेत्
तत्रैवोड्याणपीठं जगदाकर्षणसिद्धिदं भवति

तृतीयं नाभिचक्रं पञ्चावर्तं सर्पकुटिलाकारम्
तन्मध्ये कुण्डलिनीं बालार्ककोटिप्रभां तटित्प्रभां ध्यायेत्
सामर्थ्यशक्तिः सर्वसिद्धिप्रदा भवति

मणिपूरकचक्रं हृदयचक्रम्
तन्मध्ये ज्योतिर्मयलिंङ्गाकारं ध्यायेत्
सैव हंसकला सर्वप्रिया सर्वलोकवश्यकरी भवति

कण्ठचक्रं चतुरङ्गुलम्
तत्र वामे इडा चन्द्रनाडी दक्षिणे पिङ्गला
सूर्यनाडी तन्मध्ये सुषुम्नां श्वेतवर्णां ध्यायेत्
य एवं वेदानाहता सिद्धिदा भवति

तालुचक्रम्
तत्रामृतधाराप्रवाहः

घण्टिकामूलचक्ररन्ध्रे राजदन्तावलम्बिनी
विवरं दशद्वादशारम्
तत्र शून्यं ध्यायेत्
चित्तलयो भवति

सप्तमं भ्रूचक्रमङ्गुष्ठमात्रम्
तत्र ज्ञाननेत्रं दीपशिखाकारं ध्यायेत्
तदेव कपालकन्द वाग्सिद्धिदं भवति
आज्ञाचक्रम्

अष्टमं ब्रह्मरन्ध्रं निर्वाणचक्रम्
तत्र सूचिकागृहेतरं धूम्रशिखाकारं ध्यायेत्
तत्र जालन्धरपीठं मोक्षप्रदं भवतीति परब्रह्मचक्रम्

नवममाकाशचक्रम्
तत्र षोडशदलपद्ममूर्ध्वमुखं तन्मध्ये कर्णिका त्रिकूटाकारम्
तन्मध्ये ऊर्ध्वशक्तिः
तां पश्यन् ध्यायेत्
तत्रैव पूर्णगिरिपीठं सर्वेच्छासिद्धिसाधनं भवति

Saubhāgyalakṣmī Upaniṣad
(Mystical Teaching on the Goddess of Great Good Fortune) [Part III Translation]

The gods then asked Him: Please tell us how to discern the nine chakras, in their order.

He said: Let it be so. At the base is the chakra of the Absolute (*brahma cakra*). It has three coils and is shaped like the perineal region. At its root is *śakti* (energy). Meditate on it in the form of fire. There itself is the seat of desire and it bestows every desire. Such is the foundation (*ādhāra*) chakra.

The second is the six-petalled *svādhiṣṭhāna cakra* (one's own basis). At its centre is a west-facing linga. Meditate on it as resembling a bud of coral, about to open. There itself is the 'girdle seat' (*uḍyāṇa pīṭham*), which gives the ability to attract the world (to oneself).

The third is the *nābhi cakra* (navel). It is five-petalled and shaped like the coils of a snake. At its centre is the *kuṇḍalinī*, as brilliant as ten million rising suns or lightning. Meditate on it. It gives dexterity and the power to attain all (psychophysical) perfections (*siddhi*). It is the *maṇipūraka* (gem-filled) chakra.

The *hṛdaya cakra* (heart) has eight petals and faces downwards. At its centre is a liṅga of light. Meditate on it. It indeed is of the form of a swan (*haṁsa kalā*). She is the beloved of all and brings all worlds under her spell.

The *kaṇṭha cakra* (throat) is of the breadth of four fingers. On its left is *iḍā,* the moon nerve; on the right is *piṅgalā,* the sun nerve. In the middle is the white *suṣumnā.* Meditate on it. He who knows it thus comes to have the supreme perfection of the 'unstruck' (*anāhata*).

The *tālu cakra* (the palate): There flows the elixir of immortality. Shaped like a small bell, at its base-opening is the 'royal tooth' (uvula?), the tenth opening. The *śūnya* (void) there should be meditated upon. The mind merges (there).

The seventh is the thumb-sized *bhrū cakra* (eyebrow). Meditate there on the eye of wisdom, in the form of a lamp's flame. It is the root of the skull, the *ājñā cakra*, the bestower of power over words.

The eighth, *brahma randhra,* is the *nirvāṇa cakra*. Meditate on it shaped as a thread of smoke, thinner than a needle. There is the *jālandhara pīṭha* (seat of meshes), which gives liberation. This is the chakra of the Supreme Absolute (*para brahman*).

The ninth is the *ākāśa cakra* (space). It is shaped like a lotus of sixteen petals, facing upward. At the middle is its pericarp, shaped like triple peaks. At its centre is the ascending energy. See this and meditate on it. There indeed is the (royal) seat at the crest of the peak (*pūrṇa giri pīṭha*). It is the instrument for the fulfilment of all desires.

Appendix II

योगराजोपनिषत्

योगराजं प्रवक्ष्यामि योगिनां योगसिद्धये
मन्त्रयोगो लयश्चैव राजयोगो हठस्तथा

योगश्चतुर्विधः प्रोक्तो योगिभिस्तत्त्वदर्शिभिः
आसनं प्राणसंरोधो ध्यानं चैव समाधिः

एतश्चतुष्टयं विद्धि सर्वयोगेषु सम्मतम्
ब्रह्मा विष्णु शिवानां मन्त्रं जाप्यं विशारदैः

साध्यते मन्त्रयोगस्तु वत्सराजादिभिर्यथा
कृष्णद्वैपायनाद्यैस्तु साधितो लयसंज्ञितः

नवस्वेव हि चक्रेषु लयं कृत्वा महात्मभिः
प्रथमं ब्रह्मचक्रं स्यात् त्रिरावृत्तं भगाकृतिः

अपाने मूलकन्दाख्यं कामरूपं च तज्जगुः
तदेव वह्निकुण्डं स्यात् तत्त्वकुण्डलिनी तथा

तां जीवरूपिणीं ध्यायेत् ज्योतिष्ठं मुक्तिहेतवे
स्वाधिष्ठानं द्वितीयं स्याच्चक्रं तन्मध्यगं विदुः

पश्चिमाभिमुखं लिङ्गं प्रवालाङ्कुरसन्निभम्
तत्रोड्याणपीठेषु तं ध्यात्वा कर्षयेत् जगत्

तृतीयं नाभिचक्रं स्यात् तन्मध्ये तु जगत् स्थितम्
पञ्चावर्तां मध्यशक्तिं चिन्तयद्विद्युताकृतिम्

तां ध्यात्वा सर्वसिद्धीनां भाजनं जायते बुधः
चतुर्थं हृदयं चक्रं विज्ञेयं तदधोमुखम्

ज्योतिरूपं च तन्मध्ये हंसं ध्यायेत् प्रयत्नतः
तं ध्यायतो जगत्सर्वं वश्यं स्यान्नात्र संशयः

पञ्चमं कण्ठचक्रं स्यात् तत्र वामे इडा भवेत्
दक्षिणे पिङ्गला ज्ञेया सुषुम्ना मध्यतः स्थिता

तं ध्यात्वा शुचिः ज्योतिः सिद्धीनां भाजनं भवेत्
षष्ठं च तालुका चक्रं घण्टिकास्थानमुच्यते

दशमद्वारमार्गे तद् राजदन्तं च तज्जगुः
तत्र शून्ये लयं कृत्वा मुक्तो भवति निश्चितम

भ्रूचक्रं सप्तमं विद्याद् बिन्दुस्थानं च तद्विदुः
भ्रुवोर्मध्ये वर्तुलं च ध्यात्वा ज्योति प्रमुच्यते

अष्टमं ब्रह्मरन्ध्रं स्यात् परं निर्वाणसूचकम्
तं ध्यात्वा सूतिकाग्रामं धूमाकारं विमुच्यते
तत्र जालन्धरं ज्ञेयं मोक्षदं नीलचेतसम्

नवमं व्योमचक्रं स्याभदत्रौः षोडशभिर्थुतम्

संविद् ब्रुयाच्च तन्मध्ये शक्तिरूर्ध्व स्थितो परा
तत्र पूर्णो गिरौ पीठे शक्तिं ध्यात्वा विमुच्यते

एतेषां नवचक्राणां एकैकं ध्यायतो मुनेः
सिद्धयो मुक्तिसहिताः करस्थाः स्युर्दिने दिने

एको दण्डद्वयं मध्ये पश्यति ज्ञानचक्षुषा
कदंबगोलकाकारं ब्रह्मलोकं व्रजन्ति ते

ऊर्ध्वशक्तिनिपातेन अधः श्क्तेनिकुञ्चनात्
मध्यशक्तिप्रबोधेन जायते परमं सुखं जायते परमं सुखम्

Yogarāja Upaniṣad

(Mystical Teaching on the Royal Yoga)

(Translation)

I shall declare the royal science of yoga (*yoga rāja*) so that yogis may attain perfection. *Mantra yoga, Laya yoga, Rāja yoga* and *Haṭha yoga.*

Yoga is of four kinds, say the yogis who know the first principles: *āsana* (posture), *prāṇa samrodhaḥ* (regulation of vital-energy), *dhyāna* (meditation) and *samādhi* (emancipation).

Know these four to be equally acceptable to all yogas. The mantras (sacred chants, letters) pertaining to Brahmā, Viṣṇu and Śiva are to be chanted by all of clear intelligence.

Thus was the attainment through mantra yoga, as wiṭh Vatsaraja and others. Krishna Dvaipāyana (Vyāsa) and his followers found perfection through the one named *laya* (merger).

Verily, by immersing themselves in the nine chakras, the Great Ones (reached perfection).

Of these, the first is the *brahma cakra*, with three coils, and of the form of the perineum.

In the *apāna* (downward vital-tendency), named the primal root (*mūla kanda),* know it to be of the form of desire (*kāma*). That indeed is the (sacred) fire-pit, as well as the principle of the *kuṇdalinī*.

She should be meditated upon as the immanent life-form, established on light, so that one is liberated.

The second chakra is the *svādhiṣṭāna* (one's own basis). At its centre is to be known the liṅga facing the west, bright like a coral bud, established on the 'girdle seat.' Meditating on it, one attracts the whole world.

The third is the navel chakra (*nābhi*). The phenomenal world is established in the middle of it. Of the form of lightning, this five-coiled chakra should be meditated on as the central energy (of the mid-region).

Having meditated thereon, the wise one becomes a vessel of all psychophysical perfections (attainments).

The heart chakra (*hṛdaya*) is to be known as the fourth, facing downwards. Of the form of light, at its centre is a swan (*haṁsa*). Meditate on it with intense effort. By such meditation the whole world becomes subdued. Herein, there is no doubt at all.

The fifth is the throat chakra (*kaṇṭha*). On its left side is *iḍā* and on its right, *piṅgalā*. Between the two is the *suṣumnā*. Meditating on this pure light, one becomes the abode of all perfections (*siddhi*).

The sixth, the palate chakra (*tālukā*), is called the place of the small bell. It is in the path of the tenth orifice, also known as the 'royal tooth' (*rāja danta*). There, in the void (*śūnya*), having merged, one becomes liberated indeed.

Know the seventh as *bhrū cakra* (eyebrow); also known as the locus of meditation (*bindu sthāna*). Meditating on it in the middle of the eyebrows, circular, a bright light, one is fully liberated.

The eighth is the *brahma randhra* (the absolutist orifice), indicative of supreme emancipation. Meditating on it in the form of a streak of smoke, one is liberated from birth-cycles. There is to be understood the mesh-like *jālandhara,* blue hearted, bestowing liberation.

The ninth is the *vyoma cakra* (sky), with sixteen angles. Consciousness (*saṁvit*) is said to be at its centre, as positively oriented energy, well-established and transcendent. There, at the crest of the peak, meditating on this energy, one is freed of all.

The contemplative recluse, meditating on these chakras one by one, attains all psychophysical perfections, as well as final release, day by day.

Certain wise ones, with the eye of intuitive knowledge, seeing the globe-like *kadamba* flower between the two staves, go to the world of *brahman*.

By the descent of the upward energy, by the ascent of the downward energy and by arousing the central energy, arises supreme happiness, yes, there arises supreme happiness.

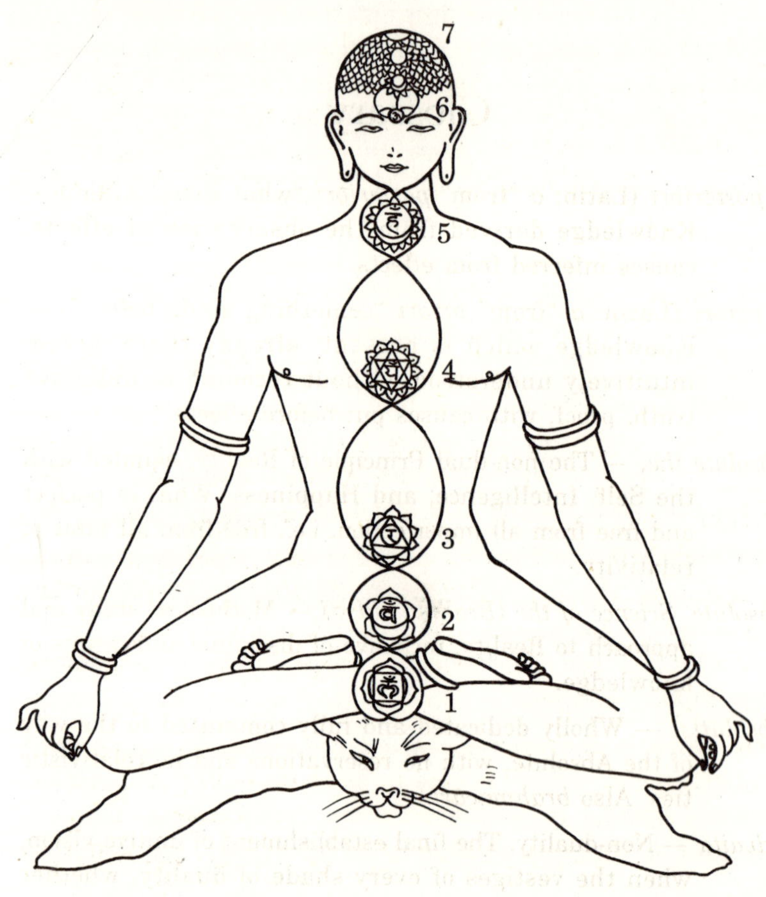

1. *mūlādhāra cakra*
2. *svādhiṣṭhāna cakra*
3. *maṇipūra cakra*
4. *anāhata cakra*
5. *viśuddhi cakra*
6. *ājñā cakra*
7. *sahasrāra cakra*

Glossary

A posteriori (Latin: *a* "from" *posteriori* "what comes after") — Knowledge derived from the observation of effects; causes inferred from effects.

A priori (Latin: *a* "from" *priori* "something going before") — Knowledge which is present, already there, given, intuitively understood without recourse to inductive truth, proof, with causes put before effects.

Absolute the, — The non-dual Principle of Reality, equated with the Self, Intelligence, and Happiness. What is perfect and free from all imperfection, i.e., free from all taint of relativity.

Absolute, Science of the (*Brahma-vidyā*) — Methodical study and approach to Reality, inclusive of discipline and means of knowledge.

Absolutist — Wholly dedicated and fully committed to the way of the Absolute, with no reservations and no relativistic ties. Also *brahmacārī*.

Advaita — Non-duality. The final establishment of unitive vision, when the vestiges of every shade of duality, whether psychological or cosmological, have been transcended by the man of philosophical vision.

Advaita Vedanta — Philosophy of non-dualism, based on a contemplative unitive approach. Unitive understanding.

Alpha — The first letter of the Greek alphabet denoting the first of a series of items or categories.

Ānanda — Bliss. Should be understood in the context of the Good in Western philosophy as a supreme value. Bounty, goodness and kindness are all conceptions depending upon a notion of value. *Sat,* existence; *Cit,* substantial being in a rational sense; and *ānanda* as a supreme value, are terms conjointly used to describe the Absolute in Vedanta, representing three stages in the appraisal of the true from the point of view of human intelligence. *Ānanda* is thus supreme bliss or goodness and describes the Absolute in terms of human feelings.

Androgynous (Greek: *andros* "man" *gune* "woman") — Uniting the characters of male and female. Hermaphrodite. *(Ardhanārīśvara* is the androgynous form of Śiva.)

Arivu (From Malayalam) — The Word or pure Knowledge. Also refers to that which is prior to a thing that is being known. The great dynamic whole which includes within it the conscious and the unconscious, the potential and the actual, the transcendent and the immanent, the creative and the created. Narayana Guru elucidates *Arivu* in his poem by the same name.

Aruṇa — Dawn. Refers to the magenta colour seen at morning twilight, caused by the combination of ultraviolet and infrared wavelengths of the electromagnetic spectrum.

Āryan — Name applied vaguely by historians to tribes who crossed over the Himālayas and penetrated into the matrix of the Indian life of prehistoric time which consisted of various amorphous formations including the so-called proto-Draviḍians.

Ātman — The Real viewed psychologically as the Supreme or universal Self. The *ātman* is further distinguishable as the *paramātman,* the Supreme Self, and the *jīvātman* or Individual Self.

Auṁ — According to the *Maṇḍukya Upaniṣad, auṁ* is the Absolute itself. As the Word of Words, this represents the Absolute, combining *Logos* and *Nous* as understood in the Greek context. The three letters *A, U,* and *Ṁ,* are said to correspond to the open, the half-open or subtle and the closed or the purely psychic worlds, thus inclusively covering the cosmological, the psychological and the spiritual grounds of Being or Reality as conceived in terms of the Absolute.

Axiology (Greek: *axia* "value, worthiness") — Theory of value. The term was probably first used by Lotze, and then by Brentano, Husserl, Hartmann and others.

Cartesian — Derived from or relating to the works of Descartes, especially the algebraic representation of planar geometry.

Cartesian co-ordinates — A system for the representation of a point in space in terms of its distance, measured along a set of mutually perpendicular axes from a given origin (the point of intersection of the two axes and of which the co-ordinates are all zero). By convention, the positive directions of the axes point to the right and upwards. The first quadrant is that in which both quantities are positive, and the other quadrants are numbered anticlockwise from the first. This system extends naturally to three or more dimensions; in three dimensions the convention is to use right-handed set of axes, and many standard formulae presuppose this.

Cakra — Wheel, disc, whirlpool, the term is applied to the basic seven psychic centres outlined in *Yoga* and *Tantra*. *Cakra* implies a vortex, and is a psychic centre or "whirling vortex of psychic energy at the conjunction points of the mind and the body." *Cakra*s can be perceived as psychosomatic, outside the space-time continuum and equivalent to the Euclidean "point" without magnitude, possessed of location but not dimension.

Contradiction, complementarity, cancellation, reciprocity — Four epistemological principles in science and Vedanta to arrive at sound methodology to observe, discuss, interpret and conclude. Based on mathematical theory, the four ways that opposite poles in a dialectic situation are related. For instance, the statement "*X* is true" *contradicts* the statement "*X* is false." They are *complementary* in that both hinge on the relative truth of *X*, and the degree of truth in one affects the degree of falsity in the other. Taken together, each *cancels* out the other, which is the way absolute neutrality is revealed in dialectical (*yogic*) thinking. The statements are also *reciprocal* or mutually related in such a way that their product produces unity; in other words, taken together *X* and not *X* comprise the totality of the universe of *X*.

Conic section — One of a group of curves formed by the intersection of a plane and a right circular cone. This curve is either a circle, if the plane is parallel to the base of the cone; an ellipse, if it is at any other angle at which the intersection is a closed curve; a parabola, if it is parallel to any line joining the vertex of the cone to a point on its base; or an hyperbola, if it is at any other angle.

Cybernetics (Greek: *kubernetes* "steersman") — Term coined by Norbert Weiner in the 1940s. The science of communications and automatic control systems in both machines and living things. The study of control systems that exhibit characteristics similar to those of animal and human behaviour. Cybernetics is a broad-based discipline which includes information, message and noise theories, and can reconcile the work of neurophysiologists, physiologists and computer engineers.

Dialectics — Greek name for the method of discovering the two sides of every problem, and of resolving it by the neutral unitive approach. The same as the word *Yoga* as revalued in Vedanta.

Draviḍian — Referred to by historians as being unlike the Āryans in colour and physiognomy and supposed to represent the most important proto-Āryan ethnic group, especially persisting to the present day in the south of India, and also represented by various hill-tribes in pockets and in isolated areas all over India.

Élan vital — Life force, vital force, vitality. A hypothetical force (not physical or chemical) thought by Henri Bergson to cause the evolution and development of organisms.

Epistemology (Greek: *episteme* "knowledge, understanding, science" *logia* "doctrine") — That branch of philosophy which deals with the basis and methods of knowledge and ways of knowing, as well as inquiry into the nature and the possibility of knowledge. It deals also with the scope and limits of human knowledge, and with how it is acquired and possessed. It also investigates related notions, such as perception, memory, proof, evidence, belief and certainty.

Erotic mysticism — Sensual imagery and male-female attractions used as forms to describe the relationship between the individual person and the all-encompassing divine reality. In the Christian Catholic and Hindu Vaiṣṇava traditions the male or female aspirant is likened to the lover of God, either as the bride of Christ or as Rādhā and Kṛṣṇa. Sex is not the ultimate union, but rather the functional dynamics of the word of God. In the Western tradition, Plotinus and St. Augustine speak of it as the attraction of the individual towards God or the Good.

Existentialism — Philosophy popular during mid twentieth century European, stemming from the Danish philosopher Soren Kierkagaard (1813-55), supported by many European thinkers like Jean Paul Sartre, and based upon the importance of the living present, without reference to time past or to come.

General Theory of Relativity — The geometric theory of gravitation developed by Albert Einstein, incorporating and extending the theory of special relativity to accelerated frames of reference and introducing the principle that gravitational and inertial forces are equivalent. The theory has consequences for the bending of light by massive objects, the nature of black holes, and the fabric of space and time.

Hierophantic (Greek: *hieros* "sacred" *phainein* "to show") — Pertaining to the visible display of the divine, usually by a priest.

Horizontal and vertical — Based on the co-ordinate axes of Descartes, everything can be studied schematically by assessing its horizontal and vertical components. Broadly, the horizontal are physical and spatial, while the vertical are metaphysical (ideas) and temporal.

Hypostatic (Greek: *hypo* "under, below" *histasthai* "to stand under, subsist") — Pertaining to substance or essence which underlies attributes. For example the Christian trinity are hypostatizations.

Indeterminism — Unpredictability. The philosophical doctrine that there are some events, particularly some human actions or decisions, which have no cause.

Intelligibles, Platonic world of the — Part of Plato's scheme, referring to an intellectual series of values beyond the senses.

Kalīdāsa — Poet and dramatist, who lived sometime between the reign of Agnimitra, the second Śuṅga king (*c.* 170 BC) who was the hero of one of his dramas, and the Aihole inscription of AD 634 which praises Kālidāsa's poetic skills. Most scholars now associate him with the reign of Candragupta II (*c.* 380 - *c.* 415).

Kāma or Kāmadeva — The Eros of India. Rati is his consort. The central eye of Śiva which erupts fire is said to have burnt Kāma to ashes when Kāma aimed his flowery-arrow at Śiva in order to make him erotic, as commissioned by the gods who needed a martial deity. The war-god was born, however, without erotic love in circumstances portrayed by Kālīdāsa in his poem called *Kumārasambhava* (The Birth of the War-God).

Kāvya — A poem, poetical composition with a coherent plot by a single author (as opposed to an *Itihāsa*). An example is Kālidāsa's *Kumārasambhava,* a heroic poetical work in Sanskrit.

Khyātivāda — The general term for different theories on errors in knowledge.

Kumārasambhava — A Sanskrit *kāvya* of Kālīdāsa, literally "The Birth of the War-god Kumara." In their struggle against the demons (*asuras*) the gods (*devas*) badly needed a warrior god and approached Brahmā to this end, who counselled that they should somehow make Śiva, who was then steeped in meditation, fall in love with a woman. Kāmadeva (Eros) was selected to tempt him for this purpose, and Kāmadeva came with his wife Rati, choosing the moment when Umā came with offerings, to let fly at him the flowered dart of erotic temptation. Śiva caught Kāmadeva before the arrow left his bow, and in his anger, Śiva opened his third eye whose glance reduced Kāmadeva to ashes.

Kuṇḍalinī — Spoken of in *Yoga* as a snake lying coiled three and a half times at the base of the vertebral column (*mūlādhāra*). It represents a ganglion, plexus or storehouse of nervous energy which irradiates upwards to the higher centres of the nervous system. It symbolizes the creative consciousness of the lower mind. Attempts to locate this basic nervous energy (*kuṇḍalinī śakti*) in histologic, organic or functional terms in modern scientific language remain unconvincing for the simple reason that this psychic energy is not reflected directly in objective organs or functions.

Liṅgam (Phallus) — Image of the male organ of generation, the penis, as used for religious worship. Literally anything that constitutes a sign or symbol. The male and female sex-organs as symbols are referred to as *liṅgams*, *pulliṅgam* meaning male sex symbol and *strīliṅgam* marking the feminine. The *śiva-liṅgam* which is the phallic symbol of Śiva is a spherical stone which is an object of worship in India from prehistoric times. It is dressed up, anointed or washed with ablutive waters by way of respect or adoration in memory of the antique god Śiva.

Kali (From *kāla* time) — Dark and terrible aspects of time personified as the process of creative becoming. In its (feminine) tragic aspect it is *Kali*. The smoky flame of a sacrificial fire is also called *Kālī* or dark, in the *Muṇḍaka Upaniṣad* (I.II.4).

Lingua mystica (Latin: *lingua* "uttering" *mystica* "mystical") — Mystical literature and its mode of expression found mainly in ancient scriptures.

Mahāvākya — Literally, "great word". Name of twelve sacred utterances of the Upaniṣads, such a *ahaṁ brahma asmi* (I am *Brahman*), *tat tvaṁ asi* (That Thou art); *auṁ tat sat* (aum, This is Real); *ayamātmā brahma* (This Self is *Brahman*); *prajñānam brahma* (*Brahman* is consciousness). Also of the mystic words *tattvam* and *auṁ*. *Mahāvākya*s are the conclusive formulae of Vedantic wisdom.

Mantra, yantra, tantra — *Mantra* is the nominal, verbal, acoustic aspect of *nada,* the primordial sound considered to be the original cause of the universe. *Yantra* is the formal, visual symbol that delimits the potential of the *mantra* to manifest in a chosen field. *Tantra* is the special device that relates the *mantra* to the *yantra* so as to derive the psychodynamics implied in both. *Mantra* is considered to be the algebraic aspect and *yantra* the geometric one, while *tantra* is the activating dynamics that conjoins *mantra* and *yantra* to make a functional whole.

Maya — The principle of indeterminism, ambiguity or error. Connotes a factor of epistemological and methodological importance in Śaṅkara's Vedanta especially, and in the Upaniṣadic lore generally. Whatever is postulated as the cause of the unreal spoken of in the most generic of categorical terms in philosophy, as against theology, is to be laid at the door of Māyā. It is the basis of duality or synergic antinomies. The nearest Western equivalent is the *Negativitat* of Hegel's system.

Metalanguage — (Greek: *meta* "after") Word-based language. Whenever an investigation is made about a language, we call this language the *object-language* of the investigation, and the language in which the results of the investigation are formulated, the *meta-language* (Carnap quoted, p147, Vol. 1 *Part 1 Int. Ency. of Unified Science*, Chicago, 1955).

Methodology — The discipline which investigates and evaluates methods of inquiry, of validation, of teaching, etc. A theory within that discipline. Note that methodology is *about* method and not the same as method.

Monomark — A single symbol representing an idea; a particular combination of letters or figures used as an identification mark.

Neti Neti — This refers to the method of negative reasoning which is at the basis of the Vedantic approach to wisdom. Literally it means, "Not this, not this." By the elimination of the irrelevant and extraneous factors which prevent the dawning of wisdom, illumination results automatically, without effort or action. This corresponds to the *via negativa* of the European mystics, such as Eckhart, Tauler, Boehme, and Dionysius the Areopagite. The *nivṛtti mārga* or path of withdrawal, which is often opposed to the *pravṛtti mārga,* or path of action, means also the same attitude of disciplined negation.

Numinous (Latin: *numen* "divine will") — Word coined by German theologian Rudolph Otto, to signify the absolutely unique state of mind of the genuinely religious person who feels or is aware of something mysterious, terrible, awe-inspiring, holy and sacred. The feeling or awareness is a *mysterium tremendum,* beyond reason, beyond the good or the beautiful. The numinous is an *a priori* category and is the basis of man's cognition of the Divine.

Occasionalism — A theory of knowledge and of voluntary control of action, in which mind and matter are non-interactive but events in one realm occur in correspondence with events in the other realm. Thus, God sees to it that an idea of noise occurs in a mind on the occasion of the occurrence of a physical noise; or, He makes a physical event happen when a mind wishes it.

Ontology (Greek: *ontos* "being, existence" *logia* "doctrine") — branch of philosophy which treats of the nature of being, or existence.

Orthodoxy — Beliefs which are declared by a group to be true and normative. Heresy is a departure from and relative to a given orthodoxy.

Paradox (Greek: *paradoxos* "beyond belief") — An apparently sound proof of an unacceptable conclusion, or an unacceptable conclusion of an apparently sound proof. These are the two closely related senses in which the word is used in more strictly philosophical contexts. In general and non-philosophical usage paradox is a statement that seems strikingly implausible, but which in fact conveys an interesting or important truth.

Parity — An essential equality between counterparts.

Pārvatī — The consort or *śakti* aspect of Śiva. She is the daughter of the Himālayas and is also a huntress, and known under various aspects in mythology and iconography.

Phenomenology — Since the middle of the eighteenth century *Phanomenologie* like its English equivalent has been a name for several disciplines, and expression for various concepts. Since the twentieth-century phenomenology is used exclusively for the philosophical method and movement that had its origin in the work of Edmund

Husserl. It is the attempt to describe our experiences directly, as it is, separately from its origins and development, independently of the causal explanations that historians, sociologists or psychologists might give.

Protolanguage — (Greek: *protos* "first, earliest") The earliest form of thought given *a priori* to man. Pictorial or gestural language that does not rely on words as such. In Oriental countries protolanguage was mainly conceived as a language in stones. This is a silent language, profound, conveying the impressions of its original designers, who used symbols which are easily deciphered. Protolinguistics is polarized, as it were, negatively at the bottom of the vertical axis. Intellects conforming to what Pascal calls the '*esprit geometrique*' are those best suited to an understanding of the structure of this aspect of language.

Quaternion structure — A fourfold structure, which for Nataraja Guru is perfectly expressed by the four quadrants produced by the Cartesian co-ordinates. This structure can be applied to any ponderable situation or thing in order to analyse its relation to the Absolute.

Rati — Passions. Forms of affectivity or attachment and considered impediments to spiritual progress. Rati is the propelling force which activates the ego into finding its gratification. It is the libidinal enjoyment of erotics. In mythology Rati is personified as the wife of Kāmadeva.

Relative, the — Whatever is partial, dependent on something else, comparative and imperfect; referred to philosophically for what is not absolute.

Renormalization — A process by which counterparts abolish their differences in respect of an axiomatic or experimental certitude.

Res cogitans (Latin: *res* "thing" *cogitans* "thinking") — Something that thinks; Descartes' designation for thinking substance which along with extended substance (*res cogitans*) constitute his dualism. The term presumably designates not only the individual mind which thinks but also the substance which pervades all individual minds.

Res extensa (Latin: *res* "thing" *extensa* "extended") — Something that has extension in space. In Descartes, material substance, matter.

Revaluation dialectical — To re-estimate and restate in keeping with the principle of unity, avoiding duality and rivalry in the process.

Śakti — The female or generative principle; wife of Śiva and a benevolent form of Devī.

Schema — (Greek: *skhema* "form, figure") Figure, external form or structural plan, specifically in Aristotle's logic, a syllogistic figure. In Kant's *Critique of Pure Reason*, The procedure of the imagination by which the categories of the understanding are applied to the manifold of sensuous intuitions. Imagination working with the pure form of time, connects sense and understanding. This is possible because the imagination contains an element of both sense and understanding, and thus is capable of formulating the rules and procedures by means of which sensuous representations may be subsumed under pure concepts. Kant uses the word in a technical sense that in order to apply non-empirical concepts to empirical facts a mediating representation is necessary. Such a third element he calls a schema. Kant reviews the categories (the pure concepts of the understanding) and indicates their correlated schemata. For example, the schema for *causality* is *temporal succession according to a rule*; the schema for *necessity* is *existence of an object at all times*.

Schema moteur — bringing into Kantian schematization an element of vital movement.

Selective subjectivism — The interplay of physical observations and geometry in the scientific epistemology of Eddington which he also called structuralism. He believed that a great part of physics simply reflected the interpretation that the scientist imposes on his data.

Subrahmaṇya — Synonymous with Kārttikeya and Bahuleya who was supposed to be born in a lake by the light or glance of Śiva which fell there. Subrahmaṇya rides the peacock and is six-headed, being born to six mothers. This myth is supposed to be astronomical also in its import, as there is a group of six stars with the same name (the Pleiades). Subrahmaṇya is younger brother to Gaṇeśa, the elephant-headed son of Śiva. Subrahmaṇya is much adored in south India, and is mentioned in the Vedas.

Sub specie aeternitatis (Latin: "under the aspect of eternity") — Expression of Spinoza, used in his *Ethics* to characterise the highest form of knowledge, which he calls intuitive knowledge, in which things are seen from the standpoint of timelessness or eternity.

Teleology (Greek: *telos* "end, result" *logia* "doctrine") — Doctrine that all things in nature were created to fulfil a specific purpose. Dialectical counterpart of ontology.

Transcendent (Latin: *transcendere* "to step over, surmount, surpass") — Of a character which is *a priori,* beyond the empirical, gained by intuition.

Umā — One of the *śakti*s of Śiva, as the beautiful and radiant daughter of the Himālayas, portrayed in Kālidāsa's *Kumārasambhava* and in the *Kena Upaniṣad* (Khaṇḍa III, 12), as the feminine Absolute. When the being of the *yakṣa* could not be comprehended, Umā is revealed in that very same space.

Unitive understanding — The essence of Advaita Vedanta. Non-dual or absolutist way in which two sides or aspects are clearly recognized and distinguished and treated as dialectical counterparts to be ultimately resolved in terms of a single neutral normative notion. Unitive understanding equates the Self and non-Self as interchangeable terms, reversing the natural tendency of thought to divide and find differences, whether in the world of facts, ideas or values. It is a contemplative way of solving the problems and conflicts of life.

Bibliography

Adams, Robert M. and George M. Logan, eds., *Paradise Lost* "The Seventeenth Century" in *The Norton Anthology of English Literature*, 6th edn., vol. I, Norton, 1993.

Atkins, Stuart, ed. and trans., *Goethe, Collected Works, Faust I & II,* Princeton University Press, Reprint edn., 1994.

Avalon, Arthur, *The Great Liberation: Mahānirvāṇa Tantra,* Madras: Ganesh and Co., 1913.

Bader, Jonathan, *Conquest of the Four Quarters : Traditional Accounts of the Life of Śaṅkara*, Delhi, 2000.

Baierlein, Ralph, *Newton to Einstein: The Trail of Light, An Excursion to the Wave-Particle Duality and the Special Theory of Relativity*, New York: Cambridge University Press, 2001.

Beck, Lewis White, trans., Kant, Immanuel, *Critique of Practical Reason*, Bobbs-Merrill, Indianapolis, 1956.

Bergson, Henri, *Key Writings*, ed., Keith Ansell Pearson and John Mullarkey, Continuum, London, 2002.

———, *Creative Evolution*, tr., Arthur Mitchell, Dover, New York, 1998 [1911].

———, *The Creative Mind*, tr., Mabelle L. Andison, translation of La Pensée et le mouvant, The Citadel Press, New York, 1992 [1946].

———, *Duration and Simultaneity,* Robin Durie (ed.), Manchester L Clinamen Press, 1999.

———, *Laughter*: An Essay on the Meaning of the Comic, trs. Cloudsley Brereton and Fred Rothwell, Green Integer, Los Angeles, 1999 [1911].

———, *Matter and Memory,* tr. N.M. Paul and W.S. Palmer, Zone Books, New York, 1994.

———, *Mind-Energy*, tr. H. Wildon Carr, translation of L'energie spirituelle, McMillan and Company, London, 1920 .

———, *Time and Free Will*: An Essay on the Immediate Data of Consciousness, tr. F.L. Pogson, Montana: Kessinger Publishing Company, original date, 1910.

———, *The Two Sources of Morality and Religion,* trs. R. Ashley Audra and Cloudsley Brereton, with the assistance of W. Horsfall Carter, Notre Dame, IN: University of Notre Dame Press, 1977 [1935].

Bernstein, Jeremy, *Albert Einstein and the Frontiers of Physics*, New York: Oxford University Press, 1996.

Bloom, Harold (ed.), *Homer's The Iliad*, NY Chelsea House, 1987, [Modern Critical Interpretations].

———, (ed.), *Homer's The Odyssey*, NY Chelsea House, 1987, [Modern Critical Interpretations].

Bloomfield, Leonard (1933), *Language*, Henry Holt and Co., NY.

Bloomfield, Maurice, trans., *Hymns of the Atharvaveda*, Sacred Books of the East, vol. 42, Oxford: Clarendon Press, 1897.

Boucher, Wayne I., *Spinoza in English: A Bibliography from the Seventeenth Century to the Present,* Thoemmes Press, Bristol, 2002.

Bourke, Vernon J., ed.; Gerald G. Walsh, S.J., Demetrius B. Zema, S.J., Grace Monahan, O.S.U., Daniel J. Honan, trans., *St. Augustine, City of God,* [*Abridged*], Image Books, Doubleday and Co., NY, 1958.

Burnier, Radha and Tatya Tookaram, trans., *The Haṭhayogapradīpikā of Svatmarama*, The Adyar Library and Research Centre, Madras, 1972.

Calder, Nigel. *Einstein's Universe: A Guide to the Theory of Relativity*, New York: Viking Press, 1979.

Cassidy, David C., *Werner Heisenberg : A Bibliography of His Writings, Second, Expanded Edn.,* Whittier Publications, Inc. (January 20, 2001).

Chaitanya, Swami Vinaya, trans., "Kali Natakam," *Indian Literature*, no. 206, Dec. 2000.

Chand, Devi, trans., *The Atharvaveda,* Munshiram Manoharlal, Delhi, 1982.

Dickens, Charles, *David Copperfield,* Jerome H. Buckley, ed., Norton Critical Edition, 1990.

———, *The Pickwick Papers,* Penguin Books, Reissue edn., 2000.

Eddington, A.S., *Space, Time and Gravitation, An Outline of the General Relativity Theory*, Cambridge University Press, 1920; reissued, 1987.

Eddington, Arthur Stanley, *The Nature of the Physical World,* Cambridge: Cambridge University Press, 1928; Reprinted Ann Arbor: University of Michigan Press, 1958.

Edwin, Arnold, *The Light of Asia,* Robert Brothers, Boston 1891.

Eliade, Mircea, *Patañjali and Yoga,* Schocken, 1975.

———, *Patterns in Comparative Religion,* University of Nebraska Press; Reprint edn., 1996.

Finch, Henry Le Roy, *Wittgenstein, The Early Philosophy,* Humanities Press, New York, 1971.

Gambhirananda, Swami, trans., *Brahma Sūtra Bhāṣya of Śrī Śaṅkarācārya,* Advaita Ashram, Calcutta, 1983.

———, trans., *Māṇḍūkya Upaniṣad, With the Commentary of Śaṅkarācārya*, Advaita Ashrama, Calcutta.

———, trans., *Chāndogya Upaniṣad, With the Commentary of Śaṅkara,* Advaita Ashram, Calcutta.

Ganesh Vasudeo Tagare, *The Bhāgavata Purāṇa,* trans., Ancient Indian Tradition and Mythology Series, vols. 7-11, Motilal Banarsidass, Delhi, 1976-78.

George, Karimpumannil Mathai, *Kumaran Asan*, Sahitya Akademi, New Delhi, 1972.

Gibbs, Laura, trans., *Aesop's Fables,* Oxford University Press, New York, 2002.

Goldman, Robert, and Pollock, Sheldon, trans., *The Rāmāyaṇa of Vālmikī*, 2 vols., Princeton, New Jersey: Princeton University Press, 1984-86.

Guru, Nataraja, *An Integrated Science of the Absolute* (based on *Darśanamālā*), D.K. Printworld, Revised edn. (in two volumes), New Delhi, 2001.

———, *Bhagavad-Gītā,* trans., and commt., Narayana Gurukula Foundation, Varkala, 1989.

———, *One Hundred Verses of Self-Instruction,* trans. and commt., *Life and Teachings of Narayana Guru,* Part II, Narayana Gurukula Publication, Varkala, Revised edn., 1990.

———, *The Search for a Norm in Western Thought,* Narayana Gurukula Foundation, Varkala.

———, *The Philosophy of a Guru*, Narayana Gurukula Foundation, Varkala.

———, *Vedanta Revalued and Restated*, Narayana Gurukula Foundation, Varkala.

Hamilton, Edith, Cairns Huntington, ed., *The Collected Dialogues of Plato* (Bollingen Series LXXI), Princeton University Press, 1961.

Heifetz, Hank, *Origin of the Young God* (*Kalidasa's Kumārasambhava*), Motilal Banarsidass.

Horn, Christopher, Augustinus, *De Civitate Dei,* Akademie Verlag, 1997

Hugo, Victor, *Les Miserables* (Various editions).

Hume, R.E., trans., *The Thirteen Principle Upaniṣads,* Second edn., Revised, Oxford University Press, New York, 1979.

Infeld, Leopold, *Albert Einstein: His Work and its Influence on Our World,* Charles Scribner's Sons; New York, 1950.

Jha, Mahamahopadhyaya Ganganath, trans., Bhatta, Kumarila, *Tantravarttika* : A Commentary on Śabara's Bhāṣya on the *Purvamīmāṁsā Sūtra*s of Jaimini/Kumārila Bhaṭṭa, Reprint edn., Delhi, Pilgrims Book Pvt. Ltd. 1998.

Kale, M.R., *Abhijñānaśākuntalam of Kālīdāsa,* Motilal Banarsidass, Delhi.

Kale, Moreshwar Ramchandra (ed.), *Daśakumāracarita of Daṇḍin,* Motilal Banarsidass, Delhi, 1993.

Keats, John, *The Complete Poems of John Keats,* Modern Library, 1994.

Lacombe, O, *L'Absolu Selon le Vedanta,* Paris, 1937.

MacKenna, Stephen, trans., Plotinus, *The Enneads,* NY, Penguin Books, 1991 (extensive introduction, including Porphyry, but the text is abridged).

Madhvananda, Swami, trans, *Vivekacūḍāmaṇi,* Advaita Ashrama, Calcutta, 1960.

McAlister, L.L. (ed.), *The Philosophy of Franz Brentano*, London: Duckworth, 1976.

McLuhan, Marshall, *Medium is the Massage: An Inventory of Effects*, with Quentin Fiore, Random House/Simon and Schuster, 1989.

Miller, Barbara Stoler, trans., *Love Song of the Dark Lord: Jayadeva's Gitagovinda*, Columbia University Press, New York, 1997.

Mitra, Vihari Lala, trans., *The Yoga Vāśiṣṭha Mahārāmāyaṇa of Vālmikī*, 4 vols., Indological Book House, Delhi, 1994.

Morgan, Dermot, *Introduction to Phenomenology,* Routledge, London, 2000.

Müller, Max, ed., Eggeling, Julius, trans., *Śatapatha Brāhmaṇa*, The Sacred Books of the East, Kessinger Publishing Company, 2004.

———, ed., *The Upaniṣads* in Two Parts, Sacred Books of the East, Dover, New York, 1962.

Musa, Mark, transl. and with notes, Alighieri, Dante, *The Divine Comedy*, vol. I: *Inferno*, vol. II: *Purgatory*, vol. III: *Paradise*, Harmondsworth: Penguin Classics, 1984.

Narang, Satya Pal, *Kalidasa Bibliography,* Heritage, New Delhi, 1976.

Panoli, V., *Upaniṣads in Śaṅkara's own Words : Īśa, Kena, Kaṭha, and Māṇḍūkya with the Kārikā of Gaudapāda: With English translation, explanatory notes and footnotes*, Mathrubhumi, Calicut, 1991-94.

Pole, David, *The Later Philosophy of Wittgenstein,* The Athlone Press, University of London, 1963.

Prasad, Swami Muni Narayana, trans. and commt., *Chāndogya Upaniṣad* (Unpublished).

———, trans. and commt., *Kena Upaniṣad,* D.K. Printworld, Delhi, second impression 2004.

———, trans., and commt., *Kaṭha Upaniṣad,* D.K. Printworld, Delhi, 1998.

Prasada, Rama, trans., *Pātañjal Yoga Sūtras with commentary of Vyāsa and the gloss of Vachaspati Misra,* Munshiram Manoharlal, Delhi, 1998.

Rajan, Chandra, *The Complete Works of Kalidasa*, vol. 2: *Plays,* Sahitya Akademi, 2002.

———, *Kalidasa, The Loom of Time,* Penguin Books (India) Ltd., New Delhi, 1989.

Ramanathan, A.A. Prof., Critically ed. with Introduction, *Amarakośa* (in three volumes), Adyar Library and Research Centre, Madras, 1971.

Richard Wilhelm trans. rendered into English by Cary F. Baynes, *I Ching,* Bollingen Series, Princeton University Press, USA, 1967.

Russell, Bertrand, *The Basic Writings of Bertrand Russell, 1903-1959*, George Allen and Unwin London, 1961; Simon and Schuster, New York, 1961.

Ryder, Arthur W., trans., *The Pañcatantra*, University of Chicago, Chicago, 1956.

Scholem, Gershom G., *On the Kabbalah and its Symbolism*, Routledge & Kegan Paul, London, 1965.

Shakespeare, William, *The Complete Works,* Deluxe Edition, [Unabridged], Gramercy, 1990.

Shastri, J.L., ed., *Śiva Purāṇa Volume*, 4 vols., Delhi: Motilal Banarsidas, Delhi, 2000.

Shelly, Percy Bysshe, *The Complete Poems of Percy Bysshe Shelley,* Modern Library; Reissue edn., 1994.

Siegel, Lee, *Sacred and Profane Dimensions of Love in Indian Traditions as Exemplified in the Gitagovinda of Jayadeva,* Oxford University Press, Delhi, 1990.

Sinha, Biswajit, *Kalidasa,* Raj Publications, New Delhi, 2002.

Smith, Norman Kemp, trans., Kant, Immanuel, *Critique of Pure Reason,* St. Martin's Press, New York, 1929.

Svatamarama, Swami, Hans-Ulrich Rieker, *Haṭha Yoga Pradīpikā: The Classic Text of Yoga,* Harper Collins Publishers, 1992.

Tapasyananda, Swami, trans., *Śivānanda Laharī of Śrī Śaṅkara,* Vedanta Press. 1987.

Tennyson, Alfred, *Tennyson: Selected Poems*, Penguin Books, Reprint edn., April 1, 1992.

The Holy Bible, New King James Version (1982). Various Editions based on the Authorized Version of 1611, commonly called the King James Bible.

Thibaut, George, trans., *Badarayana, Vedanta Sutras of with commentary by Śaṅkara*, Dover, New York, 1962.

Vasu, Rai Bahadur Srisa Chandra, *The Gheraṇḍa Saṁhitā:* Sanskrit text with English Translation, Munshiram Manoharlal Publishers Pvt. Ltd., New Delhi, 2003.

Warrier, Dr. A.G. Krishna, trans., *The Śākta Upaniṣads*, University of Kerala.

Whitney, William Dwight, trans., Lanman, Charles Rockwell (Revised and Edited) (1984) *Atharvaveda-Saṁhitā,* vol. VIII, Harvard Oriental Series, Motilal Banarsidass, Delhi.

Wittgenstein, Ludwig, Pears D.F. and McGuinness B.F., trans., *Tractatus Logico-Philosophicus*, Routledge & Kegan Paul Ltd., London, 1961.

Wittgenstein, Ludwig, *The Blue and Brown Books,* Harper Torchbooks, New York, 1958.

Woodroffe, Sir John. *Introduction to Tantra Śāstra*, Madras: Ganesh and Co., 1956.

Woods, James Haughton, trans., *The Yoga System of Patānjali with the Bhāṣya of Vyāsa, the Tattvavaiśāradī of Vacaspati Misra and the Vṛtti of Bhoja*, Motilal Banarsidass, Delhi, 1988.

Wordsworth, William, *William Wordsworth: The Major Works* Oxford University Press, 2000.

Yati, Guru Nitya Chaitanya, trans., and commt., *That Alone,* D.K. Printworld, New Delhi, 2003.

———, *Love and Devotion,* D.K. Printworld, New Delhi.

———, *The Psychology of Darśanamālā,* D.K. Printworld, Reprint edn., New Delhi, 2004.

———, trans. and commt., *Arivu (Epistemology of Gnosis)*, Narayana Gurukula Foundation, Varkala, 1989.

———, trans. and commt., *Experiencing the Īśāvāsya Upaniṣad,* East-West University of Unitive Sciences, Bainbridge, USA, 1992.

———, trans. and commt., *Māṇḍukya Upaniṣad* (Unpublished).

———, trans. and commt., *Neither This nor That but Aum,* D.K. Printworld, New Delhi, 1995.

———, trans. and commt., *Daivadasakam,* Narayana Gurukula Foundation, Varkala, 1981.

Zuckert, C.H., *Postmodern Platos: Nietzsche, Heidegger, Gadamer, Strauss, Derrida*, University of Chicago Press, 1996.

Index